4

THE LONG DISPUTE

John Prothero

THE LONG DISPUTE

*Maori Land Rights
and European Colonisation
in Southern New Zealand*

HARRY C. EVISON

CANTERBURY UNIVERSITY PRESS

First published in 1997 by
CANTERBURY UNIVERSITY PRESS
University of Canterbury
Private Bag 4800
Christchurch
NEW ZEALAND

ISBN 0-908812-57-4

Maps designed by Benjamin Evison, Sydney
Printed by Spectrum Print, Christchurch

For my grandchildren
and their generation

Mo o tatou mokopuna
Me o tatou uri kei te heke mai

ACKNOWLEDGEMENTS

I should like to thank staff at the following institutions for their generous help in making available their valuable manuscripts, illustrations and other documents for study:

Archives Office of New South Wales, Sydney
Auckland Museum & Institute Library, Auckland
Auckland Public Library Manuscript Room, Auckland
The British Library, London
Canterbury Museum Archives, Christchurch
Canterbury Public Library New Zealand Room, Christchurch
Department of Survey and Land Information, Dunedin
Department of Survey and Land Information, Wellington
Hocken Library, Dunedin
Land Titles Office, Sydney
Maori Land Court, Christchurch
Methodist Archives, Christchurch
National Archives, Christchurch
National Archives, Wellington
New Zealand Royal Society, Wellington.
Otago Early Settlers Museum, Dunedin
Public Record Office, London
State Library of New South Wales, Sydney
Turnbull Library, Wellington
Wellington City Council Archive, Wellington

I should also like to thank my son Benjamin for his excellent maps, and my brother Frank for commenting on the first draft, and my wife Hillary for her constant support.

H.C.E.

CONTENTS

Introduction		9
One	*The Maori World of Southern New Zealand*	15
Two	*Civilisation*	27
Three	*Te Rauparaha*	46
Four	*Survival*	68
Five	*Colonialism Reborn*	83
Six	*The Treaty of Waitangi*	95
Seven	*Sovereignty*	110
Eight	*The Old Order, and the New*	127
Nine	*The Otago Purchase*	139
Ten	*Governor Grey*	158
Eleven	*Kemp's Purchase*	177
Twelve	*Commissioner Mantell*	193
Thirteen	*A New Invasion*	214
Fourteen	*Honorable Proceedings*	235
Fifteen	*The Final Ngai Tahu Awards*	253
Sixteen	*Civilising the Natives*	271
Seventeen	*A Whiff of Justice*	289
Eighteen	*In Naboth's Vineyard*	301
Nineteen	*Left Out of New Zealand*	318
Twenty	*The Twentieth Century*	337
Appendices	*1: The Treaty of Waitangi*	355
	2: Signatures to Kemp's Deed, 1848	360
Glossary		363
List of maps		367

List of abbreviations   369
Key to Smith-Nairn Commission references   371
Bibliography   373
Index   387

INTRODUCTION

This book was written in response to requests for a shortened version of the author's *Te Wai Pounamu, the Greenstone Island* (Aoraki Press, Wellington, 1993). At the same time, further research has provided some significant revision.

Histories and educational texts have long been fired with admiration for the deeds of explorers, missionaries, and conquerors who paved the way for the annexation and colonisation of 'backward' territories by 'civilised' states – and fired equally with condescension or contempt for the 'savage' inhabitants of such territories. Until fairly recently, colonial empires have been considered the hallmark of greatness. Rudyard Kipling's 1897 'Recessional', with its reference to 'dominion over palm and pine' and to 'lesser breeds without the law', and his admonition, 'Take up the White Man's Burden' written in 1899, still echo down the years.

World literature is now showing the other side of the coin. From Southern Africa to the Americas, and from the Arctic to Australasia, the viewpoints and experiences of the so-called backward peoples are at last becoming known. To take an example far distant from the South Pacific, it is now twenty-five years since the Sami patriot Nils-Aslak Valkeapaa published in Finnish his *Greetings from Lappland** describing the plight of the Sami people (formerly called Laplanders) under the encroachment of the Fenno-Scandian states Norway, Sweden and Finland. A wealth of controversy followed. The law school at the Finnish University of Lapland now has a department of Nordic Law encouraging the study of Sami customary rights. Recently Pekka Antikainen published the moving photographic essay *Koillinen Tunturituuli*, about the destruction of the traditional way of life in northern Finland by modern land development, and of the Skolt Sami way of life in the Petsamo region of Russia by unbridled industrialism.** Indigenous and aboriginal

---

* See Valkeapaa, Nils-Aslak (transl. Wahl). *Greetings from Lappland: The Sami, Europe's Forgotten People*, London 1983.
** Antikainen, Pekka. *Koillinen Tunturituuli*, Oulu, 1994.

peoples are everywhere raising their voices against colonialism and its consequences, and they have many sympathisers.

To this burgeoning literature on the impact of European expansion, the present volume contributes an account of the experiences of the Maoris of southern New Zealand – a former hunter-gatherer society, and one of the world's southernmost 'native' peoples.

~

Our modern era, broadly speaking, has been characterised by the privatisation of land and other economic resources that were formerly available for common use. In recent centuries, the use of land and natural resources for community livelihood, whether based on law or custom, has been steadily eroded by state control and privatisation. Under the designation of 'improvement', or 'development', this process has been almost worldwide, and continues today. In Britain the assumed ancient rights of ordinary people to use the commons and so-called 'waste' lands, were gradually overthrown by parliamentary Enclosure Acts and Gaming Acts which confined these rights to the gentry. The Scottish crofters, among many others, suffered deprivation and eviction.*

With the advent of modern colonialism the same process was extended to lands and resources used by tribal peoples. These peoples were required to surrender their customary common-use rights and make way for private or state ownership as dictated by colonial governments. This confiscation of land rights might be accompanied by deliberate genocide, as Darwin instances in his *Beagle* diary regarding South America (August 1833). There, on the Argentine pampas, 'Indians' were killed indiscriminately by the colonial soldiery. 'All the women who appear above twenty years old are massacred in cold blood,' noted Darwin – because 'They breed so!'** In North America, many of the First Nations ('American Indians') suffered partial genocide from being forced by the Federal Government to leave their homelands for exile in the 'reservations' of the American West. The Tasmanians suffered complete extinction after being officially exiled from their lands.

---

* Hunter, James. *The Making of the Crofting Community*, Edinburgh 1976, pp. 25, 39–49.
** Darwin, Charles. *Voyage of the Beagle* (edited by Browne & Neve), London 1989, p. 111.

Indigenous populations generally, whether offering resistance to colonial encroachment or not, suffered disastrous mortalities from the introduction of European epidemic diseases formerly unknown to them. Their plight was compounded by racial prejudices of biblical origin, to which were added social evolutionist theories such as Darwin's racial theory of history expressed in his *The Descent of Man*,* and Engels's account of 'savage' and 'barbarous' societies in his *The Origin of the Family*.** Such theories served (and still serve) to justify the expropriation of tribal societies, and the treatment of formerly tribal peoples as inferior. Many former Scottish crofters who had been considered an inferior class in their own homeland were able to assume 'racial' superiority over the 'natives' when they emigrated to colonial territories.

This book relates the colonial experience of the Maoris of southern New Zealand. At first European contact these people combined a hunter-gatherer economy, accompanied by some inter-tribal trading, with the classic Maori political and social organisation. As European contact with New Zealand increased during the pre-annexation period (1790–1840), southern Maoris gradually adapted to the European commercial system, and a few chiefs eventually pursued capitalist activities themselves. In the first decade after British annexation, before their lands were taken by the colonial state, the Maoris of southern New Zealand successfully supplemented their hunter-gathering activities with European horticulture, including the growing of wheat, while maintaining their customary rights of commonage. We can therefore examine the effects of the abolition of these customary aboriginal rights by colonial governments.

≈

'History is written by the victors,' it has been said with some truth. Colonial histories which are derived essentially from official sources can give little of the viewpoint or experiences of indigenous peoples. With this in mind, every effort has been made in the present work to balance information from official sources, of which there are

---

* Darwin, Charles. *The Descent of Man, Selection in Relation to Sex*, 2 vols, London, 1870–71.
** Engels, Friedrich. *The Origin of the Family, Private Property, and the State*, Sydney, 1942.

plenty (as can be seen from the Bibliography), with information from contemporary Maori sources and unofficial observers. From these conflicting primary sources our 'Long Dispute' emerges.

In 1776, before the dawn of the modern colonial era, the historian Edward Gibbon assessed his task according to scientific principles, thus:

> Diligence and accuracy are the only merits which an historical writer may ascribe to himself, if any merit indeed can be assumed from the performance of an indispensable duty. I may therefore be allowed to say that I have carefully examined all the original materials that could illustrate the subject which I had undertaken to treat.*

Gibbon's work is unique, but his precepts are universal to the scientific method of using evidence. For the historian, the most telling evidence comes from primary sources: that is, contemporary sources unaffected by subsequent editing.

An unusual wealth of primary sources, both Maori and non-Maori, has been available for the present work. Among the most vital of these are the submissions of Maori witnesses to the Royal Commission of Judge Smith and Francis Nairn in 1879–1880, which survive in the National Archives, Wellington, in Maori and in translation, miraculously preserved – although somewhat charred at the edges from past Native or Maori Affairs Department fires. These documents bring us the speeches of Maori chiefs across more than a century in time, recalling their own experiences of the period of European colonisation in southern New Zealand. The comments of whalers and missionaries, and of Edward Shortland as ethnographer, add a perspective of their own, as do the whaling and shipping records. Also important as primary sources are the diaries, journals, letters and field books of government officials. Some of these contradict the official reports: Commissioner Walter Mantell's journal contradicts his own official reports.

No historian should ignore what has been written by others. For this reason, reference has been made to every available work, published or unpublished, which touches on southern New Zealand history during the colonial period. These are listed in the 'Unofficial' sections of the Bibliography published or manuscript.

---

* Gibbon, Edward. *The Decline and Fall of the Roman Empire*, London 1994, Vol. 6, p. 650.

Of course, even the use of such numerous sources as these cannot prove the absence of bias, or selective use of the sources. For this reason, the sources are listed in full detail so that readers may go and check for themselves, if they wish, and delve into them further. Colonial history is a serious and contentious subject, and no reader should be expected to take the accuracy of a book for granted. Besides, colonialism is a continuing belief, sustained by the economic conditions it has justified. The controversy that surrounded it in 1840 continues still, as if in 'steady state'.

The account of pre-European Maori life in Chapter 1 is derived from the secondary archaeological and ethnological sources indicated in the chapter notes, which include the most distinguished modern writers in these fields. Topographical descriptions in the text are derived from my own observations and experience during some seventy years, and may appear to that extent subjective.

Many histories analyse events and attempt to explain them. This book is a narrative, and the story it tells is left to readers to analyse and explain if they can. Some histories and biographies say who the great people are, and who are the villains. This book contains many characters, as befits a drama: but as to their relative merits, the reader again must decide. Some historical works take a moral stand, and say what was right and what was wrong. This book does not sit in judgment. The reader must be the judge, if any judging is needed. *The Long Dispute* has been written to give readers a vicarious experience of the past, or at least some insight into it. What readers may make of the experience is their prerogative. It is not for the historian to tell people what to think.

H.C.E.
Christchurch, September 1997

A note on the use of references given in chapter notes

To save space, abbreviations have been used in the chapter notes when referring to the sources used. This system can be followed by using the List of Abbreviations on page 369, and the Bibliography commencing on page 373. For items with the abbreviation 'SNC' (Smith-Nairn Commission), refer also to the Key to Smith-Nairn Commission references on page 371 to see whose submission is referred to or quoted.

Examples:

'Te Kahu 1901; Taki Ms: 19–20; WJ 24.8.1840.'
Semicolons are used to separate one reference from another. Colons are used to introduce page numbers. Each reference begins with the name of the author. If this is followed by 'Ms', the work will be found listed in the manuscript section of the Bibliography. Abbreviations such as 'WJ' given here are explained on page 369. Numerals following a colon are the page numbers on which the information was found.

'Wills–Wakefield, 21.9.1848 (2), Wills Ms Letters.'
The use of a dash denotes a letter or communication: thus 'Wills–Wakefield, 21.9.1848 (2), Wills Ms Letters' means a letter from Wills to Wakefield, the second one dated 21.9.1848, and source is Wills Ms Letters.

'Eyre–Fox 26.2.1849 & Grey–Eyre 26.3.1849, in Mackay I: 222.'
The word 'in' indicates that a secondary source has been used, not a primary source. This note refers to a letter from Eyre to Fox on 26 February 1849, and another from Grey to Eyre on 26 March 1849, and tell us that source used is the letters as published in Mackay Volume One, page 222.

'Mantell–Grey, 5.6.1846, Mantell Ms 83/418A.'
The stroke (/) means a subsection or folder: this reference is to a letter from Mantell to Grey dated 5 June 1846, in the Mantell Manuscripts, folder 418A.

'Wai-27 R35: 71ff, and U10c: 6ff.'
'Wai-27' is our abbreviation for the Waitangi Tribunal's records of theNgai Tahu Claim (1987–1990). Thus this reference is to submission R35, page 71 and following, and submission U10c, page 6 and following, in the Waitangi Tribunal's Ngai Tahu Claim documents.

'Loc cit' means 'the source last mentioned'; 'Ibid' means 'the same'; 'Op cit' means 'the work last mentioned'. 'Passim' means at various places.

I

~

The Maori World of Southern
New Zealand

NEW ZEALAND evidently remained uninhabited until late in
the human settlement of the Pacific Islands. It lay at a distance
of 1,500 kilometres from the nearest inhabited land, across sub-
tropical ocean fraught with baffling winds, and further still from
the tropical islands first settled by seafaring Polynesians. When
Polynesian Maori settlers – whether by design or accident – at last
arrived in New Zealand from the tropics, in the twelfth century
A.D. or earlier,[1] they found a pristine land.

At the southern shore of New Zealand's North Island is the
dividing sea of Raukawa Moana. Here strong winds and tides con-
tend, patrolled by the restless albatross and dolphin. Beyond the
blue of this deep sea lies the deeper blue of distant hills, half hidden
by ocean haze. The far coastline looms dreamlike: when far above
all soars the pure white peak of Tapuae o Uenuku, floating in the sky.
Thus beckons Te Wai Pounamu.[2]

Te Wai Pounamu is an island some 200 kilometres wide, stretching south-west for 850 kilometres between latitudes 40°30'S and
46°S, from Raukawa Moana to Murihiku, 'stern of the waka'. The
long coastline is a succession of rocky bluffs and reefs, deep inlets
and fiords, and broadly sweeping bays pounded by ocean surf. The
island's interior is commanded by steep mountain ranges, whose
remoter valleys in winter are gripped by conditions too harsh for
human habitation, except where large glacial lakes moderate the
climate. But the coastal harbours, estuaries and plains are habitable
throughout the year.

Note: Readers unfamiliar with Maori terms in the text should consult the
Glossary on page 363.

Te Wai Pounamu's first inhabitants found the coastal waters alive with fish and waterfowl. Forests, rich in bird life, clothed coastal hills and plains on both sides of the island. Here were many flightless birds innocent of any hunters, including several species of the huge, browsing moa. But to Maoris the island's greatest treasure was its jade, or pounamu, the most valued material both for implements and for ornaments, sought in mountainous country everywhere.[3] Its durability and beauty made it the most desirable of substances, despite the immense labour required in fashioning it. The tough, green nephrite from Arahura, on the island's west coast ('Te Tai Poutini'), was the pounamu preferred for tools, while tangiwai, an exquisite, translucent bowenite from Piopiotahi, 350 kilometres further south, was a pounamu highly prized for ornaments.[4]

Seven days' journey inland from the Murihiku coast lay Wakatipu Waimaori, the freshwater Wakatipu – a great glacial lake fed at its northern end by the powerful Awa Wakatipu. In the remote, glaciated reaches of the Awa Wakatipu's wild valley, adventurous Maoris sought pounamu. They struggled among towering peaks, dense forests, dangerous bluffs, turbulent rapids, treacherous quicksands, and icy tributaries – until a sudden bend in the valley revealed a mountain like a recumbent giant. In his mouth was the priceless inanga – the pale pounamu.[5] The fame of this marvellous pounamu place gave the name 'Te Wahi Pounamu' to the whole island – which eventually became commonly known as 'Te Wai Pounamu'.

By the year 1500 AD, fire had largely denuded eastern and inland Te Wai Pounamu of its forests, either through natural causes, during dry and windy seasons, or by Maori agency – deliberate or accidental. With this loss of natural habitat, the moa was soon hunted to extinction.[6] Some authorities suggest, on archaeological evidence, that the Maori population then declined through food scarcity – 'a descent into a scrabbling for shellfish'.[7] However, given the evident abundance of other protein-rich foods, and assuming that the Maoris would have learned to use these during the two centuries before the extinction of the moa, this 'descent' may be doubted. The coasts were washed by the nutriment-laden westerly current that circles the globe in southern latitudes. The sea was 'full of fish'.[8]

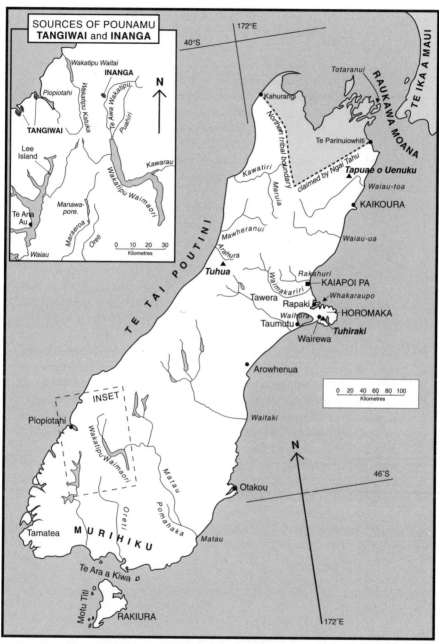

Southern New Zealand (unshaded) in pre-European times.

These in turn supported myriads of sea birds and marine mammals, whose eggs and flesh were nutritious. Seals were culled for meat in winter.[9]

The many estuaries, inlets, wetlands, lakes, streams and rivers of Te Wai Pounamu provided plentiful eels, inanga, flatfish, lampreys and other freshwater species, as well as shellfish, waterfowl and their eggs. The grasslands and surviving forests supported numerous edible birds, and kiore. In addition, food was prepared from aruhe and other plants. Ti-kauka was cultivated, and from its pith and roots the Maoris in summer made kauru, a sweet and nutritious cake.

In all, Te Wai Pounamu supported some two hundred edible plant and animal species after the extinction of the moa.[10] More than 1,400 mahinga kai have been recorded between the Waimakariri and Matau Rivers in the east,[11] and more elsewhere.[12] Eels provided a never-failing food supply in most parts of Te Wai Pounamu, particularly in coastal streams and hapua. At Wairewa and Waihora great quantities of eels were caught and dried in the open air, in summer.[13]

Varieties of harakeke provided clothing, footwear, mats and baskets, and fishing nets. The coastal pingao grass was valued for decorative work. Durable timber for canoes, buildings and fortifications, was obtained from the totara. The countryside provided stone of various kinds besides pounamu, suitable for adzes, chisels, saw-edges, and grinding implements. Fish-hooks, needles, ornaments and weapons were made from bones of whales and other animals.

The titi bred prolifically on the islands off Rakiura, where Maori whanau from various parts of southern New Zealand established their designated wakawaka to which they resorted for culling the fat juvenile birds from their burrows in late autumn. The prepared fowl were stored and transported in bags punched out from giant kelp and protected by totara bark bound with harakeke.[14] These valuable poha titi were traded with northern tribes.

The seas around Te Wai Pounamu were dangerous, dealing death to the unwary. Tidal currents were strong, waves often mountainous, and submerged rocks and reefs all too common. Sudden storms and raging gales were frequent. Survival required organisation and discipline, with proper regard for nature's forces and the gods who ruled them. Like other peoples living close to nature, the Maoris of southern New Zealand had to respect the natural world.

In the Maori view, the world was inhabited by numerous atua and wairua, potent for good or evil. There were terrifying ghosts, and baleful taepo. Taniwha were jealous deities living in water.

Tangaroa, taniwha of the sea, was especially important for the sea-faring Maoris. Mountains and other remarkable landscape features were inhabited by atua. There were tribal and family atua, and atua assigned to particular individuals, bestowing favour or disfavour according to the strictness with which the demands of tapu were obeyed. Tapu was a powerful principle concerning the sacredness of things.

The Maori gods, like those of other nations, were expected to punish wrongdoers and reward the virtuous. Tohunga skilled in consulting and influencing the spirit world were prominent in every community. Every important chief had his tohunga, or was a tohunga himself[15] – just as the English gentry had their parsons. In time of war, Maoris, like other peoples, expected their priests to pray for victory. Defeat was evidence of divine displeasure, or bad praying.

~

Food and pounamu attracted people to Te Wai Pounamu, and held them there. The distinctive flavours of local varieties of bird, eel, mollusc, fish, and other natural foods, bound people to the land and to the waters. Infants were weaned on to these foods, and grew up in the love of them and of the places that provided them. With each succeeding generation the bonds grew stronger. Each district had its specialties – such as the titi of the islands off Rakiura; the kanakana of Murihiku; the blue and pink tuangi of Otakou; the ti-kauru of Arowhenua; the kereru, paua and kina of Horomaka; the patiki, eels and putangitangi of Waihora and Kaparatehau; the weka, kumara and taiwhatiwhati of Kaiapoi; the kakapo, karaka and koura of Kaikoura; and the many varieties of fish in the sea.

The prominent landmark Te Parinuiowhiti – 'the great cliff of Whiti' – is a long, striated, whitish-grey cliff fronting the broad promontory dividing the estuaries of the Awatere and Wairau Rivers. It rises to an angled summit 270 metres above the sea, and faces north-east across Raukawa Moana towards Tera Whiti and Kapiti at the North Island. South of Te Parinuiowhiti the usually cooler climate made cultivation of the kumara often difficult, and south of Taumutu the kumara could not be grown at all. Thus southern New Zealand (i.e. the territory south of Te Parinuiowhiti) differed markedly, as a Maori habitat, from territory to the north where milder conditions allowed the widespread, regular cultivation of the kumara as a staple crop supplementing food-gathering. In southern New Zealand the Maori economy was chiefly or entirely one of hunting and food gathering. Since these activities required much more territory than cultivation did, the Maori population of southern New Zealand was more dispersed, more mobile, and less numerous, than that of the territory to the north.

For centuries Te Wai Pounamu is said to have been occupied by the Waitaha tribe, and others known as Rapuwai and Hawea had reputedly preceded them. But in the sixteenth century the island's riches attracted warlike tribes from the North Island. Ngati Wairangi occupied Te Tai Poutini, the source of much pounamu, while Ngati Mamoe settled in the east, south of Te Parinuiowhiti. Feuding among quarrelsome northern chiefs, and the universal desire for pounamu, caused more invaders to come south. The Ngati Kuri hapu of Ngai Tahu overran the Kaikoura Ngati Mamoe, and by 1700 AD other Ngai Tahu led by Moki, son of Tuahuriri, were dominant from the Hurunui River to Waihora.[16] To secure Ngai Tahu's conquests, Moki's elder brother Turakautahi established a pa on a hapua of the Rakahuri River. Questioned about this swampy site, which yielded only eel and waterfowl in any quantity, Turakautahi declared that kai could be 'poi' (swung in) from other places.[17] Hence the pa was called Kai-a-poi. Later, some of Tuahuriri's people ('Ngai Tuahuriri') seized control of Te Tai Poutini from Ngati Wairangi, and became known as 'Poutini Ngai Tahu'.[18] Kaiapoi then became the greatest pounamu trading centre in the land.

Maori tribes, however warlike, needed a proper také* to justify disrupting other people's customary rights by warfare. Any insult to an ariki or an ancestor was a potent také for war, and required utu. Otherwise, gods and ancestors would be offended, and might angrily withdraw their protection. The usual fighting season began in the latter part of summer (January or February) after the main food supplies had been garnered. Fighting ended when honour was satisfied, or when the titi season started in April. As in most human societies, warfare was considered the most exciting and honourable activity for able-bodied men. Skirmishing with rival tribes on disputed frontiers was therefore common.[19]

---

* The Maori term 'take' (pretext, reason) is rendered in the text as 'také', to avoid confusion with the English 'take'.

The independent survival of a Maori community depended on its being able to field an effective taua, commonly comprising the seventy or so men needed to work a war canoe. If a quarter of the population were able-bodied men, as some authorities have suggested was usual,[20] a community of three or four hundred people could field a taua while keeping some warriors in reserve. Several taua from allied communities might combine in a single expedition, but only under a leader whose mana was impeccable and whose tohunga promised victory. Even then, the slightest adverse omen or breach of etiquette could disrupt the expedition. Like the barons of feudal Europe, the Maori ariki were jealous of one another, and touchy regarding their personal honour. An ariki on a war expedition would rather take his taua home than put up with an indignity or taunt from an ally.

Warfare was esteemed by the warriors, for there was no greater honour than to die in battle. Such a death pleased both gods and ancestors. But no matter which chiefs gained ascendancy, life for the majority in southern New Zealand was a hard seasonal round of hunting, food-gathering, and food-preservation and storage. If warfare interrupted these vital activities, winter starvation could follow – especially if storms or snow prevented the gathering of emergency supplies. For non-combatants, as in other lands the world over, war often brought misery and disaster. Warriors could plunder non-combatants of the opposing side, rape the women, and enslave or slaughter everybody at will.[21] Recurring warfare could lay waste whole territories. The aristocratic obsession with mana, tapu and utu could disrupt the creative and productive activities of a tribe, and lead to its destruction.[22] As in other lands, successful chiefs won the honours and spoils of war; common people bore the costs. Victorious taua usually returned with captives, whose life or death depended on their captor's whim.[23] Such captives might be enslaved, or subjected to cannibalism – an insulting fate.[24] But to be a slave was more shameful than to be eaten.[25]

∾

In southern New Zealand, the preparation of food gathered at mahinga kai was concentrated at adjacent kainga nohoanga – some of which were far from home, among the rivers, plains and lakes of the lonely interior. Inland camps were busily occupied in summer, but generally deserted in winter.[26] Managing the mahinga kai required expert knowledge and skill in harvesting and preparing the foods and other produce for future use.

The organisation of work reflected and sustained the social rankings derived from birth, inheritance, or prowess in war. Distinguished ancestry conferred aristocratic rank – the status of rangatira. Like aristocracies elsewhere, the Maori aristocracy despised their commoners, and scorned menial work. Maori rangatira were preoccupied in peace and war with enhancing their personal honour and prestige.[27] As in Europe, commoners were expected to die for their rulers, even though socially they were beneath their notice. Humble ancestry meant humble rank – that of tutua or tangata hara.[28] Like the Christian and Islamic traditions, Maori tradition held that the female sex, however esteemed, was inferior to the male.[29] Men did the hunting, fishing, bird-snaring, tool- and weapon-making, cultivation, tree-felling, canoe-making, carving, religious observances, and fighting. The women of a tribe, unless ample slaves were available, did the food-gathering, preparation and dyeing of fibre, weaving and basket-making, cooking, and most of the carrying.[30]

The most prominent warrior among the rangatira became the acknowledged fighting chief and led the taua in war. The highest-born rangatira of a hapu was acknowledged as ariki. He personified the mana of his hapu or tribe just as a European monarch personified the prestige of his nation. The greater his mana, the greater his tapu. There was no higher rank than ariki,[31] but it was a social and religious distinction, not a political or military one. An ariki had ceremonial precedence, but no universal right of command. He was acknowledged as leader only if his mana remained above reproach. The tribe, or iwi, was a loose grouping of related but autonomous hapu and communities, not a political organisation. Only when a highly successful leader emerged was an iwi likely to act in a united fashion.

Free-born Maoris had the right to use mahinga kai in their own residential or ancestral territories, just as Englishmen, however humble, traditionally had a right to use commons and so-called waste lands for sustenance. Thus the Maori hunter-gatherer economy of southern New Zealand was based on common rights to the use of land and resources. But as in England, the apportioning of these common rights among the community was defined by custom, and was not 'free for all'.

No Maori chief, however powerful, was entitled to override the customary rights of free-born members of his tribe. Disputes over such matters were aired publicly on the marae, and decided by a consensus of chiefs and elders largely on the basis of whakapapa and precedent.[32] Thus the accurate memorizing of whakapapa and tribal tradition was essential. On the marae, as in a Roman forum or a Germanic tribal moot, every free man could have his say, and everyone's conduct or argument was open to debate. Oratory, skill in debate, accurate memory, and truthfulness were therefore highly esteemed. Dishonesty and lying were considered disgraceful. A chief's mana was derived in the first place from his ancestry, but it was sustained by his reputation. To avoid disgrace he had to keep his personal integrity above suspicion, and avenge all insults.[33]

∼

Customary Maori land rights were of two main kinds: také tupuna, derived from inheritance, and ahi kaa, derived from occupation of the land. Newcomers might obtain temporary rights by making a suitable koha acknowledging their obligation, or more lasting rights (také tuku) by paying acceptable utu. As in Europe, another way of acquiring rights was by marriage. Spouses acquired something of each other's status and rights. The offspring of a marriage inherited the rights of both parents. The tribal lands accommodated all these rights, and were in that sense held in common, although particular areas or resources might be tapu to particular chiefs and their followers.

Any of these rights might be disrupted in warfare by rau patu, which gave permanent title if followed by three generations of occupation. Defeated people regained their land rights if they reoccupied their land within three generations; otherwise they lost them.[34] One reason for the constant visiting and travelling by Maoris in southern New Zealand was to keep occupation rights alive. Another reason was to maintain kinship ties; a third was the universal love of travel. Te Wai Pounamu was a dangerous, splendid land, and travel whether by land or water was the spice of life.

A Maori viewing his tribal lands did not see hectares to rent, lease, sell or 'develop'. Instead, he saw resources for feeding, housing, clothing and equipping himself and his whanau, just as the rural Englishman looking at his local commons and 'waste' lands saw resources for his family's sustenance. The Maori, like the rural Englishman, was thoroughly familiar with his countryside,[35] associating particular physical features with spirits, gods, ancestors or traditions. For Maoris, as for country-dwellers the world over, the loss of ancestral lands brought spiritual anguish, as well as deprivation and disgrace.

The Maoris of southern New Zealand probably enjoyed better health, better diet, and purer drinking water than did their contemporaries in Europe and Asia where diseases unknown in Te Wai Pounamu were rife – for example, bubonic plague, typhus, typhoid, smallpox, venereal diseases, tuberculosis, cholera and influenza. Maoris suffered from pneumonia, arthritis, dental decay, a type of leprosy, and cancer.[36] They thought illness was due to sorcery, or was a punishment from the spirit world for a religious offence such as a breach of tapu[37] – just as contemporary Europeans commonly feared witchcraft and thought plagues were a punishment from God. Cures for serious illnesses, as distinct from injuries, were therefore probably not sought, except through the spells of a helpful tohunga.[38]

In Maori society, as in Europe, the privileged classes had better prospects of long life than did ordinary people, because the privileged endured less hunger, privation, and drudgery, and commanded the best of food. Some recent authorities[39] have suggested an average life span of only thirty years for pre-European Maoris, based on the pathology of bones from burials which appear, from the literature, to have been of a type accorded to commoners. Bones of the Maori upper classes, however, were buried secretly so that they could not be discovered and desecrated,[40] and in southern New Zealand chiefs were often cremated.[41] In the absence of samples from upper-class burials, thirty years may be considered too low an estimate for the average pre-European Maori life span.

One summer day in February 1770, the Ngati Kuri lookouts at Kaikoura saw an unknown pora out at sea, riding high in the water, with two tall masts and a prodigious quantity of sail strangely set. Four double war canoes were launched to investigate this vessel as she lay becalmed. The Maori warriors watched her closely until evening, prudently refusing all invitations to go on board. The strangers dubbed them 'The Lookers On', and sailed away into the night, appearing afterwards off Akaroa, Otakou and Murihiku.[42] Three years later, a similar vessel visited Tamatea, and its occupants befriended the Maoris there with gifts of hatchets, spike nails and medallions.[43] These vessels were commanded by Captain James

Cook, of the British navy. In Te Wai Pounamu he landed only at Totaranui in the north and at Tamatea in the south. His 1773 interpreter, who spoke Tahitian, understood the Maoris at Totaranui but not those at Tamatea[44] – who spoke the guttural dialect of southern Te Wai Pounamu, pronouncing the usual 'ng' as 'k' or 'g', 'r' as 'l', and 'p' as 'b'.[45]

By the time of Captain Cook's visits, the successive southward movements of Waitaha, Ngati Mamoe and Ngai Tahu had blurred the distinctions of hapu and iwi south of Kaiapoi. Marriages between persons from different hapu or different districts produced offspring with multiple rights, giving them a choice of residence. Most communities included members of various hapu. But if they were to prosper, everybody – regardless of hapu – had to co-operate in the management and use of mahinga kai.[46] Nevertheless, the noblest ancestry always conferred the greatest privileges.

About the year 1780, the leaders of Ngai Tahu and Ngati Mamoe formed a marriage alliance to end their constant feuds.[47] Honekai, son of the Ngai Tahu ariki Te Hau Tapunuiotu, married Kohuwai, granddaughter of the Ngati Mamoe ariki Rakiihia, and Rakiihia married Hinehakiri, Te Hau's cousin. The new allies turned on Ngati Mamoe dissenters and scattered them.[48] Ngai Tahu now became the dominant tribal identity in southern New Zealand.[49] But the dozen or so major Maori communities of southern New Zealand remained autonomous, their leaders co-operating only when it suited them. The aggrandisement of one was resented by the rest, for if one became greater the others felt belittled.

Notes

1. Irwin 1992: 105–10 and passim. Ngai Tuahuriri whakapapa recite forty-four generations since first arrival (Tau Ms 1992). Archaeologists on present evidence date first human settlement of southern New Zealand at between 800 and 1,100 years 'before the present' (Anderson 1983, 1991).
2. Tapuae o Uenuku ('Footsteps of the Rainbow God'), 2,885 metres high, is in Maori oratory the gateway to Te Wai Pounamu (Te Maire Tau pers. comm. 1992).
3. See Anderson in Wai-27 H1, H3 regarding Maori presence in the mountainous interior.
4. Beck 1984: passim.
5. Beck 1984: 51–56. The verification of this site in the 1970s vindicated Maori traditions, by then generally doubted, that the eponymous 'Wai Pounamu' was at or near Lake Wakatipu (see Kent Ms 'Remarks'; Shortland 1851: 155, 205).
6. Trotter & McCulloch 1989: 53.

7. Houghton 1980: 126; Anderson 1983: 27a.
8. Tortell 1981; McNab 1907: 216.
9. Bathgate 1969: 358.
10. Anderson in Wai-27 H1: 82.
11. Wai-27 R30 and H1: passim.
12. Lee Island in Lake Te Anau, for example, was regularly occupied for seasonal birding in the sixteenth century (Anderson & McGovern 1991: 17).
13. Beattie 1994: 316ff and passim; Shortland 1851: 199.
14. Boultbee 1986: 114; Kent Ms 2.7.1823; Turner 1930; Wilson 1979.
15. Buck 1950: 462ff; Dobson 1930: 96; Tikao 1990: passim.
16. Tikao 1990: 120ff; *AJHR* 1890 G-1: 22.
17. Tikao 1990: 123.
18. Mackay 1873 I (iii): 44–45.
19. Ibid.
20. Dieffenbach 1843 II: 74; Yate 1835: 164.
21. Shortland 1856: 247.
22. 'In the miserable account of war the gain is never equivalent to the loss, the pleasure to the pain.' (Gibbon 1994 6: 195.)
23. See e.g. Boultbee 1986: 100.
24. Ballara 1976: 492.
25. Buck 1950: 401; Kent Ms, 'Remarks'. Kent says the ransoming of prisoners was rare.
26. Bathgate 1969: 344ff; Anderson 1983; Wai-27 H1.
27. Barratt 1979: 62; Buck 1950: 345ff; Kawharu 1977: chapter 2; Mahuika 1981: passim.
28. Shortland 1851: 231.
29. Winiata 1967:28.
30. Anderson Wai-27 H1: 80; Heuer 1972: 20; Kent Ms 'Remarks'; Shortland 1851: 30, 59–60.
31. Buck 1950: 344.
32. Ibid: 382; Evison Ms 1952: 57–58; Firth 1959: 375 ff; Kawharu 1977: 60–62; Shortland 1856: 295 ff.
33. Kawharu 1977: 58ff; Tikao 1990: 136; Winiata 1967: 38–39.
34. *AJHR* 1890 G-1: passim; Firth 1959: chapter 11; Kawharu 1977: 58, passim; Shortland 1851: 284ff; 1856: 279ff; SIMAC Decision 15.11.1990.
35. Stack in *AJHR* 1890 G-1: 22.
36. Brailsford 1981: 13; Houghton 1980: passim; Tikao 1990: 39, 75.
37. Shortland 1851: 30ff.
38. Buck 1950: 404ff.
39. Brailsford 1981: 8; Houghton 1980: 148; Trotter & McCullough 1989: 91.
40. Buck 1950: 425; Kawharu 1977: 45; Shortland Ms Waiata Book 321.
41. Te Kahu 1901; Taki Ms 19–20; WJ, 24.8.1840.
42. Beaglehole 1962 I: 467ff; 1974: 217.
43. See Boultbee 1986: 54.
44. Forster 1982 II: 242–49, 273.
45. Harlow 1987: passim. Because 'Ngai' was pronounced 'Gai' or 'Kai' in the southern Maori dialect, some writers spell 'Ngai Tahu' as 'Kai Tahu'. The present writer nevertheless regards standardised spelling as desirable for written Maori, as it is for written English, regardless of the innumerable differences of pronunciation to be found among the various spoken dialects. Where southern dialect survives in established place names, however, a corresponding spelling is maintained (e.g. Waitaki = Waitangi, Akaroa = Whangaroa, Whakaraupo = Whangaraupo).
46. Anderson Ms 1991.
47. Anderson 1983: 38ff; Mackay 1873 I (3); Shortland 1851: 98ff; Stack in Jacobson 1914.
48. Tau Ms 1992; Tau, Goodall, Palmer & Tau 1990: 3–9a; SIMAC, evidence T. O'Regan.
49. Shortland 1851: 102; Tikao 1990: 125; Mackay 1873 II: 60, 123.

2

~

Civilisation

CAPTAIN COOK'S expeditions made no attempt to spread
Christianity. The Pacific Ocean was claimed by England's richest company, the East India Company, which banned missionaries
from its territories. And according to Protestantism's most revered
apostle, St Paul, heathens had already rejected Christ and were
irrevocably damned for it.[1] 'The holy things of God are not to
be cast before such dogs and swine,' declared one Lutheran church-
man.[2]

Since God had damned the heathen, Christians, in their own
view, could buy and sell them as slaves with a clear conscience.
European ships took firearms, rum and other merchandise to West
Africa, where armed local slave-traders delivered African slaves in
exchange.[3] These were forced on to the ships, and shackled on fetid
platforms below decks for the dreaded six-week 'middle passage' to
America. The survivors were bought there by Christian gentlemen, for forced labour under the tropical sun, or to serve as prosti-
tutes or concubines. Merchants could make £20 on each slave sold:
perhaps £8,000 for a shipment. The ships then loaded West Indies
sugar and molasses for Europe, where more rum was manufac-
tured for West Africa. So profitable was this 'Triangular Trade' that
Christian Britain, France, Spain and Holland fought fiercely for
the spoils. By Captain Cook's time, about a hundred thousand
African slaves were transported across the Atlantic annually, mostly
in British ships.[4]

Transportation across the Atlantic was not for Africans alone. It
had been imposed on British convicts, as 'banishment from the
realm', since the seventeenth century. In Cook's time, transportation or hanging were the usual penalties in Britain for theft or
forgery.[5] Seven years' transportation could be imposed for petty

theft, and fourteen years for prisoners reprieved from hanging. About a thousand convicts annually were assigned to private contractors in Britain, for forced labour in America.

In medieval Britain, the ancient customary right to use local commons and 'waste' lands for food gathering and other sustenance, had been curtailed by the feudal system, under which land was said to be held 'in fee', directly or indirectly, from the monarch or his powerful retainers, the hereditary nobles. Such customary rights as had survived to the eighteenth century were now being whittled away by Enclosure Acts to provide for private land 'development', and by Gaming Acts which gave the gentry exclusive ownership of rabbits, hares and other wild animals that commoners had traditionally trapped or hunted for food. Fortunes made from the Triangular Trade provided capital for agricultural development on the enclosed lands, and for the mechanisation of manufacturing. Many British yeomen and craftsmen lost their livelihoods, and small tenants such as Scottish crofters were forced off the land in the so-called 'Clearances'.[6] The natural resources of the British countryside, once available to all, were being privatised by Parliament in an increasingly market-driven economy, dispossessing more and more people of their traditional rights.

In eighteenth-century England life was cheap, and often short. Public health was considered no business of the government. Sewage might flow in the streets, around drinking wells, and into the nearest swamp or stream. Epidemics of smallpox, typhoid, plague and typhus were prevalent. Window taxes deprived the poor of proper ventilation in their wretched hovels, and urban industrialisation condemned thousands to living in cellars. Times were hard, unemployment was rife, crime against property was widespread, and the poor were desperate. The authorities too were desperate – to rid the country of its 'criminal class'. Hundreds of convicted thieves and forgers were hanged in public each year, to warn others – attracting thousands of spectators.[7]

Into this world of hardship, violence and despair there burst a religious movement which aroused depressed communities in town and country alike. A small band of Anglican clergy led by John Wesley, disregarding the official restraints of their church, took to open-air preaching with a fervour that captivated thousands. The message of these Wesleyans, or 'Methodists', taken directly from St Paul, was both simple and liberating: forget the cares of this world, and gain entry to the next by becoming dedicated Christians. Armed with the New Testament and the thrilling hymns of Wesley's brother Charles, the Wesleyans soon converted tens of thousands in England, and by the year 1800 the 'Methodist Connexion' functioned as an independent church.

⌇

The rebellion of Britain's chief American colonies in 1776 interrupted the transportation of British convicts to America. Many were therefore held in floating hulks in English ports, where they laboured in chains on harbour works. Others languished in overcrowded gaols where typhus ('gaol fever') killed more people than did the hangman.[8] The disease and rebelliousness in the gaols and prison hulks threatened to spread into the community at large. At last, in 1786, the government decided to 'effectually dispose of convicts by the establishment of a colony in New South Wales.'[9]

New South Wales had been claimed for Britain in 1770 by Captain Cook, under so-called 'right of discovery'. This derived from the doctrine of *terra nullius*, by which 'civilised' states, according to their own jurists, had the right to take over lands inhabited by 'savages' – who, again according to the jurists, had no systematic laws or settled government. Aboriginal Australians, like Maoris, of course governed themselves and their resources with unwritten laws of which European jurists were ignorant. Eventually Britain based her claim to Australia not on *terra nullius* but on the establishment of British law through colonisation.[10]

The first fleet carrying convicts for Australia left England in May 1787, commanded by Captain Arthur Phillip. About 750 convicts, male and female, aged from nine to eighty-two years, were crowded into six prison ships guarded by marines and accompanied by two warships and three store ships. Convict discipline was harsh even under a mild commander like Phillip, but for Navy men it could be harsher. For insubordination, sailors and marines could receive two hundred blows of the lash. Under this torture men could die.[11]

On its way to Australia, Phillip's fleet loaded supplies at Rio de Janiero for a month, and again at Cape Town, the dreaded convicts being always confined to their ships. Ashore at Cape Town, an English officer watched the public execution of an African condemned for running amok with a knife. This heathen offence was dealt with hastily by the local Dutch authorities, for fear that the offender might

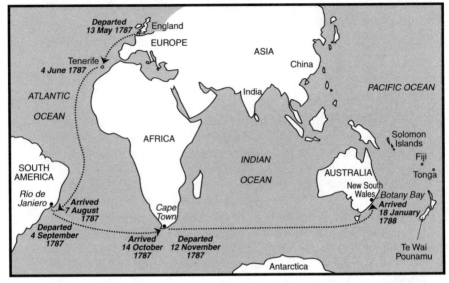

Voyage of the first convict fleet to Australia, 1787.

die first from a bayonet wound inflicted when he was arrested. At the place of execution the Englishman saw the prisoner spreadeagled on a wooden cross:

> The executioner then took pinchers which were made red hot and took all the fleshy part of the arms, legs and thighs out. The bones of his arm were then broke by an iron bar both above and below the elbow. One of his hands was then cut off and the bloody end drawn across his face. His legs and thighs were next broke. He seemed just then expiring when his head was severed from his body at two blows and stuck on a pike about eight feet high ... After the executioner had fulfilled his office he turned round and made a bow to the audience as if he expected applause.[12]

Captain Phillip's fleet arrived at Botany Bay, New South Wales, eight months after leaving England, and then settled at 'Sydney Cove' in nearby Port Jackson. Once landed, the convicts – some of whom had already been confined to their ships for over a year – were virtually marooned, whatever their sentences. 'The Government exported criminals, but it neither guaranteed nor attempted to restore them to their native land.'[13] Unrepentant convicts received the penalties of the law,[14] with flogging for disobedience, and death for theft. Thus it was that civilisation arrived within fourteen days' sailing time of Te Wai Pounamu.

∽

A second convict fleet reached Port Jackson in 1790. On this voyage, private contractors had charge of the convicts – nearly two-fifths of whom died before arrival, or soon after.[15] With this fleet came the first of the New South Wales Corps under Major Francis Grose, to replace Phillip's marines. Army officers had to purchase their commissions, and expected to profit from them. In 1792 Grose and others invested £4,200 in chartering the convict transport *Britannia*, under Captain William Raven, to sail to Cape Town via Cape Horn to get clothing, liquor and stores, for sale to the Sydney convict station.[16]

Convict transports were usually contracted with the East India Company for the return voyage to England, loading tea from China en route. In Raven's case, the East India Company agreed to his

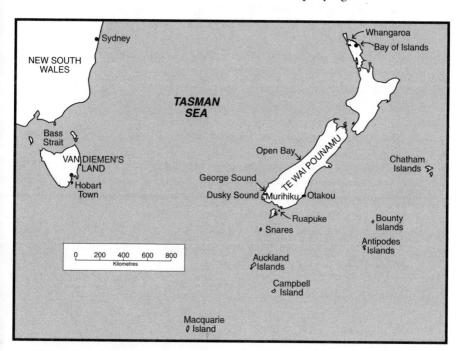

The southern sealing grounds, 1790–1830.

31

leaving sealers at Dusky Sound on his way to Cape Town, to get sealskins for sale in China. But when Raven later returned to Dusky Sound the sealers had got only 4,500 skins. The sealing speculators then turned to Bass Strait, where large herds had been found.[17]

Sealers were left at the breeding grounds by their employers for months, or years. Afterwards they were paid for their tally of skins. The sealer was 'ready to kill anything that looked at him',[18] dealing a crushing blow to the snout of adult seals and cubs alike before they could take to the water. The Bass Strait herds were destroyed after a few seasons of such slaughter, and sealers again turned to New Zealand. To deceive competitors and evade the East India Company, sealing destinations beyond Australia were generally kept secret.

Sealers were again busy on Murihiku coasts between 1803 and 1810, and on the uninhabited islands to the south and east. Ships' captains tricked their sealers and each other, and sealers tricked other sealers, for the profits to be won.[19] In the desperate quest for gain, men endured stormy seas, treacherous coasts, and relentless gales, and some large tallies were taken.[20] By 1810, the slaughter of seals had produced a glut on the world sealskin market. Only large cargoes remained profitable. The sealers' attention shifted to Macquarie Island, where vast herds of fur seals and elephant seals had been discovered. In 1811, a cargo of 35,000 skins reached Sydney. But soon the great sub-Antarctic herds too were destroyed, and sealing was in decline.[21]

～

By the 1790s, the Ngai Tahu chief Te Hau Tapunuiotu had died and was buried at Taumutu. His son Honekai was ariki in Murihiku. European ships had begun calling at Te Wai Pounamu for fresh water, vegetables and firewood. The first to visit Akaroa was an English ship which anchored about 1791 near Onuku. The local Maoris, astonished and alarmed at so large a vessel, mustered at their pa overlooking Pakaariki Bay.

Fifty years later, the tohunga Tuauau recalled his father's cautious boarding of this ship:

> He was well received, and returned on shore with the news that he had seen men with eyes, a mouth, ears, hands and feet; that he had eaten with them and had obtained an axe, which he showed us. Then the desire to have more of these made us all

want to go on board. We were dressed in cloaks of harakeke, which we left in exchange for axes and spike nails.[22]

Potatoes had been left by Captain Cook at Totaranui (Queen Charlotte Sound), and were a great boon for the Maoris of southern New Zealand when they acquired some of them. Using traditional Maori cultivation methods, fifty to a hundred men would clear the vegetation from a suitable area, burn it when dry, and afterwards turn the soil with the ko. Seed potatoes were then planted by hand, in small mounds, like kumara. Cabbages, carrots, turnips and wheat were also grown.[23] Murihiku potatoes were in great demand among visiting ships by 1810, enabling Maoris to obtain iron and steel tools in place of their traditional stone implements.

The Maoris of southern New Zealand generally welcomed Europeans, whom they called tangata pora. Ships' officers could consort with chiefs, and lower ranks with commoners. If the visitors traded fairly, and sought permission before using mahinga kai or erecting a building, they were treated as friends. But any flouting of Maori conventions invited reprisals. Tapu was the strictest convention, some breaches of it being punishable by death.[24] As a Maori elder later explained: 'Any breach of good manners might lead to a man being killed, as the Maoris were the worst people in the world for killing offenders against the rules.'[25]

Some Europeans made enemies by helping themselves to seals, timber, fish, and other resources as they pleased.[26] About the year 1810, Honekai was offended by some sealers from the ship *Sydney Cove*, and five of them were killed and eaten. Only sixteen-year-old James Caddell was spared, to be taken into the tribe. This, and similar incidents, gave Murihiku Maoris the reputation of being 'exceedingly fierce and cruel.'[27]

Meanwhile, fierce and cruel wars had gripped Europe. Hundreds of thousands of men at the behest of their rulers marched into one another's countries to kill and lay waste. The artist Francisco Goya depicted the sufferings of the Spanish people under occupation by French soldiers. Rape, torture, dismemberment, and massacre abounded in this war between Christian neighbours.[28] During this savagery in Europe, English Christians became concerned at savagery elsewhere. Baptists and other Nonconformists, Anglicans, and finally Methodists, set up missionary societies to give the heathen a second chance of escaping the damnation promised them by St Paul. Methodists saw the defeat of Napoleon at Waterloo as a sign from God, obliging them to become 'a world-missionary force' – especially in the South Pacific, a reputed stronghold of God's most dreadful curse: cannibalism.[29]

In 1814 the Anglican Church Missionary Society (CMS) started a New Zealand Maori mission at the Bay of Islands, supervised by the New South Wales colonial chaplain, Samuel Marsden. He believed in teaching heathens agriculture and crafts before evangelising them. 'Civilisation must pave the way for the conversion of the heathen,' he declared.[30] In Sydney in July 1819, Marsden hired Captain Abimelech Riggs of the American sealer *General Gates* to take him and a fresh CMS mission party, including the Reverend John Butler, to the Bay of Islands. By the end of the voyage, Marsden and Butler knew that Riggs's crew included escaped convicts. The two waited until Riggs next visited the Bay, in April 1820, when HMS *Dromedary* was present. Butler then informed on the convicts, in his capacity as Resident Magistrate, and called on the *Dromedary*'s captain 'to secure and return them to the colony and Government of New South Wales.'[31] Riggs and his ship were arrested and sent under naval guard to Sydney,[32] where he was fined £6,000 for 'seducing' convicts. The convicts protested that Riggs had ill-treated them, but they were returned to prison.[33]

The New South Wales Government now revived a project attempted in northern New Zealand thirty years before – the commercial development of harakeke, called 'flax' by the English, for ships' cordage and sails. Captain William Edwardson was sent in the government sloop *Snapper* to look for suitable flax in southern New Zealand. Soon after he reached Chalky Bay in November 1822, some *General Gates* sealers sought refuge with him, Riggs being virtually at war with the Maoris of Murihiku. The sealers had been pursued from Preservation Inlet by three war canoes commanded by the southern Ngai Tahu chiefs Pahi, Te Wera and Te Pai, Honekai's nephew. James Caddell and another European had been guiding the Maoris to the hideouts of the sealers, some of whom had already been killed and eaten. Caddell, 'much tattooed', was now a rangatira of consequence through being married to Tokitoki, Te Pai's sister. The Maoris, noted Edwardson, 'behaved very well' on the *Snapper*, and agreed to give back the sealers' boats.[34]

Captain Edwardson took Pahi and Caddell aboard the *Snapper* and spent weeks visiting Murihiku villages in search of suitable flax and methods of preparing it. Thriving Maori communities were reported, with substantial houses 'up to thirty feet long and twenty feet high'.[35] Edwardson presented chiefs with pigs – a novelty at Murihiku. He found that Maori women prepared flax fibre better by hand than could be done with his Sydney machines, and he arranged for them to prepare some for him.[36] At Ruapuke, Bluff, and Pahi's village, Edwardson loaded flax fibre and a large quantity of potatoes in return for knives and iron tools. He took Caddell, Tokitoki and a Maori youth back to Sydney in March 1823 with some samples. Great interest was aroused there in the flax trade,[37] which remained profitable for some years.

∿

Sydney by 1823 was a thriving commercial centre. Although several thousand convicts arrived from Britain each year, the free population of Sydney now almost equalled the number of convicts. Free labour was scarce nevertheless, and most of the work force were convicts. Convicts not needed for official forced labour were assigned to private employers, who could have them flogged for disobedience.[38] Thus in New South Wales a landed gentry arose on prison labour, just as in America the plantation gentry had arisen on slave labour.

Governor Phillip, as was customary for colonial governors, had in 1787 been instructed by the British Government to be considerate towards any Aboriginal Australians he encountered.[39] The initially helpful attitude of Aborigines towards the English is well documented.[40] Phillip wanted them to move to reserves and cultivate wheat, and thus become 'civilised'. But the Aborigines preferred their own foods and way of life to those of the penal colony. This was widely seen as proof of their incorrigible savagery, and common arrogance soon overshadowed the well-intentioned official policies towards them.[41] Contempt for 'savages' was shown by colonists and convicts alike, and was tempered only by the savages' fierceness in defending themselves and their womenfolk.

The plundering of settlers' crops by Aborigines in retaliation for European intrusion was reported in New South Wales as early as 1795.[42] Subsequently, huge areas of Aboriginal territory were granted to settlers for sheep and cattle runs. The introduced flocks and herds damaged or destroyed the habitats of native animals and polluted the waters, threatening the Aborigines' food supplies. Those who resisted the occupation of their lands were violently suppressed.[43]

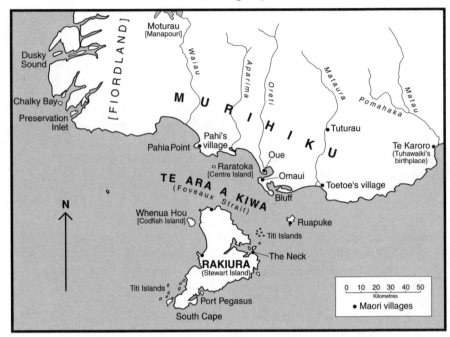

Murihiku in the 1820s.

Faced with starvation, some sought employment with the runholders. Others sought survival by moving off. Those who sought refuge in town were scorned by convicts and free men alike. Maoris visiting New South Wales could observe these aspects of civilisation, and reflect on them.

~

In May 1823 Captain John Kent was sent from Sydney to Muri-hiku in the government cutter *Mermaid*. With him, after spending two months in Sydney, went Caddell's party of three. Kent was to obtain more flax, and bring back some Maori flax-dressers. On 14 June a fire east of Preservation Inlet led Kent to a party of Pahi's people, pitching camp for their winter sealing and birding. They said that the Bluff and Ruapuke people had been busily pre-paring flax for trade. 'I was much pleased with the manner of our reception by these southern savages,' wrote Kent. They did not intend killing any more Europeans, he said, 'now that we had become friends by commencing trade'.[44] Kent went on to Ruapuke, and was welcomed. But unknown to him, Pahi with his main winter sealing and birding party on Rakiura had again killed and eaten a party of *General Gates* sealers – the third such incident in three years.[45]

On 25 June 1823 the chief Taiaroa, while returning to Otakou from the titi islands, called at Ruapuke with his birding party. He was described as a slender young man, 'not so manly' as other chiefs, but showing 'great ingenuity in understanding and imitating' European ways.[46] He brought grim news. Crossing from Rakiura that day in heavy seas, Pahi's two double canoes had broken up simultaneously, drowning all fifty people aboard. The storm had prevented assistance from other canoes in the offing. Among these was a small craft from distant Kaikoura carrying about twelve men, women and children. Kent marvelled at their making so long a journey 'for their winter food'.[47] Pahi's disaster made a deep impression on the Maoris. The atua, it seemed, now frowned on the killing of Europeans. Pahi's *General Gates* victims were the last Europeans killed by Murihiku Maoris.[48]

Kent noticed the enmity between the Murihiku and Otakou chiefs. Te Wera warned Kent against Taiaroa, and Taiaroa warned him against Te Wera. 'There is certainly a very great jealousy existing between the parties,' noted Kent, 'and their only care at present seems to be in watching each other's motions.' At Ruapuke, Kent loaded green flax for Sydney, taking on board Te Pai, Caddell and Te Wera, and their wives, and Te Wera's child. The two women were to demonstrate the dressing of New Zealand flax in Sydney.

When Kent called at Otakou for more flax, the Maoris there thought they were going to be attacked, as there was a second ship in the offing. Two hundred warriors mustered for battle, among them a Lascar from the brig *Matilda* whose boat-mates 'had all been eat'. However, peace prevailed. The Otakou Maoris had prepared no flax, having heard from Murihiku that none would be wanted. They undertook to prepare flax forthwith, however, and told Kent that more was available at Akaroa, Kaikoura, and Cook Strait. Kent found no regular European traders on the coast of Te Wai Pounamu, nor any firearms.[49]

Kent returned his Maori passengers to Murihiku in the government brig *Elizabeth Henrietta* later in 1823, under instructions to promote the civilisation of the Maoris 'by supplying them with British manufactures in exchange for their flax'. The brig grounded at Ruapuke and was not refloated by the carpenters until a year later. Mice from the ship were the first seen on Ruapuke, and were called 'henriettas'. The ship returned to Sydney in March 1825 with a cargo of flax fibre.[50]

~

Honekai was dead by 1825, and his mana had passed to his son Te Whakataupuka – 'the boldest and most active man amongst the whole tribe'.[51] His pre-eminence as ariki in southern Te Wai Pou-namu was secure, for the leading chiefs were his relatives[52] and his own mana was above reproach.

The ariki Te Maiharanui, Te Whakataupuka's northern cousin, had such distinguished ancestry that his tapu was intense, and his mere presence caused concern lest his shadow falling upon a garden might cause plants to die.[53] But such a high-born ariki did not rule the tribe. Rather, his position resembled that of a medieval king – a sacred personage among commoners, but merely 'first among equals' among the proud and jealous barons. Not all Ngai Tahu chiefs acknowledged Te Maiharanui as their superior.[54] He was among the first Maori chiefs of southern New Zealand to en-courage European trade. He established a trading post at Taka-puneke in Akaroa, and organised flax production to encourage European shipping to visit there. He allowed his son Tu Te Hounuku to sail off on a whaling ship.

While Te Maiharanui was away at Kaikoura about 1824, a woman named Murihaka tried on one of his precious cloaks at Waikakahi. This sacrilege caused such resentment among his rela-tions that they attacked those of Murihaka, and two chiefs of Ngati Irakehu hapu were killed by warriors from neighbouring Taumutu. Te Maiharanui, on returning from Kaikoura, decided to punish not those who had interfered with his cloak, but the people of Taumutu. He raised a taua from Wairewa, Waikakahi and Banks Peninsula. With the help of Taununu (chief at Ripapa) he captured Taumutu. Some Kaiapoi warriors in his force, however, having relatives there, forestalled a massacre.

The Taumutu chiefs had now to retaliate to restore their mana. They appealed to their southern relatives for help. In the follow-ing fighting season (1825–1826), several taua from the south, as well as one from Kaiapoi, rallied at Taumutu and prepared to attack Wairewa pa. The Murihiku warriors had brought two muskets – the first ever seen on a southern Maori battlefield.[55] Taiaroa, who accompanied the Otakou taua, belonged to Taumutu himself. But he had relatives at Wairewa Pa, and warned them about the muskets. The Wairewa people escaped on the lake in their canoes. The Kaiapoi taua, unwilling to be taunted for returning home bloodless, sought out and killed a nephew of Taununu. Taununu, in revenge, surprised the distant Ngai Tuahuriri outpost at Whakaepa, and killed everyone there.[56]

∾

In 1824, three New Zealand colonisation schemes were being canvassed in London. One had been floated by the French émigré Charles de Thierry; another by a 'New Zealand Company'; and a third by William Stewart, a former sealer now masquerading as Stewart the cartographer after whom Stewart Island had been named in 1816. Late in 1824, sponsored by a London firm,[57] Stewart the adventurer sailed from England in the schooner *Prince of Denmark* to recruit settlers in Sydney – but could find none. He went on to the Bay of Islands early in 1826, where he persuaded eight sawyers and shipwrights with their Maori wives to accompany him to Port Pegasus, an extensive uninhabited harbour at Rakiura that his namesake had skilfully charted. Awaiting him there, as arranged in London, was Captain James Herd with sixty-five New Zealand Company settlers in the ship *Rosanna*, direct from London via the southern ocean with the cutter *Lambton* as tender.[58]

Soon after Herd's ships had reached Port Pegasus in March 1826, they had been visited by Maoris with the chiefs Te Wera, Toetoe and Taiaroa. The men wore sailors' clothing, but the women were 'nearly naked'. The Maoris performed songs and dances. Their food while visiting included young seal, unsalted dried fish, potatoes, biscuit, salt beef and pork, and rice. They preferred water with sugar to any other drink. James Caddell was there, and confided to the Englishmen his general distrust of Maoris. 'Arms is the only sure way of civilizing them,' he said. 'Missionaries are of little or no use.'[59]

Herd and Stewart were now visited by Captain Kent in the brig *Elizabeth*, on a sealing venture from Sydney. Herd, realising that Port Pegasus was unsuitable for settlement, sailed north. At Otakou he traded amicably for potatoes, flax and pigs, and sailed on to Horomaka, where he was also invited to trade. But adverse winds drove him off, and he finally landed his settlers at Hokianga in the far north.[60] Stewart left his sawyers and shipwrights at Port Pegasus with six months' supplies and a contract to build him a 100-ton vessel. But he never returned. The workmen, led by William Cook, began work on a smaller vessel. Eventually, after some hardship, they left Port Pegasus.[61]

Among Kent's sealers in 1826 was John Boultbee, a young Englishman who kept a journal of his experiences. His first sealing gang was driven from Open Bay (Jackson Bay) in a fight with local Maoris wanting 'to acquire some of the white man's treasures' – particularly their sealing boat. Retreating to Dusky Sound, Boultbee's gang got too few sealskins to satisfy Kent. Boultbee then gave up sealing, and lived among the Murihiku Maoris for more than a year. They approved of his Open Bay fight, saying that the attackers were an 'enemy tribe' from Akaroa.[62]

The southern musket trade, encouraged by Te Whakataupuka, was now in full swing. The exchange was mainly for flax and potatoes. But Boultbee noted that 'the father of a family will sell a daughter, or two, or three, if required, for a musket each.' At Ruapuke and Otakou, a trader could obtain 'two large fat hogs for two muskets, and 100 baskets of potatoes each weighing 35 pounds, for an adze'. Boultbee became friendly with chiefs who had visited Sydney. These warned their more truculent colleagues against molesting Europeans, 'as their trade depended on them'.[63]

Boultbee considered Maori sailors timid in rough weather, and described their vessels as they arrived from their various coastal settlements for the 1827 titi season:

> Some of their canoes were eighty feet long, these canoes have no outriggers, and are about three feet wide; the lower part is one solid piece hollowed out, and risen upon by a plank of eight inches wide; at the stem and stern are high pieces of carved wood fixed. They are pulled by oars and steered with an oar. The sails are made of flax matted together, and formed like a lug, but their depth, or hoist is much greater than the width. With a fair wind they sail well, but when the wind is abeam, they lower the sail and pull.[64]

Boultbee found that the Maoris liked entertainment and song. He described a comic song with 'something of an amatory nature in it,' in which the singers generally stood on their heads.

Of Te Whakataupuka, Boultbee wrote:

> He was the most complete model of strength, activity and elegance I had seen in any man. He was in height five feet ten

inches; his muscular well formed arms and handsome falling
shoulders, well turned limbs, and erect stature, together with
his active, lively gait, were such as could not be witnessed by
anyone without exciting their notice. His countenance was not
exactly handsome, but very prepossessing, and bespoke a quick
intelligent mind.[65]

Peter Williams, who later ran a whaling station under Te Whakataupuka's protection, recalled:

Tabuki [Te Whakataupuka] was more powerful than any other
man in southern New Zealand, but one who permitted no
infringement of his power as a chief. His word was law . . . He
is said to have been more than honest in all his dealings with
his pakeha friends, always true to his word, and one who permitted neither his own nor other tribes to molest the pakeha
trader even by petty thefts without condign punishment.[66]

His fellow-tribesmen saw a different side of Te Whakataupuka:

There is no one like Te Whakataupuka when he is angry. He is
awesome. There is no exception for the women, he would just
take them whether married or not. His reputation for this was
known throughout the island.[67]

Te Whakataupuka encouraged European contact, and forbade
the killing of Europeans, allocating them Whenua Hou as a sanctu-
ary.[68] He personally protected Europeans he liked. Boultbee noted:
'I have seen the white people playing and joking with him in as
careless a manner as if they were amongst their own countrymen.'
Te Whakataupuka always wore Maori dress. He told Boultbee that
'if he would leave off wearing European clothes and dress in a kakahu
he would be well liked, and as long as he stayed amongst Maoris
he would not want . But – 'White people are too selfish,' said Te
Whakataupuka.

∾

The news that Taununu had insulted the chiefs of Ngai Tuahuriri
by massacring their people at Whakaepa soon reached Ngai
Tuahuriri's relatives in the south. When the 1827 fighting season
approached, Te Whakataupuka got about twenty muskets and
trained and drilled his musketeers. He then sailed his war canoes
500 kilometres northward to Wairewa to join taua from Otakou
and Kaiapoi. He decided first to attack Wairewa pa. Again Taiaroa

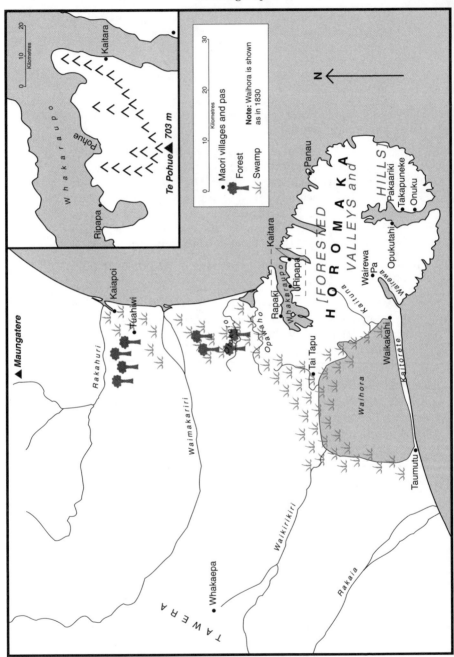

Maori villages and pas
Forest
Swamp
Note: Waihora is shown as in 1830

Te Pohue ▲ 703 m

Whakaraupo

Pohue

Kaitara

Ripapa

N

Maungatere ▲

Kaiapoi

Tuahiwi

Rakahuri

Panau

HOROMAKA and HILLS

Pakaariki
Takapuneke
Onuku

Opukutahi

Wairewa
•Pa

Wairewa

Kaituna

Kaitara

Ripapa

Rapaki

Whakaraupo

Opawaho

Tai Tapu

Waikakahi

Kaitorete

Waihora

FORESTED VALLEYS

Waimakariri

Waikirikiri

Whakaepa

TAWERA

Rakaia

Taumutu

Kilometres
0   10   20   30

Kilometres
0   10   20

Kilometres
0   10   20

went ahead and warned the defenders, who again took to the lake. But Te Whakataupuka ambushed them on the water, and the bush-clad hills echoed to the terrifying sound of the new weapons. The Wairewa canoes were overwhelmed. Even the bravest warriors succumbed to trained musketeers who could kill without coming to blows, and could shoot those who jumped overboard as well. So many were eaten by their own relatives after this uneven battle, that the murderous Ngai Tahu feud became known as Kai Huanga.[70]

The victors then sailed for Taununu's island pa of Ripapa. Taununu had already left, crossing Whakaraupo to safety. The Otakou taua approached Ripapa from the landward side, and Taiaroa shouted his usual warning. All on Ripapa who could crowd into their canoes set out after Taununu. But Te Whakataupuka emerged from a neigh-bouring cove and headed them off, ordering his canoes in line ahead so that his musketeers could fire broadside:

> About twenty men, who had muskets and ten rounds of cart-ridges, each of which contained a ball cut into four quarters, made a serious havoc at the first volley. They then loaded and fired until the canoes were sinking and their inmates swim-ming wounded in the water. These were soon despatched; the dead were left without anything being done to them. The con-querors then went on shore, and killed women and children and plundered the settlement of all that was valuable.[71]

The more active fugitives were allowed by Taiaroa to flee up the mountainside of Te Pohue, whence they repelled their pursuers with boulders. But Te Whakataupuka's taua exacted the usual retribution on the captives. Boultbee noted:

> It was horrid to hear of the cruelties that were practised on defence-less women and children. Several of the latter were tied up in lots and hung around the sterns of the canocs so that as they went along, they were choked by the waves. Some of the flesh of the unfortunate victims was eaten with potatoes. Te Whakataupuka had taken a woman as his cooky or slave, she had been with him a few days when he asked her to sing, which she declined, on this in the wantonness of his anger, he dispatched her with a tomahawk. On another occasion he killed a chief, whom he offered his choice to be his cooky or to die, the latter alternative was preferred by the heroic prisoner, Te Whakataupuka thereupon drew out his toma-hawk from underneath his mat, and with one blow killed him.[72]

Opposite: *Scene of the Kai Huanga feud, 1824–1830.*

Their honour satisfied, the victors dispersed to their homes. But Te Maiharanui, who had avoided Te Whakataupuka, still had scores to settle. With promises of peace, he persuaded the Taumutu refugees at Otakou to return home. Then, with the aid of a Kaiapoi contingent, he ambushed them as they approached Taumutu. Both sides had muskets, but the Taumutu people, fatigued from their 350-kilometre journey, were massacred.[73] Rumours now reached Murihiku that Te Maiharanui would attack Te Whakataupuka next season with the aid of a North Island ally, Te Rauparaha. The Murihiku people left their more easterly settlements for the greater safety of Ruapuke and Foveaux Strait.[74]

Notes

1. Romans 10: 18 and 11: 22.
2. Findlay & Holdsworth 1921 I: 24–25.
3. Hamilton 1947: 451.
4. Sherrard 1959: 66–69; Hamilton 1947: 449.
5. Molesworth 1838: 7b; Oldham 1990: 27–29.
6. Mingay 1989: 55–58; Hopkins 1985: 30-31; Williams 1961: passim; Thompson 1993: chapter 3.
7. Williams 1961: chapter 1.
8. Oldham 1990: 24.
9. Oldham 1990: 33–64, 122; Tench 1979: x–xii.
10. Bartlett 1993: ixff.
11. Hughes 1987: 66ff.
12. Fowell 1988: 105–6.
13. Oldham 1990: 139.
14. Tench 1979: 41.
15. Ibid: 173.
16. Kociumbas 1992: 47.
17. Hall-Jones 1945: 10.
18. McNab 1907: 39ff, 250.
19. Coutts 1969: 500ff; McNab 1907: chapters 8–10
20. Richards 1995: 28.
21. Bathgate 1969: 345; McNab 1907: 152 and 1908 I: 304ff.
22. Lavaud 1986: 24.
23. Coutts loc cit; Shepherd Ms: 24–25.3.1826; Wade 1842: 19.
24. Boultbee 1986: 88.
25. Tikao 1990: 127.
26. Bathgate, Wai-27 V5: 4.
27. Hall-Jones 1945: 30n; McNab 1907: 109, 217, 235. Stewart Island was early known as 'South Cape' (Richards 1995: 19n).
28. Goya 1967: passim
29. Deuteronomy 28: 53; Findlay & Holdsworth 1921 I: chapter 1.
30. Harvard-Williams 1961: 15.
31. Butler–Skinner, 11.4.1820, in Butler 1927: 88.
32. Cumpston 1977 I (1): 121.
33. Marsden 1932: 143n. Riggs's alleged brutality was not part of the missionaries' complaint.
34. McNab 1907: 202, 250ff.
35. Boultbee 1986: 57; McNab 1907: chapter 19.
36. McNab 1907: 216.
37. Ibid: chapter 18.
38. Molesworth 1838: 10, passim.
39. Woolmington 1988: 1–12.
40. See e.g. Tench 1979: 52, 229, 239–40, passim.
41. McBryde 1989: passim.
42. Woolmington 1988: 35.
43. Butlin 1993: 129, 209; Kociumbas 1992: 141–44; Woolmington 1988: 34–56.

44. Kent Ms: 14.6.1823.
45. McNab 1907: 182–88; Wohlers 1895: 142.
46. Shepherd Ms: 25.3.1826.
47. Kent Ms: 25–27.6.1823.
48. Boultbee 1986: 102.
49. Kent Ms: 17–20.7.1823.
50. McNab 1907: 230ff.
51. Boultbee 1986: 102.
52. Shortland 1851: 94ff, tables.
53. Te Maire Tau pers. comm. 1992
54. Tikao 1990: 141n. Tikao (ibid) says Te Maiharanui was 'upoko ariki' ('supreme chief') of Ngai Tahu.
55. Note: Carrington Ms (1934: 156) puts this incident at 1827, but Boultbee's journal confirms it as 1826.
56. Stack in Jacobson 1914: 20ff.
57. Boultbee 1986: 92n.
58. Ross 1987: 113 ff, chapter 12, passim; Shepherd Ms: 18.4.1826. Ross says Stewart preceded Herd at Port Pegasus, but Shepherd

(5.3.1826) confirms the reverse.
59. Shepherd Ms: 23–25.3.1826. Caddell is here referred to as 'Tommy'.
60. Ross 1987: 139; Shepherd Ms: 2–15.5.1826.
61. Hall-Jones 1994: 43–50.
62. Begg & Begg 1979: 149ff; Boultbee 1986: 42.
63. Boultbee 1986: 59, 78ff, 102.
64. Regarding Polynesian voyaging, see Houghton 1996: passim; Irwin 1992: passim; Sharp 1957: 38; Sutton 1994: 52–76.
65. Boultbee 1986: 114.
66. Richards 1995: 50.
67. Taki Ms: 20–21.
68. Begg & Begg 1979: 213n.
69. Boultbee 1986: chapters 4–5.
70. Stack in Jacobson 1914: 20ff.
71. Boultbee 1986: 68.
72. Ibid: 71.
73. Stack in Jacobson 1914: 20ff.
74. Boultbee 1986: 101.

3

Te Rauparaha

EUROPEAN NATIONS rose or fell by warfare, and successful military commanders were their most celebrated heroes. So it was with Maori tribes. In the North Island of New Zealand there were many more tribes than in Te Wai Pounamu, so that pretexts for warfare among quarrelsome chiefs were endless. Ngati Toa of Kawhia, caught between the warring tribes of Waikato and Taranaki, had to struggle to survive. Late in the eighteenth century a chief arose among them who, although not of the noblest birth, became pre-eminent. As a child he was nicknamed 'Te Rauparaha' (The Convolvulus Leaf), when a Waikato chief proposed to eat him with a garnish of that plant. Te Rauparaha was of short but powerful build, narrow but thoughtful features, resounding voice, and great personal magnetism. Through his shrewd judgment, skilled diplomacy, and audacious stratagems, his fame spread far and wide. Clearly his atua was a powerful one.

In 1819 northern New Zealand was engulfed by musket wars unleashed by Nga Puhi, the first tribe to acquire muskets, under their fighting chief Hongi. Te Rauparaha, to escape this danger, led a heke of Ngati Toa 400 kilometres southward towards the straits of Raukawa Moana, hoping to secure his own musket supply by trading with ships there. At Horowhenua, within sight of the straits, the resident Muaupoko tribe were suspicious of Te Rauparaha. Their chiefs invited him to a feast, then attacked him in the night. He narrowly escaped, but his children were killed.

Rugged Kapiti Island, at the northern entrance to Raukawa Moana, was an ideal base for the musket trade. Te Rauparaha wrested it from Muaupoko and Ngati Apa in 1823. He then by a ruse captured Hotuiti, a stronghold of local Rangitane and Ngati Apa, killing many of their chiefs. These tribes together retaliated, and

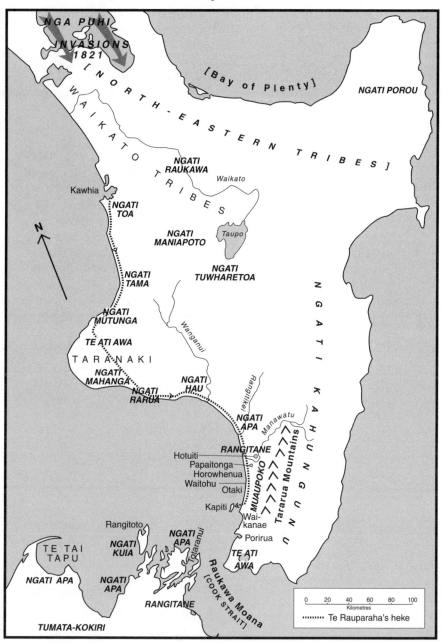

Te Rauparaha's heke, with some tribal locations in the 1820s.

with numerous allies they tried to recapture Kapiti in 1824. They were defeated.[1] Te Rauparaha's musket-trading base was now secure.

At Te Rauparaha's urging, sections of Te Ati Awa[2] and Ngati Raukawa (his relatives) from the north now joined him. Ngati Toa were determined to kill off the defeated tribes – 'but it was Te Rauparaha who was the most determined', according to contemporaries. By 1827 the fugitives were confined to the Tararua mountains, afraid to light their fires by day lest their smoke should betray them.[3]

Te Rauparaha now wished to conquer Te Wai Pounamu.[4] Defiant and insulting words from southern chiefs came to his ears, which he had to avenge. In the fighting season of 1827–1828, not long after Te Maiharanui's Taumutu ambush, Te Rauparaha armed a strong force with muskets and crossed the straits. The traditionally armed Ngati Kuia, Ngati Apa and Rangitane of northern Wai Pounamu were overwhelmed and their settlements devastated. The victors sailed on to Kaikoura, where Ngati Kuri mistook their visitors for friends and greeted them on the beach, only to be set upon

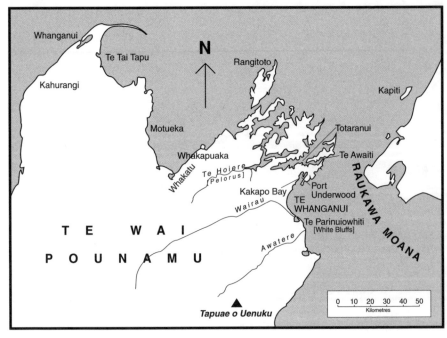

Northern Te Wai Pounamu.

with musket fire. All were massacred or captured, except those who escaped to the mountains.[5]

∼

The Wai Pounamu chiefs who had challenged Te Rauparaha were thinking of traditional warfare, with hand-to-hand weapons. Such warfare, during a succession of fighting seasons, might favour now one side, now the other, depending on the prowess of the contending warriors and their tohunga, and the favour of the gods. Captured communities might be annihilated. But the extermination of whole tribes, while it might be desired, had rarely been heard of. Traditional hand-to-hand combat was too exhausting to be sustained for long. But musket warfare was comparatively easy. Warriors with two muskets each to use at alternate intervals could fire for hours, and still have energy to pursue the vanquished.

Thus firearms brought unforeseen consequences to New Zealand. Just as armoured, stirruped horsemen became invincible in medieval Europe,[6] so musket-armed Maori warriors, well drilled and in sufficient numbers, carried all before them in New Zealand. The new warfare engulfed not only the defeated chiefs but their tribes as well, on an unprecedented scale. Medieval barons with their mounted retainers laid waste to their rivals' territories in their quest for glory and plunder; so did Maori fighting chiefs with musket-armed taua. Only the possession of sufficient muskets could avert disaster. 'Those who lagged behind in the race for arms faced destruction at the hands of those who forged ahead.'[7]

With the multitude of prisoners accumulating from his victories, Te Rauparaha organised the production of flax and potatoes and the provision of tattooed heads and slave women on a grand scale. European shipping flocked to Kapiti, enabling Te Rauparaha and his enterprising chiefs to get yet more armaments to enslave or exterminate yet more Maoris.[8] This musket economy, perfected by the genius of Te Rauparaha, rivalled the North Atlantic Triangular Trade in the degree of devastation and human suffering it caused. In New Zealand as in Africa, whole tribes were annihilated and whole districts were depopulated. At Kapiti, as at Sydney, the hardest toil and the severest punishments were meted out to prisoners. But whereas executed British convicts were consigned to quicklime in unmarked graves, executed Maori prisoners were eaten. Their heads, suitably tattooed, went to the preserved-head trade.[9]

The distinguished Ngati Toa chief Te Pehi Kupe returned from England in 1829 with a large consignment of muskets and ammunition. Te Whakataupuka too was enlarging his armoury. In 1829 he let Peter Williams establish a whaling station in Preservation Inlet for Bunn and Company of Sydney, in return for the promise of firearms, ammunition and other merchandise. Te Whakataupuka further enhanced his reputation by getting two twelve-pound carronades and two 'air-guns' from Williams.[10] Williams employed William Cook's party from Port Pegasus to build houses, a shed for sixteen whaleboats, and a large trading store at 'Port Bunn'. The adjacent Fiordland sounds yielded plenty of whales during calving, and the station prospered until they were exterminated.

Ngati Toa again invaded Te Wai Pounamu in the 1829–1830 fighting season. The také was that Kekerengu, a Ngati Kahungunu chief, had taken refuge with Ngati Kuri at Omihi after seducing a female protégé of Te Rauparaha's nephew Rangihaeata, a famous fighting chief. The invaders rounded up surviving Rangitane and Ngati Apa, ate many of them, and then proceeded to Omihi. They greeted the residents as friends, then attacked them. Those who failed to escape were butchered or enslaved.[11]

Ngati Toa then hurried on to Kaiapoi. But Ngai Tuahuriri were on their guard. Since the Kai Huanga feud the great pa had been adapted for musket warfare. Protected naturally on three sides by a deep lagoon and impenetrable swamp, the pa could be assaulted only on the southern side, where the massive wooden defences were now bullet-proof. With abundant eels in the waters, the pa could not be starved out. The defenders' confidence was expressed thus:

Ko Maungatere te maunga ki runga	Maungatere is the mountain standing above,
Ko Waimakariri te awa	Waimakariri is the river,
Ko Tuahuriri te tangata	Tuahuriri is the man.

But Kaiapoi had one disadvantage: it was exposed to changing winds. Of these, the cool easterly wind from the coast and the boisterous nor'westerly from the mountains blew from behind or across the southern ramparts of the pa. But the third wind in the cycle, the southerly gale that heralded every cold front, blew straight at the wooden defences. It was Kaiapoi's Achilles' heel.

At Kaiapoi, Ngati Toa announced their peaceful intentions. While their slaves pitched camp, some of their chiefs were admitted to the pa to trade for pounamu. Te Maiharanui was in residence, and Ngati Toa exchanged powder, flint and guns (later found to be defective) for pounamu.[12] Ngai Tuahuriri now learned that Ngati Toa had secretly desecrated the recent grave of Te Maiharanui's late relative, Te Ruaki. The old woman's remains had been cooked and eaten. This mortal insult had to be avenged.[13]

Conflicting accounts describe what happened next. According to a Ngai Tuahuriri eyewitness,[14] a Nga Puhi man, Hakitara, who was a guest at Kaiapoi, had friends in the Ngati Toa camp. While spending a night there with a woman, and having uncommon powers of concentration, Hakitara overheard Ngati Toa plotting to capture Kaiapoi. They would perform a haka in their own camp, and then offer to repeat it in the pa, and thus gain admission. The haka party would then seize the gate. Hakitara returned to the pa and warned the defenders.

In the morning, the haka sounded from the Ngati Toa camp. Those in the pa heard some mistakes – a bad omen for Ngati Toa. Then some of the haka party, with Te Pehi and other chiefs, were admitted to the pa. The haka commenced. A Ngai Tahu elder, annoyed by the sound, came from his house and fired a blank shot. The haka party hurried to leave, but were rushed by warriors of the pa. Te Pehi and others were killed trying to scale the palisade, Te Pehi falling to the mere of Tangatahara, Te Maiharanui's uncle. The bodies were eaten.

Ngati Toa accounts, however, describe the killings as pure treachery. Te Rauparaha's son says the victims were asleep in the Kaiapoi pa when they were attacked. Another account says they were killed entering the pa 'to see Te Maiharanui'. Others say that Te Pehi was quarrelling over greenstone when the attack was started by a Kaiapoi man whose brother had been taken at Omihi.[15] But whatever the circumstances, Te Rauparaha was bound to avenge the deaths. Judging the present omens unfavourable, he struck camp and retired northwards, capturing Ngai Tahu stragglers on the way. His canoes arrived at Te Awaiti on 10 May 1830 with captives from Omihi and elsewhere. A European eyewitness recalled:

> The party numbered about two thousand all told, including women and children, and they brought some five hundred prisoners with them. Altogether there must have been sixty or seventy canoes, the bow of each of which was decorated with dead men's hands and heads. Te Rauparaha would send a party

of slaves, or prisoners, to the bush to cut firewood and make a hole in the earth with a fire in it in which stones were heated. When everything was ready the chief despatched with his tomahawk the slaves that had fetched the wood and prepared the oven, and the remainder of the slaves were required to cook the bodies of their friends and serve up the joints in baskets.[16]

Meanwhile Te Maiharanui, helped by Ngati Irakehu and Ngai Tarewa of Akaroa, resumed his reprisals against those of Ngai Tahu who had offended him.[17]

⁓

Te Rauparaha and Te Hiko, Te Pehi's son and heir, decided to avenge Te Pehi's death by smuggling a taua into Akaroa on a European ship before the next fighting season. Te Maiharanui at his peacetime village of Takapuneke would then be taken by surprise. In October 1830 the twelve-man British brig *Elizabeth* visited Kapiti under the command of John Stewart.[18] On being told by Te Rauparaha that Te Maiharanui had murdered Europeans, Stewart agreed to convey a taua to Akaroa in return for a cargo of flax.[19]

The *Elizabeth* anchored off Takapuneke early in November 1830, with Te Rauparaha and his warriors concealed below decks. Te Maiharanui, at Stewart's urging, left off supervising flax production and went aboard the brig to discuss trade, accompanied by his young daughter Nga Roimata. Stewart's trading master, Cowell, invited him below decks to receive a present of gunpowder. There he was seized, and Clementson the chief mate shackled him hand and foot. Te Rauparaha and Te Hiko emerged and taunted him. More unarmed Ngai Tahu came aboard for the 'trading', including Te Maiharanui's wife Te Whe and others of his family. All were seized. Those still ashore at Takapuneke suspected nothing, for chiefs were often entertained at length on board trading ships.[20] Stewart sent a ship's boat across the harbour with an invitation for Tangatahara to come aboard, but he declined.[21]

When darkness fell, Stewart took an armed boat's crew ashore with Ngati Toa warriors. Takapuneke was set ablaze and its unsuspecting occupants were massacred as they stumbled from the flames. Next day, Stewart took part in further raids ashore. About eighty people were captured, and flesh from the dead was prepared for feasting.[22] Meanwhile, on the *Elizabeth*, Te Maiharanui tried to persuade his unshackled fellow-captives to free him and help seize the ship, but to no avail. Nga Roimata was then strangled by her parents to frustrate Ngati Toa's presumed intentions. Clementson, on his return to the ship, threw the body overboard.[23]

Stewart sailed off with Ngati Toa and his prisoners to attack Ngai Tahu at Whakaraupo. But a captive escaped overboard and gave the alarm. Stewart then set sail with his dejected prisoners and jubilant Ngati Toa for Kapiti. There the captives were taken ashore to see Ngati Toa feast upon the flesh of their relatives.

Stewart kept Te Maiharanui in irons on the ship for six weeks until the promised Ngai Toa flax was delivered. He then handed him over to Te Rauparaha, to be paraded to the mockery of Ngati Toa. With his wife and other high-born captives, Te Maiharanui was ceremoniously tortured to death at Waitohu near Otaki, and was eaten.[24]

~

The brig *Elizabeth* arrived at Sydney from Kapiti on 14 January 1831 with its cargo of flax, and with two Sydney merchants as passengers. Also on board was Pere, a fifteen-year-old relative of Te Maiharanui who had survived the massacres. The merchants, Montefiore and Kemmis, knew of Stewart's Akaroa exploit but said nothing. Pere, however, told the story to Gordon Browne, a Sydney merchant who had lived in New Zealand and understood Maori. Browne told the police, who brought in Pere, Montefiore, Kemmis and two of Stewart's crew for questioning, Browne acting as interpreter. Stewart, Cowell, Clementson, and some of the crew, were clearly implicated in the massacres, and in the subsequent deaths of Te Maiharanui and others. The depositions were sent to the Governor of New South Wales, Ralph Darling.[25]

Governor Darling was indignant to hear that Englishmen had done such deeds, and called for the culprits to be punished. He instructed the Crown Solicitor, W. H. Moore, to start criminal proceedings against Stewart, Cowell, Clementson and the two crew members.[26] But Moore, instead of having the men arrested, asked the police to obtain their 'proper Christian names'. During the resulting delay, all except Stewart disappeared.

Browne now complained to Darling about the growing Sydney trade in Maori heads, to which Stewart's ship had evidently contributed. In New Zealand, said Browne, a slave's tattooed head was now 'more valuable than the living man'.[27] The Reverend Samuel

Marsden urged Darling to hasten Stewart's trial. Two months passed, and an envoy from Ngai Tahu, accompanied by Pere, visited Darling and asked about punishment for Stewart and his men. 'This man appeared extremely intelligent,' reported Darling.[28] But when he asked Moore how the prosecutions were going, the reply was that although murder charges had been laid, only Stewart had been arrested, and Moore had released him on bail.

The *Elizabeth* affair, unfortunately for Ngai Tahu, had become entangled in New South Wales politics. The continued use of military trials and other authoritarian powers by colonial governors was being increasingly criticised in Sydney, where political reformers wanted an elected legislature with a measure of responsible government. Prominent in this agitation was William Charles Wentworth, a rich barrister, speculator and publicist, later dubbed 'Australia's greatest native son'.[29] Darling, because of a brutal court-martial punishment, had become the particular target of Wentworth's attacks.

The murder trial *R. v. Stewart* came before the Sydney Supreme Court on 16 May 1831, with Moore as prosecutor. There were no Maori witnesses, because as heathens Maoris could not take the court oath.[30] Stewart was defended by Wentworth's legal colleague Wardell, who immediately challenged the prosecution for its lack of 'material witnesses'. Moore then abandoned the case 'for the time being', and Stewart later left Australia – on Wentworth's advice, according to Darling.[31]

In reporting this outcome to the British Government, Darling bitterly criticised the New South Wales police and Crown Solicitor's office for allowing Stewart and his accomplices to escape justice. However, Darling's term as Governor had now expired. He was replaced late in 1831 by the more flexible Richard Bourke. Wentworth celebrated the night of Darling's departure for England with a public fête at his Vaucluse mansion just inside Sydney Harbour, with illuminated signs visible for miles across the water, proclaiming, 'Down with the Tyrant!' and 'God Save the King!'[32]

The London Crown law officers severely criticised their Sydney counterparts for their handling of the *Elizabeth* case, and Governor Bourke was urged to bring Stewart and Clementson to justice.[33] But they were never found. Sydney's European population now approached forty thousand,[34] and few outside Government House, except missionaries, would put the interests of 'natives' above those of commerce.

To the British authorities, the *Elizabeth* affair showed the close links between Sydney commerce and New Zealand tribal wars. To Ngai Tahu, it showed the Governor's inability to curb Sydney traders, and left a lasting distrust of the British flag. The musket trade continued unabated.[35]

~

For the fighting season of 1831–1832, Te Rauparaha decided to exterminate the people of Te Wai Pounamu. The také was that Ngati Kuia were said to have made fish-hooks of Te Pehi's bones. A large combined expedition was organised against the surviving tribes of northern Te Wai Pounamu to avenge this affront – although some say the story was false.[36] Te Ati Awa were assigned the inhabitants of Arapawa and Totaranui. A combination of Te Ati Awa, Ngati Tama, and the Ngati Rarua hapu of Ngati Toa were marshalled against the people of Whakatu, Motueka and Tai Tapu. Ngati Toa under Te Rauparaha were to deal with Ngati Kuia, the prime suspects.

The invading allies crossed Raukawa Moana early in the season, and surprised their victims with the suddenness of their attack. Those not massacred or enslaved fled to the mountains, to be hunted relentlessly. The once-thriving northern regions of Te Wai Pounamu from Totaranui to Tai Tapu were depopulated. Only where the invaders decided to settle, attracted by the country and its rich fishing grounds, were some survivors spared as slaves.[37]

Of the Wai Pounamu tribes, only Ngai Tahu remained to be conquered. Poutini Ngai Tahu were soon overrun by Ngati Rarua under Niho and Takere. They were spared, with their chief Tuhuru, to carry on their pounamu work while their conquerors took over the trade.

Meanwhile, Te Rauparaha at Kapiti gathered reinforcements against Ngai Tahu, 'his intention being to kill out that tribe until he had destroyed it'.[38] An expedition of a hundred Ngati Toa, two hundred Ati Awa, and a hundred Ngati Raukawa was mustered. During the customary religious preliminaries, the Ati Awa tohunga Kukurarangi went into a trance to consult the spirit world, and uttered this electrifying prophecy:[39]

He aha te hau	What is the wind?
He uru, He tonga	It is north-west, it is south,
He parera Kai waho e	It is east in the offing, oh!
Nau mai ra e Raha	Come then, O Rauparaha!

Kia kite koe i te Ahi   That you may see the fire
I Papakura ki Kaiapohia.   On the crimson flat of Kaiapohia.

Expressing 'Kaiapoi' as 'Kaiapohia' was a pun of great significance, for 'Kai-apo-hia' in this context was a curse meaning 'the piling-up of bodies to eat'.[40] As an expression of their undying hatred of Ngai Tuahuriri, Ngati Toa and their supporters thenceforth called Kaiapoi 'Kaiapohia'.

Ngai Tuahuriri also sought allies. Momo, their leading diplomat, visited Otakou to seek assistance, but was rebuffed. The Ngati Huirapa hapu of Ngai Tahu meanwhile strengthened their pa at Waiateruati against the expected invasion.[41]

Te Rauparaha's expedition landed north of Kaiapoi early in 1832 with plenty of firearms and ammunition, and found Ngai Tuahuriri off their guard, working at cultivations and mahinga kai. Tuahiwi, near Kaiapoi, was sacked at once – the survivors, led by Haukeke Iwikau, eventually reaching Waiateruati.[42] Te Rauparaha then besieged Kaiapoi pa. The defences were formidable, but Ngai Tahu were still divided by their feud. Taiaroa was visiting Whakaraupo with a party from Otakou. He came on to Kaiapoi, and was allowed entrance. After a time he parleyed with Te Hiko, who offered him and his party safe conduct out of the pa. Taiaroa then invited everybody in the pa to leave with him during the night. But the Ngai Tuahuriri chiefs declined to desert the sacred place of their atua. 'I shall not go,' said Tawaka. 'Let me die in this pa. Let my guts decay in the swamp of Taerutu.' So Taiaroa departed, with his adherents.[43]

The attackers assailed Kaiapoi's defences with scaling nets, shields to protect attackers from musket-fire, and firebrands to set fire to the palisades. They sapped up to the ramparts, piling up brushwood to be burned at the first southerly wind. But the defenders removed the brushwood, and the defences held. After three months, Niho arrived overland from the Poutini Coast with a hundred Ngati Rarua. He urged on the besieging forces. The brushwood began to accumulate faster than the defenders could remove it. But it was useless for Te Rauparaha to fire it, for the wind was blowing north-west from Maungatere. Yet, as everybody knew, a northwesterly often ended with a southerly gale.

Opposite: *Te Rauparaha's southern campaigns.*

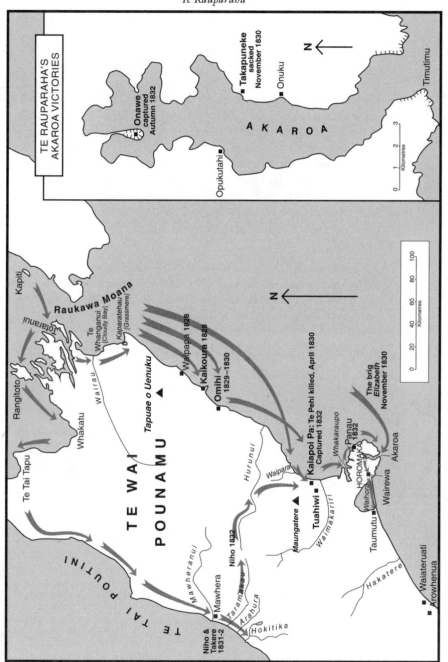

TE RAUPARAHA'S
AKAROA VICTORIES

Takapuneke
sacked
November 1830

Onawe captured
Autumn 1832

AKAROA

Opukutahi

Onuku

Timutimu

N

Kilometres
0   1   2   3

Kapiti

Rangitoto

Jolaranui

Raukawa Moana

Te Whanganui [Cloudy Bay]

Kaparatehau [Grassmere]

Wairau

Waitapa 1828

Kaikoura 1828

Omihi
1829–1830

Kaiapoi Pa: Te Pehi killed, April 1830
Captured 1832

Whakaraupo

Panau 1832

HOROMAKA

Akaroa

The brig *Elizabeth*
November 1830

Whakatu

Tapuae o Uenuku ▲

TE WAI
POUNAMU

Te Tai Tapu

Hurunui

Waipara

Maungatere ▲

Tuahiwi

Waimakariri

Whakahora

Wairewa

Taumutu

Waiateruati

Arowhenua

Mawheranui

Niho 1832

Taramakau

Arahura

Hokitika

Mawhera

Niho & Takere 1831-2

TE TAI POUTINI

Hakatere

N

Kilometres
0   20   40   60   80   100

57

At last, seeing an assault being prepared, some of the defenders made a determined sortie. Others within the pa fired the brushwood in the buffeting norwester so as to send the smoke among the besiegers. Ngati Toa were about to retreat, when the wind suddenly changed to the south and blew from behind them. They rushed to the palisades, bringing up more brush wood. In the confusion caused by the raging gale carrying a blast of choking smoke and dust into the pa, with flames and flying debris, Te Rauparaha's men were soon inside the defences.[44]

With Kaiapoi in flames, the siege was over. Pandemonium reigned. Some defenders fell where they fought. Others disappeared into the smoke with their families to escape through the swamp – in some cases only to be taken by Te Rauparaha's Rangitane slaves posted at the other side. Te Rauparaha's son later recalled the victors' elation:

> So the war-party dealt out blows, nor could the inner part of Kaiapohia pa be seen because of its being so overcrowded by the multitude of women and children, who were taken without effort. Heoi ano hopuhopu kau ana ta te taua pai! What a splendid taua! There lay everywhere the slain of Ngai Tahu.

According to this account, five hundred men and eight hundred women and children were captured.[45] But according to Ngai Tuahuriri sources there were only twenty-four kaumatua and 110 warriors inside Kaiapoi when it fell, besides women and children.[46]

Captured chiefs who had killed relatives of the attackers were, in accordance with custom, ceremonially hanged by the heels, disembowelled, and eaten. Others were spared, including Momo. In the manner of victorious warriors everywhere, takahi taua scoured the countryside, raping and killing. People fled to the hills to escape them.[47] Te Rauparaha took his forces on to Whakaraupo, but everyone had fled. He then went on to Akaroa.

~

At Akaroa, Tangatahara had rallied the local hapu, together with some fugitives from Kaiapoi, on the fortified peninsula of Onawe. They had only eight firearms, but it was a strong position. The invaders arrived before dawn, and after beating back a sortie by the defenders[48] they pitched camp nearby. When night came on,

Mautai of Ngati Mako hapu tried to burn Te Rauparaha's canoes, but rain foiled the attempt.

After several days' stalemate, Te Rauparaha hit upon a characteristic ruse. Ngai Tuahuriri resented Tangatahara's failure to come to the aid of Kaiapoi, when he himself had killed Te Pehi. Te Rauparaha now brought some leading Kaiapoi captives to the Onawe gateway to propose peace. The disconcerted defenders slackened their guard to hear what was going on, and Ngati Toa slipped inside and began killing. The defenders fired their few muskets point-blank, one shot missing Te Rauparaha only because someone pushed the barrel aside. Before they could reload, the defenders were overpowered. The customary massacre followed, after the chiefs had selected their captives. Te Hiko claimed Tangatahara.[49] About twenty Ngai Tahu men and women escaped from Onawe across the water and into the forests – including Mautai, Tuauau, Parure, Tamakeke, Ruaparae and his son Hakaroa.[50] Te Rauparaha's marauders went on as far as Taumutu.

After this disaster, the Akaroa people harboured a deep resentment against Ngai Tuahuriri for interfering with their defence. But 150 kilometres away, at Waiateruati, Te Rehe and Kaikoareare had raised a 350-strong taua to attack Te Rauparaha. At Kaikoareare's urging, the taua set out immediately.[51] Meanwhile, at Akaroa, the Ngati Toa leaders discussed whether they should proceed to attack Waiateruati. Some favoured this, but others had heard from their captives that Te Whakataupuka was there with his carronades:

Pu huri whenua – guns that can turn over the earth. These guns are unlike yours. If a shot lands among us it will burst and kill us all with just one shot. It is a gun so heavy that one man cannot lift it. When it fires, the ground is rent asunder by the shot.[52]

Te Rauparaha now decided to go home to fight his northern enemies. Te Pehi's female relatives demanded Tangatahara from Te Hiko so that they could torture and eat him. Te Hiko, to assert his mana against such impertinence, then set free Tangatahara, his father's killer.

The Ngati Toa canoes left for Kapiti. Some captives escaped in the surf near Kaiapoi, and others further north, some even at Totaranui: but there they were caught and killed by Rangitane.[53] Five days later, Tuauau and his companions emerged from their forest refuge above Akaroa. They gathered the human remains at Onawe and buried them near Pakaariki.[54] Meanwhile, the avenging taua from Waiateruati had been delayed by Kaikoareare's falling ill. By the time it reached Taumutu, Te Rauparaha had gone.[55]

Thus ended a disastrous eight years for Ngai Tahu. Their once-thriving economy had been devastated over half their territory, first by the Kai Huanga feud and then by Te Rauparaha. His victories at Kaikoura, Omihi, Kaiapoi and Onawe, together with the Kai Huanga killings, had reduced the tribal population from perhaps eight or nine thousand to probably about five and a half thousand.[56] Turakautahi's pa had fallen, and the place of its atua lay desecrated. The pounamu of Arahura, and the Poutini Coast as far south as Hokitika, were in the hands of the enemy. But on the eastern coasts of Te Wai Pounamu, except from Kaikoura northwards, Ngati Toa and their allies did not linger.[57]

~

Where musket warfare prevailed, muskets must be had. But the constant demand for flax, potatoes, fish, women and pigs, to exchange for muskets, powder and ammunition, was severely taxing Ngai Tahu's resources.[58] In November 1832 however, six months after the fall of Kaiapoi, Te Whakataupuka received Williams's promised payment for Port Bunn: sixty new muskets and half a ton each of powder and ball. He was now the best-armed chief in the south. In the Maori view, Williams's payment purchased Te Whakataupuka's protection – which he effectively provided against Taiaroa's threats to interfere with the whaling station.[59] In the European view, the payment purchased the land itself.

Just as purchasing land in New Zealand was an investment for Sydney merchants, a local whaling station was an investment for Maori chiefs. It gave access to steel adzes and axes, iron tools, nails and implements, and the skills of European carpentry and boat-building. It brought tobacco and rum, which were valuable currency. But the greatest of all treasures it brought was the whaleboat. The Maori had no equal to this craft. Some ten metres long and two or three in the beam, the whaleboat was easy to launch and handle. Its capacity, speed under sail, and simple elegance, made it a prized possession.

When Te Rauparaha returned to Cook Strait from Kaiapoi and Onawe in May 1832, John Guard bought his permission for a whaling station at Kakapo Bay to replace his former station at nearby Te Awaiti, which he had relinquished to Dicky Barrett. Te Awaiti and Port Bunn had been the first shore whaling stations on Te Wai Pounamu, established at opposite ends of the island under the patronage of Te Rauparaha and Te Whakataupuka respectively.[60] These rival Maori patrons viewed each other's whaling stations as valid military objectives.

∾

After Te Rauparaha's victorious taua had gone home following the sacking of Onawe, Ngai Tuahuriri still had to rely on trade to get more muskets and powder, for there was as yet no demand for whaling station sites in their territory. But they got enough to arm a hundred warriors,[61] and then proposed to the southern Ngai Tahu chiefs a joint campaign. The také was that some Ngati Toa were living on the Kaikoura coast. The territory would belong to them if they were allowed to stay there for three generations. This would so offend Ngai Tahu's tribal atua and ancestors that they would withdraw their protection, jeopardising the tribe's survival.

A strategy was agreed upon. In the coming fighting season (1832–1833), a comparatively small force would clear Ngati Toa from the Kaikoura coast and as far north as Te Parinuiowhiti. This Tauaiti would be led by Tuhawaiki of Murihiku and Karetai of Otakou. Te Whakataupuka and the senior chiefs would stay behind with most of the warriors, in case Ngati Toa came through the mountains as Niho had done at the siege of Kaiapoi. But the following season, when more armaments had been obtained, Te Whakataupuka would lead a Tauanui to defeat Te Rauparaha decisively.[62]

When the fighting season of 1832–1833 approached, the Murihiku taua set sail from Ruapuke for the Tauaiti, after the customary rituals, ceremonies and farewells, with Tuhawaiki, Paitu, Whaitiri and other chiefs. The planned return voyage of 1,800 kilometres was perhaps the longest yet attempted by a Maori taua. At Otakou more taua joined, under Karetai, Haereroa and Te Whaikai Pokene. The Ngati Huirapa taua were led by Rangiwhakatia and Tarawhata. Tangatahara led the Akaroa taua, and Ngai Tuahuriri with the Whakaraupo people manned their own canoes. The expedition comprised some 350 warriors, in six double canoes.[63]

When the Tauaiti reached Kaikoura in January 1833, they caught and killed some Ngati Toa.[64] They also learned that Te Rauparaha was intending to visit Kaparatehau to net moulting putangitangi – January and February being the customary months for this. The

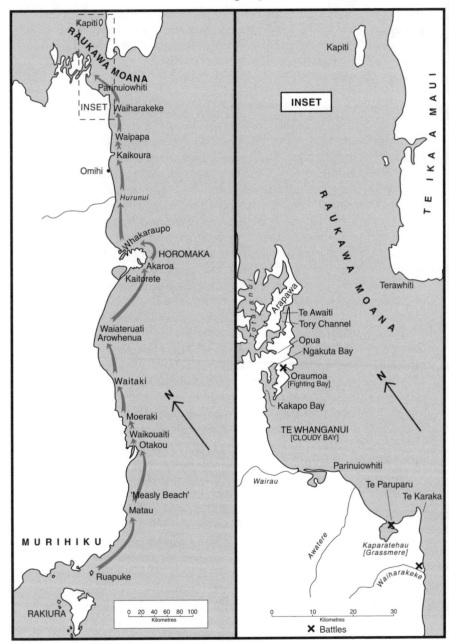

The Tauaiti and Tauanui field of operations.

Tauaiti, continuing north, recaptured Waiharakeke, where seven Ngati Toa were killed and others escaped. Tuhawaiki then took a small force over the hills to reconnoitre Kaparatehau.[65]

～

Te Rauparaha by this time, with his companions and two young sons, was camped at Wairau, waiting for suitable weather to proceed to Kaparatehau. One night while they slept, their tohunga Te Raho heard the tangata o te po singing in their strange voices:

Kei Wairau ia:	He is at Wairau now:
Kei Waiharakeke ka tumau atu.	At Flaxbourne he will be detained for ever.

The tohunga started up from his sleep and warned Te Rauparaha to go no further or he would be killed. But Te Rauparaha scoffed at this.[66]

The next day, from a hill above Kaparatehau, Ngai Tahu saw four canoes and a whaleboat approaching from Wairau. They went down to the landing place and hid. People landed from three of the canoes, and from the whaleboat came Te Rauparaha with his young sons. He paused to inspect some footprints and cabbage leaves, and someone's excrement lying on the beach.[67] Ngati Toa's dogs scented the ambush party and began barking. Ngai Tahu charged out, and a fierce hand-to-hand fight began.

Surprised and outnumbered, Ngati Toa were beaten back. Te Rauparaha and his sons and closest companions regained their whaleboat, but jumped out when they saw that the oars were missing. Te Rauparaha was seized by his pokeka. But before any blow was dealt him, the old chief slipped the garment's toggle and dived under the water. He hid in the kelp until he was rescued by his reserve canoe waiting offshore. Ngati Toa then headed back to Ngakuta Bay, leaving the frustrated Ngai Tahu to look over the dead. Among them was the tohunga Te Raho.[68]

At nightfall, Ngai Tahu launched their war canoes from Waiharakeke and set out for Ngakuta, hoping to get there before dawn. But a thick fog intervened and they arrived too late for a surprise.[69] Their advance guard fought Te Rauparaha's outnumbered party over the hill to Opua in Totaranui, while the rest of Ngai Tahu attacked Guard's whaling station, driving out the whalers and seizing their flour, sugar and tobacco. The whalers headed for Kapiti in their boats, while Ngai Tahu fired their houses and fifty tuns of oil, and dug up their potatoes. Ngai Tahu then sailed to Oraumoa to build a fortified camp. Meanwhile, Te Rauparaha sent to Kapiti for reinforcements.[70]

Two days later, a flotilla of thirty war-canoes arrived from Kapiti, manned by Ngati Toa, Ngati Raukawa, Ngati Rarua and Ngati Mutunga. When Waruwarutu, a thirteen-year-old Ngai Tuahuriri boy with the Tauaiti, saw this mighty fleet approaching, he thought to himself, 'Well, this must be the end.'[71] The next morning, Ngati Mutunga, anxious for battle honours, attacked Ngai Tahu but were routed. A general musket engagement followed, raging inconclusively among the trees and broken ground around the beach. By nightfall Ngai Tahu had little ammunition left. Under cover of darkness, they sailed for Kaparatehau with their dead and wounded, and some of the enemy's dead as well, leaving the field to Te Rauparaha.[72]

Ngai Tahu continued home next day. While putting in to Waipapa for the night, two of their canoes capsized and two Otakou chiefs were drowned. They were cremated, to prevent desecration by enemies. The Tauaiti then journeyed homewards. Tuhawaiki returned to Murihiku with his trophies of war. Ten heads were sold to Americans for two muskets, or a keg of gunpowder, apiece.[73]

～

John Guard's whalers returned from Kapiti five weeks after the Tauaiti had left, to rebuild their houses. They had a successful whaling season that winter (1833), but lived in dread of Ngai Tahu.[74] Their fears were well founded, for next summer, when the fighting season arrived, Te Whakataupuka summoned his warriors for the Tauanui, launched his war canoes, and set sail northwards. All the leading Ngai Tahu chiefs joined the Tauanui, including Te Maiharanui's long-lost son Tu Te Hounuku, who had landed at Otakou from a whaling-ship after years overseas. When the combined Ngai Tahu fleet left Horomaka in February 1834, there were six or seven hundred warriors, in thirty war-canoes and whaleboats, most of the canoes being lashed together in pairs for the voyage.[75]

The Tauanui sailed north along the Kaikoura coast, killing the Ngati Toa they found.[76] They expected the news of their approach to bring Te Rauparaha from Kapiti to Cloudy Bay to defend his whalers. But Te Rauparaha was away fighting his Taranaki enemies, including Ngati Ruanui.[77] On 6 March 1834 four hundred Ngai Tahu sacked the whaling-stations around Cloudy Bay, killing the Maoris they captured. The European whalers again escaped to Kapiti in their whaleboats. When the schooner *Harlequin* unexpectedly arrived at Cloudy Bay, Te Whakataupuka urged her seizure under the Maori custom of utu, for attempting to trade with the enemy. But Taiaroa and Tuhawaiki dissuaded him from thus antagonising European shipowners. The schooner was plundered, but was allowed to sail for Kapiti.[78]

The Tauanui waited around Totaranui for Te Rauparaha for two months, in vain. The majority then, rather than attack Kapiti, decided to head for home. Off Te Karaka, Tu Te Hounuku's canoe was upset in a storm and he perished with all his men. Taiaroa with his taua stayed in the Wairau to attack the few Rangitane remaining there, while Haereroa with his taua waited at Omihi to intercept Te Rauparaha's expected counterattack. But none came.[79] Thus ended the Great Taua – a disappointment, after so arduous a voyage, both for the warriors wanting to prove their prowess and for the fighting chiefs hoping to outgun Te Rauparaha. But it had reasserted Ngai Tahu's claim to their Parinuiowhiti boundary, and Te Rauparaha could again be challenged next fighting season.

Notes

1. Burns 1980: 115.
2. Te Ati Awa of the North Island west coast were distinct from Ngati Awa of the east coast, although both have been called 'Ngati Awa'.
3. Adkin 1948: 127; Urlich 1970: 399ff; Williams 1873, App. xxxiv–xxxix. Adkin says Muaupoko were allowed back to Lake Horowhenua.
4. Tamihana Ms (Graham).
5. Biggs 1959: 272; Burns 1980: 146; Elvy 1949: 34–35; Sherrard 1966: 32; Taki Ms: 2.
6. Trevor-Roper 1966: chapter 3.
7. Vayda 1960: 106. Regarding musket warfare, see also Allan 1965: 22ff; Kawharu 1977: 64ff; McKillop 1849: 251; Oliver & Williams 1981: 46; Pool 1977: 133 and 1991: 53; Winiata 1967: 52.
8. Burns 1980: 139, 157, 163.
9. McNab 1913: 161.
10. Hall-Jones 1943: 98, 136; Hall-Jones 1976: 22.
11. Hamer & Nicholls 1990: 21; Carkeek 1966: 27; Sherrard 1966: 33. Sherrard dates the sacking of Omihi at 1828–29, but Heberley's Ms Reminiscences clearly date Te Rauparaha's return from this campaign at about April 1830.
12. Taki Ms: 3ff.
13. Stack 1893: 36; Travers 1906: 136.
14. See Taki Ms.
15. Stack 1893: 38ff; Taki Ms: 3ff; Tamihana Ms (Graham): 47–48; Te Kanae Ms (Graham): 14.
16. Heberley Ms Reminiscences: 44.
17. Stack in Jacobson 1914: 33.
18. *Elizabeth* Ms Articles; Ross 1987:

154–66.

19. McNab 1913: chapter 2.
20. Darling–Goderich, 13.4.1831,
    No. 37, NSWSL Micro CY773;
    Shortland Ms 'Narrative': 43.
21. WJ, 1.9.1840.
22. SNC 6/68: 169.
23. Taki Ms: 8.
24. Shortland Ms 'Narrative': 35;
    Stack 1893: chapter 4; Taki Ms: 8;
    Tamihana Ms (Graham): 35.
25. Darling–Goderich, 13.4.1831, loc cit.
26. McLeay–Moore, 12.2.1831, in
    Darling–Goderich 13.4.1831, loc.
    cit.
27. Browne–Colonial Secretary,
    30.3.1831, in Darling–Goderich
    13.4.1831, loc cit; Marsden 1932:
    498.
28. Darling–Goderich, 13.4.1831, loc
    cit.
29. Cramp 1922: passim.
30. Maule–Stewart, 23.4.1832,
    NSWSL Ms A1269.
31. Darling–Goderich, 10.10.1831,
    NSWSL A1209: 845ff. According
    to Ross 1987 (loc cit) Stewart went
    to Hokianga and later disappeared.
32. Cramp 1922.
33. Darling–Goderich, 13.4.1831, loc
    cit; Goderich–Bourke, 31.1.1832,
    28.5.1832, NSWSL Ms A1269;
    McNab 1913: 34.
34. NSWSL Ms A1267/12: 692.
35. Price Ms Reminiscences.
36. See Harvey 1936: 7.
37. Allan 1965: 24ff; Burns 1980: 71;
    Carkeek 1966: 28–29; Naera Ms
    (Graham): 14; Tamihana loc cit.
38. Tamihana Ms (Graham): 63.
39. Tikao 1990: 123; Travers 1906: 212.
40. Te Aue Davis, pers. comm. 1992
41. Price Ms; Tamihana Ms (Graham):
    63; Tikao 1990: 127.
42. Green Ms Papers; Waruwarutu
    Ms Narrative.
43. Taki Ms: 9–10.
44. Taki Ms: 13ff; Tamihana Ms
    (Graham) loc cit; Tamihana in

45. Tamihana Ms (Graham), loc cit;
    Tamihana in Shortland Ms
    Narrative: 39.
46. Green Mss.
47. Couch 1987: 21; Taki Ms: 12ff.
48. Taki Ms: 13.
49. Stack in Jacobson 1914: 41; Tikao
    1990: 127.
50. Lavaud 1986: 26 (author's
    translation); Taki Ms: 14.
51. Waruwarutu Ms.
52. Taki Ms: 14–16.
53. Ibid.
54. Lavaud, loc cit.
55. Waruwarutu Ms.
56. See note 75 below.
57. Harvey 1936: 46. Burns (1980:
    168, 170, 189) claims that Te
    Rauparaha retained control of
    Ngai Tahu territory and 'colo-
    nised' some of it, citing as an
    example 'Te Whanganui' men-
    tioned in Tamihana Ms (Graham):
    77. However, 'Te Whanganui' was
    Cloudy Bay (see DOSLIW Maori
    place-name map 'Aotearoa [Te
    Waipounamu]'), and was outside
    Ngai Tahu territory. The Ngati
    Toa 'colonists' there were
    associated with Guard's whaling
    station. See Grady 1978: 48;
    McNab 1913: 3, 18.
58. See Kawharu 1977: 65 for a
    North Island parallel.
59. Richards 1995: 50–52.
60. Grady 1978: 48; Hall-Jones 1976:
    22–23; McNab 1913: 85–89;
    Mackay 1873 I: 92.
61. Waruwarutu Ms.
62. Pybus 1954a: 52ff; Taki Ms: 17ff.
63. Sherrard 1966: 21; Smith 1910:
    537ff; Taki Ms: 17ff.
64. Smith 1910: 537ff; Taki Ms: 17.
65. Te Kahu 1901: 98ff. Smith 1910:
    537ff; Tiramorehu 1849: 3. The
    newspaper translation of Tira-
    morehu's account (*NZS*, 7.2.1849:
    3) says, 'Waiharakeke and I were

Shortland 1856: 254ff.

defeated', suggesting a Ngai Tahu defeat. However, it should read 'Waiharakeke fell to us', 'mana' in the Maori original having been misprinted as 'maua' in the newspaper's transcript (Te Aue Davis, pers. comm., 1992)

66. Shortland Ms 'Narrative': 43; Shortland 1856: 259ff.

67. Carrington (Ms: 181) says Tarawhata was blamed for the excrement. But Taki's account (Ms: 17) exonerates him: the sample was too old to arouse Te Rauparaha's suspicions, and thus could not have been from Ngai Tahu.

68. Elvy 1949: 40ff; Te Kahu 1901: 98ff; Pybus 1954a: 52–53; Shortland Ms 'Narrative': 43; Taki Ms: 17–18; Taylor 1950: 21–22.

69. Waruwarutu Ms Narrative.

70. Elvy 1949: 41–42; Heberley Ms: 47; Te Kahu 1901: 98; McNab 1913: 60; Taki Ms: 19; Waruwarutu Ms Narrative.

71. Waruwarutu Ms Narrative.

72. Carrington Ms: 183; Te Kahu 1901.; Shortland Ms 'Narrative': 47ff; Taki Ms: 19; Tamihana Ms APL 27a, 27b: 91; Waruwarutu Ms Narrative.

73. WJ, 24.8.1840.

74. Heberley Ms; McNab 1913: 68, 100. Heberley dates the Tauaiti attack at 1831, some months

before the loss of the schooner *Waterloo*. However, McNab (1913: 428) says the *Waterloo* was lost in 'October 1833', which confirms the year of the Tauaiti as 1833.

75. Te Kahu 1901: 98ff; McNab 1913: 70; Pybus 1954a: 52–53; Stack in Jacobson 1914: 45–46; Taki Ms: 19; Taylor 1950: 21. If some hundreds were kept back for home defence, the fighting strength of east coast Ngai Tahu in 1834 would thus have been a thousand men. If these constituted less than the usual quarter of the population, because of the Kai Huanga feud (see Boultbee 1986: 102), the east coast population was by now reduced to perhaps 5,000. Poutini Ngai Tahu (Hooker 1986) comprised another 500. But Anderson (Wai-27 H1:79) suggests the population in 1820 was only 3,000–4,000.

76. Patuki 1878: 3.

77. Tamihana Ms APL 27a, 27b: 91ff.

78. Grady 1987: 55–59; Heberley Ms: 51; Te Kahu 1901: 98ff; McNab 1913: 69ff; Taki Ms: 20.

79. Te Kahu 1901: 98ff; Stack in Jacobson 1914: 45–46; Taki Ms: 21. Ngati Toa sources do not mention the Tauanui. Tamihana (loc cit) erroneously says that Tu Te Hounuku was killed leading the Tauaiti.

4

~

Survival

TE WHAKATAUPUKA returned home with his taua in leisurely fashion after the Tauanui campaign, presumably visiting the various communities on the Ngai Tahu coast to strengthen his standing with them, and to secure their support for future campaigns. It was not until July 1834 that he reached Otakou, where the Weller brothers now operated a whaling station under the patronage of Taiaroa and Karetai. The whaling season was in full swing. Among the vessels at anchor was a schooner owned by Captain James Kelly of Hobart. In 1817, Kelly and his crew of the brig *Sophia* had fought Ngai Tahu near Otakou after allegedly molesting their women and being suspected of trading in Ngai Tahu heads.[1]

Since Kelly had been warned to keep his ships away from Ngai Tahu coasts,[2] Te Whakataupuka ordered reprisals against his schooner, and against the Wellers for harbouring it. Unfortunately for the Wellers, their Maori patrons Taiaroa and Karetai had gone with Tuhawaiki to Sydney, where Karetai and his wife were receiving Christian instruction from Samuel Marsden.[3] Te Whakataupuka's men, numbering about five hundred, plundered the Wellers' whaling station and Kelly's ship, and threatened others in the harbour. The Europeans feared for their lives. Captain Anglem got away to Sydney in his ship, having kidnapped several Otakou Maoris, and arrived there on 16 August.[4]

Meanwhile the Cloudy Bay whaling master John Guard, a protégé of Te Rauparaha, had been wrecked on the Taranaki coast in his ship *Harriet*. Under the Maori custom of muru, shipwrecked people were liable to be chastised for having offended Tangaroa. The *Harriet* castaways had been plundered by Ngati Ruanui, traditional enemies of Te Rauparaha, and by another Taranaki tribe. Ngati

Ruanui had killed some of Guard's men, and injured his wife. The other tribe, however, had rescued the survivors from Ngati Ruanui, including Guard's wife and children, and had released Guard to go and get some gunpowder as ransom for them. But Guard went to Sydney in the Wellers' schooner, arriving there the day after Anglem's arrival. Guard and Anglem together raised a hue and cry in Sydney, demanding that the government punish the 'savages' of Taranaki and Murihiku, including the 'horrid cannibal' Te Whakataupuka, 'to teach them to respect the British'.

The *Elizabeth* affair had prompted Governor Darling to ask for an official Resident to be sent to New Zealand with military support, to control British subjects there. James Busby was eventually appointed Resident, and had arrived at the Bay of Islands in May 1833, but with the promise of occasional naval visits as his only support. Governor Bourke, in line with this, sent two warships in September 1834 with a strong punitive force to Taranaki. There the naval force attacked not Ngati Ruanui, but the tribe that was protecting Guard's survivors.[5] Egged on by Guard, the British bombarded and assaulted the Maoris mercilessly both before and after they freed their captives, behaving like 'insulted buccaneers, more than an expedition of His Majesty's forces', it was afterwards said.[6] The warships then sailed to Kapiti. After conferring with Te Rauparaha, who applauded the British action against his enemies, the naval commander issued a proclamation promising similar treatment for other 'offenders'.[7]

The British punitive force did not go on to attack Te Whakataupuka, for Te Rauparaha was about to do so himself in retaliation for the Tauanui. Hearing of this, Te Whakataupuka sent a peace embassy inviting Te Rauparaha to Ruapuke to receive some precious mere pounamu 'which were lying about his house'. But Te Rauparaha spurned this stratagem. He replied that he would come to Ruapuke with an army, and spare Te Whakataupuka if he submitted. He then summoned a large expedition for the 1834–1835 fighting season, 'to go to Otakou and Rakiura, even as far as Rarotonga [Centre Island], and kill the people of Te Wai Pounamu'.[8]

Te Rauparaha's insulting rebuff gave Te Whakataupuka the necessary také to attack first, and he made preparations accordingly. Early in 1835, when Te Whakataupuka's warriors were mustering at Ruapuke, Karetai and his wife returned from Sydney. They had been ill with measles.[9] After greeting them, Te Whakataupuka and his force left to join other Ngai Tahu taua at Horomaka before leading them north once more against Te Rauparaha.

But now a dreadful disaster overtook Ngai Tahu. The measles from Sydney had infected Te Whakataupuka's expedition, which was soon forced ashore by the illness at a place now known as Measly Beach. So many died of the strange fever, that of the hundreds of warriors who had sailed from Ruapuke only enough remained to man one canoe. The Murihiku taua went no further. Te Whakataupuka was dead.

Unaware of this disaster, taua from Otakou, Moeraki and Arowhenua sailed for Horomaka as arranged. Off Kaitorete they were struck by a violent storm that wrecked several canoes and drowned many of their occupants. The expedition was abandoned, for clearly the atua had somehow become offended.[10] Meanwhile Te Rauparaha continued his own preparations. In March 1835 the Wellers were warned that the 'Cook Strait tribes' were coming south with '1,400 stand of arms'. But Te Rauparaha's forces did not come: perhaps an epidemic had affected them as well.[11]

The southern epidemic, which reached Otakou by July 1835, was a crippling blow for Ngai Tahu. Te Whakataupuka's death in his prime of life was an irreparable loss, for he was the only ariki with the mana to unite the tribe. He had rallied the battered northern communities and restored them to the fighting ranks, and had upheld Maori rangatiratanga consistently.

Renewed Ngai Tahu attacks were expected at Cloudy Bay in the following fighting season (1835–1836),[12] but none occurred. Te Rauparaha, still determined to attack Otakou and Murihiku, now moved to detach Ngai Tuahuriri, who had fortified themselves at Puari after the loss of Kaiapoi. He sent a peace embassy with three of their captive chiefs, including Momo. The peace was accepted, and formalised by marriages, exchanges of names, and the symbolic gift of a boy parented by a Ngati Toa father and a Ngai Tuahuriri mother.[13] The Ngati Toa view of this peace was that Ngai Tuahuriri were now vassals, or slaves, of Te Rauparaha.[14]

～

European disease had now replaced warfare as the main abnormal cause of death among Maoris of southern New Zealand. Far more died of measles than had previously died in warfare. In the years ahead, recurring epidemics of measles, influenza and tuberculosis were to cause appalling mortality.[15] In 1842, the aged Waikouaiti tohunga Koroko, a patriarchal, white-bearded figure who remembered Cook's visit and the introduction of the potato,[16] recalled: 'Before we were visited by ships, disease was rare amongst us. Few died young. Now few live to be old.'[17]

Because of their long isolation in the South Pacific, Maoris lacked resistance to diseases common among Europeans, and epidemics with high mortalities were inevitable when infected persons arrived from overseas.[18] The earliest southern measles epidemic is said to have occurred in Murihiku in 1817.[19] Measles was a child's disease among Europeans, but it struck down Maoris of all ages, turning quickly to pneumonia. For this, the tohungas prescribed sitting in cold water up to the neck. Such 'hydropathy' was also fashionable in Europe, where tuberculosis sufferers were immersed in cold baths and wrapped in wet sheets.[20] But cold water cured neither pneumonia nor tuberculosis.

Europeans introduced other debilitating diseases to the Maoris of southern New Zealand. Venereal diseases came with the first European visitors.[21] Tuberculosis, usually a chronic complaint with Europeans, took an acute and fatal course among Maoris. Te Whakataupuka's son was probably a victim in 1827, when Europeans present were suspected of witchcraft because of the boy's sudden decline and death. Influenza was common in Sydney, and in September 1836 the ship *Sydney Packet*, belonging to John Jones, a self-made Sydney trader and ship-owner, brought another lethal epidemic of it to Murihiku and Otakou.[22] Introduced diseases probably killed more than half the Maoris of southern New Zealand in the 1830s. As in fourteenth-century Europe during the Black Death, which caused mortalities of similar proportions,[23] such widespread deaths among all ranks and all ages had far-reaching consequences. The gods' manifest and unprecedented displeasure caused uncertainty and despair. The loss of labour power crippled the commercial production of flax and potatoes. Traditional ocean-going canoes were finally abandoned for the labour-saving whaleboats and sealing boats, whose advent made backpacking on coastal walking tracks obsolete. Most inland settlements were abandoned.[24]

～

Tonga, like New Zealand, was included in the province of the Sydney District Wesleyan Mission. The Tongan Wesleyan mission was joined in 1831 by James Watkin, a sturdy, energetic, young Manchester man who arrived newly wed with his wife. In 1834 Watkin and his colleagues reported a pentecostal revival in Tonga – 'a piercing conviction of personal sin against God, a flood of penitential sorrow and shame'. They baptised a fifth of the Tongan population,[25] then turned their attention to neighbouring Fiji. In 1837 Watkin wrote an impassioned appeal to the Methodists of England, calling on them to 'save' the Fijians – 'a most interesting but deeply depraved people', said Watkin. He described live burials, the strangling of widows, tribal warfare, cannibal feasts, and other horrors. He urged young men to volunteer for the mission, artisans to give equipment for it, and rich and poor to give money. 'Christianize them,' cried Watkin, 'and civilization will follow!'[26]

Watkin's epistle caused a sensation in England, where he was seen as a St Paul of the Pacific.[27] Published under the title *Pity Poor Fiji*, it helped extinguish the eighteenth-century vision of the 'noble savage' and replace it with the Victorian vision of the 'depraved savage'. But in Tonga meanwhile, Watkin came under a cloud. He confessed to 'a deep attraction' for his wife's Tongan maid,[28] and his colleagues decided that he must go. Embarking in July 1837 for Sydney with his wife and family, he wrote in his journal: 'My feelings since my last date I cannot describe. God be merciful to me.'[29]

~

Te Puoho o te Rangi, high chief of Ngati Tama, was an old comrade-in-arms of Te Rauparaha. He had taken part in conquering Te Tai Tapu, and in the siege of Kaiapoi. But he came to resent Te Rauparaha's control of the Cook Strait trade. Te Rauparaha's avowed intention of taking Otakou and Murihiku as well now prompted Te Puoho to try to forestall him and take them for himself.[30] At his base at Parapara he organised a taua of perhaps a hundred men. With them, he proposed to march the thousand kilometres down Te Tai Poutini and into Murihiku in the 1836–1837 fighting season, and then 'scale the fish from its tail', bringing Ngai Tahu captives back like cattle.[31]

Setting out in the spring of 1836, Te Puoho reached Mawhera pa a month later. There he was denied entry by his old ally Niho, who did not want Poutini Ngai Tahu and their greenstone work interfered with. Te Puoho pressed on southwards with his taua, and crossed the Main Divide many weeks later north of Wanaka. They surprised a small Ngai Tahu kainga at Makarore, capturing the adults

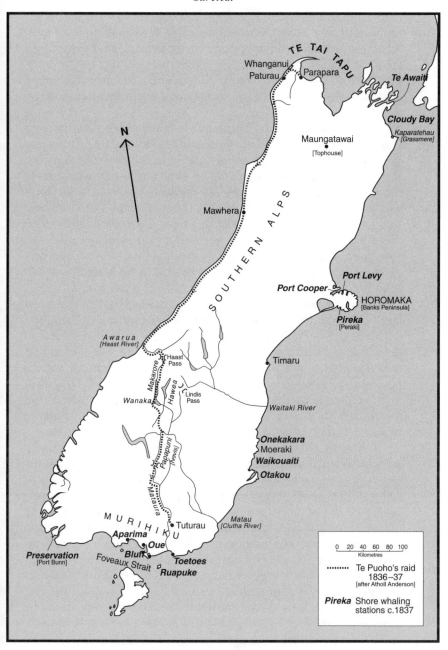

Te Puoho's raid, and shore whaling stations, 1836–1837.

and eating two children. But one youth escaped to warn the neighbouring Hawea kainga, whose people fled to Waitaki to warn their relatives. Te Puoho did not pursue them. Instead, after capturing a family at Wanaka, he maintained his advantage of surprise by heading south to the upper Mataura River, where his men captured a Ngai Tahu eeling party. They were now, after three months, nearing the heart of Murihiku.

The invaders reached Tuturau, a lamprey-fishing kainga forty kilometres from the Murihiku coast, early in January 1837. Te Puoho paused there to rest his warriors and their twenty-four captives. But some local Ngai Tahu evaded him. Uncertain whether Te Rauparaha was himself leading the invasion, they got to the Bluff whaling station and chanced to find Tuhawaiki and Taiaroa. These two hastened to Ruapuke to raise a taua. Only about sixty Ngai Tahu were available to fight, because of an influenza epidemic brought by another of Jones's ships from Sydney. 'Great numbers of those affected by the ailment were said to be lying about half dead.'[32]

Tuhawaiki with his hastily raised taua hurried back to the mainland. Through his tohunga, he consulted the omens by campfire. The heart of Te Puoho materialised in the fire light 'as if carried on the wings of a bird', signifying victory. The tohunga predicted that only two men would die. With these assurances, Tuhawaiki and his taua reached Tuturau by night and set an ambush. As the stars faded, Te Puoho was shot dead by Topi Patuki in the opening volley,[33] and a slave was shot also. Taiaroa entered the enclosure proclaiming peace, and Te Puoho's taua surrendered.

Te Puoho's brother-in-law Ngawhakawa, a former Muaupoko warrior, escaped from Tuturau and returned to Parapara alone the way he had come, believing his comrades were all dead. He evaded Niho and his people, who would have punished him as a harbinger of defeat. When Niho eventually heard of Te Puoho's defeat, he released his Ngai Tahu vassals and retired northwards to Whanganui Inlet, expecting a Ngai Tahu attack. Thus Tuhuru and Poutini Ngai Tahu regained the rangatiratanga of the Poutini Coast.[34] But at Parapara, Te Puoho's widows demanded utu for his death. Two taua of Ngati Rarua were organised to attack Ngai Tahu down the east coast. One gave up at Maungatawai in the wintry conditions. The other reached Cloudy Bay, hoping to get a ship to take them south as Te Rauparaha had done in 1830.

In Sydney meanwhile, the Church Missionary Society and the

Wesleyan mission had been petitioning for a stronger British presence in New Zealand, and Governor Bourke had sent the twenty-eight-gun frigate *Rattlesnake* under Captain William Hobson to show the flag and report on the situation. With Samuel Marsden as his adviser, Hobson arrived in Cook Strait from the Bay of Islands on 16 June 1837, and anchored at Cloudy Bay for wood and water. He heard, presumably from Guard's whalers, that the Maoris of southern New Zealand were wild savages and that Te Rauparaha was their overlord.

The Ngati Rarua taua abandoned its plans for attacking Ngai Tahu, perhaps because Ngati Toa and Te Ati Awa had fallen out, and because the British frigate was on the coast.[35] Bad weather prevented Hobson from calling at Kapiti, but had he gone there he would have found trade thriving. A contemporary English visitor recalled that every free man and boy of fourteen years upwards on Kapiti had his own gun, preferably a flintlock. 'Te Hiko used to parade his slaves before the purchaser and sell the head alive, killing the slave and preparing the head in the oven after the bargain for the purchase was completed.'[36]

On returning to Sydney, Hobson advised Bourke that treaties should be sought with Maori tribes to permit trading posts at strategic coastal points, leaving the rest of the country under Maori control. A similar policy had been followed in India and Africa. When Hobson's report and the missionaries' petitions reached England, they had far-reaching consequences for New Zealand, and for Hobson.[37]

∼

The dwindling numbers of sperm whales in the South Pacific caused whalers to turn to the slower-moving southern right whale, which provided both oil and baleen ('whalebone'). These huge mammals, as they came inshore to calve during the New Zealand winter, could be easily caught from shore-based boats, for when the calf was killed the mother stayed by it. Whalers, like the sealers before them, made no attempt to conserve the breeding stock on which their industry depended. Dozens of shore stations flourished briefly on Te Wai Pounamu coasts, until the southern right whale in its turn reached the brink of extinction.[38]

The master of a shore whaling station depended on the local Maori chief both for protection and for permission to fish along the coast from the chosen site,[39] as we have seen in the cases of Peter Williams and John Guard. If the protecting chief died, his successor's permission was needed. Thus Williams's tenure at Port Bunn was renewed by Tuhawaiki when Te Whakataupuka died.[40] Maori landing places were generally chosen as the best sites for shore whaling stations, which thus tended to be close to Maori settlements. Maoris frequented whaling stations, bartering food and services in return for merchandise. The stations got plenty of potatoes and pigs simply by carrying spare whaleboats, sails and tobacco, for which Maoris paid high prices.[41] The whalers got Maori wives to tend their huts and gardens, and paid the relatives for the service.

Maoris found ready employment on the shore stations, and on ocean-going whalers. For example, nine Stewart Island Maoris returned home via Sydney on 14 January 1837, their whaling ship having been wrecked at the Solomon Islands.[42] Wellers employed eighty-five men at Otakou in 1835, a quarter of them Maori, and by 1839 half their staff were Maoris. When Hughes established his whaling station at Onekakara in December 1836, half his experienced men were Maoris.[43] With what feelings Maoris joined in the unrelenting slaughter of whales, which they are said to have venerated,[44] is not clear. The whaling industry brought Maoris and Europeans closer together, ensuring the constant re-infection of the Maori population with imported diseases. European shore whalers have been depicted as dissolute drunkards,[45] except by their many descendants.

∼

Halfway along the exposed eastern coast of Te Wai Pounamu the rugged, sprawling, 100,000-hectare volcanic peninsula of Horomaka[46] rises from the surrounding sea and wetlands like an island, crowned by the noble dome of Te Ahu Patiki – 'sacred mound of the flatfish'. The traveller beholds Horomaka from afar. Approached from the ocean, its coastline looms in dark basalt ramparts, veined red and orange with burnt earth from the fires of the legendary voyager Tamatea, and splashed with white. Towering cliffs and strange rock formations stand boldly against the ceaseless ocean swell. On closer approach, the mariner is greeted by the small, friendly Hector's dolphin. The white patches on the forbidding cliffs mark the nesting places of the elegant and industrious parekareka.

to trade was crippled by epidemics. To survive, Ngai Tahu fighting chiefs had to find some additional means of getting money for firearms, whaleboats and ammunition. Such a means was at hand.

∽

William Wentworth, befriended by Governor Bourke, had in 1835 helped form the Australian Patriotic Association to campaign for representative and responsible government. Wentworth favoured restricting the vote to men of property. Sir George Gipps replaced Bourke as Governor of New South Wales in 1838, and had hopes of winning Wentworth to his side.[65] But when rumours reached Sydney that Britain planned to annex New Zealand, Wentworth and other Sydney speculators, to Gipps's annoyance, hastened to buy 'deeds' for large areas of New Zealand, signed by Maori chiefs, with a view to cornering the market in land for European settlement.[66]

John Jones was active in this 'land sharking'. Through a judicious alliance with southern Ngai Tahu chiefs led by Tuhawaiki, he became owner of seven whaling stations, from Onekakara to Port Bunn, among which he claimed to employ 280 men.[67] Jones's ship the *Magnet* arrived at Sydney under Captain James Bruce on 4 October 1838 with Tuhawaiki, Taiaroa, Karetai, Topi Patuki and Haereroa as passengers. These chiefs, according to Sydney sources, proceeded to sell 'vast tracts' to Jones and his confederates, Green, Small and Peacock. Taiaroa was back in Sydney on 1 February 1839, 'selling' more land to the Weller brothers,[68] and Karetai at Otakou 'sold' land as well.[69] Bruce during his visits to southern New Zealand 'purchased' more land for Jones. A subsequent investigation suggested that the Maori 'vendors' intended selling merely the permission to occupy or operate along a stretch of coast.[70] But whatever their intentions, no Maori chief had the right to alienate other Maoris' hereditary or occupation rights to land without their prior consent – as we have seen in Chapter 1.

With Maori chiefs vying for funds, and European speculators vying for 'deeds' to ever-larger tracts of land, disputes were inevitable. While Taiaroa was in Sydney 'selling' land to Weller in February 1839, he 'sold' Leathart the south-eastern half of Horomaka, including the whole Akaroa basin, for £40.[71] Tuauau, perhaps hearing of this, prepared to defend his right against the southern chiefs, and in April 1839 he obtained ammunition and muskets from Hempleman, reportedly to fight Tuhawaiki.[72] Koroko in turn was annoyed to hear of Horomaka being 'sold', since he had rights there himself.[73] To show his displeasure, in October 1839 he 'sold' the whole peninsula to the Wellers for goods valued at £67. With this 'deed', the Wellers made thousands of pounds selling parts of Horomaka to gullible parties in Sydney.[74]

Clayton and Leathart in 1837, as we have seen, had got Tuauau to sign a document purporting to convey the peninsula to Clayton, and Leathart got Taiaroa to 'sell' him half of it again for £40 in 1839. Leathart sold his Taiaroa deed to the Sydney syndicate of Cooper, Holt and Rhodes, for £325.[75] On the strength of this, William Rhodes landed a herd of short-horn cattle at Takapuneke for a cattle station.[76] Clayton sold his October 1837 deed for the whole peninsula to a Frenchman for £1,500 in August 1840.[77] In Sydney, such transactions promoted the fiction that the tribal lands of Te Wai Pounamu were privately owned by chiefs, and ripe for the picking. But in southern New Zealand the transactions caused resentment against the land-selling chiefs, and fresh dissension.

Notes

1. McNab 1907: 161ff; Richards 1995: 93–99.
2. McNab 1913: 100–1.
3. Stack 1936: 114; Taki Ms: 21.
4. McNab 1913: 103–8.
5. Skinner 1910: 108–9.
6. Thomson 1859/I: 274.
7. McNab 1913: 112–32.
8. Tamihana Mss APL 27a, 27b. Tamihana says Ngati Toa abandoned their 1835 expedition because they were converted by missionaries. However, the CMS missionaries who converted Ngati Toa did not reach them until 1839.
9. Stack 1936: 114ff.
10. Begg & Begg 1979: 301; Hocken 1898: 223; Pybus 1954a: 53; Taki Ms: 21; Waite 1940: 36ff.
11. McLintock 1949: 92; Weller Ms 'Papers', 16.3.1835.
12. Grady 1978: 84; McNab 1913: 110, 135–6.
13. Patuki 1878: 3; SIMAC, evidence

H. R. Tau 20.11.1989; Stack in Travers 1906: 242; Te Kahu 1901: 99–100. Te Kahu says the peace embassy was sent to all Ngai Tahu after the Tauanui. Evidently Ngai Tuahuriri alone accepted it.
14. Biggs 1959: passim.
15. Durward 1933: 69; Hay 1915: 10; Hocken 1898: 223; Pool 1991: 49ff; Shortland 1851: 65; SNC 3/ 17: 435; Thomson 1858: 313–14; WJ, 29.6.1843.
16. WJ, 5.7.1842.
17. Ibid.
18. Bathgate 1969: 360ff; Pool 1977: 141. Houghton (1980: 131) says, 'In 1848 every child born in Hawaii is said to have died of measles. Even allowing for exaggeration, the mortality must have been great. As recently as 1874, twenty thousand Fijians died of measles introduced from Australia.'

19. Stack 1972: 82; cf Clarke 1903: 63.
20. Desmond & Moore 1991: chapter 24; Godley 1951: 42. Prolonged hydropathy failed to cure J. R. Godley's tuberculosis, but Darwin claimed that it relieved his stomach disorders. Gideon Mantell cautioned his son Walter against it.
21. WJ, 5.7.1842.
22. Anderson 1986: 74; Boultbee 1986: 94–97; Dieffenbach 1843 II: 14; Gluckman 1976: 46, 191–96 and passim; McNab 1913: 109, 175. Pybus 1954a: 57; Savage 1807: 88ff; Wright 1967: 64; Watkin (WJ, 24.6.1840) mentions a Waikouaiti Maori who 'lost six children in quick succession' from tuberculosis, which 'carried off a great, great many New Zealanders'.
23. Ziegler 1982: chapter 14 and passim.
24. Bathgate 1969: 360ff; Shortland 1851: 171ff.
25. Findlay & Holdsworth 1921 III: chapter 2.
26. Watkin Ms 'Fiji' NSWSL A381.
27. Findlay & Holdsworth 1921 III: 381ff; Ironside 1891: 730ff.
28. Williment 1985: 113.
29. WJ, 14.7.1837.
30. Tamihana Mss 27a, 27b: 106ff.
31. Anderson (1986) is authoritative on Te Puoho's raid, and is largely followed here.
32. McNab 1913: 175–76.
33. Patuki 1878: 3.
34. Anderson 1986: 59–61.
35. Heberley Ms: 74; Harvey 1936: 10.57.
36. McNab 1913: 159–61; Marsden 1932: 464, 530.
37. Orange1987: 23ff; Shortland Ms 'Narrative': 489.
38. McNab 1913: 175.
39. Karetai Ms; Shortland 1851: 86–87.
40. McNab 1913: 96.
41. Bathgate 1969: 360ff; Shortland 1851: 108–17; Wai-27 V5: 6 (Bathgate).
42. McNab 1913: 176.
43. McNab 1913: 110, 263; Richards 1995: 116.
44. Orbell 1985: 144–46.
45. Shortland 1851: 109–11; WJ passim.
46. Horomaka was the traditional Maori name for Banks Peninsula according to Teone Taare Tikao (Mr Bill Gillies of Rapaki, pers. comm. 1994). Tainui (1946: 223) records 'Horomaka' as a small islet in Port Levy, but Carring-ton's 1849 plan of Koukourarata Reserve has this islet as 'Horo-mongo' (CMA Pictorial: 'Maori Places South Island').
47. McNab 1913: 150, 157ff.
48. Wai-27 L3 II: 198–99.
49. Wai-27 L3 I: 11–12.
50. McNab 1913: 246ff.
51. Ibid: 236–37, 246.
52. Hight & Straubel 1957: 238–39; Tremewan 1990: 3–68.
53. Tremewan (1989: 5ff) suggests that the principal 'vendor' was Te Whakarukeruke.
54. Hempleman 1911: 59–66.
55. McNab 1913: 236ff.
56. Tamihana Mss 27a, 27b: 106ff.
57. McNab 1913: 222.
58. Tamihana loc cit.
59. Pybus 1954b: 67.
60. Oliver 1990: 540–41; McDonald 1940: 9; McLean 1986: 51; Taylor 1950: 21.
61. Tikao 1990: 78.
62. McLean 1986: 17 and passim; Shortland 1851: 131; SNC 7/93: 719.
63. WJ, 23.6.1840.
64. Tamihana, loc cit.
65. Gipps–Glenelg, 3.4.1839, in HRA1/20.
66. McNab 1913: 292; Shortland 1851: 83ff.
67. McNab 1913: 277.

68. Hall-Jones 1943: 62; McNab 1913: 239, 279.
69. Karetai Ms.
70. Shortland 1851: 86–87.
71. Wai-27 L3/ I: 49ff.
72. Hempleman 1911: 82–83, 168. Hempleman's Log here spells Tuauau as 'Tuwoowo'. Anson (his editor) reads this as 'Taiaroa', to whom he imputes baffling and conflicting behaviours. Andersen (1927: 155) takes this up: 'Whilst Taiaroa and Tuhawaiki ("Bloody Jack") had combined in attacking Te Rauparaha, once his power was broken these two chiefs resumed intertribal quarrels, and on 10th April 1839 Hempleman supplied Taiaroa with powder, shot, musket, and balls, who then started for "the river" (Wairewa) to fight Tuhawaiki.'
73. Shortland 1851: 87.
74. Wai-27 L2/I: 7ff.
75. Wai-27 L3/I: 52ff.
76. Hight & Straubel 1957 I: 51.
77. Wai-27 L3/I: 11n.

5

~

Colonialism Reborn

ADAM SMITH, in his influential book *Inquiry into the Nature and Causes of the Wealth of Nations* (1776),[1] challenged the idea that colonies were beneficial for their 'mother countries'. He described their economic and political effects as needlessly burdensome. Sure enough, after Britain lost her main American colonies in 1783 her trade and industry prospered. But in 1815 the European peace brought economic depression and widespread unemployment for Britain, with severe hardship for the underprivileged. Yet Parliament, still dominated by country gentlemen, continued to pass Enclosure Acts and Gaming Acts to further the private ownership of the English countryside and its natural resources, and to stiffen the penalties for those who persisted in asserting common rights to them.[2]

The social unrest and rebelliousness that accompanied these developments in Britain,[3] along with an apparently insupportable population growth, prompted some theorists to look favourably on overseas colonisation again. The famous English political economist Thomas Malthus had cast doubt on the effectiveness of colonial emigration as a means of relieving overpopulation, except as a 'partial and temporary expedient'.[4] But Edward Gibbon Wakefield, son of an English farmer and land agent, attracted interest with a scheme for 'systematic colonisation' which he claimed would benefit the British poor by drawing off 'surplus population', and benefit the rich by creating a new field for profitable investment.

Wakefield proposed to promote the private ownership by British capitalists of tribal lands overseas – which he called 'waste' lands. 'The whole object of the proposed measure,' wrote Wakefield in 1829, 'is to diminish the evils of pauperism in Britain, and to promote colonization by rendering the purchase of waste land a very profitable employment of capital.' Wakefield claimed that the so-called 'waste' land could be got overseas for 'next to nothing'.[5] Reselling it to prospective landowners at a 'sufficient price', he argued, would provide funds for bringing an ample and competent labour supply to the 'systematic' colonies – which would thus be assured of prosperity. The 'sufficient price' would be low enough to attract investors, but high enough to keep wage-earners landless until they could save enough to buy their own land.

Wakefield was in personal disgrace through having been convicted and imprisoned for abducting a young heiress. But his colonisation scheme was assured of support, for he advocated for his colonies the same wholesale privatisation of common land that had become fashionable, and profitable, in Britain. 'Land, to be an element of colonization,' he wrote in 1833, 'must not only be waste, but it must be public property, liable to be converted into private property.'[6] Among colonial régimes, private ownership of land was now widely regarded as the hallmark of civilisation, while the communal ownership characteristic of tribal societies was regarded as absolute backwardness. In the United States of America the Commissioner of Indian Affairs declared, 'Common property and civilization cannot co-exist.'[7]

Wakefield's influential supporters formed a New Zealand Association in 1837, followed by a New Zealand Land Company in 1839, soon renamed the 'New Zealand Company'. According to the Company's governor, John Lambton, Earl of Durham, 'new' lands across the seas were 'the rightful patrimony of the English people, which God and Nature have set aside in the New World for those whose lot has assigned them but insufficient portions in the old'.[8] New Zealand was ideal for colonisation, declared Wakefield, for it was 'a moral wilderness', and Maoris were 'a thoroughly savage people' whom British colonisation would 'improve' and 'civilise'.[9] The 'improvement' of tribal peoples and their lands became a catch-cry of Wakefield and other colonial reformers – yet their insistence on privatising tribal lands implied the destruction of tribal economies based on common land rights, such as the Maori economy.

～

The New Zealand Company announced in 1839 that their first colony would be at Port Nicholson, the splendid harbour on the northern shore of Cook Strait. One-tenth of the land purchased by the Company was to be allocated as private property amongst the 'chief families' of the Maori tribes from whom the Company planned to acquire the land. Wakefield told a House of Commons Select Committee in 1840 that these 'tenths' were to support 'a Native aristocracy, a Native gentry', whose land the Company would deliberately intermingle with colonists' land, and who would therefore quickly become civilised.[10] Thus Wakefield envisaged the same kind of land distribution for New Zealand Maoris, as had already been imposed in Britain – that is, a land-owning minority and a landless majority.

Colonel William Wakefield, E. G. Wakefield's brother, was appointed New Zealand agent for the Company, and left England for Port Nicholson with an advance expedition in the Company's ship *Tory* in May 1839. His instructions included the statement: 'Wilderness land is worth nothing to its Native owners, or worth nothing more than the trifle they can obtain for it.' Maori land, said the Company, was merely a 'barren possession', and valueless without 'a great outlay of capital on immigration and settlement'.[11] E. G. Wakefield and the Company repeatedly referred to tribal land indiscriminately as 'waste', 'barren' or 'wilderness'. A modern editor of E. G. Wakefield's works has even written of 'waste countries': 'He [Wakefield] knew that a waste country could not be made fruitful without capital and labour in close and useful co-operation.'[12]

But as we have seen, pre-European New Zealand had long been fruitful for its tribal inhabitants – as had Australia.[13] The description of Maori tribal lands as 'waste' lands was mere doctrine, based not on any first-hand observation of Maori land occupancy in New Zealand, but on the aspirations of salesmen of colonial real estate in Britain. Mistaken as it was, or dishonest, it gave the colonial reformers a supposed justification for appropriating Maori tribal lands for private profit, as had been done with common lands in Britain by means of Enclosure Acts.

~

There was vigorous lobbying of the government in London in 1839 as to whether Britain should annex New Zealand. The humanitarians of the British and Foreign Aborigines Protection Society wanted to save the Maoris from exploitation,[14] the missionaries wanted to save their souls, and the colonialists wanted to make money. Each group favoured annexation, provided its own interests were secured.

All were agreed that 'natives' could not be left to themselves, and needed management.

When the government finally leaned towards annexation, it was with a note of caution. Maoris were warlike, and war cost money. The Lords of the Treasury therefore advised the government to annex only such parts of New Zealand as Maori chiefs were prepared to cede peacefully to the Queen.[15] This would require a treaty such as Captain William Hobson, as we have seen, had suggested in 1837. Accordingly, a treaty was decided on, and Hobson was invited to return to New Zealand to arrange it.

Hobson accepted appointment as British Consul to New Zealand in August 1839, with authority to assume the powers of Lieutenant-Governor under Governor Gipps of New South Wales, over such parts of New Zealand as Maori chiefs might agree to cede. Elsewhere, the authority of the chiefs would remain undisturbed.[16] But as to Te Wai Pounamu, Hobson was authorised to proclaim British sovereignty by 'right of discovery' if (as he himself had suggested) the 'wild state' of the inhabitants made a treaty impossible.[17]

In his official instructions to Hobson, the Secretary of State for War and the Colonies, Lord Normanby, stated:

> The price to be paid to the natives by the local government will bear an exceedingly small proportion to the price for which the same lands will be resold by the Government to the settlers. Nor is there any real injustice in the inequality. To the natives or their chiefs much of the land of the country is of no actual use, and, in their hands, it possesses scarcely any exchangeable value. Much of it must long remain useless, even in the hands of the British Government also, but its value in exchange will be first created, and then progressively increased, by the introduction of capital and of settlers from this country. In the benefits of that increase the natives themselves will gradually participate.[18]

Thus the British Government's view of Maori lands agreed perfectly with that of the New Zealand Company. That benefits from British colonisation would (in present-day jargon) 'trickle down' to the Maori people, was arguable. But to say that much of New Zealand was 'of no actual use' to Maoris was to ignore the widespread use they had been making of it for centuries. Moreover, despite the alleged worthlessness of Maori land, the New Zealand Company began selling Port Nicholson land in London for £1 an acre before any capital or settlers had been despatched to give it its so-called 'value in exchange'.

Lord Normanby's instructions differed from the New Zealand Company's plans in one significant respect: the buying of Maori land was to be a government monopoly. But the Company was allowed the profitable role of middle man. It had to obtain its land from the government, or with government approval, but it was authorised to resell it to settlers at a profit.[19] Thus Maori land was to be the basis for the colonial economy, with revenue for the government, profits for the Company, and prosperity for the colonists.

Hobson left England for Sydney in August 1839. In September, without waiting for official approval, the first New Zealand Company settlers were despatched from London on their four-month voyage to Port Nicholson. 'Colonists' paid their own fares, while the more numerous 'emigrants' had their fares paid or subsidised by the Company. At a farewell banquet on the Thames, Dr George Evans, a lawyer and scholar, proclaimed the colonists' devotion to Maori rights:

> There are no men on the face of the earth who have a more sincere or heartfelt desire to preserve the rights of the Aborigines than we have who are about to depart to those distant shores. We feel that they are our adopted countrymen (Cheers) and that a wrong or an injury inflicted upon them would be an injury upon ourselves (Hear, Hear.) We will be parties to no transaction in which their rights are not consulted equally with our own (Cheers).[20]

Aboard the three New Zealand Company ships which departed for Port Nicholson were many persons with capital or skills they planned to apply to farming, trade, industry or speculation in the new land. Others simply wanted to escape from England. Among these was Walter Baldock Durrant Mantell, a tall, gangling, bespectacled youth of nineteen years, with swarthy countenance and sardonic manner. He was the elder son of Dr Gideon Mantell, a prominent English physician, surgeon and palaeontologist from Lewes. Gideon Mantell was active in the scientific movement that shook the foundations of established thought and religion in the 1830s. His startling discoveries in the fossil beds of southern England, his brilliance as a public lecturer, and his vigorous and impressive presence, had won him fame and influential friends. He was ambitious; but as the son of a religious non-conformist he was shut out of the English establishment. In the struggle for social success he was consumed by a relent-less ambition that destroyed his happiness and that of his family.[21]

Walter Mantell had shown promise at boarding school and was indentured as an apprentice surgeon.[22] But just when Gideon Mantell had moved to a fashionable medical practice in London in September 1839, his wife and elder daughter left him. Walter, at the urging of his adventurous young friend George Duppa, broke his apprenticeship and, with his father's reluctant consent, took a cabin passage to Port Nicholson with Duppa in the New Zealand Company ship *Oriental*, as a colonist. Duppa's acquaintances Sir William Molesworth and the Honourable Henry Petre were fellow passengers.[23]

∽

Meanwhile, with the approach of the 1839–1840 fighting season, Tuhawaiki with other southern Ngai Tahu chiefs prepared a taua, for word had come that Ngati Toa had killed a Ngai Tahu man.[24] A flotilla of boats mustered at Otakou in September 1839[25] and made a leisurely trip north, reaching Horomaka in late October. At Wairewa the southern chiefs seized a Pireka whaling boat's crew, which included a Ngati Toa man. He was killed and (some said) eaten, along with a girl slave. But Tuhawaiki released the European members of the crew, to avoid giving offence in Sydney.

At Pireka, the taua demanded utu from the proprietor, Captain Hempleman, for employing Ngati Toa. Taiaroa got a new six-oared boat as ransom for a second Ngati Toa employee, while Tuhawaiki got 'the Big Boat with three new sails, as payment for the Place'. Hempleman got a signed 'certificate' in return, with which he later claimed about half of Banks Peninsula.[26] The flotilla left Pireka for Akaroa on 4 November, en route to the north. News of their movements reached Te Ati Awa at Cook Strait, where an attack was expected daily.[27]

But William Wakefield had now arrived at Cook Strait in the *Tory* to buy land for the New Zealand Company. On 27 September, 25 October and 8 November 1839, while the Ngai Tahu war party was still at Horomaka, Wakefield got Te Rauparaha and his allies to sign deeds 'selling' the southern quarter of the North Island, and the South Island as far south as 43°S.[28] Whether Wakefield knew it or not, Te Rauparaha and his fellow 'vendors' had no right under Maori custom to make these 'sales', which encompassed the lands of tribes other than their own, including a third of Ngai Tahu's tribal territory.

The Maori 'vendors' received from Wakefield 220 muskets, fifteen fowling pieces, twenty-four single- and double-barrelled guns, sixty-two kegs of gunpowder, eight kegs of ball cartridges and lead, and other merchandise.[29] Thus Te Rauparaha was in a stronger position than ever, with the New Zealand Company as his client. Tuhawaiki's war party evidently got wind of this, for they abandoned further action and hurried back to Murihiku. There the chiefs sold land to Captain Cattlin of Jones's ship *Success*,[30] and then embarked with him and Jones and his agent Henry Hesketh for Sydney. Tuhawaiki wanted to see Governor Gipps, 'to have the rights of Ngai Tahu established, and to get the protection of the Queen of England'.[31]

Te Rauparaha's son Katu and Rangihaeata's nephew Te Whiwhi had meanwhile gone to the Bay of Islands to ask the Church Missionary Society for a missionary for Ngati Toa. In response, the Reverend Henry Williams arrived at Waikanae with Katu and Te Whiwhi in November 1839, bringing Octavius Hadfield as the new missionary. Te Rauparaha visited Williams, who noted in his journal: 'The old man told me that now he had seen my eyes and heard my words, he would lay aside his evil and turn to the Book.'[32] Before long, at Hadfield's urging, Te Rauparaha began releasing his prisoners, including Ngai Tahu. However, Ngati Toa chiefs still regarded these people as their vassals and their lands as Ngati Toa property by right of conquest.[33]

When the *Success* reached Sydney on 27 January 1840, no one there yet knew that the New Zealand Company's first settlers were at Port Nicholson. But Sydney speculators were already worried, for Hobson had just called at Sydney aboard HMS *Druid*, en route to New Zealand to pave the way for British sovereignty. He had discussed with Gipps the wording of a treaty with the Maoris. On 19 January 1840, Gipps had issued proclamations (dated 14 January) regarding New Zealand, in line with Hobson's official instructions, reaffirming the basic principle of British sovereignty regarding land: that legal title can derive only from the Crown. Future private purchases of Maori land were disqualified, and existing claims were now subject to a Land Claims Commission. Hobson made similar proclamations on 30 January after arriving in New Zealand.

Speculators like Wentworth, Jones, Cattlin, the Wellers and Green by now had 'deeds' to millions of acres in New Zealand.[34] Such land sharking was soon to be condemned in the Sydney press,[35] and Governor Gipps abhorred it. His proclamations were anathema to the land sharks – as was the New Zealand Company's rival claim to have purchased much of New Zealand from Te Rauparaha. Wentworth and his supporters denounced Gipps's proclamations, declaring them an infringement of British liberties and beyond his powers.[36]

The presence of Tuhawaiki and his fellow chiefs in Sydney in the company of land sharks came to the notice of Governor Gipps. To further Hobson's objectives, Gipps invited the chiefs, together with others from the North Island, to meet him to consider a treaty acknowledging the Queen's sovereignty, and her sole right to purchase Maori land, in return for which the Maoris would have the rights of British subjects, and education and Christian instruction funded from the resale of their lands.[37] On 14 February, Tuhawaiki, Taiaroa, Tohowaiki and the North Island chiefs visited Gipps with John Jones.[38] Gipps gave Tuhawaiki a British flag and the chiefs ten sovereigns each, thinking that they would return next day and sign his treaty.[39]

Instead of revisiting the Governor, however, Tuhawaiki and seven other southern Ngai Tahu chiefs went with Jones to his solicitor's office. There they signed duplicate deeds purporting to convey to Wentworth and Jones all the South Island and its offshore islands that they had not already 'sold', except for Ruapuke. Tuhawaiki, as 'king' of this vast territory, received £100 in cash and the promise of a life annuity of £50, while the others each received £20 in cash and the promise of an annuity of £10.[40] Gipps received this message from Jones:

> I have been advised not to be instrumental in getting the New Zealand Chiefs (my friends now here) to sign away their rights to the Sovereignty of the Crown, respectively owned by them, until my purchases are confirmed as far as they can be by the Crown. I write to inform you I shall act on that advice.[41]

Although the eight Ngai Tahu 'vendors' could hardly have understood the thousand words of archaic legal jargon in which the Wentworth-Jones deeds are written, the idea that they actually sold Wentworth and Jones most of the South Island has had credence ever since.[42] Tuhawaiki is said to have asserted his right to make such a sale.[43] Yet the deeds were invalid, for the 'vendors' were selling what they did not own. There were at least sixty other Ngai Tahu chiefs and heads of whanau with customary rights in the Ngai Tahu territory covered by the deeds[44] – including those of Ngai Tuahuriri and of the Poutini Coast, Kaikoura, Arowhenua and the Horomaka district, over whom Tuhawaiki and his colleagues had no authority. The northern tenth of the South Island belonged to other tribes entirely. The exclusion of Ruapuke from the Wentworth-Jones 'purchase' suggests that the 'vendors' intended abandoning the South Island to the Europeans and pursuing their own commercial interests from Ruapuke. In 1843, however, Tuhawaiki told the Land Claims Commission at Otakou that he had signed no deed of sale while he was in Sydney in 1840.[45]

In Sydney, the Wentworth-Jones 'purchase' was seen simply as a challenge to Governor Gipps[46] – who, thanks to Jones's intrigue, saw the Maori chiefs no more.[47] Jones soon sold half of his half-share in the Wentworth-Jones 'purchase' to his lawyer, for £500.[48] Tuhawaiki got a dress uniform for himself and red-coated uniforms for a bodyguard, and embarked at Sydney with his party on Jones's ship *Magnet* under Captain Bruce on 12 March for New Zealand, accompanied by Henry Hesketh, now his own secretary. Hesketh took the Wentworth-Jones deeds with him. The *Magnet* was 'crowded like a slaver with men and women and goods and cattle'. Some of the cattle had been purchased by Tuhawaiki for Ruapuke, while the rest, and the men and women, were bound for Jones's new farming colony at Waikouaiti.[49] A Maori contemporary recalled:

> They loaded on to the ship food, guns, powder, clothes, everything in preparation for an army. Tuhawaiki himself was proclaimed general, and when they arrived back at Ruapuke they began to train to become soldiers. Tuhawaiki wore his General's uniform complete with sword around his waist. He cut a striking figure. Because of these activities, he began to look upon himself as the Maori King of New Zealand.[50]

Disembarking at Ruapuke, Tuhawaiki raised his flag and proclaimed himself 'Principal Chief of the Middle Island and its Dependencies', declaring Ruapuke exclusively the property of himself, Haereroa, Patuki, and others of his supporters.[51] Hesketh got the Wentworth-Jones deeds counter-signed on 2 April 1840 by Cattlin and Hoyle as attorneys for Tuhawaiki and his colleagues, 'delivering possession' of Te Wai Pounamu to its new Sydney 'owners'. Bruce and two other Europeans signed as witnesses to this hardy imposture.[52]

∽

When James Watkin arrived in Sydney in disgrace from Tonga in 1837, he could have gone on to England. But he chose to stay in Sydney, preaching for the Wesleyan mission. In 1839 he was asked to start a mission at Cook Strait, but when John Jones offered to sponsor a Wesleyan mission at Waikouaiti to serve his whaling station and farming settlement, Watkin accepted that call instead. He embarked at Sydney for Waikouaiti in Jones's ship *Regia* on 1 May 1840 with his wife and five small children, together with horses, sheep and cattle for Jones's farm settlement.[53] Reaching Waikouaiti, he became the first European missionary in Te Wai Pounamu. He preached his first sermon – to whalers, settlers and Maoris – to a text from St Paul: 'This is a faithful saying, and worthy of all acceptation, that Christ Jesus came into the world to save sinners; of whom I am chief.'[54] 'The attention paid was great,' wrote Watkin. 'May the word spoken not have been in vain. Amen.'[55]

Watkin's arrival at Waikouaiti was 'hailed with pleasure by the natives' and 'apparent satisfaction by the whites.' But Watkin felt it a heavy penance for his Tongan lapse: 'The scenery hereabout is fine, and a lover of New Zealand would perhaps be enraptured, but it is to me something like Botany Bay to a convict.'[56] Neither his Methodist upbringing nor his missionary experience had prepared Watkin for the pandemonium of a southern whaling station. The Maoris were 'deteriorated by their connection with wicked whites', he wrote. 'The horrible use of the word "bloody" is universal.' Watkin's mission house, provided by John Jones, lay between the whalers' settlement at the river mouth and the Maori kainga 500 metres upstream, while four kilometres northwards across the bay were Jones's farming settlement and his private estate, Matanaka, which was managed by his brother Thomas while he himself was in Sydney.[57]

The Waikouaiti Maoris spoke the southern Maori dialect laced with whalers' jargon. The Anglican Church Missionary Society books were hardly intelligible to them, being written in the northern, Nga Puhi dialect. 'It will be necessary to begin afresh,' noted Watkin, 'and write this hitherto unwritten language.'[58] Helped by

Haereroa, he soon listed hundreds of southern dialect expressions. He wrote a catechism in southern Maori for printing at the Hokianga Methodist mission, but had to wait eighteen months for copies to arrive.[59] Meanwhile he preached in English to Jones's settlers. 'A considerable number of Natives were present to witness the karakia bora (English worship),' wrote Watkin, 'though they could not understand anything that was said.'[60]

Notes

1. Smith 1890: 460.
2. Hopkins 1985: 31 and passim
3. Hobsbawm & Rudé 1985: 15–16 and passim.
4. Malthus 1986 III: 353.
5. Wakefield 1929a: 101–6.
6. Wakefield 1929b: 130–34.
7. Dippie 1982: 109.
8. Durham 1912 I: 13. Durham was here referring to Canada.
9. Wakefield & Ward 1837: 27–28.
10. Jellicoe 1930: 9; Ward 1840: 94, 116ff.
11. Jellicoe 1930: 8–11.
12. Prichard 1969: 26.
13. Regarding the Australian Aboriginal economy, see Butlin 1993 and Rose 1987.
14. British & Foreign APS Appeal 1840.
15. Pennington–Stephen, 22.6.1839, NSWSL CO 209/5: 96–98.
16. Williams 1941: 32 and passim;
17. Hobson–Labouchere, 1.8.1839 and Normanby–Hobson, 15.8.1839, NSWSL Ms A1280: 83, 591ff.
18. Normanby-Hobson, 14.8.1839, in Mackay 1873 I (iii): 13ff.
19. Mackay 1873 I: 43: NZ Company Charter.
20. NSWSL Ms A1281: 527.
21. G. A. Mantell Ms Journal; Spokes 1927: passim; Vallance 1984: 91ff.
22. Mantell Ms 83/495; Spokes 1927: 117.
23. Duppa–G. Mantell, 30.7.96,

Mantell Ms 83/36; G. A. Mantell Ms Journal: passim.
24. Patuki 1878: 3.
25. Harwood Ms Journal; McNab 1913: 281–82.
26. McNab 1913: 293; Wai-27 L3 I: 18.
27. Dieffenbach 1843 I: 115; Hempleman 1911: 102–3; McNab 1913: 292.
28. Jellicoe 1930: 18.
29. *AJHR* 1888 I-8: 57–60; *IUPBPPNZ* 5: 102ff; Jellicoe 1930: 18.
30. Boultbee 1986: 89 (illus); Chisholm 1994: 82.
31. Harwood Ms Journal; McNab 1913: 283; Patuki 1878: 3.
32. Williams 1968: 453–54. Williams wore spectacles and was known for his 'four eyes'.
33. Te Kanae Ms: 17.
34. Mackay 1873 I (ii): 5; (iii): 81ff.
35. *The Australian*, 10.3.1840.
36. McLintock 1958: 54–55; Shortland Ms Annexation of NZ: 25–27; Sweetman 1939: 57–59.
37. Sweetman 1939: 64.
38. Ibid: 60–61.
39. Tuhawaiki said later, 'This money was given for our consent to sell land to the Queen.' (*HCBB*, 29.7.1844: 437.)
40. Wentworth Ms Indenture; Wentworth-Jones Deed. The eight chiefs named were as follows [author's interpretations]: Tuhawaiki as 'King' of Te Wai Pounamu and Stewart Island;

Karetai, Kaikoareare, Tukawa,
Taiaroa and Te Whaikai Pokene
as chiefs of Otago; and Tohowaiki
and Topi Patuki as chiefs of
Ruapuke. See Evison 1995.
41. Sweetman 1939: 60–62.
42. See, for instance, Sweetman 1939:
65; McLintock 1949: 104–5;
Oliver 1990: 212b; Kociumbas
1992: 192; Tremewan 1994: 17.
43. Taki Ms: 33.
44. Evison 1993: 512–16.
45. HCBB 29.7.1844: 437.
46. Sweetman 1939: 67-68.
47. Shortland Ms Letters Shortland–
Clarke, 18.3.1844 (2).
48. AONSW, Reg. Gen. 9/7694
(R.1593); LTO 1825–1848 R.1-
520, No. 144.
49. Eccles & Reed 1949: 42ff, 62;
Hall-Jones 1943: 64.
50. Hall-Jones 1943: 70, 80ff; Patuki
1878: 3; Taki Ms: 21.
51. Tuhawaiki Ms Proclamation.
52. Evison 1995.
53. McNab 1913: 481.
54. I Timothy 1: 15.
55. WJ, 17.5.1840.
56. WJ, 14.6.1840; Watkin–J.Buller,
14.9.1840, Watkin Ms Letters
HL.
57. See maps in Knight & Coutts
1975: 14b, and Shortland 1851:
129.
58. WJ, 30.5.1840, 8.9.1840.
59. Ibid, 5.6.1840, 15.2.1841; Harlow
1987: vi ff; Harlow 1994: passim.
60. WJ, 5–7.6.1840.

6

❧

The Treaty of Waitangi

CAPTAIN WILLIAM HOBSON was a frail, conscientious naval officer with a rather overbearing 'quarter-deck' manner.[1] At forty-eight he was prematurely aged from twenty years' service in the West Indies, where yellow fever had left him prone to frequent headaches. As the son of an Irish lawyer he lacked influence in England, and had to be thankful for his New Zealand appointment. He reached the Bay of Islands from Sydney on 29 January 1840, and proclaimed his official powers at about the same time as the New Zealand Company's first colonists were landing without official sanction at Port Nicholson.

Hobson's proclamations echoed those of Governor Gipps in affirming that the Crown alone could grant private ownership of land, and that private purchases of Maori land were now disqualified. He arranged for the translation into Maori of the treaty that he and Gipps had drafted, and for Maori chiefs to be invited to James Busby's house at Waitangi to consider signing it. On 6 February 1840, after a public discussion, the amended document was signed there by forty or fifty chiefs, and became known as the Treaty of Waitangi.[2]

The Treaty of Waitangi's preamble emphasised the Queen's wish to stop lawlessness among Europeans and Maoris, and its three articles in turn conveyed the following meanings:

1. The Queen would have complete kawanatanga (right of government.)[3]
2. The Queen would protect the chiefs, the hapu, and all Maoris in exercising their tino rangatiratanga (absolute or unqualified chieftainship) over their lands, villages and valued possessions. The chiefs would sell land to the Queen at a price agreeable to the Maori owners and to the Queen's agent sent to buy it.

3. The Queen granted the Maoris the rights and duties of Englishmen.[4]

Hobson, now Lieutenant-Governor under Gipps, established his government at the Bay of Islands settlement of Kororareka, which he renamed Russell in honour of the new British Secretary of State for War and the Colonies, Lord John Russell, who had succeeded Lord Normanby in September 1839. As we have seen, Hobson in 1837 had suggested that British sovereignty in New Zealand could be limited, at least initially, to coastal trading posts. But the New Zealand Company's freelance colonising activities convinced Hobson of a need to extend the Queen's authority in New Zealand as widely as possible, by means of the Treaty.

Hobson had quarrelled over matters of protocol with Captain Joseph Nias, the diminutive, peppery commander of his supporting warship, the twenty-six-gun frigate HMS *Herald*. He nevertheless prevailed on Nias to take him around the New Zealand coast to get more Treaty signatures. Eight days out on this venture, Hobson suffered a stroke and was brought back to Russell. Nias took the *Herald* to Sydney and informed Gipps that Hobson's ability to govern was at an end. But the ship's surgeon told Gipps that Hobson was already recovering, and that his illness had been brought on by Nias's antagonism.[5] For this and other rumoured perversities, Nias was comprehensively blackguarded in the *Sydney Gazette*, which suggested that he should be tarred and feathered, and that his officers could hardly be expected to obey such a 'mean-souled abortion of humanity'. The newspaper's editor, despite apologising publicly, was prosecuted, fined, and imprisoned for incitement to mutiny.[6]

Among copies of the Treaty of Waitangi issued to New Zealand missionaries and officials for obtaining further signatures was one in English. This differed significantly in meaning from the original Maori treaty. 'Kawanatanga' was translated as 'sovereignty', a much wider term, and 'tino rangatiratanga' was diminished to mean 'possession'. In Article 2, the chiefs' agreement to sell land to the Queen at a mutually agreeable price was translated as giving the Queen the exclusive 'right of pre-emption' over Maori land. This English document became the official version of the Treaty, despite receiving only thirty-nine of the final total of more than five hundred signatures.

In English law, the Crown's right of pre-emption had long meant the monarch's right to commandeer necessities (usually in time of war) at specially reduced prices, to the exclusion of other buyers.

Extending this right to the buying of Maori land clearly negated the Treaty's guarantee of 'tino rangatiratanga'.[7] There appears to be no evidence that the complex implications of 'sovereignty' and 'pre-emption' were explained to Maoris who signed the Treaty of Waitangi, in either version, or that Maoris were given to understand that their 'tino rangatiratanga' was to mean merely 'possession'. But from this point on, the government's intention to claim overriding rights over Maori land was clear.

∼

In Sydney, William Wentworth lost no time in organising opposition to Governor Gipps's New Zealand proclamations of January 1840.[8] He chaired a public meeting on 2 April 1840,[9] at which a 'New Zealand Association' was formed to contest the matter on behalf of those with commercial interests in New Zealand. Gipps promptly sent Major Thomas Bunbury to New Zealand in the naval store ship *Buffalo*, as Hobson's deputy, with a few supporting troops, and with instructions that British sovereignty over the South Island was 'very urgently required', and could be proclaimed by 'right of discovery'.[10] Gipps politely ordered Nias back to Russell with the *Herald* to support Hobson.[11] He then had a bill prepared for the New South Wales Legislative Council to confirm his proclamations, and nullify such speculations as the Wentworth-Jones 'purchase' of 15 February.[12]

Hobson, still apprehensive that the Port Nicholson colonists might prejudice Maori chiefs against accepting his authority, now sent Bunbury in the *Herald*, under Nias, to get eastern and southern signatures to the Treaty of Waitangi – especially Te Rauparaha's, 'whose adherence', said Hobson, 'will secure to Her Majesty the undisputed right of sovereignty over all the southern districts'.[13] The expedition left Russell on 29 April 1840, taking Edward Marsh Williams as interpreter. His father, the Reverend Henry Williams, had already sailed for the western coasts of the North Island to get Treaty signatures.

Captain Nias was evidently impatient with his orders, for the *Herald* had obtained only six Treaty signatures before reaching Akaroa Heads on 24 May. For three days the ship lay there, and Nias lost his best bower anchor and thirty-six fathoms of cable in a tidal drift.[14] To Ngai Tahu watching from the shore, the ship's gun ports and British flag no doubt looked suspicious. Perhaps she was about to repeat the brig *Elizabeth*'s exploit of 1830, and had brought Te Rauparaha to avenge the killing of Hempleman's Ngati Toa whaler at Wairewa the previous October.[15]

Nias brought HMS *Herald* into Akaroa on 27 May, and anchored her in the dark near Onuku.[16] Meanwhile, Iwikau of Puari and Tikao of Pigeon Bay had decided to find out the visitors' intentions. These two chiefs could afford to be sanguine about Te Rauparaha, for they had been among those captured by him in 1830 and later released. Tikao, who had taken the name 'John Love', had been overseas for several years, and understood several languages besides English.[17]

When the *Herald*'s boat approached Onuku in the rain on 28 May, Iwikau and Tikao were waiting on shore. They were greeted in the southern dialect by William Stewart, whom Nias had taken on at Mercury Bay as pilot, still masquerading as Stewart the cartographer.[18] Linen had been brought from the ship to be washed. In the ship's boat also were Bunbury and Williams, who insisted no Ngati Toa were in the *Herald*. Williams read the two chiefs the Treaty of Waitangi in Maori, and explained the Queen's desire to bring peace to the country.[19] With bad weather approaching, the Europeans then returned to their ship.

They landed again with the Treaty on 30 May. Iwikau and Tikao signed 'after a little more explanation', and received the usual complimentary blankets. Williams put up Hobson's proclamations and went shooting ducks and 'plenty of pigeons'. Next morning, Nias ordered the washing aboard 'wet or dry', and sailed for Stewart Island.[20] Bunbury reported 'preposterous claims by Sydney land traders' at Akaroa, including Leathart and Rhodes. He recommended that 'Banks Peninsula should be surveyed as soon as possible, and thrown open to public competition in allotments of convenient size, to stop further claims of doubtful origin and character'.[21] But he did not suggest seeking Maori permission for this.

Hobson meanwhile had heard that the Port Nicholson settlers had set up their own administration. To counter this apparent challenge, on 21 May he proclaimed British sovereignty over the North Island by virtue of the Treaty of Waitangi, and over the South Island by 'right of discovery'. He then sent officials with soldiers and police to Port Nicholson to assert his authority. But in explaining these latest proclamations to the British Government, Hobson wandered from the truth. He claimed 'universal adherence' to the Treaty by North Island chiefs, when he had as yet received word of Treaty signatures by only a minority of them, and he claimed 'a perfect knowledge of the uncivilized state of the natives' of the South Island, when he had never been there except on his brief visit to Cloudy Bay with Samuel Marsden in 1837.[22]

Hobson thus disregarded Lord Normanby's instructions that no territory was to be annexed without the consent of the Maori inhabitants, and that the South Island could be annexed by 'right of discovery' only if the inhabitants proved incapable of understanding a treaty.[23] As it happened, however, although the news had yet to reach Hobson, more chiefs in the western and southern North Island had now signed the Treaty. Henry Williams had revisited Te Rauparaha, obtaining his signature on 14 May.[24] Nevertheless, Hobson's proclamations, like Bunbury's Akaroa report, showed little regard for Maori rights. Hobson was more concerned about settler insubordination at Port Nicholson.

～

When HMS *Herald* arrived off Stewart Island, William Stewart guided her to Port Pegasus, the extensive harbour where he had abandoned his boatbuilders in 1826. The place was deserted. Stewart claimed that his 'fifty' former colonists had moved to Paterson Inlet.[25] At Port Pegasus on 5 June 1840, Bunbury and Nias proclaimed British sovereignty over Stewart Island by virtue of Captain Cook's 'discovery', without attempting to visit its Maori settlements.

Nias was now anxious to return north. After several days shut up in Port Pegasus by adverse winds, he crossed to Ruapuke.[26] Henry Hesketh came off to the *Herald* with some Europeans and Maoris. Afterwards, noted Bunbury:

> The Chief Tuhawaiki came on board in the full dress staff uniform of a British aide-de-camp, with gold lace trousers, cocked hat, and plume, in which he looked extremely well, and his behaviour at Captain Nias's table, where he took tea, shewed that the examples he had seen had not been lost on him. He was also accompanied by a native Orderly Sergeant, dressed in a corresponding costume. The Chief spoke a little English, and appeared to be aware of the nature of the treaty, but which I thought it necessary to have read and explained to him in the presence of Mr Hesketh; and he signed it without hesitation.

Hesketh wrote Tuhawaiki's name on the Treaty as 'John Touwaick', as he had done on Tuhawaiki's Ruapuke proclamation, and Tuhawaiki signed, as usual, by penning a flourish across his name.[27] Henry

Comber, a midshipman in the *Herald*, thought he 'never saw a finer man'.[28] According to Bunbury, Tuhawaiki submitted for his signature a paper written in English, declaring his ownership of Ruapuke, but made no claim to own the South Island, although he claimed to be principal chief of it.[29] Next day (11 June), Tuhawaiki and twenty of his Maori soldiers watched military drill on board the *Herald*, accompanied by two other chiefs whose names Stewart wrote on the Treaty as 'Kaikoura' and 'Tararoa', and who signed with plain marks.[30]

The *Herald* reached Otakou Heads on 13 June, in adverse winds. Nias had a signal gun fired, and Bunbury and Stewart went in aboard the ship's boat. They found Karetai and Korako,[31] whose names Stewart wrote on the Treaty and witnessed together with Bunbury.[32] But in fact only Korako signed.[33] The landing party hurried back to the ship, which sailed at once for Cloudy Bay, ignoring the Maori settlement of Waikouaiti across the bay, where James Watkin was already busy with his Wesleyan mission. Nias was perhaps more concerned for his bower anchor and cable lying off Akaroa Heads, where he unsuccessfully tried to retrieve them the following day.

The *Herald* reached Cloudy Bay on 16 June, and Bunbury got nine Ngati Toa chiefs to sign the Treaty, including Te Rauparaha's brother Nohorua. Others declined, for fear of losing their lands. Undeterred, Bunbury and Nias on 17 June proclaimed British sovereignty over the South Island by virtue of the six Ngai Tahu and nine Ngati Toa signatories having 'ceded' it to the Crown. In the previous month, Henry Williams had obtained signatures from Te Ati Awa and Ngati Tama at Queen Charlotte Sound and D'Urville Island.[34]

Bunbury and Nias reckoned fifteen Maori Treaty signatures sufficient to justify British annexation of the South Island. But these signatories did not represent the twenty or so Maori settlements in southern New Zealand that had *not* been visited with the Treaty, nor is there evidence that these settlements were fully informed of the Treaty from the three that had been visited. Nor did the government ensure for Maoris of southern New Zealand the promised 'rights of Englishmen'. European lawlessness remained unchecked by the government, and more than three years were to pass before another official ventured south of Banks Peninsula.

∾

The Treaty of Waitangi in southern New Zealand. Inset: Waitangi region.

IOI

On 28 May 1840, the day that Bunbury promised the chiefs at Onuku the tino rangatiratanga of their land, Governor Gipps introduced his New Zealand Land Claims Bill in the New South Wales Legislative Council, to codify the provisions of his controversial January proclamations. The bill provided that private land purchases from Maoris later than 14 January 1840 were disqualified, and that a land claims commission would investigate alleged earlier purchases and report to the Governor. The maximum to be awarded for any one claim was 2,560 acres, an area specified elsewhere in New South Wales land regulations.

Five objectors contested Gipps's bill – including James Busby, who claimed to own 50,000 acres and a town site worth £30,000 in the North Island, and Wentworth, who claimed about 100,000 acres in the North Island, and much of the South Island through his joint 'purchase' with Jones. The relative merits of Gipps's bill and the Wentworth-Jones 'purchase' were bitterly contested. Wentworth argued that the bill violated Magna Carta by confiscating private property without compensation. Ngai Tahu chiefs, he said, had been entitled to sell land to Jones and himself in February 1840, since British sovereignty was not proclaimed until May. In reply, Gipps argued that Ngai Tahu, as 'savages', could not legally sell land. He warned that Wentworth could be hanged if he tried to start an unauthorised colony in New Zealand, while Wentworth accused the Governor of overriding British property rights.[35]

Gipps's bill was passed on 4 August 1840. Wentworth resigned his magistracy, and his nomination to the Legislative Council was cancelled by Gipps.[36] Wentworth and Jones pursued their claim no further. The greatest value their 'deeds' were to retain was in their magnificent sets of full-face moko of the 'vendors'.[37] The British Government accepted Gipps's bill, but deferred its implementation because of their own independent decision to send a land commissioner to New Zealand, and because the bill would have compromised the New Zealand Company's land purchases – and Lord John Russell sympathised with the Company.[38]

But Gipps, in his anxiety to defeat Wentworth and his faction, had laid bare the contradiction in British policy. On the one hand he argued that Maoris were too uncivilised to sell land privately, while on the other hand he maintained that they were civilised enough to sell it to the Crown. Of course, the government, the New Zealand Company, the land speculators, and the colonialists were all agreed that Maori land should be sold for 'next to nothing'. Their disagreement was over whether the Crown should have a monopoly of buying it.

∽

Captain Jean Langlois deposited his 'purchase deed' for Banks Peninsula with the Nanto-Bordelaise Company in France in March 1840. He then took command of a converted naval transport re-named *Comte de Paris* after the King's grandson, and sailed for New Zealand with the cautious blessing of the French Government. The ship carried some sixty colonists, and supplies and equipment for a French settlement at Akaroa – which would expand, it was hoped, to include the South Island, Stewart Island, and Chatham Islands. To guard the new colony and the local French whaling fleet, the cor-vette *Aube* of twenty-two guns and 160 crew had already left France under Captain Charles Lavaud.[39]

Lavaud reached the Bay of Islands on 10 July 1840, and was dismayed to find the British flag flying and the ten-gun sloop *Britomart* at anchor. She had replaced the frigate *Herald* on station. Her commander, Owen Stanley, was a moody but talented young officer, already distinguished in Arctic exploration. He spoke French, and took Lavaud to hear from Hobson the facts of British sover-eignty, and of the land claims commission proposed by Gipps. After due courtesies had been exchanged, Lavaud returned to his ship. From local Frenchmen he learned that others besides the French also claimed Banks Peninsula, and that William Rhodes was already farming there. On 20 July Lavaud formally protested to Hobson, who reported to Gipps:

> The conversation was introduced by Captain Lavaud denying the right of the British Government to investigate the titles of French subjects to lands obtained from the natives. I resisted this principle – contending that it would be the duty of the British Government, under any circumstances, to enquire into the validity of all titles on behalf of the natives, who had become British subjects.[40]

Hobson and Lavaud reached a gentlemen's agreement, in the pres-ence of Bunbury and Stanley, that neither side would pursue the question of sovereignty at Akaroa until the wishes of their home governments became known.

But Hobson still had his official responsibilities. On 21 July he instructed Stanley to sail as if for Port Nicholson, but to proceed instead to Akaroa, urgently and secretly, to forestall any French probing of British sovereignty there. Two new and untried police magistrates, Michael Murphy and Charles Barrington Robinson,[41] sent from Sydney by Governor Gipps, were to sail with Stanley. They were to 'show the flag' and hold courts to demonstrate the reality of British sovereignty. Hobson gave Stanley a copy of Bunbury's Cloudy Bay proclamation to show that 'the principal chiefs have ceded their rights to Her Majesty', and that British sovereignty over the South Island need not be proclaimed again.[42]

Before the *Britomart*'s departure, Lavaud again called on Hobson with Stanley. They agreed privately, as naval men of honour, that Langlois's settlers could land at Akaroa under Lavaud's protection and under British sovereignty, pending their home governments' decision.[43] That night, the two magistrates boarded the *Britomart* thinking they were going to Port Nicholson – which secretly amused Stanley. At daybreak the vessel slipped her moorings from alongside the *Aube*, and put to sea.[44] Lavaud, still unaware that the Treaty of Waitangi had been signed at Akaroa, now informed his government that if the Banks Peninsula chiefs had not already signed the Treaty, he would persuade them against it and get them to accept French protection instead. If this failed, the colonists could be moved to the Chatham Islands, where, Lavaud advised: 'I think it would be necessary to send out an expedition of combat troops to take it by force, chase the natives into the interior, guard it, fortify the vicinity of the roadstead, and immediately declare French sovereignty.'[45]

∼

HM sloop *Britomart* reached Akaroa on 10 August 1840, battered by storms. Unknown to Commander Stanley, Langlois's *Comte de Paris* was already in Pigeon Bay, also storm-battered, having arrived from France the previous day. With Langlois was the Nanto-Bordelaise Company's agent, Pierre Joseph Sainte-Croix Crocquet de Belligny – an elegant and well-connected gentleman sponsored by the Paris Museum of Natural History. Maoris had gone to Pigeon Bay from various parts of Banks Peninsula, attracted by the ship. Langlois was busy negotiating with them for land, unaware that Lavaud was already in New Zealand waters and that Britain had annexed New Zealand.

The French now witnessed the bitter divisions among Ngai

Tahu. The 'sale' of Banks Peninsula by southern chiefs such as Taiaroa, discussed in Chapter 4, was resented both by the chiefs of Akaroa and by those in the north of the peninsula led by Iwikau – including Ngai Tuahuriri of Puari. All these chiefs wanted to assert their rights. Iwikau's group agreed to sell Langlois a foothold in each of the three northern harbours – Te Pohue in Port Cooper, Kaihope in Port Levy, and Kakongutungutu (or 'Ngakomutumutu') in Pigeon Bay.[46] Langlois got their marks on blank sheets of paper,[47] and promised them, as payment, merchandise from his stores when he reached Akaroa – including 600 clay pipes, 400 tea and coffee cups, forty-eight pairs of stockings, twenty-four woollen neckties, twenty-three rifles, 150 pounds of gunpowder, and some kitchen utensils, garden implements and carpentry tools. The Akaroa chiefs sold Langlois nothing; but after their departure from Pigeon Bay, Iwikau 'sold' Langlois the four north-eastern bays in Akaroa Harbour.

Langlois left Pigeon Bay for Akaroa six days later, and fired two cannon shots across the bows of a passing whaleboat – which happened to be carrying Magistrates Murphy and Robinson back to Akaroa after their holding court in the south of the peninsula. The boat's naval officer boarded the *Comte de Paris* with Robinson, who explained to Langlois in French that British sovereignty was now in force. Langlois, pointing to the guns he had brought, scoffed at this.[48]

Commander Stanley meanwhile was lunching with Lavaud on board the *Aube*. He was recalled to his ship to visit the *Comte de Paris* and see its guns for himself. Langlois was 'thunderstruck' to hear from Stanley that Britain had indeed annexed New Zealand, that courts had been held at Akaroa and elsewhere on Banks Peninsula, and that Lavaud had acquiesced in all this. To Stanley afterwards, Lavaud denied all knowledge of Langlois's guns. 'The French, I think,' Stanley wrote home, 'are playing a deep game.'[49]

Stanley noted having made the following agreement with Lavaud:

> He[Lavaud] would cause the immigrants to be landed in some unoccupied part of the bay, where he pledged himself they should do nothing which could be considered as hostile to our Government, and that until fresh instructions should be received from our respective Governments the immigrants should merely build themselves houses for shelter and clear away what little land they might require for gardens.[50]

No French guns would be landed. Langlois's 'purchase' could be investigated, and Robinson would remain at Akaroa as magistrate.

Lavaud graciously offered Robinson the use of his cabin table until he could be housed on shore.

Commander Stanley watched the French settlers disembark on 19 August 'in a sheltered, well-chosen part of the bay where they could not interfere with anyone'.[51] Stanley then made an excellent chart of the harbour, and some fine watercolours and sketches,[52] before leaving for Pigeon Bay, Port Nicholson (where he left Murphy), and the Bay of Islands. Stanley disliked the Akaroa climate, and the French colony's future prospects.[53] But his diplomatic success with Lavaud delighted Hobson, who praised him highly. Owen Stanley later conducted hydrographic surveys north of Australia, his name being given to high mountains in Papua. He died of sickness at Sydney, aged thirty-nine years.

≈

Ngai Tahu of Akaroa at first welcomed the French presence. They supposed the English to be still in league with Te Rauparaha, since Wakefield had supplied him with muskets and gunpowder. 'Your

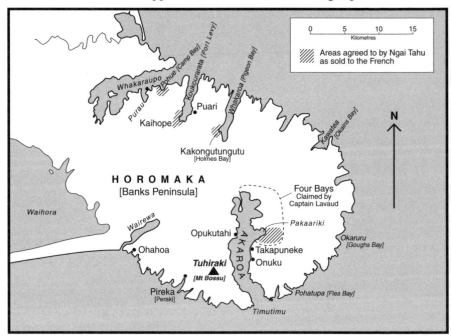

The French at Banks Peninsula.

presence among us is henceforth a protection,' Tuauau told Lavaud.[54] When HMS *Favorite* visited Akaroa later in the year, Lavaud told her commander he had no instructions from Paris beyond being 'on the coast of New Zealand for the protection of the French Whale Industry'.[55]

But when Lavaud found that the Akaroa chiefs knew nothing of Langlois's 1838 'purchase', he had a fresh deed prepared. The French again evidently used Iwikau to entrap the Akaroa chiefs, knowing that if Iwikau signed the deed, his rivals would do likewise to protect their mana. Thus the new deed, in French, was signed by Iwikau, Tuauau, Tikao, Mautai, Tamakeke, Pukenui, Nohomutu, Te Whakarukeruke and others. Under its terms, the Maoris supposedly agreed to sell the whole 100,000-hectare peninsula except for the rugged south-western corner of some 4,000 hectares. It was absurd, of course, to suppose that the Maori inhabitants would willingly abandon the most favoured haunts of their ancestors and be bundled into the peninsula's least hospitable corner.

Under Lavaud's new deed, the price of Banks Peninsula was increased to 6,000 francs (£240), to be paid in the merchandise promised by Langlois at Pigeon Bay – an assortment of clothing, tools, armaments and baubles. This illicit 'purchase' contravened Hobson's proclamations. But Police Magistrate Robinson, as he made use of Lavaud's cabin, raised no objection. The new French deed was dated 2 August 1838 so as to pass it off as Langlois's original deed – a forgery certified as 'true' by Lavaud and three of his officers, and by Belligny. Lavaud reported to Paris: 'I confess to my shame, for it is dishonest, that it was necessary, in order that in the eyes of the British authorities we have at least a semblance of a right to the ownership of the land at Akaroa.'[56]

The South Island Treaty of Waitangi signatures obtained by Bunbury had enabled Hobson to dispense with the British 'right of discovery' over the South Island, which the French could well have challenged.[57] The signatures also forestalled any French attempt at making their own treaty with the Banks Peninsula Maoris. The Ngai Tahu Treaty signatures were useful to the French Government in 1844, in defending their acceptance of British sovereignty at Akaroa against bitter criticism by French colonialists in the National Assembly.[58]

But Ngai Tahu's Treaty signatures were not so helpful to themselves. Hobson had told Lavaud that he would protect the Maoris as 'British subjects'. But at Akaroa he abandoned them to the French, and to Police Magistrate Robinson. The tall, courteous Belligny and the stout, hot-tempered Robinson soon shared the same house on shore, and became the best of friends.[59] After Commander Stanley's departure they continued to take advantage of the enmity between Iwikau and the Akaroa chiefs.[60] Belligny soon began selling land for the Nanto-Bordelaise Company in the four Akaroa bays 'sold' by Iwikau, and Robinson abetted him in this by buying some of it for himself.[61]

Lavaud had originally acknowledged that the 'unoccupied part' of Akaroa agreed to by Stanley for the French settlement was to be simply 'the cove [l'anse] where we were'[62] – that is, Pakaariki, where the French built their town. But on his return to France in 1843 Lavaud claimed that Stanley and the Akaroa Maoris had agreed to the French having the four Akaroa bays 'sold' by Iwikau.[63] Robinson obligingly concurred. Until 1848, the francophile Robinson and his successor at Akaroa were the only New Zealand Government officials resident among the Maoris of southern New Zealand.

Notes

1. Hocken Ms NZ Notes: 12.
2. Orange 1990: 66ff,130.
3. Shortland Ms Annexation of New Zealand: 31.
4. For full Treaty text and translation, see Appendix I, p. 355.
5. Comber Ms, 31.1.1840 and 3, 12, 30.3.1840; Scholefield 1934: 107 and passim.
6. *Sydney Gazette*, 14–18.4.1840; Gipps–Russell, 20.7.1840, CO[Ms]/201/298: 149, PRO.
7. See Haast 1938: 387ff.
8. Sweetman 1939: 59–60, 77–102.
9. *Sydney Gazette*, 31.3.1840, advertisement.
10. Gipps–Hobson, 3.4.1840, in HRA1/ XX: 591.
11. See Hall 1938: 52–53.
12. Sweetman 1939: 68-69.
13. Hobson–Bunbury, 25.4.1840, in *IUPBPPNZ* III: 139. The 'Southern Districts' officially comprised the South Island and the southern half of the North Island.
14. Comber Ms, 24–27.5.1840.
15. Hempleman 1911: 103.
16. Comber, loc cit; Williams Ms: 24ff.
17. Tikao 1990: 1.
18. Comber Ms 8, 13.5.1840; Ross 1987: passim.
19. Bunbury 1861 III: 100.
20. Williams Ms: 29–30.
21. Bunbury–Hobson, 28.6.1840, NSWSL A1267-19.
22. Hobson–Russell, 25.5.1840, in *IUPBPPNZ* III: 138.
23. Normanby–Hobson, 14–15.8.1839, in Mackay 1873 I (iii): 13ff.
24. Orange 1990: 130ff.
25. Comber Ms, 4–10.6.1840.
26. Bunbury–Hobson, 28.6.1840, loc cit; Comber Ms, 10.6.1840; Hall-Jones 1994: 51–59.
27. Treaty of Waitangi Ms: 3. Tuhawaiki's name on the Treaty is in the same hand as his Ruapuke 'proclamation', also written by Hesketh.
28. Comber Ms 10.6.95.

29. Bunbury–Hobson, 28.6.1840, loc cit.
30. Evison 1993: 147 n31. The reports of Bunbury or Marsh do not identify these two chiefs. 'Tararoa' has been read as 'Taiaroa', but Bunbury says that Taiaroa was at Moeraki at the time, not Ruapuke. 'Kaikoura' was probably Kaikoareare, named on the Wentworth-Jones deeds as 'Kaikoraira' and on the Ruapuke Proclamation as 'Kikora'. Sweetman (1939: 60) also has Kaikoareare as 'Kicora'.
31. Ross 1987: 186–88.
32. Treaty of Waitangi Ms: 3.
33. Evison 1993: 147 n35. Of the seven Ngai Tahu names on the Treaty of Waitangi, judging from the handwriting, Williams wrote Iwikau's and Tikao's, Hesketh wrote Tuhawaiki's, and Stewart wrote the rest.
34. Orange 1990: 146–48.
35. Sweetman 1939: passim.
36. Gipps–Russell, 16.8.1840, in HRA1/20: 760–62.
37. See Evison 1995.
38. Russell–Gipps, 21.11.1840, CO[Ms]/201/297: 187ff.
39. McNab 1913: 250ff; Tremewan 1990: chapter 4.
40. Hobson–Gipps, 21.7.1840, in Gipps–Russell, 24.8.1840, NSWSL CO 201/297.
41. Hill 1986 I: chapter 3. A 'police magistrate' ran the local police force and local court.
42. Hobson–Stanley, 23.7.1840, in Gipps–Russell, 24.8.1840, loc cit.
43. Tremewan 1990: 96ff.
44. Lubbock 1968: 128ff.
45. Lavaud–Minister of Marine, 19–24.7.1840, in Wai-27 G2: 199–202.
46. W. Shortland–Lord Stanley, 15.11.1843, in ARSCNZ, *HCBB*, 29.7.1844: 433ff.
47. *NTR*: 532.
48. Lavaud Ms; Lubbock 1968: 128ff.
49. Stanley to his family, 24.8.1840, CPL ZMs 43. This letter is catalogued 'Stanley to his wife', but he died unmarried (Lubbock 1968: passim).
50. Stanley–Hobson, 17.9.1840, in Gipps–Russell, 19.10.1840, NSWSL CO201/299: 420ff.
51. Ibid.
52. See Maling 1981: 25ff.
53. Best 1966: 241.
54. Lavaud 1986: 26.
55. Dunlop–Gipps, 5.12.1840, in Gipps–Russell 6.12.1840, NSWSL CO 201/299.
56. Tremewan 1990: 122–23. Although at the Waitangi Tribunal in 1988 the Crown advanced this French deed as valid, the tribunal concluded it was a forgery (*NTR*: 540–41).
57. Rutherford 1949: 23.
58. New Zealand Company 1844: 75.
59. Tremewan 1990: 259.
60. See Shortland 1851: 7.
61. Tremewan 1990: 151, 260.
62. Lavaud Ms: 48–49 (author's translation).
63. Lavaud 1986: 29; Tremewan 1990: 116.

7

~

Sovereignty

CAPTAIN HOBSON had been strongly influenced by the Reverend Samuel Marsden during his New Zealand cruise in 1837, and as Lieutenant-Governor of New Zealand he looked again to the Church Missionary Society (CMS) for guidance. After proclaiming himself British Consul at Waitangi, Hobson complied with his official instructions by setting up a Department for the Protection of Aborigines to promote 'the health, civilisation, education, and spiritual care of the Natives'. In April 1840 he appointed a CMS missionary, George Clarke, to be Chief Protector, with authority to supervise sales of Maori land.[1]

With the advent of British sovereignty, Maori fighting seasons, and slavery, were at an end – for British law forbade them. The return of Ngai Tuahuriri captives from the north made Puari the largest Ngai Tahu settlement, and the pa there was enlarged. Poutini Ngai Tahu continued as custodians of the pounamu. Tuhawaiki at Ruapuke pursued his commercial interests. From Kaikoura in the north and the Poutini Coast in the west, to Rakiura in the south, people resumed their seasonal tasks, adopting such European practices as seemed desirable.

The Secretary of State for War and the Colonies, Lord John Russell, meanwhile gave thought to his duties toward the 'native' peoples of the British Empire. In August 1840 he instructed Governor Gipps and his Lieutenant-Governors about the various 'races' of aboriginal peoples – 'some half-civilized, some little raised above the brutes':

> We, indeed, who come into contact with these various races, have one and the same duty to perform towards them all: but the manner in which this duty is to be performed must vary with the varying materials upon which we are to work. No

workman would attempt to saw a plank of fir, and cut a block of granite, with the same instrument, though he might wish to form each to the same shape.[2]

'Natives', said Russell, had to be recast in the British mould. Prompted by Gipps's report on the notorious massacre of Australian Aborigines at Myall Creek on 10 June 1838, and similar atrocities,[3] Russell urged that the 'suspicious, ignorant, indolent savages' had to be saved from themselves, and from 'rapacious, violent and armed Europeans.' Russell declared:

> Between the Native, who is weakened by intoxicating liquors, and the European who has all the strength of a superior Civilization and is free from its restraints, the unequal contest is generally of no long duration; the Natives decline, diminish, and finally disappear.[4]

Christian education alone, said Russell, with practical training in trades and domestic duties, could fit Natives for 'civilized life' and save them from extinction. This charitable work was to be funded by fifteen per cent of the revenue from the sale of native lands. Russell told Hobson that this fifteen, or perhaps twenty, per cent was for his Protectorate Department to further the 'education and the intellectual, moral and religious improvement' of the Maori people.[5]

The view expressed by Russell that 'civilized life' was morally far superior to that of the 'savage' had been already well publicised by E. G. Wakefield and the New Zealand Company, and was ardently shared by all colonialists. The duty of 'civilizing the natives' – the 'White Man's Burden', as Rudyard Kipling later called it – was widely accepted. Among the first to commend himself to Russell for this high calling was a brilliant, ambitious young English army officer, Captain George Grey, whose consuming interests were scientific inquiry and British colonial expansion – in his view, the twin pillars of human progress.

In 1837 Captain Grey had set out from England for Western Australia in charge of an exploratory expedition supported by the Royal Geographical Society and financed by the British Government. He took time en route to send Professor Richard Owen of the Royal College of Surgeons a skull and bones of the Tenerife 'race'.[6] Grey's two West Australian explorations were intrepid, but ill-conceived. Aboriginal Australians hostile to intruders repeatedly attacked Grey's second expedition, braving the Englishmen's bullets. During one such ambush the leading warrior – a stately figure – daringly speared

Grey before making for the bush. Grey, distressed by his wound, and by his companions' half-heartedness, shot his retreating adversary in the back[7] – a deed that may have preyed on his mind thereafter.

During his return to England, Grey composed a report on 'The best means of promoting the civilisation of the Aboriginal inhabitants of Australia'. Grey wrote that 'From the moment they are declared British subjects', Aborigines should be taught that 'British laws are to supersede their own'. Otherwise, he maintained, the authority of the older natives would prevent the rest from becoming civilised. Aborigines, like convicts, could be reformed by working for respectable citizens, Grey argued. Employers of Aborigines should be rewarded, he said, for thus 'rendering one, who was before a useless and dangerous being, a serviceable member of the community'.[8] After three years in the service of Europeans, said Grey, Aborigines could be allowed a plot of land.

Lord John Russell recommended Captain Grey's report to Gipps and Hobson, and appointed Grey to be Governor of South Australia. Subsequently, however, Grey's report was attacked by Wesleyan critics, who claimed that because of the 'morally degraded condition of the white population', the adoption of Grey's plan would result in the Aborigines being effectually 'annihilated'.[9]

Edward Gibbon Wakefield, as we have seen in Chapter 5, told an 1840 parliamentary select committee that the New Zealand Company's Maori reserves were to be 'tenths' occupied as gentlemen's estates by leading Maori chiefs and their families, and mingled with Europeans' holdings. According to William Wakefield's Cook Strait 'purchase' deeds of 1839, the tenths would be 'held in trust' by the Company. But the chiefs evidently expected to occupy them, for Wakefield said that they told him they would 'live with the English as with each other'.[10]

But by October 1840 the Company had embraced Lord Russell's views, and had changed its tune about the tenths. Firstly, the tenths were now to be elevenths, equal to a tenth of the land allocated to settlers. Secondly, instead of being occupied by leading chiefs and their families, they were to be administered by a trust that would lease the land to settlers and use the proceeds for 'the moral and physical well-being of the Native chiefs, their families and followers'.[11] Thus the original scheme for civilising Maoris by admitting their chiefs to the colonial gentry was abandoned in favour of civilising them by schooling and religious instruction. Instead of having land to live on out of each block purchased by the Company, Maoris were to be cared for 'morally and physically'. Thus the stage was set for the future tutelage of Maoris in the same manner as Australian Aborigines. That 'natives' needed tutelage more than economic independence, and homilies more than land, was to remain a cherished belief in colonial Australasia. Since it implied that 'natives' were inferior by nature, it also justified reducing their status to that of an underclass in colonial society.

Edmund Halswell, an English magistrate, was appointed by the New Zealand Company to go to New Zealand as Maori Reserves Commissioner and put the new reserves scheme into practice. He was told:

> It is the aim of the New Zealand Company to civilize the Native race by means of a deliberate plan, which, though confessedly experimental, is believed to be the only systematic attempt ever made to improve a savage people through the medium of colonization.[12]

Lord John Russell was of the Whig Party, which sympathised more with commercial colonisers than did their main parliamentary opposition, the Tories. The Whigs now opposed the transportation of convicts, and Sydney received its last consignment in November 1840. In the same month, Russell made the New Zealand Company an attractive offer: the Company could have a charter officially authorising their aims and activities. Of the land they purchased from Maoris, four acres would be Crown-granted for every £1 they spent on colonisation.[13] An accountant, J. A. Pennington, would inspect the Company's accounts and recommend to the Governor of New Zealand how much land they should be granted under the scheme.

The New Zealand Company accepted Russell's offer gladly. The Company's Royal Charter was duly issued on 12 February 1841, authorising them to 'purchase and acquire, settle, improve, cultivate, let, sell', and otherwise deal in land in New Zealand for the purpose of profit.[14] The Company now announced a new settlement, to be named Nelson in honour of the admiral who had saved Britain from the French in 1805. In the same patriotic spirit, the Company renamed the Port Nicholson settlement Wellington, after the victor of Waterloo, himself now an enthusiastic colonialist.

The choice of site for Nelson was to be subject to Governor Hobson's approval. Meanwhile a thousand 201-acre lots of land were offered for sale to settlers and investors, at £300 per lot.

The three ships of the Nelson advance party began leaving for New Zealand on 28 April 1841, led by Captain Arthur Wakefield – a distinguished naval officer and brother of Edward and William Wakefield. On the same day, the British Government approved the first of Pennington's awards, for half a million acres.[15] Meanwhile Lord John Russell had appointed William Spain, an English lawyer, as Land Claims Commissioner to determine in New Zealand what land the Company had properly purchased from the Maoris.

The New Zealand Company favoured the 'Port Cooper Plains' as the site for Nelson.[16] But Hobson was opposed to the dispersal of European settlements around the coast, as a burden on his meagre resources. When the Nelson advance party arrived at Wellington in August 1841, Hobson was there on an official visit,[17] and vetoed the Port Cooper site. To the Wakefields' disgust, he also announced that he would not grant Pennington's awards until Commissioner Spain had confirmed that the land in question had been properly purchased from the Maori owners.[18] Hobson was not going to risk a Maori conflict for the sake of the New Zealand Company, which (as a naval man) he regarded as a coterie of land speculators, jobbers and political radicals.

The Wakefields and their supporters, full of optimism from having won the favour of the British Government, resented being obstructed by Hobson, and execrated him as 'Captain Crimp' all the more. When Hobson went on to Akaroa, however, Lavaud agreed with him that to have Nelson at Port Cooper would unfairly prejudice the French claim.[19] Thus the site of Nelson was confined to the Company's original Cook Strait 'purchases' – an option promised them by Lord John Russell.[20] Nelson was founded at Whakatu in October 1841, with Te Rauparaha's consent. Thus 'systematic' colonisation reached Te Wai Pounamu.

At Wellington, 110 of the original 1,100 one-acre town sections had been reserved as Maori tenths, and 4,200 acres of rural land were selected as Maori endowment reserves in April 1842 by Reserves Commissioner Halswell. Halswell was soon to be replaced by a board of trustees headed by George Augustus Selwyn, newly appointed Anglican Bishop of New Zealand.[21] One-eleventh of Nelson's 201-acre lots became Maori endowment reserves, which were later leased to European settlers by Selwyn's board. From the rents on these 'tenths', a Maori schoolhouse and two hostelries were built,[22] to civilise the Nelson Maoris.

~

On 9 June 1841, six months before Commissioner Spain's arrival in the country,[23] the New Zealand Legislative Council, acting with the authority of the British Parliament, passed its Land Claims Ordinance Number 1, in place of Gipps's suspended New Zealand Land Claims Act of 1840. The ordinance (or 'act') reaffirmed the established principle of English law as it had been applied in Britain's American colonies: that all 'unappropriated lands' were Crown property, subject to 'the rightful and necessary occupation and use thereof by the aboriginal inhabitants', and that these 'aboriginal' rights could be purchased only by the Crown.[24]

Thus the real meaning of British sovereignty was spelled out. In England from feudal times the monarchy and aristocracy had claimed authority over all land, although they were often resisted in this by their subjects. In New Zealand, as in Australia, the Crown had now asserted the same authority. The Queen's subjects were to be entitled only to such land as she, through Parliament, might decide.[25] Maoris, under the ordinance, were entitled only to such land as was deemed 'rightful and necessary' for them.

The Treaty of Waitangi's guarantee of 'tino rangatiratanga' was not what it had seemed. Chiefs had signed the Treaty equally with the Crown's representatives. But this equality vanished with the proclamation of British sovereignty, for the sovereignty of the British Crown is absolute and unconditional. British subjects are subject to parliamentary statutes. These, and not the Treaty, would determine Maori rights, and what land Maoris could have. Whether ministers of the Crown would regard the Treaty of Waitangi as morally binding remained to be seen: it was certainly not going to be legally binding. This useful distinction was a refinement unknown to the Maori.

The New Zealand Land Claims Ordinance provided for a commission, as proposed by Governor Gipps, to examine and report upon all formal claims to have purchased land privately from Maoris – with the exception of New Zealand Company claims, which were the responsibility of Commissioner Spain. The new Commissioners, Lieutenant Colonel Edward Godfrey and Major Mathew Richmond, afterwards interpreted their instructions as disallowing purchases made after 14 January 1840, the official date of Gipps's proclama-tions.[26] For valid purchases, they were required to recommend to the Governor how much land should be granted, to a maximum of 2,560 acres, depending on how much value in money or goods had been paid to the Maori owners.[27] If a purchase of more than 2,560 acres were proved, the 'surplus' became Crown property. Thus the English legal convention of the 'Crown's eminent domain' became manifest in New Zealand.[28]

James Watkin, the Wesleyan missioner at Waikouaiti, was a busy man. Chiefs frequented his house to argue religion – including Koroko, whose atua was 'very angry' with him for this. Watkin made some alphabet books, and found the Maoris keen to learn:

> Tonight our kitchen furnished a scene which might have done for a painter: a considerable number of young men with their books in their hands conning over their a-e-i-o-u, etc., and,

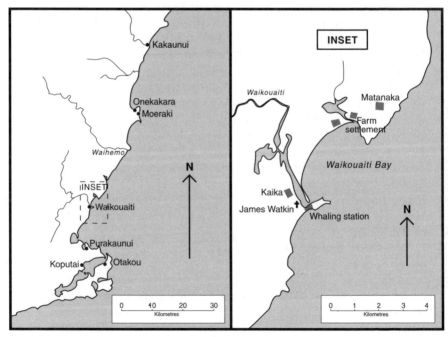

James Watkin's Wesleyan circuit, 1840–1844.

while I was teaching some, others of them would be soliciting the instruction of one of my little boys with 'E ha tene, William? (What's this, William?)' Some learn very rapidly, and before they went away could say many of the letters. Oh, that I had books![29]

Soon the Waikouaiti Maoris ceased working on Sundays – to John Jones's annoyance, it was later said.[30]

In September 1840 Watkin began preaching partly in Southern Maori, provoking much discussion:

They had thought that each country had its respective gods. My asserting that there is but one in the universe, and that the God of England is the God of New Zealand startled them, and I rather think offended some of the priests . . . They think the slightest infraction of the tapu will be visited by death, but when I ask them why the New Zealand gods don't kill me, who not only break but denounce the tapu as foolish and false, they look rather foolish and say they cannot touch me, it is only the Maori they can kill.[31]

Gradually Watkin's influence spread. In October 1840, Tuhawaiki attended a Wesleyan service at Waikouaiti with four large boat-loads of his followers. In November, Watkin began preaching entirely in Southern Maori. Although still without books, he taught regular classes with the help of his wife and sons:

A school for men and boys at early morning, and one for the women and girls in the evening, both well attended for the scant population of the place, all ages and all grades. Old, young, chiefs, people, faces furrowed with time as well as with the tattooing instrument.[32]

Watkin's great bugbear was the lawless European population, whom British sovereignty did nothing to restrain. He was particularly annoyed with Jones's farming settlement: 'Wickedness and ignorance are characteristic of the place, – one of the most drunken on the coast.'[33] Assault and theft by Europeans were commonplace. When French whalers seized a pregnant Otakou Maori mother and her child and took them off to sea, Watkin complained to Magistrate Robinson at Akaroa, noting in his journal:

Now the country is claimed by the British Crown as one of its appendages it would be well if British law were brought into operation for the protection of the Natives and the suppression of the enormities practised by Europeans, which are of the worst kind . . . Give me heathens before these Christians. Drunkenness, theft, and violence prevail among the parties who call themselves Christians. The Natives are much more free from vice than they. The foreigners have been and are a curse to the Natives.[34]

But nothing was done for the Maori victims. Watkin welcomed the decline of the whaling industry: 'A huge curse in this country: is it not an awful thought that cannibal heathens may be made worse by association with people called Christian?'[35]

In August 1840, two Catholic priests had arrived with the French colonists at Akaroa. There the Onuku Maoris were already Wesleyan – converted by a Maori preacher from the North Island.[36] Watkin was now distressed to learn that CMS missionaries were also in the field. He dreaded that these rivals might reveal his Tongan scandal:

I cannot forget my disgrace, I cannot forgive myself for being the cause of it. If my Brethren had decreed me a lighter punishment, what days of misery it would have saved me, and I might have been more useful than I have been or hope to be in this part of the world. I often wish that I had gone to England, where though my pain and shame would have been intense it would have been of briefer continuance.[37]

But Watkin was heartened when in December 1840 a fellow Wesleyan, Samuel Ironside, established a mission at Ngakuta in Cloudy Bay.

Watkin persevered at his lonely post, tortured in turn by guilt, self-doubt and despair, with no support from the Methodist authorities either in Sydney or New Zealand. He confided in his journal: 'My soul loathes the country. I am sick of the place and of the people, and low in body, low in mind, unhappy in my experience, and unsuccessful in my efforts.' After two years at Waikouaiti, he wrote: 'I teach and preach but apparently without effect. I have no enquirers, no candidates for baptism. A few can read, more perhaps are restrained from vices formerly practised, but I want to see conversions take place.'[38]

In July 1842, sunk in penitential gloom at Waikouaiti, James Watkin gave a Maori woman a Christian burial. This simple ceremony changed his fortunes, for he buried her near a white woman's grave. Afterwards, he noted:

This has given huge offence, as I am told, to some of the most Christian whites, who are highly indignant at such a blow against white superiority, for according to their notions supe-riority exists after death as well as during life – an opinion from which I am a most sincere dissenter, and gave some of my rea-sons for the same to my white congregation in the evening, by which they might learn that I thought that if superiority exists that it belongs to the natives and not to them.[39]

Most Europeans now boycotted Watkin's services, but his Maori support gradually increased. In October 1842, he preached at Otakou to 'a considerable number of southern Natives' who had assembled there with Tuhawaiki. The Otakou people wanted a Euro-pean missionary, as did Tuhawaiki (who asked again a year later),[40] but Watkin could not oblige them.

In December 1842, Hadfield sent Te Rauparaha's son Katu, now christened 'Tamihana' (Thompson), and his cousin Te Whiwhi, christened 'Henare Matene' (Henry Martyn), as missionaries among Ngai Tahu.[41] Watkin bitterly resented this intrusion by 'High Church doctrines'.[42] He wrote to Ironside:

I have seen Mr Hadfield's preaching squad of Natives – Henry Martyn and his compeers. I wish some of yours had come on – they would have been invaluable to me. I am still single-handed. I am sorry to say that these Churchmen appear to have either been instructed in the art of evil speaking or that it is natural to them. You and I and our people come under the censures of these High-churchmen – I shall be sorry if the civil feuds of the Maoris are to be succeeded by religious ones . . . I think that the sending of Native agents by Mr H (if he sent them) savours of something like impudence.[43]

The Anglicans' visit spurred Watkin on. His regime for Chris-tian conversion was strict. Penitent Maoris had to abjure tapu, muru, utu and taepo; renounce violence, profanity, slavery, polygamy, al-cohol-drinking, cursing, cannibalism, and sexual activity outside of Christian marriage; and profess belief in Christ and the Gospels. Then, as catechumens, they had to prove their diligence and devotion, to become candidates for baptism; after which the most zealous and steadfast could become mission teachers to bring others to the faith.

Watkin baptised his first Maori convert in December 1842, and gave a feast for his Maori congregation. In January 1843, at Waikoua-iti, he baptised his first rangatira converts, who thereafter assisted at his church services. In April 1843 he received religious books from the British and Foreign Bible Society, and soon had 'from forty to fifty in class'. He wrote: 'They have generally bags or little baskets of a size sufficient to contain the New Testament and hymn book slung around the neck and occupying the situation erstwhile occupied by the powder flask and the cartridge box.' Koroko told Watkin that his coming 'had put an end to cannibalism, murder, and other evils formerly frequent'. Some of Ironside's preachers came to help Watkin, who again complained that 'Hadfield's people have been preaching up the Church, and the Wesleyans down'. He was dismayed when 'the Church' won some converts at Moeraki and in the far south.[44]

In June 1843 Watkin baptised an influential group – Horomona (Solomon) Pohio, his missioner at Ruapuke; Hoani Wetere (John Wesley) Korako; Tiare Wetere (Charles Wesley) Te Kahu; and nineteen others. In July, opening his new church at Waikouaiti, Watkin achieved his greatest triumph – the baptism of Tiramorehu himself. The conversion of such chiefs was crucial, for it encouraged others to enter the fold, or at least to respect it. Tiramorehu took the baptismal name of 'Matiaha' after Matthias, the last of the original apostles, chosen for his diligence,[45] and maintained a lifelong zeal for the Wesleyan faith. Watkin admired his 'strength of moral principle', as did his successor Charles Creed. For Watkin these conversions were a great vindication of faith. But for the Maoris it was an even greater act of faith. In renouncing their tapu and their atua they were trusting to a god unknown to their fathers. The spiritual hierarchy of Maoridom was exchanged for the spiritual brotherhood of Methodism, in which Maori and European, chief and slave, were equals.

In August 1843, John Jones's family arrived from Sydney, followed by 'bustle, blasphemy and drunkenness', lamented Watkin – the worst desecration of the Lord's Day ever seen in the place, 'shocking the whalers themselves'. When Jones himself followed, Watkin's English services became 'better attended' – though without apparent conviction,[46] for the Europeans, although longer acquainted with Christianity than the Maoris, evidently cared for it less. But Watkin's Maori following went from strength to strength, with baptisms, marriage ceremonies and large congregations. In his first three years he made more Maori converts than the CMS at the Bay of Islands had done in its first fifteen. Edward Shortland (an Anglican) explained this as follows:

There was an emotional side to the Christian faith largely utilized by the followers of Wesley. The Maori was as firm a believer in witchcraft as the Methodist missionary was in the personality of the devil, and the condition of mind which clings to either conviction is, if not identical, closely allied. The Methodist missionary aspired solely to spiritualize, where the Church missionary first sought to civilize. Each Society did good work in its own way, but in later years the Church missionaries found that the Methodist plan of operation was not to be neglected.[47]

~

Meanwhile in England the Whigs had lost office to the Tories under Sir Robert Peel in August 1841, and Lord John Russell was out of the Colonial Office. His successor, Lord Stanley, was no friend of the New Zealand Company. In 1843 he rebuked their spokesman for describing the Treaty of Waitangi as 'a praiseworthy device for amusing and pacifying savages for the moment'. The Company fared poorly under Stanley, who confirmed Hobson's decision not to grant Pennington's awards until Commissioner Spain had investigated the Company's land purchases. Thus many colonists who had paid the Company in England for land, found on arrival in New Zealand that it was occupied by Maoris who showed no inclination to vacate it – proof, the colonists assumed, of the government's partiality to Maoris.

But another blow was in store for the New Zealand Company. The 'rightful and necessary occupation and use' that the 1841 Land Ordinance had made a condition for Maori land rights to be recognised, was about to be put to the test. William Wakefield's 1839 'purchases' included the large and fertile Wairau Valley, claimed by Ngati Toa by rau patu after their virtual extermination of Rangitane there in 1828. Commissioner Spain had reported to the Administrator in April 1843 that Te Rauparaha and Rangihaeata had testified to having sold Wakefield Te Tai Tapu and Whakatu, but not the Wairau. The Company had not convinced Spain otherwise.[48]

Ngati Toa 'occupied and used' but little of the Wairau, although they visited it regularly to maintain their ahi kaa. But the Nelson settlers, loyal to E. G. Wakefield's doctrine, regarded the Wairau as 'waste land' awaiting European settlement, and sent surveyors to peg it out. Survey poles, like traditional pou whenua, in Maori eyes were an assertion of ownership – and this impression was confirmed when

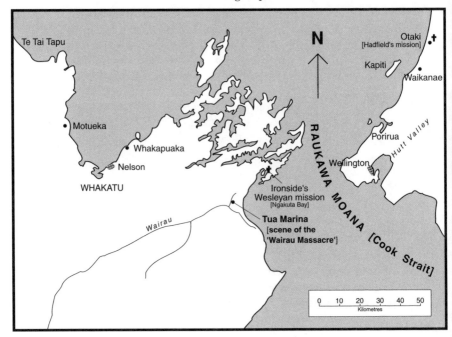

The Cook Strait region and the 'Wairau Massacre', 1843.

the Nelson surveyors took local materials to build their huts. Te Rauparaha therefore had the huts burned. The surveyors returned to Nelson with the story, and amid great excitement Captain Arthur Wakefield mustered about thirty armed men and set out for the Wairau to arrest the famous chief for arson.

On 17 June 1843 the Nelson posse came upon Te Rauparaha with about ninety of his people at Tua Marina, in the lower Wairau. He was called upon to be handcuffed. He declined, but offered to pay for the huts. The Police Magistrate, Henry Thompson, in a fury, laid hands on him, and a scuffle developed. Some Nelson men then fired at their Maori fellow citizens, perhaps accidentally, and shot one of Rangihaeata's wives, a daughter of Te Rauparaha. The Europeans lost the ensuing fight and either surrendered or fled. The twenty-two who surrendered, including Wakefield and Thompson, were then tomahawked by Rangihaeata as utu for his wife, and as satisfaction for 'another man whose father had been killed at his side'. These killings became known as the 'Wairau Massacre'. Te Rauparaha excused them thus:

Should a man be spared who commenced a fight? And having found himself in danger of being killed throws down his arms and cries out 'Enough, we will now be good friends'? No, our customs demand that the relations of the slain seek for a payment of blood for the blood of their slain.[49]

Te Rauparaha and his party, expecting war, at once crossed the sea to Otaki. The Nelson Chief Surveyor, the Quaker Frederick Tuckett, brought the fateful news to Wellington, with some survivors, the day after the fight. He himself had avoided the confrontation after trying to dissuade Captain Wakefield from his adventure. Meanwhile Samuel Ironside, having buried the dead, abandoned his mission and followed Tuckett to Wellington.

Matene Te Whiwhi and Tamihana Te Rauparaha were at Otakou during these events. When they heard that Ngati Toa were fighting Englishmen, they left off preaching peace to Ngai Tahu and hurried home to Otaki. At Akaroa, Commodore Bérard – who had replaced Captain Lavaud in January 1843 – erected forts and prepared for a Maori uprising. When word of the Wairau disaster reached England, the New Zealand Company suspended business. Civilising Maoris had lost its appeal, for the present.

∼

Two months after the Wairau disaster, Commissioner Godfrey arrived at Akaroa to hear land claims. His interpreter was Edward Shortland, one of George Clarke's Assistant Protectors of Aborigines. Shortland was aged thirty-one, and a Cambridge graduate. The Shortlands were family friends of Hobson. Edward had been Hobson's private secretary, and admired his principles.[50] Like Hobson, he was sceptical of the New Zealand Company's activities.[51] But Hobson had died in office in September 1842, and Lieutenant Willoughby Shortland, Edward's brother, now headed the colony as Administrator, pending the arrival of a new Governor.

Land Claims Commission claimants were required to pay a fee, appear or be represented at the hearing of their claims, and meet their own expenses. Of fifteen Banks Peninsula claimants, only three complied. The first was Cooper, Holt and Rhodes, of Sydney, who had paid Leathart £325 for the half of Banks Peninsula that Leathart claimed to have paid Taiaroa £40 for in 1839. Since Taiaroa was but one of many Maori owners, Godfrey dismissed the claim. But he recommended that William Rhodes be allowed later to purchase his cattle station at Akaroa Heads. The second claim was by two Frenchmen who had paid Clayton £1,500 for Banks Peninsula, which Clayton claimed to have bought from Tuauau in 1837. When Tuauau testified that Clayton had paid him nothing, and that therefore he (Tuauau) had sold nothing, this claim was also rejected.[52]

Last came the Nanto-Bordelaise Company's claim to Banks Peninsula, which they had mistakenly estimated at 30,000 acres instead of 250,000. Nearly all the Akaroa Maoris attended the hearing, as well as many from Puari led by Iwikau – whose support the French company relied on.[53] The Akaroa Maoris had been greatly annoyed by the French occupying not merely Pakaariki Bay, which they had agreed to, but the four Akaroa bays 'sold' by Iwikau as well. Te Rautahi (French Farm) had been commandeered besides by Lavaud, for vegetable gardens.[54]

To prove their claim, the French submitted their August 1840 deed, falsely dated 12 August 1838 so as to appear to be Langlois's original.[55] But Godfrey was not deceived, and concluded that the French had bought only Pohue, Kaihope, Kakongutungutu and Pakaariki. These totalled perhaps 3,000 acres, depending on how far inland their boundaries were taken.[56] The Maoris agreed, however, to sell the French more land later if they did not need it themselves.

Britain in 1842 had promised to treat the French claim like a British claim,[57] and the French therefore expected the benefit of Pennington's awards. They submitted evidence of expenditure on roads, buildings, bridges, presents to Maori chiefs, and emigration, equivalent to £15,125. At four acres to £1, this would compute to 60,500 acres of Maori land, had Ngai Tahu agreed to sell it. But Commissioner Godfrey, in view of the spurious French deed, made no recommendation.

In September 1843 Godfrey went to Otakou to hear southern land claims. Tuhawaiki arrived with his Murihiku supporters, and crossed to Waikouaiti to get John Jones. Next morning Edward Shortland watched for their return, and noted:

> Although it blew a violent storm from the north-east, we saw Tuhawaiki's squadron making for the harbour, which it soon after entered without accident. Mr J. [Jones], who came with them, told us that he, although an old sealer, would not have ventured out in such weather, had he not been persuaded by these natives, who are not only very bold, but very expert in sailing their boats.[58]

John Jones was considered a 'large-hearted Methodist' by Sydney Wesleyans for sponsoring Watkin's mission. But at Godfrey's commission he claimed reimbursement for it, in Maori land.[59] For his 20,000-acre claim at Waikouaiti he said he had paid the Maoris £3,952 7s 6d, £350 of which was the cost of Watkin's mission. At the Land Ordinance rate of five acres to £1, this £350 represented 1,750 acres of Maori land. Jones and Peter Williams (Preservation Inlet), supported by Tuhawaiki, were recommended by Godfrey for the maximum award of 2,560 acres.[60] Relying on Maori evidence, Godfrey approved twenty southern claims, for which he recommended Crown grants totalling some 9,300 acres.

Godfrey sailed for Wellington on 15 October 1843 and conferred there with his fellow Commissioner, Major Richmond. They reported the French Akaroa claim to the Administrator in Auckland, noting that it contravened Governor Gipps's proclamation of 14 January 1840 forbidding private purchases of Maori land after that date.[61] The Administrator, mindful of the international implications, sent the file to London.

Notes

1. Jellicoe 1930: 49.
2. Russell–Gipps, 25.8.1840, in HRA1 XX: 774ff.
3. See Gipps–Glenelg, 15.12.1838, quoted in Woolmington 1988: 46–49.
4. Russell–Gipps, 25.8.1840, loc cit.
5. McLintock 1958: 177.
6. Grey–Owen, Tenerife 22.7.1837, Sherborn Ms Autographs.
7. Grey 1841 I: 150ff. Woods (1865) praises Grey's courage, but not his expeditions.
8. Russell–Gipps, 8.10.1840, in HRA1 XXI: 33ff.
9. See Benjamin Hurst–La Trobe 22.7.1841, quoted in Woolmington 1988: 66–67.
10. Jellicoe 1930: 20ff.
11. Ibid: 26–28.
12. Ibid.
13. Ibid: 24.
14. NZ Company Charter, in Mackay

1873 I: 42–47.
15. Jellicoe 1930: 25, 34.
16. Wakefield 1845 II: 32ff.
17. Ibid: 49.
18. Jellicoe 1930: 25–26.
19. Hight & Straubel 1957: 77.
20. Wakefield 1845 II: 70, 144.
21. A notable Maori map of Te Wai Pounamu was drawn for Halswell: see *AJHR* 1894 C-1: 99.
22. Jellicoe 1930: 36ff.
23. Spain, shipwrecked at South Africa, did not reach New Zealand until December 1841.
24. NZ Land Claims Act 1841, 4th Vic. 2 Session 1, 9.6.1841. See 'R. v. Symonds 1847' in Haast 1938: 394 and passim; also McHugh 1991: chapter 5.
25. McHugh (1991: 98) says the Crown's purported ownership of all land in New Zealand is a 'constitutional fiction'; but the

power of the Crown in Parliament to appropriate or bestow lands by statute is hardly fictitious, as Maoris learned to their cost.

26. *AJHR* 1862 D-10: 10.
27. See Evison 1993: 149.
28. *AJHR* 1862 D-10: 18 and passim; Gipps–Russell, 16.8.1840, in HRA1 XX: 759; McHugh 1991: 103–4; Orange 1987: 97.
29. WJ, 1.8.1840.
30. Wohlers 1895: 97.
31. WJ, 21.9.1840.
32. Ibid, 21.11.1840.
33. Ibid, 9–23.8.1841, 6.9.1841 and passim.
34. Ibid, 21.9.1840.
35. Watkin–J. Buller, 13.5.1843, Watkin Ms Letters (HL).
36. Tremewan 1990: 148ff; Couch 1969: 8.
37. WJ, 9.11.1840 and 21.11.1840.
38. Ibid, 16.5.1842 and 2.7.1842.
39. Ibid, 4.7.1842.
40. Ibid, 15.10.1842 and 12.10.1843.
41. Stack Ms Report, Christchurch Diocesan Maori Mission 1882–1883; Tamihana Ms 1845 (Graham). 'All Ngai Tahu believed promptly in the word of the true God,' says Tamihana.
42. WJ, 10.12.1842.
43. Watkin–Ironside, 14.1.1843, Watkin Ms Letters (MAC).
44. McLean 1986: 20b; WJ, 26.12.1842, 16–18.1.1843, 22.5.1843, 5.6.1843 and 12.6.1843; Watkin–Ironside, 22.5.1843, 19.6.1843, Watkin Ms Letters (MAC); Watkin Ms Register of Baptisms.
45. Watkin Ms Register of Baptisms. Concerning Matthias, see Acts 1: 26.
46. WJ, 8.8.1843, 11.9.1843.
47. Shortland Ms Annexation of NZ: 8.
48. Spain–FitzRoy, 31.3.1845, in Mackay 1873 I: 54ff.
49. Shortland Ms Diaries and Journals.
50. Shortland Ms Annexation of NZ.
51. Shortland–Clarke, 19.5.1845, Shortland Ms Letters.
52. Godfrey–Hope, 2.7.1845, in Wai-27 L3 II: 169ff; Mackay 1873 I: 83–87.
53. Shortland 1851: 7.
54. Shortland–Clarke, 18.3.1844, Shortland Ms Letters; Tremewan 1990: 161–63, 260–63. See also Canterbury Crown Grant records, CMA L & S G39 40/1 and 2.
55. Godfrey–Hope, loc cit.
56. ARSCNZ, *HCBB*, 29.7.1844: 433ff; *NTR*: 541; Wai-27 J47: 6, Q22: 2–5, U10D.
57. Aberdeen–Cowley, 28.7.1842, in ARSCNZ, *HCBB*, 29.7.1844: 439.
58. Shortland 1851: 80ff. Maori coastal drownings were frequent.
59. Eccles & Reed 1949: 31–32.
60. Ibid; Mackay 1873 I: 82ff. After tenaciously contesting this award, Jones received 10,000 acres in 1867 under the John Jones Land Claims Settlement Act.
61. ARSCNZ, *HCBB*, 29.7.1844: 434.

8

The Old Order, and the New

IN 1843 several New Zealand Company colonists who could not get their promised allotments of land from the Company at Wellington or Nelson decided to select land in Ngai Tahu territory, expecting to get legal title to their selections later. In February 1843 William Deans arrived with his workers at Putaringamotu on the 'Port Cooper Plains', where European settlement had been unsuccessfully attempted in 1840. His brother John joined him with horses, sheep and cattle from New South Wales. In April 1843 the Hays and the Sinclairs landed at Pigeon Bay.

These 'squatters' shared the Company's view that land was worthless until it had been 'improved' by European capital and labour. But they happily used resources that were already flourishing without European capital or labour. John Deans wrote to his father in Scotland:

> A vast many sorts of salt water fish are to be got in many of the bays. Abouka [hapuka] I have seen nearly as large as myself, they are as rich as salmon and very fine flavoured. Baricouta are also to be got in great abundance and are very easily caught, also a good many eels as thick as a man's leg and very fat, and we are very fond of them; very fine flounders; abundance of quail, very fine eating. Also a large bittern, some of these when moulting cannot fly and a good dog can catch as many as you choose. There are a great many descriptions of ducks, all very fine eating – of the grey ducks I have seen more here in an hour than ever I saw anywhere else in my life, and have shot a dozen in a couple of hours; wood pigeons are abundant about April, May and June: a person may shoot them often in our bush as fast as he can charge his gun; a parrot called kaka, when fat it is very good; woodhen is abundant in some places.[1]

The Greenwood brothers landed at Port Levy in December 1843 and squatted at Purau, naming it 'Port Greenwood'. The old chief Nohomutu was living there with his whanau,[2] and demanded payment from the Greenwoods. But they threatened to call in Police Magistrate Robinson, and continued burning hillsides, helping themselves to timber and firewood, and building stockyards. Ngai Tahu, having attended Godfrey's commission, were well aware that Europeans could not legally seize land they had not paid for. No doubt they were also aware that they could expect no help from Robinson. John Tikao was the acknowledged authority on European business, for he understood European ways and could write letters. Therefore, anticipating Edward Shortland's return from the south, and knowing that the New Zealand Company were rumoured to be contemplating a settlement at Port Cooper,[3] Tikao sent messages to Maoris with rights at Banks Peninsula, urging them to assemble and assert their rights, for Assistant Protector Shortland could convey their concerns to the Governor.

∼

The French at Akaroa had no legal title to the land they occupied. But what they lacked in legality, they made up for with intrigue, ably assisted by Charles Barrington Robinson. As Police Magistrate he was able to keep the French informed about other Banks Peninsula claimants' activities. As we have seen, he connived at the French company's sale of land that it did not own, and he bought some for himself. Belligny reported to France:

> The British magistrate must also be on our side; his interest is that of the company, for he has bought from it and he is as concerned as we are that its title be acknowledged as valid; I have also just interested the Collector of Customs in our cause by selling him four acres.[4]

Robinson, far from enforcing Commander Stanley's arrangement that the French were to keep to Pakaariki Bay, persisted in supporting the French claim to the whole peninsula. He stopped people paying Ngai Tahu for the use of land, water and timber. When the French company faced financial difficulties, Robinson protected Belligny from his creditors.[5] While unofficially helping the French at Maori expense, he officially reported that he was protecting Maori interests. He claimed to have prevented a 'battle' between Tuhawaiki and the Banks Peninsula chiefs, and to have persuaded Ngai Tahu not to have a 'paramount chief'.[6] In May 1843 Robinson reported that 'from their own admission the Natives had sold Port Cooper'[7] – a statement that Commissioner Godfrey's findings afterwards gave the lie to, as we have seen.

Recognising Tikao as a threat to his impostures, Robinson gave him a bad name with the authorities. In May 1843 he told the government that Tikao had tried to extort money from the Hays and Sinclairs, and had threatened to attack them and the Deanses. When he warned Tikao against attacking the settlers, said Robinson, Tikao challenged him to bring 'four hundred men armed with muskets'. Robinson reported that 'troublesome natives' had pulled down the Deans's stockyard at Port Cooper, and rebuilt it only at Robinson's request.[8] When Wellington newspapers published this last story, William Deans protested that the stockyard had not been pulled down, and that he had good relations with the Maoris.[9]

Robinson's court judgments were unhelpful to Ngai Tahu. His penalty against Hay for his cattle destroying an acre of Maori potatoes was to award one blanket, one pair of trousers and one hat among four Maori owners.[10] The Crown's 'protection', with Robinson as its agent, was of doubtful benefit to Ngai Tahu. The French, however, were deeply grateful for Robinson's services, and asked the New Zealand Government to recommend him to the British Government for a suitable reward.[11]

Belligny, supported by Commodore Bérard, now hoped to buy from Ngai Tahu the whole of Akaroa Harbour and Pigeon Bay. The leading Akaroa chiefs were Tuauau and Parure at Onuku; Tikao at Ohae; and Hakaroa, his father Tè Ruaparae, Tamakeke and Mautai at Opukutahi.[12] The French therefore approached not these chiefs, but Iwikau at Port Levy – and got him to name the goods he would accept as payment for his rights on the peninsula. Bérard took his corvette to Sydney and bought the required goods for about £240. While there, he had an encouraging meeting with the incoming Governor of New Zealand, Captain Robert FitzRoy, and returned to Akaroa on 31 December 1843.[13]

≈

When Commissioner Godfrey left Otakou for Wellington in October 1843, Edward Shortland resumed his duties as Assistant Protector of Aborigines. Shortland spent three months, with two

Maori companions from the Bay of Plenty, where he was previously stationed, visiting Maori settlements from Foveaux Strait to Banks Peninsula, carefully recording Maori traditions, assessing Maori welfare, and taking a census.[14] He found the Maori economy buoyant, with traditional technology and mahinga kai being used along with European importations.[15] He observed and described traditional methods of preparing eels, fish, fernroot, tutu juice, kauru ('a very nutritious food'), taramea perfume, pounamu artifacts, and titi ('a favourite but unwholesome food'). The last four of these products, and kotuku feathers, were still traded with North Island tribes for kumara and other items. Shortland noted ti kauka plantations flourishing around Taieri and Waiateruati, where 'nearly the whole population' worked producing kauru from December to February. The distinctive items of Maori diet in southern New Zealand, he observed, were titi and kauru. Maize and kumara were rare. Pounamu was still obtained from Piopiotahi, Arahura and Wakatipu, by sea or land: 'When procured, it is fashioned and polished by rubbing down with sandstone, a work of much labour, in which every old man in a pa spends several hours of the day.'

Besides fishing, eeling and cultivating potatoes, the Maoris ran pigs on rough country, culling them when required. Shortland reported:

> They have acquired a considerable knowledge of English; whaling and sealing boats have superseded canoes, in the management of which they show great skill and boldness; they have become expert whalers, and obtain employment at the fisheries often on the same terms as Europeans. Their houses, too, have generally doors and chimneys, and within, a platform is raised two or three feet above the ground for a bed-place.

Shortland found Maori society in southern New Zealand well ordered and law-abiding, despite the absence of any British authority except that of Police Magistrate Robinson at Akaroa. Petty thefts were rare: 'The persons and property of Europeans are more often in danger from each other than from natives . . . those [serious disturbances] which do take place being almost entirely confined to Europeans at the whaling stations.'

Shortland's census recorded 1,923 Maoris for the settlements he visited, from Banks Peninsula southwards.[16] But the total Maori population of southern New Zealand was now probably about 2,500.[17] Of the 277 'whites' recorded by Shortland, (209 men, twenty-five women, and forty-three children), eighty-one were at Waikouaiti, including most of the women and children.[18] Shortland blamed the decline in Maori population on 'inordinate use of rum, now falling into disrepute', 'prostitution' and the 'sale of young women to European settlers, thereby leaving an inadequate number for the young men'. He disagreed with the prevailing view that Maoris had an 'unsound constitution', but thought that 'the alternate adopting and throwing off of European clothing must tend to develop diseases of the lungs, so prevalent among them'. He described the Maoris as 'highly intellectual human beings who will eventually take their place side by side with the white man, as equals in civilization'.[19]

Shortland thought the CMS preachers had fostered dissension:

They have busied themselves in making proselytes, with more of the native than Christian spirit, and have caused a schism between the inhabitants of almost every settlement, one party styling themselves children of Wesley, the other the church of Paihia.[20] The distraction of their minds thus caused, has essentially interfered with their happiness, by producing ill-feeling and separation between the members of the same family.

He disliked the Wesleyan obsession with sin, and seems to have avoided Watkin. The strict Wesleyan observance of Sunday vexed him when his Wesleyan guide refused to help in river crossings, and when Tiramorehu refused to discuss Maori traditions, on Sundays. Watkin, for his part, was suspicious of Shortland's interest in Maori traditions,[21] which Protestants generally condemned as Satanic.

Shortland, like Watkin, advocated the study of the Maori language, but for a different reason. The missionaries learned it in order to preach and teach religion in Maori, leaving Maoris still unable to read English. Shortland wanted people to learn Maori so that they could teach the Maoris English.[22] Like Watkin, he compiled a word-list of Southern Maori, regarding it not as a 'language' but as a dialect presenting 'not so much difficulty as a West of England man would encounter on visiting one of the northern counties'.

~

At New Year 1844, Edward Shortland decided to walk from Waikouaiti to Akaroa, a distance of nearly four hundred kilometres. This decision mystified Koroko, who had offered to take him to Akaroa in his whaleboat. Shortland began his walk on 4 January, accompanied by his North Island companions and several Ngai Tahu. Six days later he arrived within sight of the Waitaki River, the greatest natural obstacle in his path. Resting with his guides on a hillside overlooking the broad Waitaki plain, Shortland scanned the coastal ranges and alluvial plains to north and south. The summits of the Otakou hills, ninety kilometres distant, were clearly recognisable, so clear was the atmosphere on that balmy summer day. To the west lay tumbled, forest-clad coastal hills, rising to the alpine ridges of the 2,700-metre Kakaunui mountains. To the northwest, the Waitaki ('resounding waters') issued from its clouded portals, beyond which lay the mysterious interior of Te Wai Pounamu, where no European had yet set foot.

When Shortland reached the small kainga of Te Puna a Maru on the south bank of the Waitaki, the elderly Ngati Huirapa chief Huruhuru received him with due courtesy. The great river, pale with glacier milk in the summer thaw, was in full flood, over a kilometre wide, while the northwesterly föhn wind – 'hot, dry and oppressive' – chastised the plains. Huruhuru was preparing to vacate his kainga with his whanau of seven people, and cross the river to his eel traps at the Waihao hapua – eels being 'one of the chief delicacies of the land', noted Shortland.

Some of Huruhuru's people prepared aruhe, the standard sustenance for a long march, while others made mokihi of bundled raupo reeds bound in a canoe shape, with which to cross the wild river. These craft were light when dry, but once launched they became increasingly heavy in the water. The largest, five metres long, Huruhuru designed to carry himself and his wife, together with Shortland and his two North Islanders and all their gear. In the evenings, while the relentless wind shook tents and whare, and the powerful river resounded in its swollen channels, Huruhuru, with a companion, described to Shortland the interior of the island. He drew a map showing the remote mountain lakes Wakatipu, Wanaka and Hawea, which fed the Matau River – bigger even than the Waitaki. He also made Shortland a pair of torua from ti leaves plaited double, to protect his feet against the pebble beaches and the thorns of the tumatakuru.

After four days of waiting for the wind to abate, the little community at last awoke to a calm dawn. The Waitaki being lowest at that hour, like all snow-fed rivers, Huruhuru ordered a crossing. The whole party boarded their mokihi, which were launched into the swift, swirling current. To the European, the venture seemed

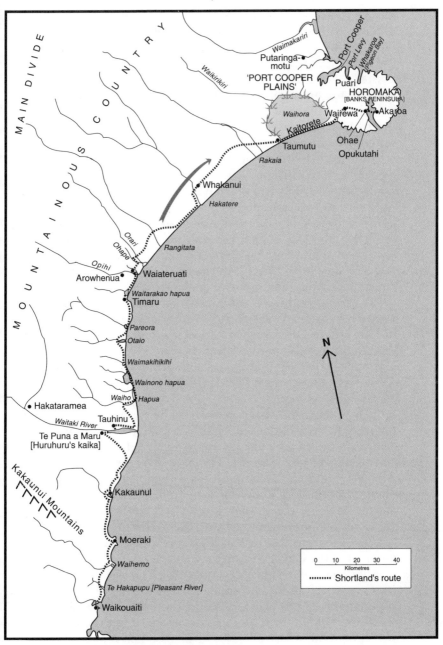

Edward Shortland's journey, January 1844.

reckless in the extreme. But to the Maori boatmen, the headlong lurching danger of a mokihi on a powerful river was pure delight. They guided their craft rearing and plunging down the deepest channels, for to strike any snag or shingle-bank could mean instant disaster. Twenty or thirty minutes later, and some seven kilometres downstream, the north bank of the Waitaki was safely reached. The mokihi were beached for other travellers to use. Huruhuru took Shortland to the coastal track that would take him northwards, and went off to his eel traps.

Shortland's footsore party reached Timaru on 18 January, having encountered Bishop Selwyn and his party travelling south. Koroko and his crew had sailed the 120 kilometres from Moeraki to Timaru the previous day, on a strong southerly wind, bringing Shortland's spare baggage and a cargo of poha titi. Shortland admired the tall poha, as high as a man and decorated with feathers. Some were destined for Waiateruati, some for Banks Peninsula, and others for the North Island. The chief Te Rehe, fishing at the nearby Waitarakao hapua, undertook to guide Shortland to Waiateruati.

Te Rehe sorted his nets while his wife cooked potatoes and white-bait for the visitors. Waiateruati now stood out clearly on the plains, 'its lofty wata at a distance looking like the ruins of ancient temples'. Shortland found that most Waiateruati people were working at their cultivations at nearby Arowhenua, or preparing kauru further inland. People were also setting off for Akaroa by land or sea, in response to John Tikao's messages.

While Shortland's baggage went on by sea to Akaroa with the poha titi, Te Rehe's elder son Tarawhata offered to guide him there on foot, in return for a blanket. Te Rehe brought Shortland a basket of kauru as a parting gift. The snow-fed rivers of the plains – Waitaki, Rangitata, Hakatere, Rakaia and Waimakariri – were clouded with sediment during their frequent freshets.[23] But the smaller streams, rising among the sweet herbs and refreshing forests of the foothills, flowed with the purest of water, providing excellent kanakana, koura, kokopu and eels – for which Tarawhata detoured to the Ohape Stream for a meal.

Shortland's party trudged on from Ohape for three hot and dusty days, across the plains and shingle beaches, towards Taumutu at Waihora. Inland, the blue forested foothills stood forth against the dry plains. Behind them rose steep and rocky ranges two thousand metres high, now bare of snow. At times, when mountain gorges cleared briefly, there were glimpses of distant icy peaks towards the

Main Divide of Te Wai Pounamu. Tarawhata told Shortland local place names, and the best methods of getting water and fording rivers. He also described the sources of the rivers and the distant mountain lakes whence they came.

The straggling, shiny green tutu shrub was found from time to time on parched, shallow soils – poisonous in the stem and seed, but a great boon to the traveller. Its juicy purple berries strained or sucked through a flax fabric yielded a most refreshing drink. Where there was no tutu, empty vessels had been left at the occasional watering places for carrying water from one place to the next. Tarawhata knew holes in cliffs where fat titi might be found. At the sight of a flock of terns hovering close inshore, the Maoris threw off their loads and rushed to get fish for dinner. On the tiring final day of their march, they had Te Rehe's kauru to sustain them.[24]

Thus Shortland enjoyed customary hospitality from Ngai Tahu of the plains – a world of broad skies, long distances, dangerous rivers, strong winds, dust, and sweat. As Shortland describes it,[25] theirs was a co-operative, well-organised life, and they shared with visitors their knowledge of the country, the bounties of their mahinga kai, and the extra gifts of nature as they befell. The vast alluvial plain stretched for 250 kilometres from south of the Waitaki to beyond the Rakahuri. It was no wasteland, but a rich and sustainable food-store.

When Shortland reached Akaroa on 31 January 1844, the French corvette *Rhin* was at anchor, together with five whaling ships.[26] Belligny promptly complained to Shortland about 'natives visiting him every now and then in a body', demanding payment for land occupied by French settlers, and trampling his flower beds. Shortland spoke to Ngai Tahu, who had assembled at Tikao's urging, and advised them rather lightheartedly to await the Queen's consent before expecting any payment. But when he went on to Port Levy he heard Maori complaints about Europeans 'spreading themselves over the country with their stock', and refusing to pay for permission to land cattle or to cut timber, on the grounds that 'all the land belonged to the Queen of England'.

As the Greenwoods were the most complained of, Shortland went to Purau accompanied by some aggrieved Ngai Tahu. Joseph Greenwood told Shortland he thought it illegal to pay Maoris anything. But, noted Shortland, Greenwood had ignored

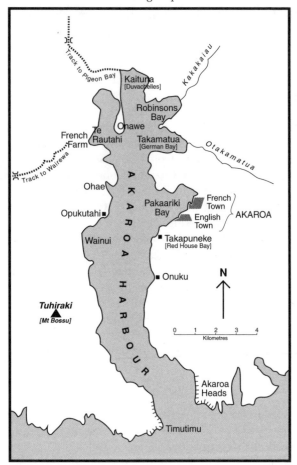

Akaroa, 1843.

'the illegality of occupying forcibly land that evidently did not belong to himself, whether the Queen claimed it or no . . . The doctrine that Mr G advocated was a very favourite one among new comers, who landed full of the idea that there were large spaces of what they termed waste and unreclaimed land, on which their cattle and flocks might roam at pleasure, and to which they had a better right than those whose ancestors had lived there, fished there, and hunted there; and had, more-over, long ago given names to every stream, hill, and valley of the neighbourhood.'[27]

Greenwood agreed to pay £3 or £4 in goods annually to the Maori owners, if he could occupy the next bay as well.[28] Shortland wrote to Magistrate Robinson advising against allowing settlers to occupy land on Banks Peninsula.[29] But Shortland had no authority over Robinson, or over the settlers. After he had gone, Joseph Greenwood decided to pay the agreed rental only for 'as long as I think proper'.[30] The squatters continued to assert their 'rights', and their stock continued to destroy Maori gardens.

Shortland, while waiting at Akaroa for a passage to Wellington, dined aboard the *Rhin* at Bérard's invitation, with Robinson and Bishop Selwyn. Bérard asked Shortland for 'a list of the Maoris who had a right to lands about the harbour, and a form of deed such as was used by the Government in purchasing land from the aborigines'.[31] Shortland provided the list, but warned that such purchases were illegal, and that it was difficult to make them dispute-proof. He advised writing to Governor FitzRoy. Bérard accordingly wrote to FitzRoy for assistance in purchasing 'the four ports of Akaroa, Pigeon Bay, Port Levy and Port Cooper'.[32]

When Shortland reached Auckland he reported the French company's activities at Akaroa to the Chief Protector, in terms that made Police Magistrate Robinson's neglect of his proper duties obvious. Shortland recommended that Robinson should visit whaling stations twice yearly 'in a small armed vessel', instead of remaining at Akaroa. The persistent French usurpation of Maori land, said Shortland, could provoke violence, and the government should intervene:

> Should the French Company be permitted to purchase any part of Banks Peninsula, in order to fulfil their engagements with their settlers, the presence of a Protector of Aborigines will be required to see that it is clearly understood and defined, what lands are to be sold, and what reserved, and to take care that all persons having just claims to the lands offered for sale be parties to the contract.[33]

But Assistant Protectors could do no more than submit reports, and make recommendations. Shortland's went unheeded by the New Zealand Government.

Notes

1. J. Deans–Deans snr, 28.9.1845, in Deans 1937: 90ff. 'Quail' – *Coturnix novaezealandiae*, or *koreke* – now extinct.
2. Greenwood Ms Diary, 16.1.1844.
3. Shortland 1851: 263n.
4. Quoted in Tremewan 1990: 260ff.
5. Robinson–Murphy, 30.4.1842, NAW IA 1842/1284, Tremewan transcript; Tremewan 1990: chapter 15 and passim.
6. Robinson–Colonial Secretary, 30.11.1842, NAW IA 1843/255, Tremewan transcript. Such a rank, even if it were merited, would not depend on a police magistrate's approval.
7. Robinson–Colonial Secretary, 10.5.1843, loc cit.
8. Robinson–Colonial Secretary, 10.5.1843, NAW IA 1843/1425, Tremewan transcript.
9. W. Deans–Deans snr, 6.9.1843, in Deans 1937: 70.
10. Shortland 1851: 254ff.
11. Buick 1928: 249n.
12. Shortland Ms Middle Island Journal.
13. Tremewan 1990: 268ff.
14. Shortland has been described as 'the first anthropologist of the Maori', and his *Southern Districts of New Zealand* as 'the seminal work of South Island Maori history and ethnography' (Oliver 1990: 397a). An acquaintance described him as 'one of the most amiable unassuming yet capable men that I ever came across' (Clarke, marginal note, Shortland Ms Waiata Book).
15. Shortland Ms Middle Island Journal; Shortland–Clarke, 18.3.1844, in Mackay 1873 II: 123ff.)
16. Mackay 1873 II: 123ff (Shortland–Clarke, 18.3.1844); Shortland Ms Middle Island Journal.
17. See Evison 1993: 191n.
18. Hocken Ms Papers: 99.
19. Shortland 1851: 41.
20. Paihia: New Zealand headquarters of the CMS.
21. WJ, 20.1.1844; Shortland 1851: 210.
22. Shortland 1851: x.
23. On 30.3.1849, Torlesse saw Tiramorehu, returning on foot from Akaroa to Moeraki, crossing the flooded Rangitata by 'running down it up to his neck' (Torlesse 1958: 71).
24. Sources for Shortland's journey: Shortland 1851: chapters X–XIII; Shortland Ms Middle Island Journal; Selwyn Ms Journal I; John Wilson 1990: 91.
25. Shortland 1851: passim.
26. Selwyn Ms Journal I, 14.2.1844.
27. Shortland 1851: 252ff. Yet McHugh (1991: 78) says, 'From the first, British settlers recognised the title of the Maori tribes to their traditional land. This recognition was made not only by the Colonial Office in London, but by those actually involved on the frontier.'
28. Shortland 1851: 260–61; Greenwood Ms Diary, 12.2.1844. These differ as to the rental.
29. Shortland 1851: 266ff.
30. Greenwood Ms Diary, 12.2.1844, 2.5.1844 and passim.
31. Shortland 1851: 272–73.
32. Tremewan 1990: loc cit.
33. Shortland–Clarke, 18.3.1844, Shortland Ms Letters.

9

≈

The Otago Purchase

CAPTAIN ROBERT FITZROY was a tall, thin, melancholy, religious man of aristocratic descent. He was impulsive by nature, and eccentric in manner. His appointment as Governor of New Zealand in 1843 was widely applauded in England. Aged thirty-seven, he was renowned as a cartographer, and his command of HMS *Beagle* on its famous expedition with Charles Darwin had earned him the Gold Medal of the Royal Geographical Society. In later life he became a distinguished meteorologist.

The New Zealand Company in Britain, still buoyed by the favours granted them by Lord John Russell in 1840, but as yet unaware of the Wairau disaster, announced plans on 1 July 1843 for another settlement. This was to be 'New Edinburgh', proposed by the liberal Scottish politician and sculptor George Rennie. He, like other colonial reformers, argued that the colonisation of New Zealand would relieve poverty and avert revolution in Britain.[1]

New Edinburgh was to be a Wakefield scheme colony with a Scottish character: the rural sections were to be only fifty acres, suitable for a community of ploughmen tilling the soil on small farms. The settlement was to comprise 120,550 fertile acres, providing two thousand properties – each with a quarter-acre town section, a ten-acre suburban section, and a fifty-acre rural section. One-tenth of the properties would be set aside as Company reserves, and the sale of the others to settlers at £120 each (about £2 per acre) would bring in £216,000 – a quarter of which was for the Company, while the rest would pay for emigration, surveying, public works, and support for churches and schooling. Two hundred town sections were to be allocated to the municipality. The Company, as agents for the scheme, would obtain the required land, while the New Zealand Government would be responsible for allocating reserves for public and Maori purposes.[2] FitzRoy met Rennie before leaving England, and agreed with the scheme.[3]

FitzRoy left England in June 1843, and learned of the Wairau disaster some months later from Governor Gipps in Sydney. He reached Auckland late in December aboard the frigate *North Star*, with fifty-six fresh soldiers, to find the colony bankrupt and land sales at a standstill.[4] Even with his reinforcements, there were only 134 British soldiers in the country.[5] The Chief Protector, and some missionaries, considered Arthur Wakefield's party to have been the aggressors at the Wairau.[6] But the Nelson magistrates still wanted Te Rauparaha and Rangihaeata arrested. The New Zealand Company settlers expected FitzRoy to attack Ngati Toa at once. 'No-one appeared disposed to give the natives credit for courage, or skill in warfare,' wrote FitzRoy later. 'No-one seemed to doubt that they would fly before a very small detachment of military.' He suspected that the desire at Wellington to have the Maoris expelled was due to the colonists wanting the land and the produce market for themselves.[7]

FitzRoy believed it his duty to reconcile colonists and Maoris, while satisfying the Company's land claims within reason. He acknowledged the Maori right to British citizenship, and often received chiefs at Government House, Auckland, however inconvenient to his household. He later wrote:

> The natives are such keen observers of character and conduct, – so quick in detecting inconsistency, and estimating individuals by their actions, that an inconsistent person – though professing to be a missionary – would have no moral influence. Among the principal chiefs a regard for truth, and a sense of honour prevail . . . An old tattooed chief, though smeared with red ochre, wrapped in a dirty blanket, and with feathers stuck in his head, like Rauparaha, Rangihaeata, Kawiti, or Heu Heu, will be found as keen a lawyer (in native usages and common sense) and as proud a democrat as may be met within the precincts of Westminster. You may reason with these men, and may convince them, if you have justice as well as truth on your side; and further, you may move them out of their intended course, if not against their self-interest. But to drive – to coerce them – will be most difficult.[8]

~

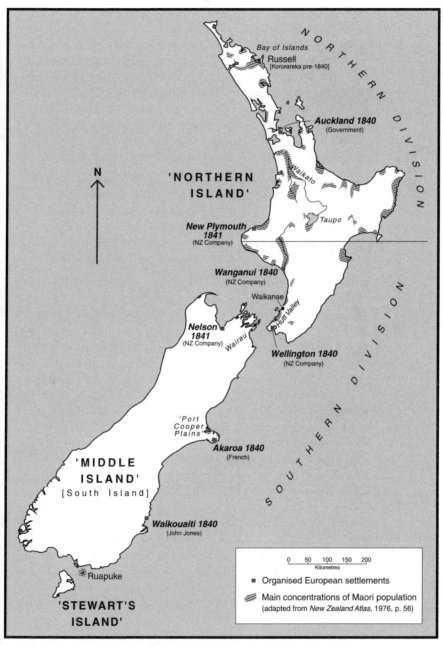

The Otago Purchase

Early European colonisation and administration of New Zealand.

141

Soon after his arrival in Auckland, FitzRoy sailed for Nelson and Wellington to investigate the Wairau disaster and decide what should be done about it. He reached Wellington from Nelson on 30 January 1844, and convened a korero to discuss the Wairau dispute. Thus on 12 February 1844, while Edward Shortland was trying to dissuade Joseph Greenwood from seizing Maori land at Purau, about five hundred Ngati Toa assembled at Waikanae to discuss the Wairau disaster with FitzRoy and his officials, who were accompanied by officers of the *North Star*. Hadfield and his missionaries were also present. FitzRoy addressed Ngati Toa about the Wairau killings, saying:

> I was exceedingly angry. My heart was very dark, and my mind was filled with gloom. My first thought was to revenge the deaths of my friends, and the other pakeha who had been killed, and for that purpose to bring many ships of war, sailing vessels, and vessels moved by fire, and many soldiers; and had I done so, you would have been sacrificed, and your pas destroyed.[9]

He had heard the Europeans' side of the story, said FitzRoy: now he wanted Te Rauparaha to explain himself. [10]

Te Rauparaha then spoke, with the Governor frequently interrupting him to have points clarified by the interpreter, Assistant Protector George Clarke junior, and with Hadfield interrupting Clarke to correct his interpreting. Te Rauparaha declared that he had never sold the Wairau, that he had not wished to fight, but that Magistrate Thompson had tried to handcuff him. When he resisted, the Englishmen had fired. The captives were killed because that was the Maori custom after bloodshed, he said.

'Tell him to sit down, so that I may think over what to say to them,' said FitzRoy. He sat making lengthy notes while the audience waited patiently, as was customary on a marae.[11] At last he rose to give his decision. Ngati Toa had committed a great crime in killing their captives, he said, but the Englishmen had been wrong to start the fighting. Therefore he would not avenge them. Let all be friends, and he would protect Maori and European alike. Maoris must not be deprived of their lands, and settlers must not be molested. The Protectors and the missionaries would guide the Maoris, said FitzRoy. With Major Richmond as Southern Superintendent, and Commissioner Spain investigating the New Zealand Company's purchases, he said, justice would be done to all.

The Wakefields' cousin Francis Dillon Bell, the Company's agent at Nelson, was present throughout this, making notes for the

Company and their supporters. They never forgave FitzRoy, and determined to destroy him.[12]

~

Colonial governors were often pestered by people wanting to get on the government's meagre payroll. Walter Mantell, when he had arrived at Port Nicholson in the *Oriental* in January 1840, had found jobs hard to get. He became Wellington's postmaster, a humble post with poor quarters.[13] The salary did not satisfy him, and he used his father's name to get money.[14] His father had sought preferment for him with Governor FitzRoy, through a reluctant Charles Darwin.[15] Walter Mantell saw FitzRoy twice in 1844, and told him that the 'sedentary nature' of being postmaster was ruining his health. He then resigned, confident that FitzRoy would get him a better job. But FitzRoy did not oblige, and Mantell was left unemployed.[16]

William Wakefield also waited on FitzRoy, early in 1844, about buying the necessary land for New Edinburgh. The British Government had authorised FitzRoy to approve a South Island site for the Scottish settlement, and the first colonists were soon to sail from Scotland. The New Zealand Company, under its 1841 charter, was entitled to buy land for the settlement; but FitzRoy, in view of the Wairau disaster, decided that the purchase should be supervised by his nominee, John Jermyn Symonds, a Wellington Police Magistrate and former Assistant Protector.[17] The Company could buy 150,000 acres, if Symonds approved. FitzRoy would then waive the Crown's 'right of pre-emption' over the purchase, to give it official sanction.[18] He told Symonds:

> You will inform the aboriginal native population that you are sent to superintend and forward the purchase of lands which they wish to sell, and that you, on behalf of the Government, will not authorize, nor in any way sanction any proceedings which are not honest, equitable and in every way irreproachable.[19]

After the Wairau disaster, William Wakefield had sent the New Zealand Company's surveyor, Frederick Tuckett, back to Nelson to take charge there on behalf of the Company – a responsibility Tuckett did not enjoy, for absentee landowners were outnumbered at Nelson only by discontented, underemployed labourers. Tuckett blamed this situation on the Company's policy of selling land in

England, which in his opinion favoured 'land jobbers'. Land, he thought, should be sold to people only when they arrived in New Zealand, and then only to genuine farmers.[20] Disillusioned with the Company, Tuckett resigned from Nelson and was about to return to England when Wakefield invited him to take charge of the New Edinburgh purchase. Tuckett accepted, on being promised complete freedom in choosing the site.[21]

Tuckett, now aged thirty-six, was strong-willed, with boundless energy, caustic tongue, and stern countenance, tolerant in religion, and hard of hearing.[22] He chartered the schooner *Deborah*, and sailed from Nelson on 31 March 1844 with two assistant surveyors, and stores and equipment for a lengthy expedition. Passengers included Nelson settler Dr David Monro, and two missionaries – Charles Creed, who was to replace Watkin at Waikouaiti, and the Lutheran Johann Wohlers, who sought a southern mission situation for himself. After collecting Symonds at Wellington, the expedition sailed for Port Cooper, William Wakefield's preference, so that Tuckett could examine it as a 'standard of comparison'.

On the day that FitzRoy had issued his instructions about the New Edinburgh purchase, Tuhawaiki was introduced to him by Bishop Selwyn, and no doubt heard of the intended colony. For months it had been rumoured that the New Zealand Company, driven from the Wairau by Ngati Toa, would want the Port Cooper plains.[23] Now that the Company had fallen out with Te Rauparaha, Tuhawaiki hoped to win them to his side.

～

The *Deborah* anchored in Port Cooper on 5 April 1844. Tuhawaiki came off to the schooner with three boatloads of Ngai Tahu, including Taiaroa, ready to negotiate a sale.[24] Tuhawaiki as usual impressed the Englishmen. Monro wrote to the *Nelson Examiner*:

> Tuawaike is probably one of the most Europeanised natives in New Zealand. He was most correctly and completely dressed in white man's clothes, even to the refinement of a cotton pocket handkerchief. His outward and investing garment was an excellent drab great-coat; and no stage coachman in England could have thrust his hands into his pockets with a more knowing air . . . On many subjects he surprised us by the extent of his knowledge; and, generally, his remarks were characterised by much shrewdness and very considerable drollery. Tuawaike

is a fine-looking man, above middle size, and well proportioned, with good features, and an intelligent expression of countenance.[25]

Meanwhile Tuckett set out with one of his surveyors to inspect the Port Cooper plains, and became marooned in the extensive swamp between the Port Hills and Putaringamotu. Alone for the night in one of the richest eel fisheries in the country, the two Englishmen considered how best it might be drained. Afterwards they visited the Deans's property, and reached the Waimakariri. Tuckett thought the plains unsuitable for small farms. Waihora, whose mild waters supported probably a greater natural food supply than any other lake in the country, was to him 'an unattractive and almost useless lagoon'.

When Tuckett returned to the *Deborah*, Symonds rebuked him for his unannounced excursion to the plains. 'The Maoris are very jealous,' said Symonds, 'and do not like or understand the spying out of the land.'[26] Tuckett resented Symonds's rebuke – for he, not Symonds, had been authorised (by Wakefield) to purchase the land, and (by Richmond) to survey the harbours if the Maoris did not object.[27] But FitzRoy had told Symonds to 'superintend and assist' Tuckett.[28] Thus each man thought he was in charge.

The *Deborah* went on to Waikouaiti, where on 20 April James Watkin welcomed his successor, saying, 'Welcome to purgatory, Brother Creed.'[29] Watkin had now registered 258 baptisms, thirty-seven marriages, 227 Bible class enrolments, and more than twenty lay preachers. He deplored the New Edinburgh scheme: 'Talk about colonization as a means of promoting Christianity, forsooth! The thing is preposterous, it never tended to that end that I have ever read or heard of.' Watkin left Waikouaiti with his wife and family on 27 June for a mission post at Wellington.[30]

At Waikouaiti, Symonds persuaded John Jones to take him back to Wellington in his ship *Scotia* to complain about Tuckett.[31] Tuckett's expedition then proceeded to Otakou Harbour, which Monro described thus:

The sky, a great part of the time, was without a cloud, and not a breeze ruffled the surface of the water, which reflected the surrounding wooded slopes, and every sea-bird that floated upon it, with mirror-like accuracy. For some hours after sunrise, the woods resounded with the rich and infinitely varied notes of thousands of tuis and other songsters. I never heard anything like it before in any part of New Zealand. It completely agreed with Captain Cook's description of the music of the wooded banks of Queen Charlotte's Sound.[32]

From Otakou, Tuckett walked southwards to inspect the country with his assistants, accompanied by Monro. They rejoined the *Deborah* at Foveaux Strait, and visited Stewart Island and Ruapuke. Monro reported of Ruapuke:

> The natives are great travellers, and well provided with capital large boats, in which they jaunt about in pursuit of profit or amusement. Everyone to whom we spoke agreed as to the most unaccountable fact of their rapidly diminishing numbers.[33]

Wohlers landed at Ruapuke to establish his mission, to which he would devote forty years. Like Watkin, he suffered loneliness and self-doubt, and detested the Maori way of life. He believed Ngai Tahu had become 'degraded' by their own 'savage' customs, and agreed with the theory that 'savage races' were degenerate, and salvageable only by Christianity:

> No savage race, no habitually indolent and improvident person, will take to patient industry – which is inseparable from a healthy civilized life, – unless the mind is first changed by an inward regenerating power.[34]

Wohlers recorded Maori traditions. As was the fashion, he called them 'myths' – a convenient term for the beliefs of others.

John Jones arrived at Otakou from Wellington on 8 June 1844 with Symonds, and Wakefield's brother Daniel and his interpreter David Scott, and with Tuhawaiki and Taiaroa.[35] Tuhawaiki sent for his Murihiku supporters, a hundred and fifty of whom arrived at Otakou within two days. Tuckett's party returned from their southern excursion, having decided there was no better site for New Edinburgh than 'Otago'.[36]

Beyond the hills at the head of Otakou Harbour lay the partly forested lower Taieri plain, which appeared to promise profitable farmland. To the west of this plain, marking the boundary of Tuckett's chosen block, rose the 895-metre escarpment of Maunga-atua, 'mountain of the atua'. Had the Europeans climbed the steep forested slopes to Maungaatua's broad, mysterious summit, carpeted with alpine herbs and sentinelled by giant rocks, they would have

The Otago Purchase

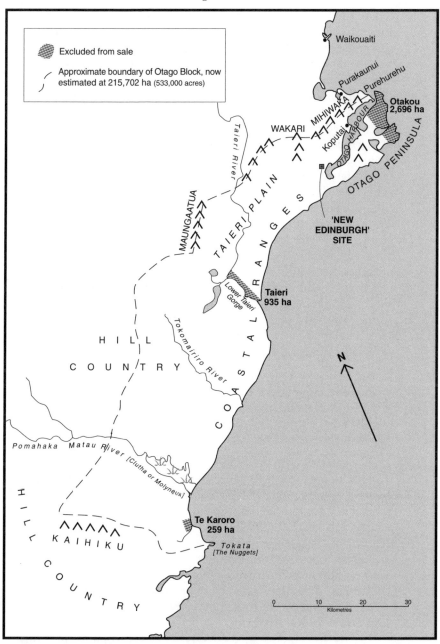

Excluded from sale

Approximate boundary of Otago Block, now estimated at 215,702 ha (533,000 acres)

Waikouaiti

Purakaunui

Purehurehu

MIHIWAKA

Otakou
2,696 ha

WAKARI

Koputai

OTAGO HARBOUR

OTAGO PENINSULA

Taieri River

MAUNGAATUA

TAIERI PLAIN

COASTAL RANGES

'NEW EDINBURGH' SITE

Lower Taieri Gorge

Taieri
935 ha

HILL COUNTRY

Tokomairiro River

N

Pomahaka

Matau River [Clutha or Molyneux]

HILL KAIHIKU COUNTRY

Te Karoro
259 ha

Tokata [The Nuggets]

0   10   20   30
Kilometres

The Otago Purchase, July 1844.

seen stretching far inland, beyond their chosen purchase, a prodigious expanse of sinuous rounded hills and gullies clothed in tall tussock grasses, golden green and tawny, interspersed with stands of New Zealand beech and darker patches of manuka and associated shrubs. Beyond were blue-black mountains splashed with snow, range upon range, extending west and north as far as the eye could see.

South of the lower Taieri plain lay eighty kilometres of fertile, well-watered lands, with ample timber, extending towards Tuckett's southern boundary beyond the Matau – a river even 'an American would not despise', said Tuckett. Here, in all, were at least 400,000 acres of land, and Tuckett intended to buy it all. Symonds agreed with Tuckett's choice, but insisted that the boundaries be traversed with the Maori owners, as Edward Shortland had advised. Tuckett objected and wrote his resignation, armed with which Symonds again returned to Wellington. Tuckett then reached an agreement with Tuhawaiki, Karetai and Taiaroa, that they would sell his chosen block for £2,400, excepting such parts as they wanted to retain.

Symonds returned from Wellington nearly four weeks later with William Wakefield, Commissioner Spain, and George Clarke junior – who had just tried unsuccessfully to buy the Wanganui tribes' land for £1,000.[37] Tuckett had by now annoyed the Maoris by surveying across their urupa.[38] Wakefield, however, admired Tuckett's choice of site:

> For picturesque beauty Otago yields only to Akaroa amongst the harbours of these islands. The waters of the harbour teem with fish of the best sorts. The hapuka is taken in great quantities near the shipping town Port Chalmers; flat fish and oysters in all the bays.[39]

The boundaries of Tuckett's block were now duly visited, or observed, leaving only the question of what land Ngai Tahu were to retain. They asked to keep the Otago Peninsula of 21,250 acres, with its ancestral sites.[40] But Wakefield objected that Europeans already squatting on the peninsula might compete with New Edinburgh. He threatened to call off the sale unless the peninsula was included. Symonds, despite his instructions to watch over Maori interests, failed to intervene. The Maoris agreed to accept the northern end of the peninsula (including Otakou), together with land at the lower Taieri gorge and at Te Karoro further south – a total of 9,612 acres.[41]

Twenty-five chiefs signed the Otago deed at Koputai on 31 July 1844.[42] Tuhawaiki kept nearly half of the £2,400 payment.[43] Karetai called on Maoris and Europeans to respect each other's land. He came to blows with Tuhawaiki after being reproached by him for dishonesty when an Otakou chief mistakenly complained of being underpaid. Wakefield praised Tuhawaiki's business acumen in facilitating the sale:

> He entered into all the details of the sale, described the boundaries exactly by name and designs on paper, and conducted the transactions on the part of the Natives with the tact and readiness of an accomplished man of business. He repeatedly expressed his determination to abstain from spirits for the future, and to take his place amongst the intending settlers as an English gentleman.[44]

But in his zeal for helping with the purchase, Tuhawaiki failed to ensure that Otago Ngai Tahu were left with sufficient land for their future needs.[45] He was drowned off Timaru two months later. He was buried first at Waiateruati, which was then abandoned because of the tapu, and finally at Ruapuke where a monument stands in his memory.[46] His death ended Murihiku dominance in Ngai Tahu affairs, and deprived European speculators and land buyers of a congenial associate.

∼

The New Zealand Company's Otago expedition contributed to one of the great controversies of the century – the reason for the 'dying out' of the Maoris of southern New Zealand. We have already noticed the epidemics of the 1830s. In 1844, William Wakefield reported to his Company:

> The population of the Southern Island has decreased with extraordinary rapidity since the establishment of whaling stations on its shores, and the visits of whaling ships to its fine harbours and bays.

He added: 'Since Mr Tuckett's first visit to Foveaux's Strait three months ago, he has learned of the death of many of the men and women who were then apparently in strong health.'[47] Wakefield blamed this extraordinary mortality on 'the introduction of new habits, and formerly unknown diseases' – identifying as 'new habits' the drinking of 'raw spirits', wearing blankets, and eating titi and whale blubber. As 'new diseases' he specified measles and venereal disease.

Tuckett discussed the population decline with local Europeans, and noted: 'At each place which I have visited, I have been assured that the Maoris are dying rapidly.' He reported only six Maoris at Te Karoro, where, he was informed, there had once been more than two thousand. Similar declines were said to have occurred elsewhere among Maoris of southern New Zealand. Tuckett blamed 'measles, other diseases, and ardent spirits', and 'two-thirds' of marriageable Maori women living with Europeans.[48] Monro, an Edinburgh-trained physician who had studied at Paris, Berlin and Vienna, thought, like Shortland, that the 'rapidly diminishing numbers' of the Maoris of southern New Zealand were inexplicable.[49]

In the 1840s no one understood epidemics. European authorities disputed whether they were caused by contagion, or infection. Some thought that the mere touching of infected persons conveyed disease, and others that infection was spread by certain winds. Some thought civilisation was itself a defence against disease, and that epidemics originated among 'barbarous' peoples, among whom they included their own slum-dwellers. Any susceptibility to epidemics, in this view, was both proof and consequence of uncivilised living.[50]

Europeans in the nineteenth century generally attributed lung diseases to 'bad air' and 'vapours'.[51] According to this 'miasmic theory' of disease, Maoris became prone to lung disease through leaving hilltop pas to live in the 'bad air' of the swamps while cutting flax – a notion that survives to this day.[52] In Europe the centuries-old belief that swamps generated 'bad air' and disease, was reinforced by the fact that when such swamps were drained, the disease disappeared. But Maoris flourished well enough in swamps in southern New Zealand before European contact. The great pa of Kaiapoi was in a swamp, as were many kainga in the wetlands between Waihora and Waimakariri. The European 'swamp disease', malaria, was in fact spread by anopheles mosquitoes breeding in the swamps. When such swamps were drained, the anopheles disappeared, and with them the malaria. But New Zealand had no anopheles, or malaria.

Some Europeans thought Maoris contracted disease through eating potatoes, 'the lowest species of human food'.[53] Others thought it 'Nature's eternal law' that 'weaker races' must die off when confronted with a more 'durable and vigorous race', such as the English 'race'.[54] Wohlers thought the high death rate among Maoris was due to their having degenerated into 'wild, stinking, heathen cannibals'.[55]

Medical science was in its infancy in the 1840s. The nature of infectious diseases was a mystery as yet unsolved. That they were due to specific bacteria and viruses was unknown, because these had not yet been identified. No one understood the process whereby repeated exposure to infectious diseases improved a community's resistance to them – a process from which Europeans had benefited over the centuries, but Maoris had not.

In European medicine, the usual treatment for chest complaints was 'copious bleedings, a fly-blister, and a purge'. The first trained medical doctor among the Maoris of southern New Zealand, Joseph Crocombe, came to Otakou in 1836 and settled at Jones's Waikouaiti station in 1838. The clinical thermometer, the hypodermic syringe, antiseptics, and anaesthetics were unknown. Compound fractures usually proved fatal. For infected wounds and abrasions, Crocombe generally found Maori remedies as good as any.[56]

On 29 July 1844, two days before the New Zealand Company's Otago deed was signed, the House of Commons published a select committee's report on New Zealand. A slim majority of the committee's members, and most of its witnesses, were New Zealand Company sympathisers.[57] The report strongly criticised FitzRoy's policies, and quoted Governor Gipps's statement of 1840 that 'uncivilised inhabitants' could not claim authority over the country they inhabited, and had 'right of occupancy only'; they could not sell or lease their uncultivated land, for 'the simple reason' that they did not own it. The Treaty of Waitangi was a mistake, said the report. British sovereignty should have been proclaimed 'on the ground of prior discovery'. The report's view of Maoris was strictly paternal: 'The rude inhabitants of New Zealand ought to be treated in many respects like children, and in dealing with them firmness is no less necessary than kindness.'

The 'natives', said the report, had been mistakenly taught that they owned land they did not occupy, whereas once British sovereignty had been proclaimed, the Crown owned it. Unoccupied land derived its only value from the application of European labour and capital, the report said, and the Maoris with their 'barbarous and superstitious customs' could not effectively use it. They were entitled only to land 'actually occupied by them, and cultivated in common', and to forests 'actually used for cutting timber'. If Maoris resisted these principles, the report declared, 'We have no doubt that civilization and intelligence, in the event of a struggle, would maintain their accustomed superiority.' The report praised Captain George Grey's 1839 proposal for civilising Aborigines, and advised that 'every effort should be made to amalgamate the two races' by 'education and training'. To hasten this process, Maori reserves should be scattered among European properties, said the report.

This select committee report was the first widely published official document to set forth clearly the twin principles of Victorian colonial policy – that the bulk of the land rightfully belonged to the Europeans, and that 'natives' would be well enough repaid with Christianity, schooling, and the superior example of the 'civilized race'. In New Zealand, the report caused dismay and anger among the tribes, and jubilation among settlers. It was not supported by the House of Commons, and Lord Stanley rejected it. But its bald prejudices held a strong attraction for colonial New Zealanders, who clung to them from generation to generation thereafter.

Despite Ngai Tahu's unchallenged evidence at Godfrey's commission, that at Akaroa they had sold the French only Pakaariki Bay, Belligny continued selling other land around Akaroa Harbour, with the full knowledge of Police Magistrate Robinson. At Te Rautahi, Belligny offered 300 acres at £2 6s an acre.[58] But the Akaroa chiefs wanted their ownership properly acknowledged, and stiffened their demands for payment. Edward Shortland had advised them to 'wait quietly' for Belligny to obtain the Queen's consent. But the Otago purchase made this advice less convincing. Some French settlers were threatened with eviction, and Commodore Bérard again prepared for a Maori uprising. Robinson could have mediated this dispute according to the law. But his own interests depended on a French success, and he did nothing.

Bérard, since getting Shortland's advice in January 1844, had waited in vain for Governor FitzRoy to visit Akaroa. In March 1845, the French decided to issue the Maoris with the goods obtained by Bérard in Sydney, together with the residue of Langlois's 1840 cargo. Some chiefs wanted schooners, so Belligny obtained the *Sisters*, valued at £200, from the Sinclairs as part payment for their French grant at Kakongutungutu.[59] He presented gifts to important chiefs, and distributions were prepared for Ngai Tahu of northern Banks Peninsula, and (with the schooner) for those of the Akaroa district. At each distribution the French required a 'deed of sale' to be signed. The 'deeds' were never published, for the 1841 Land Ordinance

disqualified such 'purchases', as we have seen. Instead, Belligny took
them to France as a bargaining counter for his company.

Robinson reported these French 'purchases' to Superintendent
Richmond in characteristic fashion. He said that the 'deeds', which
he 'had not seen', conveyed the whole peninsula to the French in
'two separate purchases', and he sent Richmond a copy of Bérard's
map showing the division.[60] Yet he was 'perfectly certain' that neither Bérard nor the French Government had any designs on the
peninsula. 'It was the natives' earnest wish to sell,' Robinson said,
and Bérard merely wanted to protect his settlers. Only three Maoris
had refused to sign, said Robinson: Hakaroa, Ruaparae and Mautai.
He omitted to add that these three were the leading Akaroa chiefs.
He said he had warned the French that their 'deeds' might be invalid.
Yet he did not attempt to stop them. He gave his usual account of
his devotion to the Maoris. 'They know well my indulgent conduct
to them,' he wrote.[61] Years later, as we shall see, it emerged that
many Maoris had bitterly opposed selling land to the French.

Superintendent Richmond, preoccupied with land disputes in
the Hutt Valley, and the threat of war there, passed on Robinson's
reports to FitzRoy – who, distracted by Hone Heke's defiance at
the Bay of Islands, accepted them without question. The timing
was fortunate for the French. Robinson resigned soon afterwards
and followed Belligny to Europe, where he resumed his intrigues
in support of French interests, and his own, at Banks Peninsula.

Ngai Tahu meanwhile turned their attention to the squatters.
FitzRoy had refused to allow the Deanses to buy Putaringamotu. But
when the Ngai Tuahuriri chief Te One Te Uki asked Superintendent
Richmond if the Deans could lease the place, the government agreed.
More than a year later, in December 1846, the Deanses signed a
lease agreement with Te Uki and his colleagues[62] for grazing rights
to land extending 'six miles in every direction' (about 29,000 hectares), for twenty-one years at £8 a year.[63] Robinson's successor
John Watson arranged a similar Maori lease for the Greenwoods
for some 25,000 hectares around Port Cooper. William Rhodes
purchased this from the Greenwoods in July 1847.[64] Rhodes and the
Deans family later turned these Maori leases to good advantage.

∽

The New Zealand Company had paid £2,400 for the Otago block,
which in reality contained more than half a million acres. Such

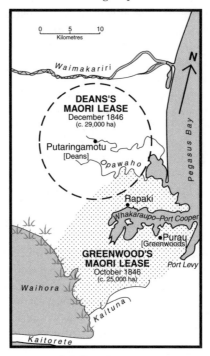

Maori grazing leases, 1846.

token prices had originally been justified by the supposed future incremental value of the Maori 'tenths', as we have seen. But the Company made no specific proposals for Maori reserves in their New Edinburgh scheme, other than leaving the matter to the government. The Otago deed referred to the 9,612 acres that Ngai Tahu had retained, as 'Nga wahi wenua kua kotia e matou mo matou mo a matou tamariki' – 'The portions of land that we have cut away entirely for us, for our children'.[65]

Lord Stanley had told the Company early in 1843 that Maoris were entitled to the benefit of tenths in addition to land they chose not to sell,[66] and FitzRoy was no doubt aware of this. Some Otakou chiefs testified thirty-six years later that William Wakefield had promised them 'wakawaka' in New Edinburgh, in addition to the land withheld from sale.[67] But the deed contained no such promise. Symonds had left Wakefield to settle the terms,[68] and had at Wakefield's suggestion referred the question of tenths to the government without making any 'express stipulation' to Ngai Tahu.[69] Tuckett,

154

Scott, Clarke, and Symonds all referred to the Maoris' unsold portions as 'reserves', as did the official translation of the deed. Wakefield told his Company that Maori reserves could not be provided within the Company's purchase until it had been surveyed.[70] He did not say *whether* they should be provided. An acquaintance of Wakefield said of him:

> One remarkable faculty of Colonel Wakefield was his reticence. No-one who had an interview with Colonel Wakefield knew what he thought and what he meant to do. His manner was attractive, and, in outward appearance, sympathetic, but the inner man was out of sight and hearing. Colonel Wakefield, like the mole, did his work underground.[71]

Wakefield returned to Wellington from Otago to find that the New Zealand Company's finances were failing, and that no colonists would be sailing for New Edinburgh. In the event, the new settlement was delayed until 1848. By then there was a new government in Britain, a new Governor in New Zealand, and a new policy for Maoris.

Notes

1. McLintock 1949: 159.
2. *NTR*: chapter 6 passim.
3. Wai-27 C1: 16.
4. McLintock 1958: 153ff.
5. FitzRoy 1846: 14ff.
6. BFAPS nd: 17ff.
7. FitzRoy–Stanley, 15.4.1844 (D), in *BPPNZ*.
8. FitzRoy 1846: 55–56. FitzRoy condoned American slavery (Desmond & Moore 1991: 120).
9. FitzRoy–Stanley, 15.4.1844 (E), in *BPPNZ*.
10. Wakefield 1845 II: 515ff.
11. Clarke (1903: 58) recalled, 'For nearly an hour no one moved or spoke, but all eyes were intently fixed on us.'
12. Wakefield 1845, loc cit; McLintock 1958: 151.
13. See Ward 1928: 106a.
14. Mantell 1940: 168, 180, 192, 197.
15. Darwin–G. Mantell, 21.4.1843,

Mantell Ms 83/ 33.
16. Hamilton–Mantell, 29.1.1844 and 9.9.1844, Mantell Ms 83/143; Mantell–Grey, 5.6.1846, Mantell Ms 83/418A.
17. Scholefield 1940 II: 355b; Wards 1968: 321.
18. See also Wai-27 R35: 71ff and U10c: 6ff.
19. FitzRoy–Symonds, 27.2.1844, in Mackay 1873 I: 96.
20. Tuckett–Hodgkinson, 16.8.1844, in Hocken 1898: 226ff.
21. Ibid.
22. Wohlers (1895: 84ff) says, 'In his all-round love of mankind, [Tuckett] made no difference between one religion and another. Jews, Heathens, Turks, and Christians were alike to him.'
23. Shortland 1851: 263n.
24. Selwyn 1847: 145.
25. Hocken 1898: 234.

26. Ibid: 203–4.
27. See McLintock 1949: 135–36.
28. Mackay 1873 I: 97.
29. Wohlers 1895: 98. Wohlers thought Watkin was 'half joking'.
30. WJ, 20.4.1844 and 29.6.1844.
31. See *NTR*: 300ff for background to Otago Purchase.
32. Monro–*Nelson Examiner*, 20.7.1844, in Hocken 1898: 243–44.
33. Hocken 1898: 250ff.
34. Mackay 1873 I (ii):21.
35. Wai-27 T1: 89.
36. The name 'Otago' was not officially adopted until 22 June 1848.
37. Wards 1968: 311ff.
38. Clarke 1903: 60ff.
39. W. Wakefield–NZ Company, 31.8.1844, in Hocken 1898: 267.
40. Clarke 1903: 62; Wai-27 V9: 11.
41. *NTR*: 306ff.
42. DOSLIW Crown Land Deeds, Otago No. 3. The Waitangi Tribunal (*NTR*: 311) concluded that the Otago purchase covered about 533,000 acres. The Company retained 150,000 acres, and the rest became Crown land.
43. Atholl Anderson in Oliver 1990: 555a; Tremewan 1994: 40.
44. W. Wakefield–NZ Company, loc. cit.
45. *NTR*: 341.
46. Oliver 1990: 553ff; Hall-Jones 1943: 115ff; Hay 1915: 47ff.
47. Clarke 1903: 62ff; W. Wakefield–NZ Company, loc cit. Clarke's 'Notes' were written from memory in 1893. His celebrated 'elegiac' speech by Tuhawaiki, often cited as if verbatim, was perhaps inspired by late Victorian belief in the inevitable extinction of 'native races'.
48. Tuckett's Journal, 22. 5.1844, in Hocken 1898.
49. Monro–*Nelson Examiner*, loc cit.
50. Delaporte 1986: 11ff, 160–66.
51. Gluckman 1976: 123.
52. See e.g. Simpson 1986: 29 and Wai-27 T1: 48ff.
53. Thomson 1859 I: 216.
54. Dieffenbach 1843 II: 15, 18ff.
55. Wohlers 1895: 189, 198.
56. Fulton 1922: 7ff.
57. 'Report from the Select Committee on New Zealand', House of Commons, 29.7.1844, in *IUPBBPNZ* II: iii–xiv.
58. CMA, L & S G39 40/1–2; Tremewan 1990: 163.
59. Belligny sold Kakongutungutu (150 acres) to the Sinclairs for £345 – more than Ngai Tahu were paid for the entire 1840 French 'purchase'.
60. A copy of Bérard's map is in Grey–Colonial Secretary, 22.3.1849 (No. 30), in *IUPBPPNZ*.
61. Robinson–Richmond, 13.3.1845 and 23.4.1845, NAW New Munster 8 1845: 131, 183. Robinson's favourable reputation seems to originate in his own reports. Sewell (1980 I: 331) said of him in 1852: 'Mr Robinson seems a clever educated man, but everybody speaks of him as dangerous and mischievous.'
62. Deans 1937: 87ff. The Deanses claimed to have already paid Ngai Tahu £20.
63. Andersen 1949: 11–12; Deans 1964: 46.
64. Rhodes Family Ms Papers, CMA Box 8.
65. Wai-27 R36a: 1ff. Dr Ann Parsonson here indicates that the transcript of the Otago deed in Mackay 1873 I: 104 is inaccurate, and she provides an accurate transcript of the original.
66. *AJHR* 1873 G-2B: 17.
67. SNC 4/38: 62; 4/39: 1–3, 83ff; 5/43: 102–3. H. K. Taiaroa (*NZPD* 25: 479a) urges that Otago Maoris were entitled to tenths. According to Mantell (*AJHR*

1872 H-9: 7), Tuhawaiki thought likewise; but it is not clear how Mantell could have known this. See *NTR*: 298–300 and *AJHR* 1891 G-7: 6–7.

68. SNC 4/37: 48–52.
69. Symonds–Superintendent, 2.9.1844, in Mackay 1873 I: 103.
70. *AJHR* 1888 I-8: 74.
71. Gisborne 1897: 16–17.

10

~

Governor Grey

George Grey was always cold, and unimpassioned. His eye was
steely blue.[1]

GOVERNOR FITZROY had been poorly funded by the British Government. The New Zealand Company resented his
decisions, and undermined him. His idealism could not disguise his
financial incompetence – and this, together with Hone Heke's uprising in the north, was enough to discredit him in the House of
Commons, where support for the 1844 select committee's proposals was growing. In April 1845 the Secretary of State for War and
the Colonies, Lord Stanley, sent FitzRoy notice of his recall, indi-
cating as his main fault a failure to report adequately to London.[2]
Six weeks later, Lord Stanley wrote a complimentary letter to the
Governor of South Australia, Captain George Grey, the young army
officer praised in the select committee's report, offering him the
governorship of New Zealand, with double FitzRoy's salary and
three times his funding. Stanley told Grey, regarding this appointment: 'You will honourably and scrupulously fulfil the conditions
of the Treaty of Waitangi,' and 'You will omit no measure within
the reach of prudent legislation or of a wise administration of the
Law, for securing to the aborigines the personal freedom and safety
to which they are entitled.'[3]

In a further despatch, Stanley suggested that Maoris might readily
surrender their 'waste lands' if the lands were taxed.[4] He then sent
Grey a secret despatch allowing him £10,000 in addition to his
official funding. With this sum, Grey was to surreptitiously buy
land for European settlement from Maori tribes, 'with their free
consent'. The New Zealand Company, unaware of this, would continue trying to buy the land allowed them under Pennington's

awards. If they failed, Grey was to make his purchases available to them. Otherwise, he could market them profitably, and buy more.[5] Grey, as it happened, did not need Lord Stanley to teach him how to dissemble.

At four acres for every £1 spent, the Pennington system by now entitled the New Zealand Company to have purchased nearly 900,000 acres of Maori land – of which they wanted about 600,000 acres for their settlements at Wellington, New Plymouth, Nelson, Wanganui, and New Edinburgh, and the rest for future needs. But Lord Stanley, despite the Company's strident protests,[6] insisted that the land could not be Crown-granted unless it had been proved to have been purchased to the satisfaction of the Maori owners.

∽

The Nanto-Bordelaise Company, as we have seen, claimed 30,000 acres at Banks Peninsula. Lord Stanley informed Grey that they were amply entitled to this area, through having spent £11,685 on colonisation at Akaroa. Commissioner Godfrey, now in London, had told the Colonial Under-Secretary, G. W. Hope, that Ngai Tahu would willingly sell 'the greater part of Banks Peninsula'.[7] Stanley therefore told Grey to have the 30,000 acres marked out, and to issue a Crown grant for it. For this, the French were to pay the Maoris compensation, said Stanley, as had been done at Wellington in 1843. There, the New Zealand Government had allowed the New Zealand Company to pay compensation to Maori owners who had been omitted from William Wakefield's 1839 'deeds of purchase', instead of requiring the Company to negotiate the purchases afresh.[8] At Wellington the 'real payment' to Maoris was supposed to have been the 'tenths'. But Stanley did not say Ngai Tahu at Banks Peninsula were to have tenths, or any other reserves. Nor did he specify the amount of compensation.[9]

Grey's most urgent task on arriving in New Zealand in November 1845 was to quell Heke's uprising in the north. This he did decisively, with the aid of Maori allies. But he had to be vigilant. Apart from his private secretary John Symonds, and the Colonial Secretary Andrew Sinclair, he could not be sure whom to trust. His restless mind constantly pondered how to undermine potential enemies. The New Zealand Company's disgruntled settlers were clamouring for land; the Chief Protector George Clarke and his assistants were openly conniving with FitzRoy, who was still in the country; while Archdeacon Henry Williams and his CMS missionaries seemed to Grey to be excessively antagonistic to him.

Grey now acquired a great advantage in dealing with his scattered responsibilities. HMS *Driver*, a brig-rigged, four-gun paddle steamer, arrived on station at Auckland from China in January 1846. Sailing ships had been known to take three weeks or more between Auckland and Wellington; but the paddle steamer, by using much coal, could make the journey in as many days. In the same month, following Grey's claim to have destroyed treasonable letters at a rebel pa, a rumour was circulated that Henry Williams had himself encouraged Heke's rebellion. The New South Wales Protectorate Department was by this time in disfavour with Governor Gipps.[10] In February 1846, after Chief Protector Clarke had refused a demotion, Grey proceeded to dismantle the New Zealand Protectorate Department.[11]

Grey was visited about this time by Commodore Bérard. Grey told him of Lord Stanley's award, and offered to send someone to Akaroa to arrange the transfer of 30,000 acres from Ngai Tahu to the French company. But Bérard hedged. Without mentioning the French 'purchases' of March 1845, he told Grey that Belligny would return from France to deal with the matter.[12] Bérard left New Zealand in April 1846. Belligny never returned.

The New Zealand Company's Wellington settlers claimed the whole Hutt Valley, with its tall forests and fertile soil, as part of William Wakefield's 1839 'purchase' of the region. But Ngati Rangatahi did not recognise the 'purchase', and maintained cultivations there, from which they refused to move without compensation. Grey arrived at Wellington in the *Driver* on 12 February 1846 with five hundred troops – some of which, presumably at Grey's orders, laid waste to Maori dwellings and urupa on the disputed land. In retaliation, Ngati Rangatahi plundered some settlers. The Company thought Te Rangihaeata had instigated this, and wanted him attacked immediately. Instead, Grey got Te Rauparaha's consent to the stationing of troops at Paremata near Te Rauparaha's pa, and ordered a military road to be constructed from Wellington through Ngati Toa territory to Porirua and Paremata, and beyond. Before returning to Auckland, he told Superintendent Richmond to defend the Wellington and Hutt

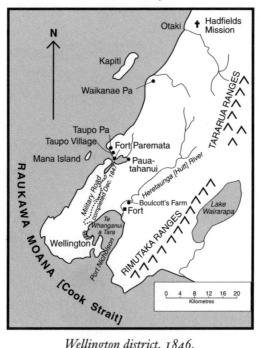

Wellington district, 1846.

Valley settlers, and punish any further Maori hostilities.[13]

Grey, on Lord Stanley's instructions, now Crown-granted the entire 1844 Otago purchase to the New Zealand Company,[14] without providing any Maori reserves within the block. The New Edinburgh leaders had opposed the provision of Maori reserves within the Otago block for the two hundred Otago Maoris, who they thought numbered only fifty,[15] saying: 'Any such reserves would be not only unnecessary but an absolute hindrance to the purposes of the settlers, by interposing unoccupied wastes, and increasing the expense of roads &c, without benefit to anyone.'[16]

Grey now dealt the CMS missionaries a telling blow. Some of them, particularly Henry Williams, had acquired extensive landed estates. In a secret despatch to London in June 1846, Grey reported that this acquisition had been at the expense of Maoris and settlers, and would cost 'a large expenditure of British blood and money'. When referred to the CMS headquarters in London, Grey's statement caused a scandal from which Williams's reputation never recovered. On 1 July, Grey dismissed George Clarke and appointed

Symonds as Native Secretary and Protector of Aborigines, responsible only to himself.[17]

The fall of George Clarke, and the rumours of Henry Williams's
'treason', signified the end of CMS influence in New Zealand government circles, and everyone needed to know it. Walter Mantell, still
unemployed at Taranaki, had shrewdly anticipated Clarke's dismissal.
He wrote to Grey asking for a job, saying that Clarke had refused to
employ him. 'It would almost appear that some obstacle existed to my
employment,' he wrote. But Grey did not lack sycophants, and held
out only a possibility of temporary employment for Mantell.[18]

Among Clarke's former CMS colleagues had been the mission
blacksmith James Kemp. His son Henry Tacy Kemp entered government service in February 1840, and rose by August 1845 to be Native
Secretary and Interpreter for the Southern Districts when Edward
Shortland returned to England. But fate could be unkind to officials of humble origin, in a world where everything depended upon
influence, and patronage. With no family connections of consequence, they had to curry favour with those in power or see their
careers come to a sudden end. Governors needed such men. Having
no alternative but to be loyal, their loyalty was absolute. The advent
of the subtle and unpredictable Grey brought new hazards for government officials. But Kemp could study Grey's foibles and gratify
his whims as he accompanied him on his official rounds in the Southern Districts. Perhaps Kemp came under his spell, as many did, for
Grey had a winning way of seeming to confide even in his juniors.[19]

The lion of Wellington society at this time was the senior military officer, Lieutenant-Colonel William McCleverty, lately arrived
from India on army pay to help the New Zealand Company with
their land problems.[20] The affable McCleverty was no tool of Grey's,
but his dual role marked the close partnership between the Company
and the State in New Zealand. At Wellington, McCleverty supervised
the Company's dealings with Maori tribes. But if the tribes turned
hostile, he would command the government troops against them.

～

The Wanganui fighting chief Te Mamaku of Ngati Haua-te-rangi
was of the traditional Maori school of thought. He abhorred
soldiers being on land belonging to chiefs, for it implied that they
and not the chiefs held the rangatiratanga of the land. On 16 May
1846 he attacked an army outpost at Boulcott's farm in the Hutt

Valley, killing some soldiers. The Hutt Valley war had begun in earnest. Ngati Toa were divided. Te Rauparaha favoured placating the government. His nephew Rawiri Puaha was helping with Grey's Porirua military road. But Te Rangihaeata agreed with Te Mamaku. Settlers could be tolerated on disputed territory so long as the chiefs' rangatiratanga was acknowledged. But as of old, the presence of a rival's warriors on disputed territory could be honourably met only by matching force with force.

Governor Grey, hurrying from Auckland in HMS *Driver* at the news of war, did not concern himself further with the rights and wrongs of the Hutt Valley dispute. Ngati Toa were the dominant tribe in the region, so Grey considered how to fasten a hold on them. His spies reported that Te Rauparaha was aiding Te Rangihaeata secretly, but was himself on a peacetime footing. Grey therefore befriended the leading younger Ngati Toa chiefs – Puaha, Te Whiwhi and Tamihana – who were Christians and no longer deferred to Te Rauparaha, let alone to Te Rangihaeata. He loaded the *Driver* with troops at Wellington, and took Te Whiwhi aboard while he patrolled the Manawatu coast to intercept a Wanganui war party said to be coming south. When heavy seas prevented Grey's intended landing, his thoughts turned to Te Rauparaha at his peacetime village inside Porirua Heads. Stealthily bringing the *Driver* up to the heads by night, Grey sent in a landing party under Midshipman McKillop, who knew Te Rauparaha and his village. Two hundred armed men were in support. At daybreak on 23 July 1846, McKillop's men surrounded Te Rauparaha's dwelling. Without warning, the great chief was seized in his bed, naked and struggling. He was abducted aboard the warship without bloodshed, and without a warrant. Te Whiwhi was on deck to greet him. The greeting was ignored.[21]

The legality of this act remained in doubt.[22] But at one stroke Grey had confounded his Maori adversaries, and had delighted settlers everywhere.[23] He now had Te Rauparaha's heirs under a compelling obligation. He returned with his prisoner to Auckland, where Te Whiwhi joined Tamihana at Bishop Selwyn's Maori missionary college.

∼

Commissioner Spain, in March 1845, before leaving New Zealand, had disallowed William Wakefield's 1839 Cook Strait 'purchases', except for the Port Nicholson block.[24] This confirmed Ngati Toa as still the customary owners of the Porirua block north of Wellington, and of the Wairau block east of Nelson. But, said Spain, Ngati Toa had not effectively occupied the Ngai Tahu territory south of the Wairau, despite their invasions of 1828–1832. Therefore, by Maori custom, Ngati Toa did not own this territory and could not have genuinely sold it to Wakefield.[25] In spite of Spain's findings, however, Ngati Toa continued to claim the South Island by right of conquest, as far south as Banks Peninsula and Arahura. Puaha leased fifty kilometres of this disputed territory – the coast between Wairau and Kekerengu – to the Wellington militia captain Charles Clifford, for a pastoral run.[26]

Grey now prepared for the purchase of the Porirua and Wairau blocks from Ngati Toa.[27] Ever in his mind was the Roman precept 'divide and rule'. In November 1846 he informed his naval commander, and Superintendent Richmond, that Ngati Toa were plotting against the government. He told Richmond to secure Tamihana and Te Whiwhi (now back at Otaki) to the government side, and sent £25 for the purpose. He sent reinforcements to Wellington in December 1846.[28]

But by 1847 the New Zealand Company's land troubles were centred at Wanganui. There the Company had sought land for their settlers to make up for what they could not get for them at Wellington or at Manawatu (which Te Rangihaeata refused to sell). Te Mamaku was now back at Wanganui with his warriors, still resentful of events in the Hutt Valley. The Christian Wanganui tribes welcomed the Company's settlers. Te Mamaku was happy to be their protector. But he would not tolerate soldiers. Amid growing war fever, Te Mamaku and Te Rangihaeata were suspected of plotting afresh the destruction of the Company's settlements.[29] Grey diverted troops to Wanganui. But he did not forget Ngati Toa.

Te Rangihaeata and his militants, driven from the Hutt Valley, had by March 1847 fortified themselves at remote Poroutawao in the Manawatu, to await Grey's expected attack. But Tamihana and Te Whiwhi were supporting Hadfield's peace policies. It was a perplexing time for Ngati Toa. After all their efforts to secure a prosperous haven on the Kapiti coast, their tribal alliances had collapsed and their two greatest chiefs were at odds – the one imprisoned, and the other withdrawn to a distant fighting pa.

For Grey, however, the future seemed assured. Late in 1846 he had learned that Sir Robert Peel had resigned as Prime Minister on 30 June, and that the Whigs were back in office under Lord John

Russell. The views of the 1844 select committee on New Zealand, so favourable to the New Zealand Company and to Captain George Grey, now reigned at the Colonial Office. Earl Grey, who as Lord Howick had chaired the select committee, had replaced Lord Stanley as Secretary of State for War and the Colonies, while Benjamin Hawes, the committee's secretary, was now Earl Grey's Parliamentary Under-Secretary.

Earl Grey had not been an advocate of Captain George Grey's appointment as Governor of New Zealand.[30] Nevertheless, Governor Grey could still be audacious in his official despatches, if he wrote with due deference. In February 1847 he sent Earl Grey a despatch explaining his abolition of the Protector's Department. It had been 'for all practical purposes an utterly useless establishment', he told Earl Grey. 'Neither the Chief Protector of Aborigines, nor his two sons, who were also protectors of aborigines, were fitted by either energy of character, or by their industry, to watch over and promote the interests of the natives,' he said.[31]

Governor Grey now learned from Earl Grey that Parliament had passed a Constitution Act for New Zealand. Two provinces, New Ulster and New Munster, each with a Lieutenant-Governor, replaced the Northern and Southern Divisions, and Grey was 'Governor-in-Chief'. An accompanying Royal Charter prescribed a complex system of government. Derided in England, it was a godsend to Governor Grey, for it was not hard to find reasons for delaying its implementation. His autocratic rule was to continue for six more years.

The Sixth Resolution of the 1844 select committee had stated:

> Means ought to be forthwith adopted for establishing the exclusive title of the Crown to all land not actually occupied and enjoyed by Natives, or held under grants from the Crown; such land to be considered as vested in the Crown for the purpose of being employed in the manner most conducive to the welfare of the inhabitants, whether Natives or Europeans.

In line with this resolution, the Queen's Instructions in the new Royal Charter laid down that no Maori claim to land was to be recognised except for 'land occupied or used by means of labour expended thereon'.[32] The Instructions provided for the registration of cultivated Maori lands, while all other lands were to be proclaimed Crown domain lands.[33] These proposals raised a storm of objections in New Zealand from supporters of the Treaty of Waitangi. Bishop Selwyn and Chief Justice Martin registered their protests in a petition to the Crown. Embarrassed, Governor Grey urged Earl Grey to be cautious over the proposal, pointing out that Maoris still used 'waste lands' for food-gathering.[34]

～

If government troops were again to fight Te Rangihaeata and his supporters, would Puaha, Te Whiwhi and Tamihana keep the rest of Ngati Toa neutral? It seemed to Governor Grey that any doubts besetting these three Christian chiefs might be relieved by suitable compliments, and by gold. After first visiting Nelson,[35] Grey asked the three chiefs in March 1847 to help him arrange a government purchase of the Porirua and Wairau blocks. A price of £2,000 (in instalments) was agreed upon for the Porirua block – an area of 68,896 acres between the Porirua coast and the Hutt River. Of this, Ngati Toa were to retain 11,020 acres in reserves.[36] The Porirua deed and the receipt for the first government payment were signed at Porirua on 1 April 1847 by Puaha, Nohorua, Te Whiwhi, Tamihana and four other Ngati Toa chiefs, and witnessed by army officers including McCleverty and Servantes.[37] Thus Grey got nearly 58,000 acres of land for the Wellington settlement for about eightpence per acre.

As for the Wairau, where Arthur Wakefield and his companions had been been killed in 1843, Ngati Toa understood Grey's request in Maori terms – 'Give me the land where my dead died.' Rawiri Puaha responded in kind: let Ngati Toa have Kaiapoi, where Te Pehi and his companions were killed in 1830.[38] Such an exchange would appease the dead on both sides, government and Ngati Toa, and signify reconciliation. Ngai Tahu, in Ngati Toa's view a vassal tribe, need have no say in the matter.[39]

Grey agreed to pay Ngati Toa £3,000 for the Wairau, with Kaikoura and Kaiapoi and the intervening coast, in five annual instalments, leaving Ngati Toa substantial reserves.[40] Thus the place of Ngati Kuri's and Ngai Tuahuriri's atua, and the bones of their dead, would be forever subject to Ngati Toa. Te Whiwhi, Puaha and Tamihana signed Grey's Wairau deed in Wellington on 18 March 1847 – not publicly in the presence of their people, but privately in the presence of Governor Grey, Colonel McCleverty, Lieutenant Servantes and other Europeans. The three young Ngati Toa chiefs received their first £600 that day.[41] Yet a belief persisted among Ngati Toa, that Grey had made them no payment, and that they

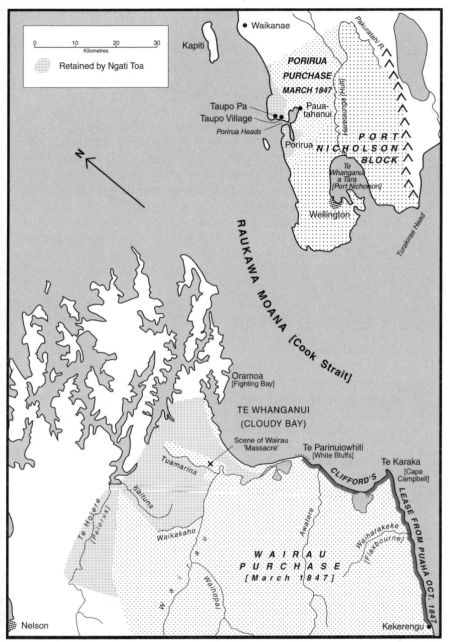

The Port Nicholson Block and Grey's Ngati Toa purchases.

in fact had paid him £200 for Kaiapoi.[42]

The Wairau purchase was worthy of Grey. By a stroke of the pen he had secured the allegiance of Te Rauparaha's heirs, solved the land problem for the New Zealand Company at Nelson, and put both parties in his debt. But he had intervened in a tribal dispute of which he knew little, or nothing. Later, Servantes was to report that the Ngati Toa claim to Kaiapoi had been considered 'doubtful'. He did not think Ngai Tahu had a better claim – or a worse one.[43]

But Grey told the British Government a different story. He said the Ngati Toa claim to the 220 kilometres of coastal territory from Wairau to Kaiapoi 'was identical with their claim to the Valley of the Wairau', implying that it had been approved by Commissioner Spain.[44] But Spain had rejected it, as we have seen. Grey did not investigate who was occupying this coastline. Kaikoura was in fact occupied by Ngati Kuri under their chief Kaikoura Whakatau, who had never been a captive of Te Rauparaha. Grey nevertheless authorised the New Zealand Company to select land for settlers throughout the districts he had just purchased.

Governor Grey gratified the New Zealand Company yet further, before leaving Wellington for Auckland in March 1847 in his new steam sloop HMS *Inflexible*. He proclaimed martial law over the Wanganui district in preparation for war against Te Mamaku and Te Rangihaeata.[45] After he left for Auckland, a Wellington newspaper expressed satisfaction with the Porirua and Wairau purchases, and reported that 'the Natives evinced considerable anxiety for the release of Te Rauparaha, but they were given distinctly to understand that for the present he would not be released'.[46]

Te Rauparaha's captivity in Auckland diminished his influence, while the influence of Puaha, Te Whiwhi and Tamihana increased. The absence of Te Rauparaha and Te Rangihaeata had given the three younger chiefs a free hand in dealing with the government. The Wairau purchase was not a surrender, much less a confiscation such as the colonists had advocated. It was an official acknowledgement that Ngati Toa's rangatiratanga encompassed not only the Wairau, but Kaikoura and Kaiapoi as well – an undoubted success for Ngati Toa, and an unpleasant surprise in store for Ngai Tahu.

On 18 April 1847, Te Rangihaeata raided Kapiti Island for gunpowder, and a settler family named Gilfillan were murdered by Maoris at Wanganui. But Ngati Toa at Porirua remained loyal to the government. Some of them were soon fighting Te Mamaku.[47] Grey could well congratulate himself on his Ngati Toa policy. He was particularly pleased with the compliance of Puaha, whom he described long afterwards as 'one of the best men I have ever known in my life'.[48] And he informed London: 'There can be no doubt that the fact of the Ngatitoa Tribe receiving for several years an annual payment from Government, will give us an almost unlimited influence over a powerful and hitherto a very treacherous and dangerous tribe.'[49]

~

Among those absent from the defence of Kaiapoi in 1832 was a youth named Pakipaki, whose grandfather had purchased residential rights at Tuahiwi in the eighteenth century.[50] Pakipaki had boarded a sailing ship, adopting the name 'Te Hau', or 'Metehau' ('like the wind'). He sailed on American ships for eight years, and returned to New Zealand about 1840, finding work on a government boat at Wellington. Metehau was a man of the times. His years at sea had accustomed him to the cosmopolitan maritime world, and the absence of tribal restraints. He called himself Teoti Wiremu (George William) Metehau, and became a competent letter-writer – an important skill in an age when political excitement was high and not many, European or Maori, could read and write. But he kept his Maori loyalties. At Wellington he became in modern terms a 'land rights activist' – an admirer of Hone Heke, Te Rangihaeata and Te Mamaku.[51] Government officials, including Postmaster Mantell, therefore regarded him as a 'bad character'. Metehau must have been a good seaman to have held his job.

While Wanganui was under martial law in 1847, Governor Grey arrived there on 4 June from Wellington in HMS *Inflexible* with Colonel McCleverty and reinforcements to fight Te Mamaku. Also on board was a dazzling entourage including Waka Nene of Nga Puhi, Te Wherowhero of Waikato, and thirty-five Te Ati Awa to fight for the government. The faithful Kemp was in attendance on Grey.[52] Metehau too was on board: but he must have made his sympathies too obvious, for Kemp had him put ashore 'on suspicion of being a spy'.[53]

Walter Mantell, on the other hand, after his humble letter of 1846 to Governor Grey, had found his fortunes improve. By 1847 he had his outdoor job, supervising Maori workers on Grey's military road out of Wellington. This allowed him time for natural history. Having heard of the Reverend Richard Taylor's discovery in 1843 of fossil flightless birds' bones at Waingongoro in Taranaki, Mantell got leave to go there.[54] He selected some of the best specimens from Taylor's caches, including fossil bones of a large rail, and sent them to his father.[55] Dr Mantell proudly lectured on these specimens at the Geological Society in London to an audience including Charles Darwin, and the fossil rail was named *Notornis mantelli* after its New Zealand 'discoverer'. Thus Walter Mantell was launched in the scientific world, and father and son were reconciled.[56]

~

Edward John Eyre was an English clergyman's son – an awkward figure with a strange gait and a slight speech impediment. He had gone to Australia as a youth in 1832 to prove himself – first as a New South Wales 'overlander', and then in the arid south of the continent while Grey was Governor of South Australia. Eyre's daring feats of exploration displayed more of endurance than of skill. Grey appointed him a resident magistrate, but soon regretted it, for Eyre was wilful. Grey eventually wrote Eyre a glowing testimonial to take back to England – to get rid of him, it was said. The Colonial Office, impressed by this testimonial, appointed Eyre in 1846 to the new post of Lieutenant-Governor of New Munster under the Governor-in-Chief, George Grey. Thus Grey got his unwanted 'protégé' back – and 'no-one was more incredulous at the news than Grey himself', according to a contemporary.[57] When Eyre arrived at Auckland in July 1847, to his surprise Grey did not install him in office but left him to cool his heels for six months.[58]

Governor Grey was informed late in 1847 that Parliament had passed an act giving the New Zealand Company the disposal, for three years, of the Crown demesne in New Munster. The New Zealand Government was to purchase Maori land with funds provided by the Company (from a British Government loan), and the Company would 'have the disposal of the lands so acquired'.[59] Thus the Company, for a period of three years from 5 July 1847, got a monopoly of the Maori land business in New Munster, and the services of the government as its buying agent. Parliament had raised the Company to a pinnacle of favour, and Grey trimmed his sails accordingly.

On 16 January 1848, HMS *Inflexible* arrived off Otaki from Auckland. On board were Grey and his wife, and the aged Te Rauparaha with his friend Te Wherowhero. Grey restored Te

Rauparaha to his people, and then spent a week in Wellington. Among the respectful citizens and government officials who saw him privately was road-construction supervisor Walter Mantell. What passed between them is unknown, but evidently Grey saw in the younger man one on whom he could depend.

Grey at last allowed Eyre to take his oaths of office at Wellington, as Lieutenant-Governor of New Munster, on 28 January 1848. But he allowed Eyre no real authority, and saddled him with tedious administration that sorely tried the 'man of action'. Wellington officials soon learned to take their cues from Grey rather than from their new Lieutenant-Governor.[60] Grey went on to Te Wai Pounamu in the *Inflexible* with his personal staff, his wife, and William Wakefield. His intention, with Wakefield, was to prepare for the purchase from Ngai Tahu of the territory between Otago and Kaiapoi (the Wairau purchase 'boundary'), and to inspect the preparations for the Otago settlement (formerly New Edinburgh), where arrival of the first settlers was at last expected.[61] Thus on a summer evening early in February 1848 the people of Pigeon Bay, both Maori and European, beheld the noisy, outlandish paddle steamer with its clouds of black smoke, clattering and churning into their peaceful, forested harbour, to anchor in the cool shadows at its head. Grey's party went ashore to visit Ebenezer Hay, the Pigeon Bay squatter.

Francis Sinclair, the other original local squatter, had perished with his eldest son on a voyage to Wellington in May 1846. His widow and her surviving children were away from the bay. But they had a French title for their 150 acres of land at Kakongutungutu, which they called Craigforth, and a guarantee from William Wakefield, dated April 1845, for another 350 acres if his company acquired Pigeon Bay within three years.[62] Hay, however, had no title at Pigeon Bay, and had refused to pay rent to Ngai Tahu.[63] When he heard from his distinguished visitors that the New Zealand Company were contemplating a settlement in the district, he asked whether he would keep his farm. Grey referred the question to Wakefield. The Company, said Wakefield, expected an agreement with the French about Banks Peninsula, and would then award Hay 200 acres at Pigeon Bay in place of what he had been entitled to receive in the North Island.[64]

Grey and Wakefield asked Hay about Ngai Tahu's likely attitude to selling land. Hay replied that they were too possessive regarding the land, but were agreeable to European settlement.[65] The *Inflexible* left Pigeon Bay with the Governor's party the following day for

Akaroa. There Grey found no agent of the French company with whom he could arrange the boundaries of their promised 30,000 acres, but he summoned the Ngai Tahu chiefs of the whole district to Akaroa to discuss selling their land to the government.

∾

At two o'clock on the appointed day,[66] Ngai Tahu assembled to hear the man who had subdued Hone Heke and the great Rauparaha. Grey probably saw in the attentive assembly a humble tribe of little account, grateful for his presence among them. He told them he wanted to buy their land for English settlers. He had already purchased Kaikoura and Kaiapoi from Ngati Toa, he said, and wished to join this purchase to the land already purchased at Otago.

When Ngai Tuahuriri heard that Grey had bought Kaikoura and Kaiapoi from Ngati Toa, they objected at once. Te Uki rose to challenge the Governor, and said: 'Ka mea atu ahau ehara tena whenua i a Ngati Toa' – 'That land does not belong to Ngati Toa.'[67] The Governor contradicted him: 'Oh, yes. According to Ngati Toa it belongs to them, and belonged to their ancestors.' At this, other Ngai Tahu protested, and Te Uki again addressed the Governor: 'Do not hide from us what you may have done wrongly with our land, but tell us that we may all know what you have done.'[68]

These words were not welcome to Governor Grey.[69] He was not used to being contradicted to his face, and still less to being admonished in front of his own officials. However, he saw that he now had an advantage. If things were as they said, Ngai Tahu would be desperate to retrieve their rangatiratanga over the land he had purchased from their enemies. The only way they could now retrieve their mana would be to sell him their remaining land in case he paid Ngati Toa for that as well. Grey and Wakefield were now able to write of Ngai Tahu's 'anxiety' to sell their lands to the government.

Grey reply was conciliatory. He promised Ngai Tahu that although Ngati Toa had been paid for Kaikoura, Ngai Tahu would be paid for Kaiapoi,[70] and could keep any other land they wanted.[71] He agreed to review the Wairau purchase according to Maori custom. He invited Te Uki and his companions to come to Wellington later, for a whakawaa. Ngai Tahu would stand on one side, and Ngati Toa on the other, and Grey would uphold whichever side could establish the best claim to the disputed territory. The Ngai Tahu chiefs agreed to this proposal.[72] Pigeon Bay was then discussed, and Tikao asked that part of it be left in Maori ownership.[73]

Finally it was agreed that if Grey sent a commissioner to Akaroa, Ngai Tahu would discuss selling the land between the Ngati Toa boundary and the Otago purchase, provided that the payment for Kaiapoi was given to Ngai Tahu and not to Ngati Toa; it was the prerogative of Kaikoura Whakatau and Ngati Kuri to be paid for Kaikoura. Wakefield understood from this discussion that the land to be purchased from Ngai Tahu was 'the level country back to the central range of mountains'.[74]

~

HMS *Inflexible*, at six knots, reached Otakou from Akaroa in twenty-four hours, and anchored near Karetai's kainga. But instead of visiting the tangata whenua, Grey set out for the head of the harbour with his wife and Wakefield, in the boat of their host Charles Kettle, now the Company's chief Otago surveyor. After spending two days satisfying himself with the preparations for the new settlement, Grey returned to his warship and sent for the Otakou chiefs. He told them he wished to join the Otago purchase to the land he had purchased from Ngati Toa, and would send a commissioner to negotiate with them. He dismissed the chiefs, and returned to Wellington in the *Inflexible*.[75]

Grey wanted to send a commissioner to Ngai Tahu from Wellington at once, but Wakefield wanted the Surveyor-General at Auckland to do the job.[76] Grey therefore instructed Eyre to prepare for the purchase – and then, from Auckland, told him that the Surveyor-General could not be spared. Eyre's Native Secretary, Henry Tacy Kemp, must be sent on the mission, said Grey, as interpreter if not as commissioner.[77]

Grey had agreed with Wakefield, without consulting Ngai Tahu, that their payment was to be £2,000, in instalments of £500 per year over four years.[78] With Earl Grey in charge of the Colonial Office, and George Grey in charge of New Zealand, the official policy on Maori lands was now identical with that of the New Zealand Company.[79] Cash payments were to be trifling, and issued in instalments. The real payment for the Maoris would be in the benefits of civilisation.

Eyre duly commissioned Kemp for the Ngai Tahu purchase, and got him a berth in HM sloop *Fly* under Commander Oliver, who had been ordered to visit the Auckland Islands to see whether the whaling stations rumoured to be operating there required some reinforcement of British sovereignty. Eyre gave Kemp some written instructions from Grey, emphasising the following duty:

> To reserve to the Natives ample portions for their present and prospective wants, and then, after the boundaries of these reserves have been marked, to purchase from the Natives their right to the whole of the remainder of their claims to land in the Middle Island.[80]

Before boarding the *Fly*, Kemp saw William Wakefield, who was providing the purchase money on behalf of the New Zealand Company. According to Wakefield, Banks Peninsula was not part of the purchase. It had all been 'sold to the French company' by Ngai Tahu, and the New Zealand Company in London were about to buy out the French.[81] Thus Kemp embarked on his mission armed with the doctrine that all 250,000 acres of Banks Peninsula were French property. Yet it would have been strange if Wakefield had believed this to be the case, for he had just been at Banks Peninsula with Grey, who had known for two years that the French were entitled only to 30,000 acres of it.

Notes

1. F. D. Bell, Hocken Ms NZ Notes: 72. Concerning Grey's character, see also Rutherford 1961; Godley 1951: 130; Gisborne 1897: 36.
2. Stanley–FitzRoy, 30.4.1845, Peel Ms Papers.
3. Stanley–Grey, 13.6.1845, in *IUPBPPNZ* IV: 574ff.
4. Wards 1968: chapter 5.
5. Stanley–Grey (secret), 28.6.1845, APL GNZ Mss 38.
6. See Aglionby–Peel, 18.7.1845, Peel Ms Papers 40571. Shown the New Zealand Company's protest against Stanley's decision, Peel remarked on the Company's 'cunning scribes'. On Under-Secretary Hope's draft reply, Peel noted: 'Your draft like Sir John Cutler's worsted stockings is so darned that it is not easy to discover the staple' (ibid, 40573).
7. Godfrey–Hope, 2.7.1845, in Wai-27 L3 II: 178–79. Stanley–Grey, 6, 7.7.1845, in *IUPBPPNZ* IV: 574ff; Tremewan 1990: 279–96.
8. See Hamer & Nicholls 1990: 50ff; Jellicoe 1930: 41ff. The idea was William Wakefield's.
9. See Mackay 1873 I: 78ff. Hawes–Mallieres,19.12.1848, (ibid) states: 'All that remains to be done is to determine the particular tract [of 30,000 acres] to be assigned to this Company.'
10. Woolmington 1988: 116–22.
11. Rutherford 1961: 97–98
12. Bérard–Navy Minister, 20.5.1846, quoted in Tremewan 1990: 290.
13. Wards 1968: 214–300.
14. Stanley–Grey, 15.8.1845, in *IUPBPPNZ* V: 252ff.
15. Mackay 1873 II: 126; Wakefield in Hocken 1898: 270.

16. Cargill–Harington, 29.8.1845, in Wai-27 C2.6: 6ff.
17. McLintock 1958: 200ff.
18. Mantell–Grey, 5.6.1846, and minute, Mantell Ms 83/418A; Hamilton–Mantell, 29.1.1844, 9.9.1844, Mantell Ms 83/143.
19. See Meredith 1935: 55–56; Reeves 1898: 176.
20. Jellicoe 1930: passim; McLintock 1958: 225–26; Wards 1968: passim.
21. Oliver 1990: 507a; Kemp 1901; McKillop 1849: 199ff.
22. Wards 1968: 296.
23. See Deans 1937: 109.
24. See DOSLIW Maps W48ff.
25. Spain–FitzRoy, 31.3.1845, in *IUPBPPNZ* V: 49–50. For Maori custom regarding rau patu, see Buck 1950: 380–81, Kawharu 1977: 41, 56, Martin 1860: 18–19.
26. SNC 4/27: 570ff; Allan 1965: 388.
27. Memo in Grey–Gladstone, 14.9.1846, in *IUPBPPNZ* V: 609ff.
28. Grey–Hayes, 14.12.1846, Grey Ms Letterbook 1847–1853: 170–97.
29. Wards 1968: 322–28.
30. Hope–Peel, 17.2.1848, Peel Ms Papers 40600.
31. Grey–Earl Grey, 4.2.1847, in *BPPNZ* 1847: 92.
32. Mackay 1873 II: 212.
33. Earl Grey–Grey, 23.12.1846, in *IUPBPPNZ* V: 520ff.
34. Grey–Earl Grey, 7.4.1847, in *IUPBPPNZ* VI: 14ff.
35. For Grey's presence at Nelson, see Grey Ms Letterbook 1847–1853: 216–217.
36. See DOSLIW Wellington 144 and Map W48.
37. DOSLIW Wellington 144.
38. See Kawharu 1977: 56-57. By Maori custom, a tribe could claim an interest in a place where a chief had been slain, but not its ownership unless the other side gifted it.
39. Te Kanae Ms 1888: 19; SNC 4/31: 624, 7/94: 2, 725. See also Servantes 'Memorandum', 4.9.1850, in Grey–Eyre, 17.10.1850, NAW New Munster.
40. Power 1849: 138; Servantes, loc cit.
41. DOSLIW Marlborough 1 ('true copy'); SNC 4/27: 569–70.
42. See Te Kanae Ms 1888: 19.
43. Servantes, loc cit.
44. Grey–Earl Grey, 26.3.1847, in Mackay 1873 I: 201–2.
45. Wards 1968: 328.
46. *NZS*, 20.3.1847. George Clarke claimed Grey had 'wrung and wrested' the Wairau from Ngati Toa by threatening not to release Te Rauparaha unless they signed the Deed (Ms Williams Papers, Folder 28.156. Letter 445). The story has had some currency (Rutherford 1961: 66, Burns 1980: 284), but Ngati Toa evidence contradicts it. See Te Kanae Ms 1888; Te Whiwhi SNC 4/27.
47. Wards 1968: 343.
48. SNC 4/31: 624ff.
49. Grey–Earl Grey, 26.3.1847, loc cit.
50. Stack, in *AJHR* 1890 G-1: 22.
51. Mantell–Colonial Secretary, 15.6.1849, NAW 97/6.62; Tau (Ms 1992: 300) says that Metehau worked in America.
52. Wards 1968: 339.
53. Kemp–Eyre, in Eyre–Grey, 21.6.1849, NAW 97/6: 62.
54. Mantell Ms Notes of a Journey; Andersen Ms typed note AMIL.
55. G. A. Mantell–Owen, 27.11.1848, Mantell Ms 83/77; *NZI* V: 95–99. Mantell subsequently apologised for 'poaching' (*NZI*, loc cit.)
56. Mantell 1940: 218–19. On 6.11.1849, Gideon Mantell received '2 boxes from Walter – a marvellous collection of moa bones – many beautiful tertiary shells' (ibid: 244–47).
57. See Hocken Ms NZ Notes.
58. Scholefield 1940 I: 235ff.

59. Earl Grey–Grey, 19.6.1847, in *IUPBPPNZ* V: 115–17.
60. Gisborne 1897: 43–44; McLintock 1958: 215ff; Thatcher–Mantell, 24.1.1848, Mantell Ms 83/143. Captain Hoseason of the *Inflexible* said Eyre was so fond of his dress uniform that he slept in it (McLintock 1958: 216n).
    E. G. Wakefield said Grey was jealous of Eyre as a 'rival explorer' (Wakefield–Rintoul, 16.4.1853, in Canterbury Papers II).
61. Wakefield–Harington, 29.2.1848, in *IUPBPPNZ* VIII: 167ff.
62. CMA, L&S G39 40/2: 35.
63. Hay 1915: 10ff; Shortland 1851: 272–80.
64. Deans 1937: 125–26.
65. Hay, loc cit.
66. Mantell Ms 1537: 34. Tikao told Mantell six months later, that Grey's meeting commenced 'at 2pm on the 14th of February'.
67. SNC 7/96: 3, 731–32.
68. Tiramorehu–Eyre, 22.10.1849, in
69. See McLintock 1958: 241, 309, regarding Grey's reaction to opposition.
70. Tiramorehu–Eyre, loc cit.
71. Mantell Ms 1537: 39.
72. SNC 7/96 Te Uki, loc cit.
73. Tikao–Grey 15.10.1850, Grey Ms G618/272: 319–21, APL.
74. Wakefield–Harington, 29.2.1848, loc cit.
75. Ibid.
76. Grey–Earl Grey, 25.8.1848, in Mackay 1873 I: 208.
77. Grey–Eyre, 8.4.1848, in Mackay 1873 I: 208.
78. Grey–Earl Grey, 25.8.1848, loc cit.
79. Harington–Earl Grey, 7.4.1848, in *IUPBPPNZ* VI: 144.
80. Grey–Eyre, 8.4.1848, loc cit; Eyre–Kemp, 25.4.1848, in *AJHR* 1888 I-8: 7ff.
81. Wakefield–Eyre, 25.4.1848, in *IUPBPPNZ* VIII: 226.

Mackay 1873 I: 227.

11

Kemp's Purchase

DURING THE 1840s the Maoris of southern New Zealand supplied the colonial market with potatoes and other produce, despite being afflicted by recurring epidemics. Enterprising chiefs operated coastal trade in their own vessels.[1] In 1844, European visitors remarked at Maori agriculture from Foveaux Strait to Banks Peninsula. They saw 'flourishing potato gardens' at Bluff and Molyneux.[2] At Waikouaiti, 'almost every Maori farmer had a patch of wheat, which seemed to have succeeded very well'.[3] At Puari, largest of Ngai Tahu settlements, there were 'numerous and extensive cultivations skirting the wood'.[4]

In 1848 Europeans saw 'excellent wheat and potatoes' grown by Maoris at Arowhenua,[5] and pumpkins, maize and vegetable marrows were grown as well.[6] The production of traditional foods was also maintained. Visitors could obtain ti-kauru and kanakana as well as flour and salt.[7] Murihiku Maoris brought wheat to Dunedin and other European settlements, along with pigs and potatoes.[8] At Taieri, the chief Te Raki grew wheat 'very large and plump in the ear'.[9] Puari was 'a fine little settlement with about 250 acres of woodland under wheat and potatoes'.[10]

Recognising the value of wool and meat on the colonial market, Maoris learned stock-farming skills from European settlers. At Pigeon Bay they were 'good shearers, capital hands in the bush with an axe, and industrious as cultivators'.[11] Benefiting from European contact, a policy initiated by Te Maiharanui and Te Whakataupuka, was thus maintained. The new settlement foreshadowed by Governor Grey now promised Ngai Tahu yet more trade, perhaps rivalling that of Ngati Toa. But trade depended on having land to raise the produce that trade required. Maori travellers knew the fate of landless people, such as the Aborigines begging on Sydney streets.

177

As we have seen, Governor Grey in 1846 demurred at Earl Grey's proposal for declaring uncultivated Maori lands 'waste lands of the Crown'. But he revived the same idea himself in a despatch to London dated 15 May 1848, after Commissioner Henry Kemp had left for Akaroa. After complimenting Earl Grey on his wisdom, and himself on his farsightedness, Governor Grey said he had 'discovered a principle' for getting Maoris to surrender their 'waste lands'. Instead of first reserving for them what they wished to keep when he bought a block of their land, Grey said, he now obtained the surrender of the entire block 'for a trifling consideration', and later gave back 'an adequate portion' as reserves. The Maoris, said Grey, regarded such reserves as 'a boon conferred by the Government', and would soon abandon and forget their 'invalid' claims to more extensive territory.[12] Although Grey described this as something he had done, he had not done it. But he evidently thought it was as good as done. In the same despatch, Grey described in glowing terms his contribution to the advancement of the Maori people. 'The payment they receive for their land,' he wrote, 'enables them to purchase stock and agricultural implements.'

Governor Grey, as we have seen, had arranged with William Wakefield for the New Zealand Company to pay Ngai Tahu only £2,000 for the new multi-million-acre block to be purchased from them – a fraction of the price per acre that Ngati Toa and the Wanganui tribes had been paid for their land.[13] What 'stock and agricultural implements' could Ngai Tahu buy for £2,000? In 1847, the Deans brothers had paid over £500 in Sydney for 600 sheep, of which 430 survived the voyage to Port Cooper.[14] William Rhodes at Akaroa thought a thousand sheep the minimum needed for a profitable sheep run.[15] Thus £2,000 could provide Ngai Tahu with stock and implements for one such farm, and perhaps a smaller one as well – and there were at least 1,333 Maoris with rights in the block.[16] Two such farms could not possibly have supported such a number of people. Governor Grey gave Earl Grey a curious reason for fixing Ngai Tahu's payment so low: 'It was as large an amount as they could profitably spend, or as was likely to be of any real benefit to them.'[17]

∽

Commissioner Kemp arrived at Akaroa from Wellington in HM sloop *Fly* on 2 May 1848, in wintry weather. He announced that the purchase of land from Ngai Tahu would be negotiated there when he had brought interested chiefs from Otago. The *Fly* then sailed for Otago, but was driven off on a stormy voyage to the Auckland Islands, and Kemp only reached Otago four weeks later.[18] The first of the long-awaited Scottish colonists had arrived there on 23 March. When the assembled Otago chiefs heard Kemp explain his proposal, Karetai was unwilling to go to Akaroa.[19] The proposed purchase came almost within sight of the Otakou marae, and could have been discussed there and then. Finally Kemp persuaded Karetai and about eleven others from Otakou and Waikouaiti to go with him to Akaroa on the *Fly*. Charles Kettle also embarked, under instructions from the New Zealand Company to assist Kemp – who, however, did not divulge his own official instructions to Kettle.[20] Kettle took surveying instruments to mark out Maori reserves, and a self-made map of the territory – for Kemp had no map.[21]

On board HM sloop *Fly*, the Maoris were quartered with the marines. On the first morning at sea, they went aft while the marines did their deck drill. The mists lifted, revealing the mountains beyond the Waitaki plain. Kemp was asked the boundaries of the land he wished to buy. The Maoris understood him to say, 'It is along the base of the hills, taking in the plain.'[22] The *Fly* reached Akaroa on 4 June. Kemp went to Captain Bruce's hotel, Kettle went to Police Magistrate Watson's house, and the Otago chiefs went to see their relations.[23]

The five-week interval between Kemp's first visit to Akaroa and his subsequent return enabled Ngai Tuahuriri to reach a decision regarding their own exclusive territory, which lay between the Hurunui and Waikirikiri Rivers. Aware that the New Zealand Company wanted Port Cooper and the adjacent plains, Ngai Tuahuriri had decided on selling the territory north of the Rakahuri River that Grey had already paid Ngati Toa for, together with the territory between the Waimakariri and Waikirikiri Rivers, which gave direct access to the port, and within which the Deanses were already farming. Ngai Tuahuriri would keep the 100,000-hectare block between the Waimakariri and Rakahuri, and thus retain the best of both worlds: their traditional heartland, and the advantage of a European colony close at hand.[24]

At noon on Saturday, 10 June 1848, after days of wintry squalls, some five hundred Ngai Tahu assembled at Akaroa in bright sunshine, in their various divisions, at the 'English blockhouse' – a wooden fort built by the French in 1843 near Bruce's hotel. Ngai Tuahuriri formed the largest contingent. Among them was Metehau, whose knowledge of the North Island land business[25] had found him a kindred spirit in John Tikao. At a tribal hui of this kind, senior chiefs were expected to defend the interests of their hapu. Others had to defend their whanau's rights. Every rangatira could have his say. All must be truthful, for watching over all was the spirit of Rakaihautu, the shaper of the land, the foot-piece of whose digging stick (the crag of Tuhiraki) towered above the harbour.

～

When Kemp appeared before the assembled Ngai Tahu, the customary speech-making began. Spokesmen for each tribal division recited the names of the lands they claimed to hold, in case others wished to challenge them. From the north, Ngai Tuahuriri named the lands from Waiau-ua to Waikirikiri. Taiaroa named those from Waikirikiri to Waitaki, Horomona Pohio those from Waitaki to Moeraki, and Te Whaikai Pokene and other Otago chiefs completed the call down to Purehurehu, the northern boundary of the Otago purchase. All these lands were on the eastern side of the island.[26] Kemp then repeated that his mission was to 'join' the Ngati Toa purchase with the Otago purchase, as Governor Grey had proposed.

Ngai Tuahuriri replied first. Paora Tau was their senior spokesman, Te Uki was their orator, Tiramorehu was their most learned man, and Tikao was their businessman. Their first concern was to see whether Governor Grey had kept his promise to return them Kaiapoi and the land northwards. Tau therefore offered to sell Kemp the land between the Rakahuri and Hurunui. Kemp asked where these rivers were. When Tau explained that they were north of Kaiapoi, Tiramorehu recalled later, Kemp 'shut him up at once', saying, 'That land has long since been sold by Ngati Toa. It is from Kaiapoi in another direction I want to talk to you about.'[27]

Thus it was clear that Grey had broken his promise to return the Kaiapoi territory to Ngai Tahu.[28] Some wanted no further dealings with Kemp. But the senior chiefs decided to bide their time for the whakawaa that Grey had promised. Tau announced that Ngai Tuahuriri would not recognise Ngati Toa's sale of Kaiapoi and the land northwards,[29] but would agree to the sale of the land from Kaiapoi south to Purehurehu, with an inland boundary along the coastal mountains from Maungatere to Maungaatua. Kemp made no reply.[30]

Opposite: *Kemp's purchase and the Port Cooper district, 1848.*

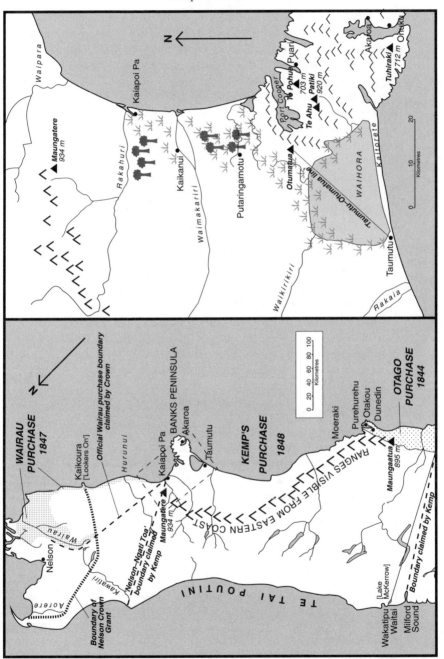

Tikao then named £5 million as the price for the territory being offered. Ngai Tahu wanted to buy plenty of sheep and cattle with the proceeds of the sale, as Governor Grey had suggested.[31] When Kemp said that he could pay only £2,000, Tikao, with the approval of the gathering, said he would not get the land for so little. Next, Te Uki rose to specify the land Ngai Tuahuriri intended to keep. He personified his hapu in traditional fashion: 'Mr Kemp, I will keep a firm hold upon the land between Rakahuri and Waimaka-riri, with my mahinga kai; also my eel weirs, I will keep possession of these, also my sacred places.'[32]

Tiramorehu then explained that in view of Kemp's small price, Ngai Tahu would have to keep all their mahinga kai, and the kainga nohoanga that went with them, and the fisheries in the rivers and lakes, and ample farm land besides, to support themselves and their children after them. The Europeans could have the rest, which would be the greater part.[33] The Maoris argued heatedly with Kemp about this, and the price, while Kemp noted down the speakers' names.[34] Among them was his old acquaintance, Metehau. At last Kemp agreed that Ngai Tahu could keep their mahinga kai and kainga nohoanga, and ample reserves besides.[35] At 4 pm the winter sun sank behind the snow-capped hills beyond Akaroa Harbour. Kemp announced he would leave Akaroa in two days' time, and the Maoris must decide by then whether to accept his terms. The meeting dispersed.

Taiaroa now saw Kemp privately, and offered him the land south of the Waikirikiri for £1,000.[36] Dissension settled also on the Ngai Tuahuriri camp. Metehau supported Tikao in vehemently opposing the sale of the land for less than its market value.[37] But the senior chiefs, veterans of the wars with Te Rauparaha, saw things differently. For them, rescuing the mana of Ngai Tuahuriri from the stigma of the Wairau purchase was more important than any commercial bargain. Ngati Toa still claimed rangatiratanga over the land as far south as the Waikirikiri, and would no doubt sell Grey all of it just as readily as they had sold him Kaikoura and Kaiapoi. In that case Ngai Tuahuriri would lose all their land. Only by signing an official deed confirming that the remaining land was Ngai Tahu's and not Ngati Toa's, could this danger be averted. Throughout Sunday, Ngai Tuahuriri argued among them-selves. All agreed on one thing: that the sale must leave ample resources for their continued prosperity. They sent Kemp a letter reaffirming Te Uki's statement that as a condition of the sale they must retain the territory between the Waimakariri and Rakahuri Rivers.[38]

~

Kemp, according to his official instructions, as we have seen, was now required to visit with Kettle all the Maori settlements in the block he was purchasing, and mark out the Maori reserves. Instead, he followed the 'principle' Governor Grey had described in his despatch of 15 May. He again met Taiaroa at Watson's house, and discussed payment by instalments. Taiaroa offered to forgo Otago's share until the second instalment. Kemp told him that those wanting a share of the first instalment (£500) were to follow him (Kemp) on board the *Fly* next morning.[39] Thus Kemp planned to get the deed signed and a payment made before allocating any reserves. As he stated many years later, he had never intended otherwise.[40]

Signing a purchase deed aboard a warship was a novel procedure, but it suited Kemp's purpose. No one could board without permission, and Kemp would invite only senior chiefs, for deck space on the sloop was limited.[41] Once aboard, the chiefs would be on a strange deck in the presence of armed men. They would recall how Te Rauparaha had been abducted on the *Driver* two years earlier, and how Kemp had been there when it was done.

On Monday morning, 12 June, Kemp and his party boarded the *Fly*, followed by Taiaroa and the Otago chiefs.[42] Kemp and Kettle went below – Kemp to engross his deed in Maori, and Kettle to prepare a 'plan', really a sketch map, to 'connect with the deed'. This showed a distorted outline of much of Te Wai Pounamu, based on the faulty charts of the time. Meanwhile, Paora Tau, Te Uki, Te Whakarukeruke, Tikao, and other senior chiefs, also boarded the sloop. Sentries guarded a rope stretched across the deck separating Maori from European. Kemp emerged and read his deed aloud:

Wakarongo mai e nga Iwi katoa – ko matou ko nga Rangatira, ko nga Tangata o Ngaitahu kua tuhi nei i o matou ingoa i o matou tohu ki tenei pukapuka i tenei ra i te 12 o Hune, i te tau tahi mano, waru rau wha tekau ma waru, ka whakaae kia tukua rawatia atu kia Wairaweke (William Wakefield) te Atarangi o te Whakaminenga o Niu Tireni e noho ana ki Ranana, ara ki o ratou Kaiwhakarite, o matou whenua, o matou oneone katoa e takoto haere ana i te taha tika o tenei moana, timata mai i Kaiapoi i te tukunga a Ngatitoa, i te rohe hoki o Whakatu, haere tonu, tae tonu ki Otakou, hono tonu atu ki te rohe o te tukunga a Haimona, haere atu i tenei tai, a, te mounga o Kaihiku, a, puta atu ki tera tai ki Wakatipu Waitai (Milford Haven) – Otira kei te pukapuka Ruri te tino tohu, te tino ahua o te whenua, – Ko o matou Kaainga nohoanga ko a matou mahinga kai, me waiho marie mo mo matou, mo a matou tamariki, mo muri iho i a matou; a ma te Kawana e whakarite mai hoki tetehi wahi mo matou a mua ake nei, a te wahi e ata ruritia ai te whenua e nga Kai Ruri – ko te nui ia o te whenua, ka tukua whakareretia mo nga pakeha, oti tonu atu. Ko te Utu kua tukua mai mo matou e Rua mano pauna moni (£2,000) – e tuawha-tia mai te utunga mai o enei moni kia matou, Utua mai kia matou inaianei, e Rima rau pauna (£500), kei tera utunga e £500, kei tera atu e £500, kei tera rawa atu, e £500 huihuia katoatia e £2,000. Koia tenei tuhituhinga i o matou ingoa i o matou tohu, he whakaaetanga nuitanga no matou, i tuhia ki konei ki Akaroa, i te 12 o Hune 1848.[43]

This conveyed the following meaning to the Maoris present:

Hear this, all people! We, the chiefs, the people of Ngai Tahu, who have signed our names and marks to this document on this 12th day of June in the year 1848, have agreed to surrender entirely to Wideawake (William Wakefield) – the shadow of the Assembly of New Zealand in London, that is, their directors – our lands, all our soil lying along the coast of this ocean, beginning at Kaiapoi where Ngati Toa sold, and at the boundary of Whakatu, continuing on to Otakou, joining the boundary of Symonds's purchase, continuing from this ocean until it reaches the mountains of Kaihiku, then continuing on to the other ocean at Wakatipu Waitai (Milford Haven). However, the particular shape or appearance of the land will be revealed on the survey map. Our places of residence and our food-gathering places are to be left to us without impediment for our children, and for those after us. The Governor will set aside some portion for us later when the land has been clearly surveyed by the surveyors – the greater part of the land will be given to the Europeans for ever. The payment made to us is two thousand pounds, to be paid in instalments. Paid to us now, £500, the next payment £500, the following payment £500, the last payment £500, making a total of £2,000. We express our agreement by signing our names and marks here at Akaroa on the 12th of June 1848.[44]

Thus the deed promised Ngai Tahu their mahinga kai and kainga nohoanga, and more land when the surveying was done, as Ngai Tuahuriri had requested.

But when Tikao heard instalments mentioned, he objected at once, as this method of payment had not been openly discussed. Others supported him. Kemp then said to Tikao, 'I thought we had finished our dispute on shore, and that the whole thing would be settled now you have come on board the vessel.' Tikao would not back down. Some of the chiefs then understood Kemp to say (although he later denied it) that if they refused the money, it would be paid to Ngati Toa, and soldiers would take possession of the land. At this, Tikao told Kemp to keep his money, and got his boatmen to row him ashore.[45]

Taiaroa then said to Paora Tau and Te Whakarukeruke, 'Why are you allowing the money for your land to be taken away and paid over to Ngati Toa? I should have thought you would be glad to get it.'[46] Others sided with Taiaroa, who again offered Kemp the territory south of the Waikirikiri. But this territory gave no access to Port Cooper, for which Kemp needed at least some Ngai Tuahuriri signatures. Tau then repeated Ngai Tuahuriri's consent to the sale of the east coast lands from Maungatere to Maungaatua.[47] Without further ado, Kemp went below for the money. The Maoris argued among themselves, and Tikao was hailed back to the ship.

Kemp returned on deck, spread out the deed, and wrote Taiaroa's name on it. Taiaroa drew a careful spiral alongside. Kemp then wrote the names of Maopo of Ngati Moki, Paora Tau and Koti of Ngai Tuahuriri, and Tainui of Kaikanui and Te Tai Poutini. Each took the pen and drew a distinctive tohu beside his name. Kemp next wrote Karetai's name, but Karetai did not sign. Next, Kiriona Pohau of Kaitorete, Wiremu Te Raki of Otakou, and Solomon Pohio of Waikouaiti wrote their names in turn. Pohio also wrote the names of Te Whaikai and Rangi Whakana, who did not sign. Potiki then signed with a tohu, and Te Kahu wrote his baptismal name, 'Tiare Wetere' ('Charles Wesley').

Tikao now returned on board. When he saw what had happened, he bitterly reproached Paora Tau. But he wrote his name on the deed, as did John Pere, Te Uki, Tiramorehu, Korehe and Pukenui, making sixteen signatures – ten by autograph and six by tohu. 'There was a great deal of confusion going on,' Te Uki recalled later. 'People were all wandering about. We thought it was simply a receipt for the money.'[48]

Kemp paid half his £500 instalment to Tikao for Ngai Tuahuriri,

and half to Taiaroa for those south of Waikirikiri. He left no copy
of the deed for Ngai Tahu, but said he would soon return and mark
out the promised reserves. The chiefs went ashore, Commander
Oliver weighed anchor, and HM sloop *Fly* sailed for Wellington.

∽

Kemp's deed states that the land purchased was to be more clearly
defined in a pukapuka ruri, or survey map. But unknown to the chiefs,
Kettle's sketch map was attached to the deed.[49] Unlike the deed,
the map showed Banks Peninsula as already sold to the French.[50]
Kettle had sketched in his idea of the 'Kaihiku' and 'Maungaatua'
mountains, with Wakatipu Waitai (now Lake McKerrow) wrongly
labelled 'Milford Haven', and Kaiapoi some sixty kilometres north
of its true position. This was the so-called 'pukapuka ruri'. But it
was certainly not a survey map.

Kettle evidently thought his sketch map faithfully indicated the
boundaries described in the deed. But what Kemp had in the deed
differed from what Kettle had on his sketch map. According to the
deed, Ngai Tahu had sold the land and soil 'Lying along the coast of
this ocean' and 'continuing on to the other ocean at Lake McKerrow'.
But Kettle's map showed the purchase to include most of Te Wai
Pounamu from west coast to east coast, with a northern coast-to-
coast boundary as a straight line devoid of the identifying place names
customary for Maori boundaries. Kemp had presumably obtained
'Wakatipu Waitai' from Taiaroa as a southern West Coast place name.
But neither the deed nor the sketch map gave any other West Coast
name.[51] No West Coast lands were named during the negotiations,
and no one had claimed the right to sell them.

Ngai Tuahuriri later denied agreeing to sell the West Coast to
Kemp. They thought they were selling the land that Tau had
described, between the east coast and the coastal ranges. People
had come to the negotiations, or stayed away, thinking Kemp was
buying only Kaiapoi, or east coast lands.[52] Otago Maoris could sell
to Wakatipu Waitai if they wished, but this did not oblige others to
sell to the West Coast. Indeed, its sale would require the consent of
its residents, especially the senior Poutini chiefs Tuhuru, Koeti and
Taetae, none of whom had been present at Akaroa.

Kemp tried to reconcile Kettle's sketch map with his deed. The
deed gave the northern boundary as 'Kaiapoi, where Ngati Toa sold,

Opposite: *Part of an official copy of Kettle's sketch map for Kemp's purchase.*

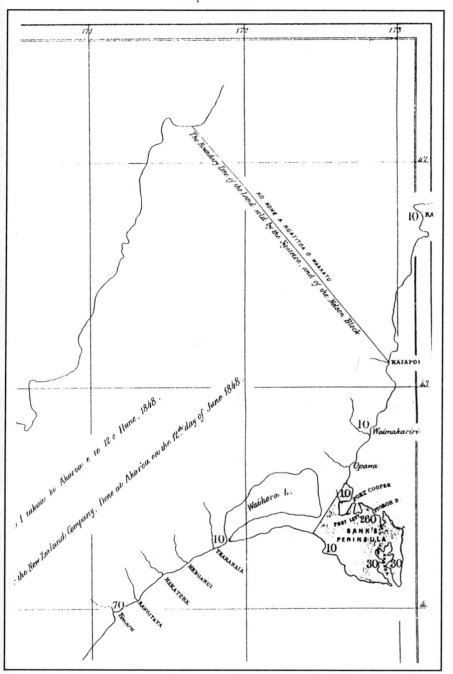

and at the boundary of Whakatu'. Therefore Kemp wrote on the Kettle's northern boundary, 'Ko rohe a Ngatitoa o Whakatu' (the boundary of Ngatitoa and Nelson), and in English, 'The boundary line of the land sold by the Ngatitoa and of the Nelson Block' – the 'Nelson Block' being the territory to be Crown-granted for the Nelson settlement.

But the Wairau deed, which Kemp himself had drawn up,[53] says, 'Ko Wairau haere atu Kaparatehau, te Karaka, haere rawa atu Kaikoura, Kaiapoi atu' ('From Wairau along to Lake Grassmere and Cape Campbell, along to Kaikoura until Kaiapoi').[54] Thus the 'Ngati Toa boundary' did not extend inland from Kaiapoi. Nor did the Nelson block extend to the West Coast. Its boundary began near the Aorere River and officially ran thence via the Nelson lakes to 'the East Coast, terminating at a place called Kaiapoi or Lookers On, thence by the East Coast to Cape Campbell'.[55] 'Lookers On' was actually Kaikoura, not Kaiapoi. With Crown officials so confused about the 'boundary of Whakatu', the expression could have meant little to Ngai Tahu.

～

Once back in Wellington, Kemp announced that he had made a vast acquisition, later estimated at twenty million acres. He had made no record of his negotiations, but reported that all Ngai Tahu had agreed to the sale. He concealed the fact that the deed had been signed aboard the warship, by stating that it had been 'duly executed by the native chiefs, in the presence and with the consent of the people'. The deed had only sixteen Maori signatures, as we have seen, but Kemp claimed it had forty.[56] Indeed, it had forty Maori names, but twenty-four were unsigned – twenty-two of them written in Kemp's hand and the other two in Pohio's. Nevertheless, all were 'witnessed' by Commander Oliver and Lieutenant Bull of the *Fly*, Watson the resident magistrate, Kettle of the New Zealand Company, Bruce the hotel-keeper, and by Kemp himself.[57]

One difficulty remained for Kemp. To get even sixteen signatures, he had had to promise Ngai Tahu all their mahinga kai and kainga nohoanga, and further reserves as well, leaving Europeans simply the 'greater part' of the land. But the New Zealand Company would never stand for this. They had been annoyed when Donald McLean, with Grey's approval, had reserved some mahinga kai when purchasing the Wanganui block.[58] But there had been war at Wanganui, and Kemp had no such excuse.

Kemp therefore made a 'true translation' of the deed.[59] The term 'Whakarite' in the deed denotes the Governor's *obligation* to provide further reserves.[60] But in Kemp's translation the Maoris conceded to the government 'the power and discretion of making us additional reserves of land'. The passage 'Ko te nui ia o te whenua, ka tukua whakareretia mo nga pakeha, oti tonu atu' meant 'But the greater part of the land will be for the Europeans for ever'. But Kemp translated it thus: 'It is understood however that the land itself with these small exceptions becomes the entire property of the white people for ever.'

The deed's wording implied that the 'survey map' and 'survey-ors' would come later. But in Kemp's translation, the 'survey map' became 'the map which has been made', making it appear that the Maoris had already seen it. 'Mahinga kai' became 'plantations', its northern meaning.[61] Kemp reported that all this had the 'consent of the people'. Yet he had told Ngai Tahu they would get ample reserves when the land was surveyed,[62] not 'plantations' and 'small exceptions' at the government's discretion. He did not report Ngai Tuahuriri's request for the land between the Waimaka-riri and Rakahuri.

Kemp was the official interpreter for New Munster, and his translation became the official version of the deed.[63] Lieutenant-Governor Eyre did not question it. But he reprimanded Kemp for not visiting the whole block and marking out the reserves, and for having made out the deed to the New Zealand Company instead of to the Crown.[64] Eyre complained at length to Governor Grey about these shortcomings.[65] But Grey made light of it, and told the Brit-ish Government that the purchase had been 'fairly and properly completed'.[66] When Grey next visited Wellington, he appointed Kemp to his North Island land-purchasing team with Donald McLean and Francis Dillon Bell.

∽

Bishop Selwyn arrived at Akaroa in his schooner *Undine* six days after Kemp had left. He met some chiefs who had signed Kemp's deed, and noted, before proceeding to Auckland:

They seemed perfectly satisfied with the sale, having received two thousand pounds, for which they had given up, as they told me, plains, mountains, rivers, etc., as far as Foveaux Straits, trusting to the faith of the Government to make suitable reserves for their use.[67]

Selwyn was mistaken about the amount received, and the southern extent of the purchase; but he correctly stated the Maoris' trust in Kemp's promises.

Ngai Tahu remained deeply divided over whether Kemp's deed should have been signed before the full price and the promised reserves had been delivered. Those who had signed believed they were upholding their mana and their people's interests against further encroachment by Ngati Toa, for the Wairau purchase had shown that those who signed land-purchase deeds at the behest of Governor Grey were recognised as true owners of the land. Since Grey had promised they could keep the lands they wanted, and Kemp had agreed to their keeping their mahinga kai, kainga nohoanga and ample reserves as well, the tribe's interests seemed well protected.

The Christian signatories – Tau, Pohio, Tiramorehu, Te Kahu and Te Raki – may have felt it their Christian duty to trust a Christian Governor who served a Christian Queen, for Christianity had wrought profound changes in Maori society. Class distinctions and aristocratic privileges were fading: 'A new concept of chieftainship arose which emphasized the New Testament qualities of peacemaking, humility, goodwill, charity, service, law-abidingness, obedience and faith.'[68] Yet many customary owners had not signed Kemp's deed. Some, like Mautai, had stayed away from the negotiations. Others had attended, and rejected Kemp's terms. Others – Karetai, Waruwarutu, Te Whakarukeruke and Naihira – had boarded the *Fly* but did not sign the deed. The land rights of these men could not be cancelled, under Maori custom, by the signatures of others.[69]

But the chiefs who signed Kemp's deed were also following Maori custom. Bishop Selwyn found it remarkable that they showed such faith in promises. But according to the 'savage' Maori code of conduct, the promise of a rangatira on a marae was entirely dependable, for if he dishonoured it he dishonoured himself. Mana was lost by those who broke promises, not by those who were deceived. Land was precious to the Maori, but mana was more precious still. The Ngai Tuahuriri chiefs discussed Kemp among themselves, and said:

> If this man does not keep his promise, we will consider he is a person of low degree, and so are all his people.[70]

Notes

1. Bathgate 1969: 368–69; Tremewan 1990: 346 n43.
2. Coutts 1969: 508–9.
3. Hocken 1898: 242.
4. Shortland 1851: 255.
5. Torlesse 1958: 65.
6. *AJHR* 1888 I-8: 37.
7. Mantell Ms Sketchbooks 3: 59.
8. Bathgate, loc cit; Coutts, loc. cit.
9. Burns Ms Diary, 21.2.1849.
10. Wills–Wakefield, 21.9.1848 (2), Wills Ms Letters.
11. Andersen 1916: 55; Hay 1915: 7ff.
12. Grey–Earl Grey, 15.5.1848, in *BPPNZ* 1847–49 7: 22ff.
13. *AJHR* 1888 G-1: 11; Downes 1915: 320; Wards 1968: 349.
14. Deans 1937: 118.
15. Tremewan 1990: 182. See also Hight & Straubel 1957: 196.
16. See *NTBB*.
17. Grey–Earl Grey, 25.8.1848, in Mackay 1873 I: 208.
18. Oliver–Maxwell, 5.8.1848, Fly Ms Letterbook.
19. SNC3/8: 316ff.
20. Kettle–Wakefield, 19 and 23.6.1848, in *IUPBPPNZ* 8: 296–97.
21. Wai-27 L8: 44ff.
22. SNC3/8: 316ff.
23. Ibid; Kettle Ms Fieldbook.
24. See Tau, Goodall, Palmer & Tau 1990: 5.11ff, on the Waimakariri-Ashley district.
25. Wills–Wakefield, 21.9.1848 (1), Wills Ms Letters. At Wellington, says Wills, Metehau had 'gained much mischievous experience of Courts of Claims'.
26. Kettle Ms Fieldbook, June 1848.
27. SNC 3/5: 223.
28. The government had paid Ngati Toa the second £600 for the Wairau Purchase in April.
29. SNC 3/7: 276.
30. SNC 3/1: 13ff.
31. Kettle Ms Fieldbook, 10.6.1848.
32. SNC 3/7: 278.
33. SNC 7/93: 720ff, 3/4: 219; *NTR*: 209ff (re Ngai Tahu use of mahinga kai at the time).
34. SNC 3/5: 226ff.
35. SNC 4/25: passim.
36. Kettle Ms Fieldbook, 10.6.1848.
37. Te Kahu told the SNC (3/8: 325–26): 'A man named Te Hau [Metehau], who is here present, objected strongly to part with the land. They withdrew the land from sale.'
38. Wills–Wakefield, loc. cit.
39. Kettle Ms Fieldbook, 11.6.1848. Te Uki (SNC 3/7: 279) says Kemp sent for Taiaroa.
40. SNC 3/1: 24.
41. Kettle–Wakefield, 19.6.1848, in *IUPBPPNZ* 8: 296.
42. SNC 3/8: 327.
43. DOSLIW Canterbury No.1, author's transcript. Maori language errors are Kemp's own.
44. Translation by Te Aue Davis.
45. SNC 3/1, 3/4: 178ff, 3/5: 228ff, 3/7: 282ff and 3/10: 381ff; *AJHR* 1876 G-7B: 5.
46. SNC 3/5: 230 and 3/7: 282ff.
47. SNC 3/4: 185ff and 3/7: 282ff.
48. SNC 3/7: 287–88.
49. Kemp's deed has Lieutenant Bull's undated statement: 'The annexed plan was attached to the deed of Sale and sealed in my presence.' Nothing indicates when this was done. Chiefs later testified that Kemp showed them no plan or map (SNC3/7: 286–87, 3/8: 337, 3/6: 270, 3/4: 192; MLCI 1B: 45 [Pohau]). At the SNC in 1879, Kemp was uncertain whether he had shown the 'plan' to Ngai Tahu (SNC3/1: 24–25). The SNC chairman, Judge Smith, remarked: 'I believe there is no proof at all that this plan was attached to the

deed, or that the Maoris saw it when the deed was signed' (SNC 4/26: 550).

50. Kettle Ms Fieldbook, 10–12.6.1848. This says Tikao confirmed that Banks Peninsula had already been sold to the French. But see also *NTR*: 545.

51. DOSLIW Canterbury No.1, 'plan'. Kettle's 'plan' shows 430 'Natives' in Kemp's block, and none on the West Coast. 'Buller River' at the northern boundary is a later inscription.

52. SNC 3/4: 192–95, 3/6: 204 and 7/84: 272–73; MLCI 1B: 40ff, 24.4.1868.

53. Kemp 1901: 9.

54. Mackay 1873 I: 204–6.

55. Mackay 1873 II: 374.

56. Kemp–Gisborne, 19 and 20.6.1848, in *IUPBPPNZ* 8: 292.

57. DOSLIW Canterbury No.1. Subsequent accounts (e.g. Mackay 1873 I: 210, Rutherford 1961: 173, Hight & Straubel 1957:106, Ogilvie 1996: 51) follow Kemp in treating all the Maori names on the deed as signatures or proxies.

58. Grey Ms Letterbook, 17.4.1846: 104ff; SNC 3/2: 694; Wards 1968: 321, 349 and passim.

59. Kemp–Gisborne, 19.6.1848, in *IUPBPPNZ* 8: 292.

60. Oral observation by Georgina Te Heuheu, member of the Waitangi Tribunal, during discussion of Wai-27 T1, Christchurch, 13.6.1989.

61. Wai-27 Q21: 29–31, S22: 11; also Kemp in SNC 3/1: 17 and passim.

62. Kettle reported, 'We explained to them that ample reserves would be made for them, and that, under those circumstances, the sum offered was in fact a gratuity' (Kettle–Wakefield, 19.6.1848, in *IUPBPPNZ* 8: 296). See also SNC 3/6: 255.

63. McHugh (1991: 326) treats Kemp's translation as if it were the original text of the deed.

64. The 1847 New Zealand Supreme Court ruling in *R. v. Symonds*, however, had affirmed that a private purchase of Native land merely conferred the title on the Crown (Haast 1938: 387ff). See Rutherford 1961: 126–27 as to how this case was brought at Grey's instigation.

65. Eyre–Grey, 5.7.1848, in *AJHR* 1888 I-8: 12ff.

66. Grey–Earl Grey, 25.8.1848, in Mackay 1873 I: 208.

67. Selwyn 1849: 119ff.

68. Winiata 1967: 51. Bishop Selwyn reported that Christianity had 'much weakened' the Native chiefs' authority over their tribes (Selwyn–Hawkins, 22.3.1845, Peel Ms Papers 40574) .

69. Shortland 1882: 102–3. See also SNC 7/83: 266–67.

70. SNC 3/4: 184.

12

Commissioner Mantell

A wild, loose, careless, clever fellow.[1]

WALTER MANTELL learned the Maori language from his workmen on the Porirua military road. This, and his shrewdness and self-confidence, marked him as a man of ability. But Mantell's bantering, sarcastic manner made him enemies, as did his private life. In November 1847 he was reported for 'abusing the Armed Police unnecessarily'.[2] According to Henry Tacy Kemp, he also caused trouble by having 'an intimacy' with wives of chiefs associated with his workmen.[3]

Kemp's purchase was a windfall for the New Zealand Company. But the bland promises of Kemp's deed had to be converted into the plain reality of the Company's requirements. On 1 August 1848, Mantell got word to finish on the Porirua road. Next day, he collected from Lieutenant-Governor Eyre notice of his appointment as Commissioner for the Extinguishment of Native Claims in the Middle (i.e. South) Island. He was to 'complete the negotiations partially entered upon by Mr Kemp', and to allocate the Maori reserves due under Kemp's deed, assisted by Arthur Wills, a Company surveyor.[4]

Lieutenant-Colonel McCleverty, the Company's adviser on Maori reserves, instructed Mantell on the subject.[5] The Maoris of southern New Zealand, McCleverty believed, should have little land; otherwise they would avoid wage labour, cling to their old customs, and perhaps compete with European settlers on the land. In Jamaica, former slaves subsisted on less than three acres.[6] For the poorer soils and colder climate of southern New Zealand, McCleverty prescribed a maximum of ten acres per head[7] – which, Mantell was assured, Governor Grey entirely agreed with.[8]

Thus, although Kemp's deed was 'signed, sealed and delivered', the government pretended that it was entitled to deny Ngai Tahu the deed's chief benefits. This was called 'completing the purchase'.[9] Its rationale was Kemp's false translation of the deed, giving the government 'power and discretion' in providing Maori reserves. It was contrary to Lord Normanby's instructions to Governor Hobson, contrary to the Treaty of Waitangi, and contrary to the 1847 *R. v Symonds* Supreme Court ruling that aboriginal title was 'entitled to be respected' and could not be extinguished 'otherwise than by the free consent of the Native occupiers'.[10] The government and the New Zealand Company ignored these supposed safeguards, and prepared to force on Ngai Tahu the basic principle of colonialism: that tribal lands were to become the property of Europeans, except for such portions as the government might allow Maoris to keep. The agent of this enforcement was to be Walter Mantell. The Company told his surveyor, Wills, to protest if Mantell allocated reserves that might be inconvenient for European settlement.[11]

Eyre's instructions to Mantell were full of generous sentiments towards the 'natives', but gave Europeans on the land absolute preference over them. According to Eyre, Ngai Tahu were to have 'liberal provision both for their present and future wants' – but only to the extent that Mantell 'might consider necessary'. Mantell was to be tireless in ascertaining Ngai Tahu's 'rights and interests' – and tireless in getting them to accept what he thought 'most just and best'.[12] But John Jones, for his grant of 2,560 acres under Godfrey's Land Claims Commission recommendations of 1843, could select his land in three blocks if he wished, said Eyre.

∽

The luckless Eyre accompanied Mantell to Akaroa on HM sloop *Fly*, unaware that Grey, his tormentor, was on his way from Auckland to Wellington. When the *Fly* arrived at Akaroa and the Ngai Tuahuriri chiefs went aboard expecting to see Commissioner Kemp, they found Lieutenant-Governor Eyre instead. They again declared that they would retain the territory between the Waimakariri and the Rakahuri, and, finding Eyre in an expansive mood, some requested more. Eyre readily agreed.[13] But Mantell, as interpreter, instead of translating Eyre's consent into Maori, warned him *sotto voce* that allowing such a large Maori reserve would be inadvisable. Eyre angrily complied.[14] But some chiefs understood English better than

Mantell supposed, and heard Eyre's initial consent. They recognised Mantell's role, and nicknamed him 'Te Tipa' – The Advance Guard.

When Ngai Tahu had gathered at Akaroa in sufficient numbers, Mantell went ashore and showed them Kettle's sketch map of Kemp's 'purchase'. Tikao, Tiramorehu, Te Whakarukeruke, Te Whaikai Pokene, and others, protested that the map was new to them. They vehemently objected to the inclusion of the West Coast in the purchase as indicated on the map. They wanted Mantell to depart, so that they could deal with Kemp as before.[15] But Mantell stood his ground. He said he was there to mark out reserves for them, starting at Kaiapoi. This provoked another outcry from Ngai Tuahuriri, who insisted that they were keeping the whole Waimakariri block, Kaiapoi included.[16]

HM sloop *Fly* now left for Wellington with Eyre, and Mantell persuaded Paora Tau and his party to take him and Wills to Kaiapoi.[17] On the way, Mantell heard from the Maoris that Kemp's deed was written, and the payment made, on board the *Fly*, and that Kemp had restricted the number allowed aboard – at first suggesting 'only four'.[18]

Mantell and Wills spent a night with the Deanses at Putaringamotu before going on to the Waimakariri. There, their crossing of the river was opposed. Metehau, who had already written to Eyre, explained to Mantell and Wills that Ngai Tuahuriri's share of Kemp's payment had been allotted to the territories south of the Waimakariri and north of the Rakahuri, to affirm that the land between these rivers (some quarter of a million acres in area), 'worth £1 an acre', was to remain Maori.[19]

But Mantell insisted that Governor Grey wanted him to inspect the boundaries of the purchase, which meant going to Kaiapoi. The Maoris argued among themselves all night about this. Some maintained that Mantell should be allowed to cross the river, since he might later persuade the Governor to overturn the Wairau purchase. But others suspected Mantell of intending to subvert their decision to keep the Waimakariri block. Mantell, listening from his tent, heard suggestions of frustrating his surveys with false place names. Next morning he announced his dislike for Maori place names, and proposed replacing them with English names.[20] At length, Mantell and Wills were allowed to cross the Waimakariri, provided they acknowledged Maori ownership of the land by paying for their firewood.

Thus, on 31 August 1848, Mantell and Wills stepped ashore on the magnificent estate that Tuahuriri's sons had occupied a hundred and fifty years before, and which their descendants had defended at such cost. It was a smiling landscape of grassland, wetlands and forest, backed by bold mountain ranges capped with winter snow. The plains and downlands, ideal for farming, abounded with weka, koreke and wild pigs. There were fine plantations of cabbage trees. Three ancient podocarp forests, the largest remaining on the plains, held a wealth of bird life and timber.[21] Streams of crystal-clear water gushed from underground sources, nourishing a maze of channels, swamps and lagoons rich in eels, lampreys, waterfowl and fish. All the useful varieties of harakeke and raupo were here, with muds to dye the fibre. Kakapo and other choice birds inhabited the vast beech forests of Tawera and Puketeraki – where kiore, which periodically teemed in millions, provided a great delicacy. The inland ranges yielded taramea, whose perfume was traded far and wide, and a celmisia whose fragrant leaves made exquisite women's capes. The sea coast, and the estuaries and hapua of the Rakahuri and Waimakariri, provided ample fish and seafood. The snow-fed waters of the Waimakariri were adequate in its lower reaches for a seaport. Here were traditional resources prized by the Maori, together with the means for future agriculture, pastoral farming, and trade with the new European colony.

∾

Judging the danger of a Ngati Toa attack to be past, Ngai Tuahuriri had been preparing to leave Puari and reoccupy the Waimakariri block.[22] A new pa had been built at Tiorori, south-east of Tuahiwi, the Kaiapoi site being highly tapu. As it was springtime, most people were away – 'some planting, some at different places in the bush, and some of them up in the hills. Some were catching weka, some at Murihiku, some at Otago, some at Moeraki.'[23]

Mantell persuaded Paora Tau to take him to Kaiapoi. Once there, Mantell got up on the sacred mound and told the assembled Maoris that Kettle's sketch map absolutely proved that Kaiapoi belonged to Ngati Toa, and that Ngai Tahu had sold Kemp all the territory from there to the West Coast. A heated argument followed, until Tau called for silence. He solemnly declared that Ngati Toa's boundary was at Parinuiowhiti near Cook Strait, 250 kilometres to the north. Ngai Tuahuriri had agreed to sell Kemp only as far inland as Maungatere and the foothills, he said. Their intention always was to keep the Waimakariri block. They would appeal to Governor Grey.

Mantell replied, 'Very good, the Governor is in Wellington.'[24] But, he added, they had accepted Kemp's payment and were therefore bound by Kemp's deed and Kettle's sketch map. He wished to reserve some land for them, otherwise their children would have nothing. If they behaved themselves, and admitted they had sold Kemp all their land, he would write to the government about their complaint regarding Ngati Toa's boundary.[25]

The following day (Saturday) Ngai Tuahuriri again insisted that they would retain the Waimakariri block. But Mantell and Wills boldly started surveying a reserve there, continuing on the Monday, while the verbal battle also continued. On the Tuesday, the survey approached Tuahiwi. Metehau now decided to assert his rights. Te Rauparaha had made his stand at the Wairau on this very point. He had stopped the New Zealand Company's survey and burned the surveyors' huts, and had afterwards been vindicated by Governor FitzRoy and Commissioner Spain, gaining the government's healthy respect.

Metehau fired Wills's hut and tried to remove Mantell's tent. Seeing Mantell, he drew his tomahawk, while Mantell hastily primed his shotgun. But other Maoris restrained Metehau. A late-night korero among the Maoris followed. Tau urged that it should be left to the Governor to honour the terms of Kemp's purchase, while Metehau urged that Mantell should be evicted. To Mantell, listening from his tent, it seemed that Metehau was winning the argument. At midnight he wrote to Wellington, gloomily predicting that he and Wills would have to move off and try again elsewhere.[26]

But at daybreak Mantell was rescued from his difficulties. A distant smoke from Puari signalled that Taiaroa had a schooner ready for Wellington, for Grey's whakawaa. Tau agreed to take Mantell's letter – which, unknown to Tau, bitterly denounced Ngai Tuahuriri.[27] Metehau left Mantell a note from 'all the people', demanding £10,000 for his own land and promising to demolish any survey poles Mantell erected.[28] The Maoris hurried off, leaving Solomon (Haukeke) Iwikau with Mantell. Some twenty chiefs embarked at Puari for Wellington, led by those who had signed Kemp's deed.

⁓

Mantell and Wills, freed from the opposition of Metehau and his supporters, marked out a 2,640-acre 'Kaiapoi reserve' around Tuahiwi – about one-hundredth of the Waimakariri block that Ngai Tuahuriri had requested. Mantell had with him Shortland's census showing 450 Ngai Tuahuriri at Port Levy;[29] but without going there, he recorded '200' at Port Levy and 'twenty-nine' at Tuahiwi.[30] He left Haukeke Iwikau a plan of the reserve,[31] and allowed Wereta Tainui just five acres at nearby Kaikanui, saying that Tainui's ten people could use the Tuahiwi reserve.

Mantell returned to Putaringamotu highly pleased with himself. The Deanses were pleased too, for they paid no further rent for their Maori lease. This remained a grievance with Ngai Tuahuriri, for the forest and spring-fed stream at Putaringamotu were valuable mahinga kai, the ownership of which had been guaranteed them by Kemp.[32] Mantell returned to Akaroa to report afresh to Eyre, giving Ngai Tuahuriri's reasons for disputing the Ngati Toa boundary.[33]

But in Wellington the Ngai Tahu deputation had already seen Governor Grey. Grey had undertaken to summon Ngati Toa for the whakawaa, but on the appointed day they did not arrive. As a compromise, Ngai Tahu asked Grey to make Te Parinuiowhiti the boundary of Kemp's purchase. This would satisfy Ngai Tahu's claim to be the true owners of the territory between Kaiapoi and Te Parinuiowhiti, and at the same time satisfy Grey's desire to buy it. But Grey declined to disturb the advantage he had given Ngati Toa, and the deputation departed empty-handed.[34]

∾

Mantell and Wills left Akaroa on 23 September 1848 to walk to Otago. Mantell now knew that at least sixteen of Kemp's 'signatures' were written by Kemp himself, and that only two chiefs between Taumutu and the Otago block had signed: Tiramorehu of Moeraki, and Pohio of Waikouaiti.[35] To bring the rest under the deed, Mantell would make it known that only those who accepted his terms would share in the reserves, and that those who wanted a share in the remaining payments would have to co-operate with him.

Kiriona Pohau, a Kemp's deed signatory, was eeling at Kaitorete when Mantell arrived there. He told Mantell that Kaitorete was not in Kemp's purchase, since (he said) the boundary crossed Waihora along the Otumatua–Taumutu line (see inset in map on page 181).[36] Mantell ignored this and walked on to Taumutu, where Te Uki was waiting for him. Mantell allocated eighty acres for the sixteen people there. They told him they owned the land outside the piece he was marking off, and needed it for their stock. Te Uki said he also would need a large area for his whanau, and named various mahinga kai and kainga nohoanga between Taumutu and the Rakahuri as their traditional property. Mantell promised Te Uki that larger reserves would be made when the country was surveyed.[37]

Once beyond Taumutu, Mantell encountered less argument about Kemp's boundaries. But enforcing the New Zealand Company's requirements was still difficult. Ngai Tahu knew that the Wanganui Maoris had been allowed to keep substantial eel fisheries. With people like Metehau active regarding Maori rights, such knowledge was readily circulated around the country. Consequently, Mantell found Ngai Tahu everywhere insistent on keeping their eel weirs, and places needed for new ones.[38] He told them to refer these matters to the government.[39]

Mantell walked on with Wills, occasionally marking out reserves on the McCleverty principle, telling the people to vacate their other land, promising that larger reserves would come later, and making geological observations for Grey.[40] Some chiefs disputed his activities, or tried to influence him.[41] He told those who requested mahinga kai, or more land, to wait. Hostile demands he refused point-blank. 'Solomon Pohio and Kahuti Blueskin demanded a reserve at Waihao,' he wrote in his journal. 'I explained that they could not have one there (likewise at Matakaea).'[42] At Timaru, Tarawhata treated Mantell well. But since Tarawhata's cultivations were 'at the most valuable part of the bay', Mantell placed his reserve further north.[43] Tarawhata wanted Mantell to reserve him a coal deposit, but Mantell refused when Tarawhata declined to say where the coal was.[44]

Tiramorehu received Mantell hospitably at Moeraki, and suggested that land-purchase payments should be entrusted to leading chiefs at each settlement, otherwise the money would 'take wing'.[45] Mantell asked Tiramorehu to move his people to Tuahiwi to be with the rest of Ngai Tuahuriri. But Tiramorehu declined to leave his people's urupa at Moeraki. Mantell then allocated only five hundred acres for the Moeraki community of nearly two hundred people.[46] Tiramorehu requested another thousand acres for their stock, as well as some forest land. But Mantell allocated only timber rights to another ten acres. About this time, Governor Grey replied to a letter from Professor Richard Owen in London, who had recommended Mantell for employment. Grey told Owen, 'If he continues to merit employment I will see that he is not lost sight of. He has a very good knowledge of the native language and is a very intelligent gentlemanly fellow.'[47]

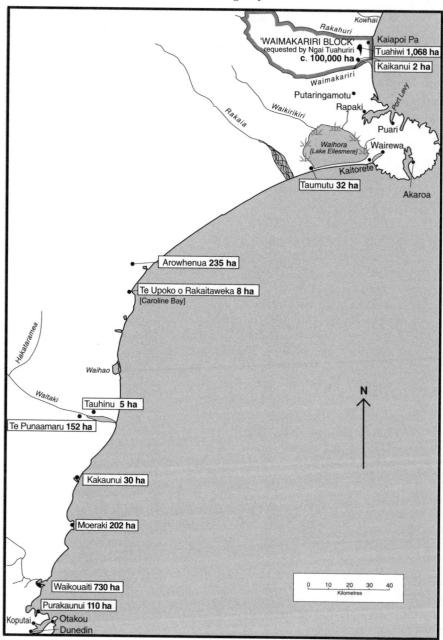

Mantell's Maori reserves for Kemp's purchase.

Scene near Tuahiwi (note the tall whata), 1848.
Watercolour by William Fox.

'Riccarton, Messrs Deans Station' (Putaringamotu), 1848.
Watercolour by William Fox.

Akaroa in 1850 (note the blockhouse, centre). Watercolour by William Fox.
HOCKEN LIBRARY

'Port Lyttelton Immigrants', January 1851. Watercolour by William Fox.
HOCKEN LIBRARY

William Fox watercolours of (above)
Wereta Tainui at Kaikanui, 1848,
and (left) *Matiaha Tiramorehu in*
his prime, 1849.
HOCKEN LIBRARY

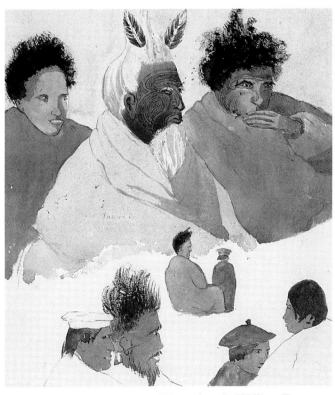

Tuahiwi Maoris, 1849. Watercolour by William Fox.
HOCKEN LIBRARY

Haereroa, a Ngai Tahu fighting chief.
HOCKEN LIBRARY

Matiaha Tiramorehu in later life.
CANTERBURY MUSEUM

Paora Taki, who dictated a Ngai Tahu account of Te Rauparaha's raids.
CANTERBURY MUSEUM

Kaikoura Whakatau in traditional dress.
CANTERBURY MUSEUM

Left: *Edward Gibbon Wakefield, theorist of the new colonialism.*
HOCKEN LIBRARY

Right: *The Reverend James Watkin, first Christian missionary
in southern New Zealand.*
HOCKEN LIBRARY

Walter Mantell MLC, in later years.
HOCKEN LIBRARY

Right: *Governor Sir George Grey in 1867.*
HOCKEN LIBRARY

Matenga Taiaroa in old age.
HOCKEN LIBRARY

H. K. Taiaroa, MHR for Southern Maori, c. 1885.
HOCKEN LIBRARY

Wiremu Potiki, an Otago chief, c. 1880.
HOCKEN LIBRARY

Left: *Horomona Pohio in later life.*
CANTERBURY MUSEUM

A Maori hangi on sports day at Tuahiwi, 1885.
CANTERBURY MUSEUM

A traditional mokihi, displayed on a dray by Arowhenua Maoris, 1902.
CANTERBURY MUSEUM

Left: *Tamati Parata, MHR for Southern Maori, c. 1906.*
HOCKEN LIBRARY

Below: *Maori children at Tuahiwi, c. 1935.*
CANTERBURY MUSEUM

The land squatted on by John Jones's whalers at Waikouaiti was the most desirable in the bay, giving access to kai moana and the best landing places. Haereroa, Kahuti and Pohio asked Mantell to include this land in the Maori reserve. But Mantell refused, saying that the request was 'unjust' and would have to be referred to Lieutenant-Governor Eyre. Against strenuous Maori objections, Mantell excluded the squatters' land from the Waikouaiti reserve of 1,800 acres, which, he said, was for 121 Maoris. The chiefs then left in disgust. Afterwards, wrote Mantell, 'Mr Jones came and made his selection of 2,560 acres in three blocks, which Mr Wills marked on his map.'[48]

Mantell reached Port Chalmers with Wills on 9 December 1848. Many years later, he described his journey through Kemp's block as 'a struggle, in which I got the land reduced as much as possible,'[49] while the Natives complained of the reserves being too circumscribed'.[50] But now he reported to the government that Ngai Tahu, except for trouble-makers, were all happy with his reserves.[51] He made careful geological observations for Grey, but recorded little of the Maori way of life. He was evicted from Otakou by Taiaroa, Potiki and Kaikoareare. According to Mantell, all were drunk, and threatened his life.[52]

For the '637' Maoris that Mantell reported in Kemp's block and Port Levy, he had allowed 6,359 acres – just under McCleverty's maximum. But in fact more than double this number of people had claims on the land.[53] Mantell had allowed not ten acres per head, but less than four. In denying Ngai Tahu some of their cultivated land, he had overstepped the sixth resolution of the 1844 House of Commons select committee, which had conceded that Maoris should keep land they 'actually occupied and enjoyed'. Mantell's severity surpassed even that of the Queen's Instructions of 1846, which had at least allowed for Maori claims when determining the 'Crown demesne'. Whether land was 'occupied and enjoyed' by Maoris, or not, did not concern Mantell. The Treaty of Waitangi was a closed book to him, as it was to McCleverty, Eyre and Grey. Under Grey, now knighted for his services, the New Zealand Government served the interests of European colonisation, and Maori interests took second place. And so it was to remain.

~

The year 1848 brought revolution to Europe, and was a worrying time for investors there. But English colonial investors were not daunted. A 'Canterbury Association' was formed by prominent Anglicans, to preserve in New Zealand the virtues of English society, including the ancient partnership of church, state and landed gentry. A colony, to be called 'Canterbury', was to be established under the auspices of the New Zealand Company, with land selling at £3 per acre. As usual, two separate classes would embark from England: 'colonists', who had bought land and paid their own fares, and 'emigrants', the future wage-earners, whose fares were subsidised subject to a suitable character reference from a clergyman. The Association could let unsold 'Canterbury' land for grazing, at £1 per year per hundred acres, with special concessions for colonists according to how much land they had bought.

'Canterbury' was to be in New Munster, away from concentrations of Maori population. The choice of site was entrusted to Captain Joseph Thomas, who already had experience in New Zealand. He returned to New Zealand in November 1848 as the Canterbury Association's chief surveyor, with Thomas Cass and Charles Torlesse (Wakefield's nephew) as his assistants. These three arrived at Akaroa on 15 December 1848 to inspect the Port Cooper plains, Thomas's personal preference. With them was William Fox, an energetic, thirty-six-year-old Durham man with an Oxford degree and a legal training. William Wakefield had died suddenly in Wellington on 19 September. Fox, who happened to be in Wellington and held power of attorney for Wakefield, and had previously been the New Zealand Company's Nelson agent, had promptly taken over as Chief Agent.[54]

Eight days after Fox and Thomas set out to inspect the plains, Mantell landed at Akaroa from Otago with fourteen southern chiefs, for the payment of the second Kemp's purchase instalment of £500, which had been due on 12 December. Among them were Topi Patuki and Tuhawaiki's son Kihau, whom Mantell championed as Ngai Tahu's highest-ranking chiefs. But the money had not arrived. Instead, a letter (eleven weeks old) from Eyre was waiting for Mantell, with more instructions. Grey, said Eyre, wanted Mantell to provide reserves 'only around pahs, residences or cultivations to the extent that may be necessary for the resident Natives', and to promise that 'the Crown will hereafter mark out for them such additional reserves as may be considered necessary for their future wants'. Mantell, as we have seen, had already done precisely this.[55]

Mantell dismissed the waiting chiefs, and sent to Fox saying that he needed the money for the instalment, which was already overdue. He then reported to Eyre, saying:

> I trust that it will be found that I have in every case given such consideration to the present and future necessities of the Natives that the Lieutenant Governor will see little cause to regret that the reserves should have been finally arranged prior to my receipt of His Excellency's letter.[56]

Fox and Thomas meanwhile walked about the Port Cooper plains, highly pleased with what they saw. They returned to Akaroa in response to Mantell's message, and found him 'playing his accordion in Bruce's grog shanty'.[57]

~

The £500 that Mantell was waiting for from the New Zealand Company arrived at Akaroa four weeks late. This allowed time for the Ngai Tahu chiefs there to discuss Mantell's activities, and compare notes. Metehau wrote to the government saying that he and many others had dissented from Kemp's purchase, and he named four land holdings he intended to keep.[58] Some Maoris warned Charles Torlesse to stay south of the Waimakariri.[59] Te Uki again asked Mantell about the promised mahinga kai and kainga nohoanga, and was again told to 'wait'.[60] Other chiefs went to Mantell, unsuccessfully. Their general conclusion was that he had no intention of fulfilling Kemp's promises, or even his own.[61]

When Mantell met Ngai Tahu on 22 January 1849 to pay out the £500 instalment, he was confronted with an angry assembly. Tiramorehu, Te Whakarukeruke, Tikao, and others, declared that his reserves were insufficient in number, and in size. They wanted Kemp's promises honoured. Otherwise, Mantell could take his £500 away, as they would require the £5 million originally asked for.[62] Mantell replied that the £250 paid to Ngai Tuahuriri by Kemp had been disproportionate to their numbers, and that this time he would pay them only £70. After further argument, Tikao proposed appealing to Eyre. On 24 January, Mantell sailed for Wellington with Topi and Tiramorehu, while Taiaroa, Tikao, Pohau and other chiefs went in their own vessel.[63]

When Mantell reached Wellington he quickly reported to Eyre before Ngai Tahu could do so, saying that the 'disturbance' was purely over the distribution of the money. Taiaroa and Tikao had again wanted half each, said Mantell, but he had refused them. Ngai Tuahuriri with their 'usual insolence' and 'dishonest clamour' had persistently obstructed him, he said, as was typical of 'returned slaves'. They had threatened to fight Taiaroa's people for the money, he said. Horomona Pohio had taken more than his share, and was 'one of the most sullen evilly-disposed Natives I have met with, reminding me much of John Tikao, though less audaciously insolent'. Mantell said that 'well-conducted' and 'well-disposed' chiefs had not opposed him. He proposed to avoid further 'disturbances' by sharing the second instalment among nineteen recipients, including four Poutini chiefs who would get £10 each for the West Coast. Mantell did not state in writing his main purpose in seeking a wider distribution of the payment: it would bring more Ngai Tahu under Kemp's deed, for anyone who accepted payment became legally bound by the deed.[64]

Eyre, in the presence of Mantell, Fox and Kemp, gave the Ngai Tahu chiefs a short shrift when they went to complain to him about Mantell's reserves and the Ngati Toa boundary. He asked Tikao and Taiaroa why the money should be paid to them. They began saying it was insufficient, but Eyre cut them short and told them to get back to their ship.[65] With the approval of Fox and Patuki, he upheld Mantell's proposal for paying the instalment that was due. Thus Ngai Tahu were again denied an opportunity of discussing their grievances with the government.

Tiramorehu now turned to the press. On 7 February 1849 he gave Ngai Tahu's view of their dispute with Ngati Toa in a long open letter to Governor Grey, published in Maori (with English translation) in the Wellington *New Zealand Spectator and Cook Strait Guardian*.[66] Tiramorehu stated:

> Te Rauparaha began hostilities against Ngai Tahu, but Ngai Tahu put an end to the war; wherefore, I conclude that our lands were not conquered by Ngati Toa. We still have a right to treat about our own lands.

Governor Grey was mistaken, said Tiramorehu, in believing 'Rawiri Puaha's dishonest claims' to the territory from Kaiapoi northwards: 'Rawiri virtually sold us along with the land. Aue! Te he o tenei whakaaro!' ('Alas! How utterly wrong is this way of behaving!')[67] Tiramorehu named places in this territory that he said belonged to Ngai Tahu: 'Kaiapoi, Te Kohai, Waipara, Tahatu, Motunau, Hurunui, Pauapirau, Waiau, and Rangitahi [Lake Tennyson]'. He called on Grey to negotiate with Ngai Tahu for these, and to negotiate with Kaikoura Whakatau for Kaikoura. The newspaper commended Ngai Tahu for 'appealing to reason rather than to force', and for 'submitting their claims to the tribunal of public opinion', and invited Rawiri Puaha to reply on behalf of Ngati Toa. But no reply followed.

Before Tiramorehu's letter could reach Governor Grey in Auckland, Grey had already informed Earl Grey that the purchase of all territory between Nelson and Otago had been completed, and that

> Although official information has not yet reached me regard-
> ing the final adjustment of those details of Kemp's purchase
> which relate to the survey, and defining the reserves kept for
> the use of the Natives, yet I have received information, which
> I believe to be authentic, that the whole of these details have
> now been conclusively and satisfactorily adjusted.[68]

Eyre sent Mantell back to Akaroa on 19 February 1849 in the naval survey paddle-steamer HMS *Acheron*, to pay the £500 instalment. Eyre thought the warship would be useful for quelling further Ngai Tahu 'disturbances', and her commander, Captain John Lort Stokes, readily agreed.[69] Topi Patuki, Taiaroa, Tiramorehu and Pohau went south in the *Acheron*[70] while Tikao and other chiefs embarked in their own schooner. On reaching Akaroa, Mantell announced that he would distribute the payment next day.

A large gathering of Ngai Tahu assembled at Akaroa on 22 February 1849 to consider the payment. Mantell had with him Police Magistrate Watson of Akaroa, and Captain Stokes, Surgeon David Lyall and Survey Officer William Hamilton from the warship, which stood conveniently by. Mantell was handed a letter from Te Uki, again requesting mahinga kai and kainga nohoanga and sufficient land. Mantell replied, 'All right.'[71] Another letter, written in Mete-hau's clear hand, explained his family's title at Tuahiwi, and why he opposed Mantell's reserve being there. He had not sold his land, said Metehau. 'It is not good that other people be paid for my land.' Tikao agreed with him, he said. He asked Mantell to read out the letter to the assembled chiefs, and have it discussed openly.[72] Mantell refused.[73]

Now came the climax of Mantell's efforts. He took out Kemp's deed and read it out again. On the back of the document, he had written in Maori:

> Hakaroa. Pepueri 22. 1849. No tenei ra i tukuna ai kia matau te tuarua o nga utunga mo a matau wenua e mau nei te ahua. £500 Erima rau pauna moni i tukuna nei kia matau. Na Mr Mantell Commissioner for Extinguishing Native Claims i tuha kia matau.[74]

This was later officially translated as:

> Hakaroa, February 22nd, 1849. On this day was paid to us the 2nd instalment for our lands herein described [or delineated]. £500 were handed over to us. Mr Mantell, Commissioner for Extinguishing Native Claims, divided the money among us.[75]

The phrase 'e mau nei te ahua' – literally, 'the likeness is attached' – was translated by the official translators as 'herein described', or 'herein delineated'. But according to Mantell, it meant 'as shown on the attached map',[76] for Kettle's controversial sketch map was attached to the deed. In the deed, as we have seen, the proposed map was referred to as 'pukapuka ruri' (survey document), not 'ahua' (likeness).

When Mantell summoned those named in his schedule to come forward and sign for their money, they refused. Kemp's promises had not been fulfilled, they said. Mantell replied that they would be: they would receive more land, and a large final payment. But the Maoris were adamant. Mantell then delivered a 'sermon' in Maori, 'preaching the gospel' of schools and hospitals.[77] There would be schools for Ngai Tahu and their children, and hospitals where their sick would recover; the government would give them atawhai, he said.[78]

This line of argument, delivered in so religious a manner, gave some chiefs food for thought, for another epidemic of measles had been raging, with many deaths.[79] Ngati Toa had access to the government hospital in Wellington. Te Hiko himself had been there when he was ill, even against his friends' advice.[80] But Ngai Tahu had no such opportunity. Mantell was closely questioned about the schools. He was understood to promise schools at all Ngai Tahu settlements, to give Maoris knowledge and understanding equal to that of Europeans.[81]

At last Taiaroa, Pohau and Kihau came forward, followed by the other named chiefs. The back of Kemp's deed received the signatures of seven who had already signed the face of it: Taiaroa, Tikao,

Pohau, Paora Tau, Te Uki, John Pere and Tiramorehu (who signed for the Poutini chiefs' £40 in their absence). More important for Mantell were the nine new signatories from south of Taumutu: Karetai, Tarawhata, Rawiri Te Mamaru, Noa Paka, Paitu, Kahuti, Topi Patuki, Kihau and Huruhuru (who had delegated Te Mamaru to sign for him). All were duly witnessed by Stokes and the other officials.[82] Mantell had thus increased from sixteen to twenty-five the number of valid signatures on the deed.

Although Kettle's sketch map, according to Mantell, was attached to the front of the deed while the chiefs signed the back of it, Mantell never claimed that he drew their attention to the map. That the chiefs saw it, or knew it was there, or knew that 'e mau nei te ahua' referred to the 'pukapuka ruri' of the deed, was never established. Pohau, the only signatory who was later questioned about this, testified that he saw no map or plan.[83] However, regardless of the deed plan with its controversial boundaries, the vital thing for the Ngai Tahu chiefs were the promises in Kemp's deed, together with those made by Mantell and Grey. They were more important even than the promises in the Treaty of Waitangi, for they confirmed Ngai Tahu's perpetual ownership of their precious mahinga kai, together with their kainga nohoanga, and additional land as well.

The nine new signatures on the back of Kemp's deed were a triumph for Mantell. Eyre praised his 'careful and zealous' work to Fox, and to Grey – who fully concurred.[84] Mantell, with Grey's approval, had promised the Maoris more reserves at a future date, during his tour of the eastern part of Kemp's block in 1848, and again at Akaroa at the payment of the second instalment. But, as we have seen, and unknown to the Maoris, he had reported to Eyre that everything was completed, including the allocation of reserves, and Grey had reported the same thing to London. The Wellington press (again, unknown to Ngai Tahu) now reported Mantell's 22 February proceedings, saying that he had 'completely and satisfactorily settled with the respective tribes, the boundaries and all other questions connected with the extensive purchase made by the Government in the Middle island'.[85]

Fox, annoyed at the New Zealand Company being saddled with the Kemp's purchase payments, denounced the purchase. He called on the government to adopt Earl Grey's recommendation of December 1846 and declare the whole South Island as Crown wasteland, since 'the few natives had occupied an almost inappreciable quantity of land'. However, Governor Grey rejected Fox's arguments, and insisted on the Company paying all instalments on the purchases he had arranged, including Porirua and Wairau.⁸⁶

⌒

On 22 February 1849, the day that Ngai Tahu signed Mantell's receipt at Akaroa, and two weeks after the newspaper publication of Tiramorehu's protest to Governor Grey, the same paper published a letter to the Queen from Te Rauparaha and twenty-seven other chiefs at Waikanae, saying:

> This is a letter of thanks from us to you for your wise choice of Governor, when you appointed our loving friend Governor Grey to be Governor of New Zealand . . . By his government all quarrels were put an end to. He brought into force that there should be but one law for us, and for the white people. He made us acquainted with your good intentions towards us, the natives. He joined his to the works of Christ, his ministers and his bishops, and now for the first time good works are the result, faith in our father which is in heaven, and in our saviour Jesus Christ, and the doing those worldly things which God thinks good for the body . . . We have now adopted him as our father, and we consequently look upon you as our mother in the love of Jesus Christ.

They asked that Grey be made permanent Governor of New Zealand: 'We are well disposed towards this Governor. If you should send him away to some other country you will cause us, who love him so much, great grief.'⁸⁷ Grey graciously forwarded the letter to the Queen, and it was duly published in the Parliamentary Papers.⁸⁸

The senior Ngai Tuahuriri chiefs had decided to trust in the promises of Grey, Kemp and Mantell. But Metehau resented Europeans 'exploring' beyond the Waimakariri, and in the mountains, as if everything belonged to them. Torlesse had been near Te Kuratawhiti, where Metehau had land rights.⁸⁹ *Acheron* people had been on Maungatere, and at the sacred Kaiapoi pa site, stealing human bones.⁹⁰ Maoris who had opposed Kemp's purchase expected to keep their land. Metehau had had no response from writing about this to Eyre and Mantell. He therefore wrote to the Queen, in Maori, in his best handwriting, as follows (in translation):

April 2 1849 Tuahiwi

Go, my friendly letter to London to Queen Victoria.

Madam, tenakoe. Great is my regard for you. Let your clemency be shown to us, as our respect for you is great even unto the end – even so you also, because you have become as near as a relation can be to us, because New Zealand has been named as a messenger of wealth to the Queen – Friend Victoria, Greetings to you, living in your own country.

My address to you is this – with regard to my pieces of land, I have retained them, because I was not one of those who consented to sell the land. I have retained them for my permanent use. They are not large pieces, they are small. Had I consented to sell the land I should not have retained these pieces. Those who consented to sell have their own way of thinking about the matter. Those pieces we are now claiming are not large pieces, they are small. Let your graciousness therefore be shown to us and to New Zealand generally, because these lands are our own and were handed down to us by our ancestors. The pieces my father had are the portions I now claim, Te Kuratawiti and Tawera. Then there is the pa of Kaiapoi. They are small pieces, but the number of acres will tell. These are the portions of land I wish to retain. This is my friendly address to you, and therefore be kind to us.

From George William Metehau, to Queen Victoria in London. Madam, send a reply to this letter.[91]

Metehau's painstaking letter, properly sealed with red wax, came to the hands of Governor Grey. He sent it to Eyre, asking for Metehau's status, character, what claim he had, and whether he had received any payment for Kemp's purchase. Eyre referred the matter to Kemp and Mantell. Kemp commented as follows:

The Lt Governor will remember the name of the writer – a troublesome young man who was threatened with imprisonment by the Governor-in-Chief for interfering with the surveyors. He was formerly a captive. He received part of the payment. The Governor-in-Chief will remember the writer as having been turned out of the steamer at my suggestion during the disturbances at Wanganui when he was supposed to have been acting as a spy.[92]

Mantell gave four pages of information, emphasising the following:

I have known the native in question since February 1841 when he was employed in the Government boat belonging to my department. Even at that time he bore a bad character. Since then he has been leading a vagabond life, principally in this the North Island, until the prospect of gain apparently induced him on hearing of the probable sale of his native district to return thither. He had before this acquired and is still known by the name of 'Flash Charley'.

His signature is attached to Mr Kemp's deed of sale and he acknowledged to me that he had signed it. In my letter dated 'Tuahiwi Sept 5 1848' I reported his conduct at Tuahiwi. I may add that he on that occasion assaulted Mr Wills, set fire to a hut erected by our men, and was forcibly held back by the other natives while rushing to attack me with a tomahawk.

Mantell added:

It is most probable that through Tikao he received some portion of the last as he did of the first instalment, but neither his rank nor his influence would have justified me in entrusting him with any portion of the money for distribution. He is respectably descended but by no means a chief. His influence if he is to acquire any can only spring from success in his opposition to Government. Finding himself a stranger in his own country and bringing with him all the low cunning and imperfect knowledge of our customs which he has acquired in his disreputable wanderings, he seeks with these to raise himself a party by which he may imitate those chiefs of this the North island of whom he is always speaking and whom he would so much wish to resemble – Rangihaeata and John Heke. He is a near relative and constant coadjutor of Tikao whose influence gained by successful defiance of the law I succeeded in shaking considerably in January last. Since his misconduct at Tuahiwi I have declined to hold any communication with him.[93]

Grey accepted these comments from his loyal junior officials. Metehau's letter never reached the Queen, and was never answered.

Notes

1. Fox on Mantell, Hocken Ms NZ Notes: 35
2. Durie–Russell, 26.11.1847, Mantell Ms 83/155.
3. Grey Ms Letters Mss 201.
4. Domett–Mantell, 2.8.1848, Mantell Ms 83/148; *AJHR* 1888 I-8: 91 q198.
5. McCleverty was now Commander of the Forces, member of the Executive Council and member of the Board of Management for

Native Reserves for New Munster.
6. Hurwitz 1971: 157.
7. MLCI 1B: 82 and1A: 13.
8. *AJHR* 1888 I-8: 88 q145, 92 q235.
9. Wakefield–Wills, 5.8.1848, NAW NZC 3/8: 432ff.
10. McHugh 1991: 110.
11. Wakefield–Wills, op cit.
12. Ormond–Mantell, 2.8.1848, Mantell Ms 83/149.
13. SNC 3/4: 199; Mantell–Domett, 30.1.1849, in Mackay 1873 I: 216.
14. SNC 3/2: 150ff; *AJHR* 1888 I-8: 89 q163ff: Mantell here agreed that 'Ngai Tahu would not have parted with the land unless they imagined they would have very large reserves.'
15. *LT*, 13.5.1879: 5e; MLCI 1B: 44; SNC 3/4: 192–94; 3/6: 241–42, 270–73; 3/7: 286; 3/10: 386.
16. Mantell–Gisborne, 30.1.1849, in Mackay 1873 I: 216.
17. SNC 3/2: 153; 3/4: 200.
18. Mantell Ms Sketchbook 3: 151.
19. Ibid: 9–10; Mantell–Gisborne, 5.9.1848, in Mackay 1873 I: 213. The block was about 100,000 hectares.
20. Mantell Ms Outline Journal Kaiapoi to Otago 1848–49, 30.8.1848, and Sketchbook 3: 2.
21. Wills–Wakefield, 21.9.1848 (2), Wills Ms Letters.
22. SNC 3/8: 400; Mantell–Gisborne, 21.9.1848, in Mackay 1873 I: 214. Mantell and Wills reported that Ngai Tuahuriri were moving because they had sold Banks Peninsula to the French.
23. SNC 3/11: 400ff.
24. SNC 7/94: 724ff, 773ff; Mantell Ms Sketchbook 3: 150.
25. Mantell Ms Sketchbook 3: 36 and passim.
26. SNC 3/2: 157; Mantell Ms Outline Journal, 5.9.1848; Mantell–Gisborne, 5.9.1848, in

Mackay 1873 I.213. Metehau is here misspelt 'Mitcham'. Mantell's journal says Metehau 'succeeded in winning many to his side', but his official report to Gisborne says Metehau had no supporters. Wills (loc cit) said Metehau was a 'cunning troublesome fellow', all too familiar with the 'Hutt question and native successes in Hutt and Horokiwi skirmishes &c'.
27. Mantell–Gisborne, 5.9.1848, in Mackay 1873 I: 213.
28. Mantell Ms 1530: 12–13.
29. Mantell Ms Outline Journal.
30. Mantell–Domett, 30.1.1849, in Mackay 1873 I: 216ff.
31. Mantell's copy is now CMA Map 140/8.
32. Te Uki took this grievance to the SNC on 5.4.1880 (SNC 8 App. 51).
33. Mantell–Private Secretary, 21.9.1848 (2), in Mackay 1873 I: 214.
34. SNC 7/96: 731–32; Domett–Mantell, 24.12.1849 and Eyre–Kemp, 13.6.1850, in Mackay 1873 I: 227–29.
35. Mantell Ms Sketchbook 3: 121.
36. MLCI 1B: 43, 45.
37. SNC 3/7: 299ff; 7/96: 730ff.
38. Mantell-Rolleston, 12.4.1866, in Mackay 1873 I: 241–42.
39. SNC 3/6.255, 4/34.711ff.
40. MLCI 1A: 12–14; *AJHR* 1888 I-8: 39 q142–48; SNC 7/95:727.
41. Mantell Ms 1530: passim.
42. Mantell Ms Outline Journal, 3.11.1848.
43. Ibid, 19.10.1848. According to Mantell, this was at Tarawhata's request.
44. Mackay 1873 I: 217.
45. Tiramorehu–Mantell, 20.11.1848, Mantell Ms 1530.
46. SNC 3/5: 234. Kettle's deed map showed a population of 185.

Mantell reported 87.

47. Grey–Owen, 3.11.1848, Sherborn Autographs. Grey had made 'a very large collection' of fossil bones for Owen, but lost them in a house fire.
48. Mackay 1873 I: 218; Mantell Ms Outline Journal, 4–6.12.1848; Kettle–Cargill, 6.8.1850, Kettle Ms Letters.
49. MLCI 1A: 14; *AJHR* 1888 I-8: 39 q148.
50. SNC 3/2: 692.
51. Mackay 1873 I: 216–19.
52. Mantell–Domett, 30.1.1849, in Mackay 1873 I: 218.
53. For Mantell's 1848 census, see Mackay 1873 I: 220 for a summary and Mantell Ms Outline Journal for details. The census is curious in that it records sixty-two 'hapu' among his 637 persons. A population of 956 persons was later proved for Kemp's block for 1848, and a further 377 outside it with rights to the land (*NTBB*: passim). Alexander Mackay thought Mantell underestimated the Kemp's block Maori population by 843 (*AJHR* 1891 G-7A: 3). With the 377 living outside the block, this would give 1,857 claimants to the reserves.
54. Oliver 1990: 135a.
55. Eyre–Mantell, 4.10.1848, Mantell Ms 83/149; *AJHR* 1888 I-8: 92 q235–38.
56. NAW G/7/4 Mantell–Eyre, 23.12.1848 (2); Mackay 1873 I: 215–16.
57. Hocken Ms NZ Notes: 36.
58. Mantell Ms 1530: 11–12.
59. Torlesse 1958: 47. Torlesse referred to Maoris as 'blackbirds' (ibid: 49).
60. SNC 7/96: 732.
61. SNC 3/6: 255.
62. SNC 3/6: 246ff.
63. SNC 3/9: 357ff.
64. Mantell–Colonial Secretary, 30.1.1849, in Mackay 1873 I: 216ff; Mantell Ms 83/150, 22.2.49; Mackay 1873 II: 201. See also MLCI 1A: 13. Mantell told the Land Court: 'When I paid the instalments I got as many additional signatures as I could to the receipts.'
65. Domett–Mantell, 13.2.1849, Mantell Ms 83/150; SNC 3/9: 357ff; Tiramorehu–Eyre, 22.10.1849, in Mackay 1873 I: 227–28. Domett repeats Mantell's story that Tikao had kept Kemp's payment for himself, but Maori eyewitnesses later testified that Tikao distributed it honestly (SNC 3/7: 291; 3/4: 208; 3/10: 387).
66. *NZS*, 7.2.1849: 3.
67. Corrected translation by Te Aue Davis.
68. Grey–Earl Grey, 10.2.1849, in Mackay 1873 I: 212.
69. Stokes–Eyre, 14.2.1849 (misdated 1848), Stokes Ms Papers.
70. Log, 19.2.1849, Stokes Ms Papers.
71. SNC 3/7: 296.
72. Mantell Ms 83/193.
73. Mantell Ms 1530: 61.
74. DOSLIW Canterbury No. 1, verso.
75. Mackay 1873 I: 211, 239.
76. MLCI 1B: 70. Mantell said the plan 'was attached to the deed when I received it from the Government, and it was attached when the receipt was signed and when I returned it to the Government'.
77. SNC 3/9: 359. Patuki recalled: 'Mr Mantell then began to preach his gospel to us. He said, "I will preach to you."'
78. SNC 3/4: 201ff, 214; 3/6: 246ff; 3/7: 297ff.
79. Hay 1915: 8ff.
80. Selwyn 1849: 87.

81. *AJHR* 1888 I-8: 44; SNC 3/2: 146ff; 4/33: 689.
82. DOSLIW Canterbury No. 1, verso.
83. MLCI 1B: 44.
84. Eyre–Fox, 26.2.1849 and Grey–Eyre, 26.3.1849, in Mackay 1873 I: 222.
85. *NZS*, 17.3.1849.
86. *NZS*, 26.5.1849, 2.6.1849.
87. *NZS*, 22.2.1849. This translation is in Grey's London despatch of 22.3.1849.
88. *BPPPNZ* 1850: 66.
89. Thomas named the whole range after Torlesse (Torlesse 1958: 45n).
90. Stokes Ms *Acheron* Journal 1849–1851: 158. The typescript 'Acheron Journal' in HL Ms 168 has transcription errors.
91. Metehau–Queen Victoria, 2.4.1849, in Eyre–Grey, 21.6.1849, NAW G7/6 No. 62 (with Mantell–Eyre, 15.6.1849, and Kemp's comments in margin of Mantell's letter). Translation by Te Aue Davis. Metehau writes 'Nui Tireni' for New Zealand.
92. Ibid. Metehau was never a captive (Te Maire Tau, pers. comm.).
93. Ibid. Metehau's distinctive signature, 'Nateoti Wiremu Metehau', does not appear on Kemp's deed or Mantell's receipts.

13

~

A New Invasion

THE ECONOMY of colonial New Zealand was depressed in 1849 – especially at Wellington, where an earthquake in October 1848 had frightened many people away. The proposed 'Canterbury' settlement was keenly awaited, as a boost to business as well as to official appointments. But the site had yet to be decided, and for this the approval of Governor Grey and of Bishop Selwyn was required. Wellington people wanted 'Canterbury' to be at nearby Wairarapa.[1] Grey also favoured Wairarapa, or Rangitikei-Manawatu,[2] while Aucklanders could only regret that the choice was officially confined to New Munster.

The chief surveyor for 'Canterbury', Captain Joseph Thomas, on 28 February 1849 formally notified William Fox, the New Zealand Company's Chief Agent, that the Port Cooper district was his choice for the new settlement. But, said Thomas, the French still claimed 30,000 acres on Banks Peninsula – yet Ngai Tahu denied having sold it. He could not begin surveying, said Thomas, until he had the government's assurance that Maori title in the region had been completely extinguished.[3] Thomas and Fox therefore sailed for Auckland to see the Governor and Bishop Selwyn, leaving Charles Torlesse to explore 'the Great Plain'.

At Auckland, Fox tried hard to persuade Governor Grey for Port Cooper, but without success. One day when they were out riding, their disagreement became heated. 'I am Lord High Admiral here,' said Grey, 'and I will prevent your taking the harbour of Port Cooper.'[4] But Fox was not to be browbeaten. From his lodgings he boldly wrote to Grey demanding Port Cooper and Port Levy for the new settlement. He 'observed from a parliamentary paper in his possession', said Fox, that the French claimed land at both harbours. Furthermore, Grey had yet to carry out Lord

Stanley's instructions of 1845, said Fox, by transferring 30,000 acres of Banks Peninsula to the French. Fox had a suggestion for Grey. Kemp's deed plan excluded the peninsula from Kemp's purchase, but the deed itself did not. The deed should prevail, said Fox: otherwise, Grey would have to repurchase Banks Peninsula.[5]

After a dignified interval, Grey approved of the Port Cooper site, as did Selwyn. Grey's consent was eased by a glowing report from Captain Stokes, who described the breathtaking view from Maungatere, Ngai Tuahuriri's sacred mountain – which he had renamed 'Governor Grey':

> I saw one entire plain stretching a hundred miles to the south-ward and watered by a multitude of streams that like silver threads meandered in their seaward course. On the east lay the deep blue sea broken in the distance by the many peaked hills of Banks Peninsula, and on the west – a distance varying from 20 to 50 miles – rose a range of mountains of sufficient elevation to have their summits capped with snow. Northwards from Maungatere further plains of considerable extent were observed.[6]

Stokes estimated that the territory 'northwards', which the Crown regarded as part of the Ngati Toa Wairau purchase, contained 934,000 acres suitable for agriculture, and another 566,000 'rugged, but good for sheepruns'. Grey, as we have seen, had already reported to London that all this was available for European settlement, even though Ngai Tahu had repeatedly asserted that it was part of their own customary tribal territory.[7]

After their Auckland disagreement, Grey never again warmed to Fox. But he had no desire to follow in the footsteps of Robert FitzRoy. He therefore informed Lieutenant-Governor Eyre that Banks Peninsula was part of Kemp's purchase – contrary to what William Wakefield had maintained. Lord Stanley's French grant could be allocated from Akaroa and Pigeon Bay, Grey told Eyre, but Ports Cooper and Levy were to be deemed 'a reserve made upon behalf of the Natives under Kemp's deed, which they dispose of to the Government for the use of the new settlement about to be established'.[8] The New Zealand Company had called the tune, the Governor-in-Chief was dancing to it, and Ngai Tahu land rights were further imperilled.

∾

The Nanto-Bordelaise Company by 1845 had been reduced to virtual bankruptcy, for the British annexation of New Zealand had cooled French enthusiasm for the Company's Akaroa venture. But Lord Stanley's promise of 30,000 acres gave the company a useful bargaining counter. Therefore, when Akaroa Police Magistrate Robinson resigned and followed his friend Belligny back to Europe, he found his way into the service of the New Zealand Company in London, as their agent in negotiating to buy out the French company. In France, Belligny found out the lowest price the French company was likely to accept, and informed Robinson, who secretly informed the New Zealand Company in return for a commission for Belligny and a fee for himself. When Belligny reported that the French were baulking at the low price being offered, Robinson prompted the New Zealand Company to threaten to close negotiations. At last, on 30 June 1849, the New Zealand Company in London bought the French company's Banks Peninsula interests for £4,500. French land titles at Akaroa were guaranteed. Belligny was awarded fifty hectares at Pigeon Bay and ten at Takamatua – all of which were later transferred to Robinson.[9]

On the very day that the news of the French sale was despatched to William Fox from London, together with the French 'purchase deeds' for Banks Peninsula, Captain Thomas and his party embarked at Wellington for Port Cooper, along with Commissioner Walter Mantell and his cat and Maori porter. Mantell had recently sent Grey his report, *The Geology of a Portion of the Middle Island*.[10] At Port Cooper, Thomas was to prepare for the arrival of the Canterbury settlers, while Mantell was to 'extinguish the Native title' on Banks Peninsula in line with Grey's decision that it was to be yielded to the government for a 'modest compensation'.[11] Mantell planned to acquire Banks Peninsula by purchasing in turn Port Cooper, Port Levy and Akaroa – the order of their importance to the New Zealand Company.

Grey's decision on Banks Peninsula accorded perfectly with the New Zealand Company's doctrine that 'Wilderness land is worth nothing to its Native owners, or worth nothing more than the trifle they can obtain for it'. But the decision also implied three assumptions, all of them false: firstly, that Ngai Tahu had agreed to sell the French Lord Stanley's 30,000 acres; secondly, that they did not want the rest of Banks Peninsula; and thirdly, that a 'modest compensation' (which Fox had fixed at £350) could sufficiently compensate the two or three hundred Banks Peninsula Maoris for the loss of their homeland.

Eyre, in instructing Mantell on his Banks Peninsula duties, had suggested that Mantell could falsely represent to Ngai Tahu that under the 1841 Land Claims Ordinance they had already forfeited the peninsula to the Crown by having sold land there to the French.[12] 'And if Ngai Tahu rejected this?' Mantell had asked. Then, said Eyre, 'Let them leave it.' Mantell must 'carry matters with a high hand'. Mantell wrote this in his notebook in Greek script, secure from untutored eyes:

Λετ θεμ λεαφε ιτ. Ι μυστ καρι ματερζ ωιθ α 'ι 'ανδ.
[Let them leave it. I must kari maters with a hi hand.]

And, Mantell had asked, what if Ngai Tahu resisted his survey, as Metehau had done at Tuahiwi? Then, said Eyre, 'Summon the Akaroa Police.'[13] Eyre, incidentally, had been writing to Grey, about

[the] political influence which is so necessary to lead on a simple and uncivilized race from one stage of improvement to another, or to secure their steady adherence to that extensive change in their habits, pursuits, and train of thoughts which it is so desirable to attain.[14]

~

Mantell arrived at Port Cooper with Thomas's expedition in the dead of winter. Ice was on the harbour. A severe measles epidemic had been raging, leaving the survivors despondent.[15] The aged Nohomutu was senior chief, and lived at Purau with his remaining ten people. Te Whakarukeruke, Te Uki, Tiakikai and Tukaha were associated with him in the rangatiratanga of the Port Cooper district.

Nohomutu asked for £2 million, with large reserves, when Mantell announced to the chiefs that Port Cooper was required for European settlement. Tukaha wanted a large payment in ships, boats and horses. But Mantell would not discuss prices. He was there, he said, to allocate reserves and award any small payments he thought appropriate. He again promised to reserve the mahinga kai that Te Uki had repeatedly requested elsewhere.[16] But at Port Cooper, he said, he would allow reserves only at Rapaki and Purau, and pay only £160. At this, Nohomutu went off to consult his kinsmen around Banks Peninsula.[17]

When Nohomutu returned, Mantell's terms were emphatically rejected, and none of his arguments could sway the Maoris. To 'cut the knot', Mantell sent his surveyor, Octavius Carrington, to mark out the Purau reserve.[18] The New Zealand Company had granted George and William Rhodes 450 acres at Purau, or 'Rhodes's Bay'.[19] Mantell allowed only ten acres there for Nohomutu and his people, despite their protests, and firewood rights at Motuhikarehu. All their other cultivations were to be vacated.

After further weeks of argument, Nohomutu and seventeen others signed Mantell's Port Cooper deed on 10 August. Those who refused to sign it would be excluded from the reserves, said Mantell.[20] His Port Cooper block encompassed the 65,000 acres of the Rhodes brothers' Maori lease. The deed transferred 'all the land, and all belonging thereto' to the Queen, in return for £200 and reserves at Purau and Rapaki – the latter of 850 acres, with less than sixty acres arable.[21] Mantell recorded that the signatories were 'highly satisfied'. He then went off to the Rhodes homestead, his source of beer.[22]

∾

Mantell's Port Levy block comprised some 100,000 acres, extending from Waihora to Pohatupa. There were Maori settlements at several bays, with valuable podocarp forests, among them Pigeon Bay and Kawatea – where Tuahuriri's son Moki had first come ashore and tended his karaka grove six generations earlier. The block also included Kaituna, a fertile, forested valley of great cultural importance to the Maori. Four Maori groups held rights in the Port Levy block: those at Koukourarata in Port Levy, led by Apera Pukenui; those at Kawatea and other bays to the east; those at Wainui, Opukutahi and Wairewa; and Ngai Tuahuriri at Puari, who claimed pre-eminence.

Mantell arrived at Koukourarata on 15 August 1849, and was told by Pukenui's party that their price for the Port Levy block was £1,000: half for those living in the eastern bays, and half for themselves. They wanted reserves at Koukourarata, Pigeon Bay and Kawatea. John Tikao reminded Mantell of Governor Grey's promise, witnessed by Akaroa Magistrate John Watson, of a reserve at Pigeon Bay where his child was buried.[23] Mantell, however, offered £300 for the whole Port Levy block. Pukenui refused this, saying that he had just been offered £100 for just 200 acres by a guest of the Sinclairs.[24] And so matters stood.

Mantell now sheltered in his tent from the wintry weather, reading books, writing to his father,[25] drinking sherry with Carrington,

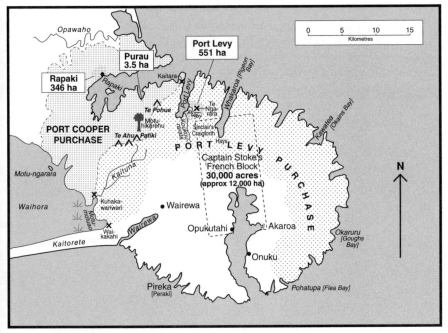

Mantell's Banks Peninsula purchases and reserves, 1849.

talking to chiefs who came to see him, and nursing a severe tooth-
ache. Gradually his hopes were realised. As more chiefs arrived,
more disputes broke out among them. Maopo, Pohau and Tamakeke
quarrelled bitterly with Pukenui when they arrived over the hills
from Wairewa and heard that Kaituna was to be sold.[26]

After ten days of arguments, Pukenui asked Mantell outside to
hear Tamakeke, an accomplished orator. Tamakeke spoke for two
hours. He denied that Ngai Tahu had forfeited Banks Peninsula by
selling land to the French, and ridiculed Mantell's offer of £300.
'£1,000 or nothing,' said Tamakeke. He would keep his own land for
his children, he said, and give some to the French if they returned.
Bérard and Belligny, before they left, had told him: 'If you sell to the
French, you will be safe. If you sell to the English, you will be driven
to the tops of the snowy mountains.'[27]

But further divisions emerged among the Maoris as more days
passed. The Port Cooper chiefs disagreed with Pukenui and his
supporters regarding Kaituna, and so did Maopo's party. Some feared
that Taiaroa and Patuki might come and interfere. Others were

impatient to be gone, for it was time for spring planting: besides, Captain Thomas was employing Maoris as road-builders.[28] At last Mantell asked Pukenui to his tent and told him the intended Koukourarata reserve would be marked out next day. Pukenui protested that the purchase had not been agreed to. He wanted to see Governor Grey about his promises of February 1848. He asked Mantell out of his tent. Unity returned to the Maori camp. Pukenui and Tamakeke both insisted on £1,000, otherwise they would keep their land. 'Everyone agreed with Tamakeke,' noted Mantell in his diary.

Mantell now adopted Eyre's suggestion, and addressed the Maoris as follows:

> Listen to me. You talk about keeping the land. How can such language apply to land for which payment has already been given? When I came here my first care was to set apart and have surveyed reserves for you so that you might not be driven off the land. As to the money which I have awarded, I shall not increase it because it is what I think just so I see no reason for exceeding the amount of £300 on which I have decided. This money you can take or not, the land will nevertheless belong to the Governor. Never mind the money, let me take care of you. If tomorrow is a fine day I shall direct Mr Carrington to begin the survey of the reserve. You have said the survey shall not proceed until I have agreed to your terms. This is foolish. If you really prevent the survey, the boundaries of your land will be vague and undefined and will most probably be narrowed.[29]

At this, Tamakeke, Maopo, Pohau, Pokene, Tikao and all the Ngai Tuahuriri chiefs departed.[30]

❧

Seth Howland, an American boat-builder, had settled at Kawatea with his wife Hari Tiki, a cousin of Pukenui. Hearing of Mantell's activities, he went to Koukourarata to confront him. He loudly ridiculed Mantell's assertion that Banks Peninsula already belonged to the Governor, and challenged Mantell to eject him from Kawatea. 'Bring him under notice,' wrote Mantell in his notebook.

Mantell now instructed Carrington to survey a Maori reserve of 1,361 acres at Port Levy, mostly steep hillside. Carrington, in the process, caused an uproar by standing on the sacred red rocks of Te Ngarara, a strict preserve of tohungas.[31] Pukenui, worn down by dissension, at last agreed to accept the reserve, with a payment of £300. 'I wanted the other £200 for people to pay their debts,' Pukenui told Mantell. 'I have no children to inherit from me, nor have most of us.'[32]

Money to pay the £300 arrived from Eyre, with the admonition: 'The Natives have already been so well compensated for their claims generally, that they can only anticipate additional payments as a matter of grace.'[33] Eyre sent Mantell C. B. Robinson's reports on the 1845 French 'purchases' – 'which it is supposed may be of some use to you in your negotiations with the Natives'.[34] The Port Levy deed was signed by Pukenui and twenty-one of his people on 25 September 1849. Mantell had five more names added to the signatures 'by proxy' – including that of Tamakeke, his strongest opponent. Of twenty-eight chiefs whom Mantell recorded as having attended some part of his 'negotiations' at Port Levy, only eight signed the deed.[35] With the £300, Pukenui by general consent bought a schooner. It was wrecked soon afterwards.[36]

Mantell now went on to Akaroa. He tried for two days to persuade the Akaroa chiefs to sell the 85,000-acre Akaroa block, but without success. Led by Tikao and Tamakeke, they insisted on keeping half the block for themselves, including the western side of Akaroa Harbour, the southern bays of Banks Peninsula, and the Wairewa basin. In reply, Mantell announced his award: £150 for the block and 1,880 acres in reserves. The Maoris rejected this, and left Mantell to himself.[37] But if they thought this was a victory for them, they were mistaken, for Mantell's Akaroa award was official, and final. The £150 remained in Magistrate Watson's safe, and the proffered reserves remained unsurveyed. Stokes had already selected the attractive upper reaches of Akaroa Harbour and Pigeon Bay as the 'most eligible site' for Lord Stanley's French grant of 30,000 acres.[38]

∼

The smallness of Mantell's reserves in Kemp's block caused bitter recriminations between those Maoris who had signed Kemp's deed and those who had not.[39] Mantell's Banks Peninsula awards now compounded the sense of outrage. Matiaha Tiramorehu, as a leading Kemp's deed signatory, wrote at length to Eyre from Moeraki in September 1849, protesting:

> When Mr Kemp came here he placed the boundary of the Ngatitoas' land at Kaiapoi. This mistake caused our hearts to be darkened. Since then, Mantell arrived here, and when the

Maoris saw the portions which he reserved for them they began to quarrel.

Grey had not kept his promise to pay Ngai Tahu for Kaiapoi, said Tiramorehu, and Eyre had wrongly dismissed their deputation in Wellington. Ngai Tahu had strenuously urged that the Maori share of the land should be large, yet Mantell had allowed, for example, only 500 acres for the whole Moeraki community. Tiramorehu asked: 'Do you, Governor Eyre, think that I should tell him to reserve for the multitude a piece of land only large enough for one man?' All Mantell's reserves should be extended, he said, so that 'we may have plenty of land to cultivate wheat and potatoes, also land where our pigs, cattle and sheep can run at large'. He admonished Eyre:

> This is but the commencement of our complaining to you, Governor Eyre. And even if you return to England we shall never cease complaining to the white people who may here-after come here.[40]

A month later, Mantell learned that one of Torlesse's trig stations had been destroyed. Torlesse wanted the culprits dealt with. A Wairewa man and his Ngati Kahungunu companion were arrested, and fined £2 by Magistrate Watson. Te Uki paid the fines, of which Watson refunded him fifteen shillings.[41] Mantell then reported his Akaroa award to Eyre. He said that he had told the Akaroa chiefs that they were entitled only to their residences and gardens, but they had conducted themselves 'as usual, in the most insolent and turbulent manner', demanding much of the block for themselves – which he had refused to allow.[42]

On 4 December 1849, Fox informed the New Zealand Government that his company had bought out the Nanto-Bordelaise Company. Mantell now received £1,000 from Wellington for the final instalment for Kemp's purchase, and sailed off to pay the southern chiefs at Koputai. There, in a whare, he saw for the first time the splendid indigo-blue, cobalt, turquoise and buff-green colours of the rare takahe, skinned, along with kakapo and kiwi. These birds had been captured in Fiordland by sealers. Mantell acquired the takahe skin from its owner and sent it to his father in London.[43] Dr Mantell exhibited the specimen at the Zoological Society and had it restored and mounted as *Notornis mantelli*, to take pride of place in his Chester Square drawing room. He urged his son to send more *Notornis*, for which the going price in London was '£20 to £25' per bird, he said.[44]

For the final instalment of Kemp's purchase, Mantell carefully prepared two fresh parchments as receipts, one inscribed in English and the other in Maori.[45] On the Maori receipt he wrote: 'Hei utunga wakamutunga mo nga wenua katoa i roto i te pukapuka tuku-wenua o Mr Commissioner Kemp i wakaaetia ai i a Akaroa i te 12 o Hunae 1848' (Final payment for all lands within the deed of sale that was agreed to with Mr Commissioner Kemp at Akaroa on 12 June 1848).[46] But on the English receipt he wrote: 'Last combined instalments on the purchase of the Ngaitahu block, including the whole of the lands specified in the deed of conveyance at Akaroa on 12th June 1848.'

'Ngaitahu block' was the official term for the block shown on Kettle's sketch map attached to Kemp's deed as a 'deed plan'. Unlike the deed, the map clearly included the West Coast and the mountainous interior of the island, the sale of which Ngai Tuahuriri had disputed. But in the Maori receipt, the expression 'within the deed of sale agreed to with Mr Commissioner Kemp' implied that the payment was for lands Ngai Tahu had *agreed* to sell to Kemp. Only the Maori receipt was intelligible to the Maoris, since their mission-trained scholars could not read English. Mantell got as many Ngai Tahu as possible to sign both parchments. Eleven signed them at Koputai on 17 December 1849, including five new signatories, and another nineteen signed at Akaroa on 28 December, including twelve new signatories. The document in English became the official receipt.[47] The Maori document was never published.

Mantell's fresh signatures brought the number of legally valid Kemp's purchase signatures to forty-two. But there were still twenty-five chiefs and heads of whanau with rights in Kemp's block who had not signed Kemp's deed, or any of Mantell's receipts, including Hakaroa, Kaikoareare, Koeti, Te Maire, Te Matahara, Mautai, Metehau, Naihira, Pokene, Te Rehe, Te Ruaparae, Taetae, Taki, Tamakeke, Tarapuhi, Tuahuru, Tuhuru, Tuauau, Rangi Whakana, and Te Whakarukeruke.[48]

Mantell, on returning to Wellington with his receipts, was given Tiramorehu's letter of protest with a 'please explain' from Eyre, who was peeved at receiving Maori complaints on a matter he supposed to be closed.[49] In reply, Mantell supplied Eyre with his incorrect estimate of 200 Ngai Tuahuriri at Port Levy and eighty-seven at Moeraki. For these 287, Mantell wrote, he had provided 3,145 acres – including the 'fine and valuable estate' of 2,640 acres at Tuahiwi, which sufficed 'for them all'. He told Eyre:

> By this you will perceive that the wants of the Natives are amply provided for in the reserves which I made, the boundaries of which, at the time of the survey, were in each case approved by them.[50]

Five months later, Eyre instructed Kemp to answer Tiramorehu:

> Reply to this that the question raised by them was long since settled by Governor Grey, who told them, on their applying to him at Wellington, that he could not disturb or reopen the arrangement made relative to the purchase of Wairau, Kaiapoi, etc., from the Ngatitoas. Neither can I now consent to reopen or alter any arrangement relative to the reserves at Moeraki. I have examined into the matter, and find that the reserve made there contains 500 acres, which is considerable for the very few Natives resident there.[51]

Tiramorehu was informed accordingly.

Thus the 'very few' Maoris at Moeraki, whom Mantell recorded as eighty-seven, but who actually numbered nearly two hundred,[52] were condemned to subsist on five hundred acres. They were worse off than their relatives at Tuahiwi. Despite Tiramorehu's efforts, and his hospitality to Mantell, Ngai Tuahuriri had been dealt a crippling blow.

Ngai Tahu were now entitled to seek a remedy in the Supreme Court, where the 1847 judgment in *R. v Symonds* had held that the Crown's exercise of its demesne rights in New Zealand was subject to customary Maori title – the 'modified title of the Natives', which entitled them to all the benefits from the land, that they had enjoyed before the arrival of Europeans.[53] Ngai Tahu could also have challenged the government's right to vary the terms of their agreement with Kemp. With Chief Justice William Martin and Justice Henry Chapman still at the Supreme Court, they would no doubt have had an attentive hearing. But with Governor Grey as their official protector, Maoris knew nothing of their legal rights. Thus the government escaped a court action.

Ngai Tahu continued to complain to Governor Grey about the Wairau purchase and Mantell's reserves.[54] But such complaints were foredoomed, for they were all referred to Mantell. Thus when Tikao protested again about the Wairau purchase, Mantell told the government that the disputed land was Crown demesne because it was so sparsely populated.[55] Only once did a Ngai Tahu protest bear fruit. In August 1850, Charles Kettle found that all the North Otago Maoris were discontented with Mantell's reserves, particularly at Moeraki and Waikouaiti.[56] Kettle was on personal terms with Grey, and arranged for him to receive the Waikouaiti chiefs during his official visit to Dunedin in November. Afterwards, on Grey's orders, Kettle added 900 acres to the Waikouaiti reserve.[57]

∽

The New Zealand Company by mid-1850 had become dissatisfied with their profits, and gave the British Government due notice of surrendering their charter and ceasing operations. To protect the Canterbury Association, Parliament on 14 August 1850 passed the Canterbury Association Lands Settlement Act, transferring to the Association the Company's former right to dispose of 'waste and unappropriated land' in the million-hectare 'Canterbury block' – defined as bounded by the sea coast on the east and the 'snowy range of hills' on the west, and the 'Ashburton' (Hakatere) River in the south and 'Double Corner' (Waipara) in the north. The Act confirmed the Association's land price of £3 per acre, and its pastoral lease charge of £1 a year per hundred acres.

Thanks to Governor Grey's despatches,[58] neither Parliament nor the Canterbury Association knew that within the Canterbury block Ngai Tahu had been promised mahinga kai and kainga nohoanga, and further reserves, and that they disputed the Wairau purchase which according to Grey included the northern portion of the Canterbury block. The Canterbury Association's first four ships arrived in December 1850 at Port Cooper, renamed Lyttelton, bringing 575 'emigrants' and 207 'colonists', coyly referred to as the 'Canterbury Pilgrims'. Grey was there to meet them; but he did not meet local Ngai Tahu to discuss their complaints.

Clause 11 of the Canterbury Association Lands Settlement Act, however, specifically protected 'the rights of any person or persons entitled or claiming to be entitled to any of the lands described in the said schedule by virtue of any deed or contract made or entered into previously to the passing of this Act'. Kemp's deed was such a contract, as were the oral promises made to Ngai Tahu by Grey, Kemp and Mantell in 1848 and 1849. A court of law would no doubt have held that these undertakings, or at least those in Kemp's deed, were binding on the Crown. Clause 11 helped the Deanses and the

Rhodeses to retain the benefits of their Maori leases. But the safeguards of the law again escaped Ngai Tahu, who knew nothing of
them.

Organised European settlement at Otago and Canterbury
quickly brought temporary advantages for Maoris of southern New
Zealand, in more opportunities for marketing potatoes, wheat and
firewood, and in enabling chiefs with schooners and whaleboats to
enlarge their coastal trade.[59] The poorer Europeans required fish,
since meat was expensive, and Maoris turned increasingly to commercial fishing.[60] But although Maoris in southern New Zealand
produced potatoes, maize, wheat, melons, cabbages and other exotic
vegetables for sale, traditional foods such as ti-kauka, eels and whitebait were still the basis of their own diet.[61]

∼

Under the Wakefield scheme, land was to be sold at a price sufficient to prevent all but the wealthy from acquiring large estates.
The New Zealand Company had achieved this with their prices of
thirty shillings per acre at Nelson, forty shillings at Otago, and sixty
shillings at Canterbury. But so little land had been sold at these
prices when the Company ceased operations in 1850, that the success of these settlements remained in doubt. Squatters like Clifford,
the Rhodes brothers and the Deans brothers, however, had shown
that in Te Wai Pounamu, as in Australia, sheep runs were profitable
where land could be got sufficiently cheaply. Lyttelton colonist James
Edward FitzGerald, later Canterbury's first Provincial Superintendent, wrote home to Britain:

> The only way to make money here is by sheep farming. Money
> may be literally coined in that trade. And it is eminently the
> profession of a gentleman. The sheep farmer may have his com-
> fortable house and gardens and a little farm producing all he
> requires, but his personal task is to ride about the country
> inspecting his vast flocks and giving directions for their man-
> agement.[62]

The Canterbury Association's resident agent, John Robert
Godley, advised by a committee headed by FitzGerald, reduced the
Canterbury pastoral rental in May 1851, so as to encourage pastoral farming, and wrote to Governor Grey asking that the Canterbury block be enlarged to include the whole of the plains, with a

percentage of the land revenue going to the Church of England. This prompted Grey to tell his Legislative Council:

> It does not appear to me – at a time when so large a portion of the population of Great Britain are in such distress – to be in accordance with any rule of Christianity, that the poor of the earth should have closed against them, by such restrictions, so large a tract of fertile country which a bounteous Providence has placed at the disposal of the human race.[63]

Grey, by means of the Crown Lands Amendment and Extension Ordinance of 28 July 1851, now extended to New Munster the favourable Crown pastoral lease regulations already operating in New Ulster.[64] Crown licences cost only £5, and the rental was based not on the area of the leased land but on the number of stock carried, at one penny a head for sheep and sixpence for cattle. The runholder was allowed five years to build up his flock, and was then allowed two acres per sheep. Thus a 20,000-acre run carrying 10,000 sheep would cost only £41 13s 4d a year. Leases were for fourteen-year terms, subject to cancellation if the land was required for closer settlement or was sold to another party; but compensation was allowed for any improvements.

In response, the Canterbury Association in February 1852 introduced further concessional lease rentals for its own block, providing for pastoral runs of up to 20,000 acres. By the end of 1852, fifty-two such runs had been taken up, half of them by Association colonists.[65] With the Canterbury Association and the Crown now vying for runholders, pastoral land in Kemp's block and the Wairau block attracted graziers even from Australia. An annual return of twenty-five per cent on money invested in sheep could be expected on these runs,[66] with cash returns coming from the sale of wool in England, and selling surplus stock to other farmers. Among the first in the field under Grey's regulations were Robert and George Rhodes, who drove five thousand of their Banks Peninsula sheep to beyond the Ashburton River and laid claim to more than 500 square kilometres of choice territory between the Opihi and the Otaio,[67] where Edward Shortland had watched Ngai Tahu at their mahinga kai seven years before.

The Deans brothers' 1846 Maori lease now came into question, since it encompassed most of the planned town of Christchurch. In 1852 Godley allowed John Deans to exchange it for Homebush, a foothills run of 33,000 acres – at that time the largest in the

Canterbury block. Because their Maori lease had been for a twenty-one-year term, they were allowed Homebush at the original Maori rental of £8 a year until 1867.[68] In the same year, the Rhodes brothers' Maori lease helped them to secure nearly a quarter of Banks Peninsula, including all Purau and Kaituna.[69] But Ngai Tahu, the authors of these handsome advantages, had to subsist on barely four acres per person.

~

The expansion of European pastoralism in southern New Zealand prompted further Maori protests in 1851. Te Poka of Akaroa wrote to Governor Grey complaining that settlers' cattle had been turned loose on his land. Grey told Magistrate Watson to look into it.[70] Watson, who had himself just applied for a pastoral lease at Akaroa, knew well that the Canterbury Association had leased out Te Poka's land, and he sent Grey's letter on to Godley.[71] Godley, of course, was empowered by the Canterbury Association Lands Settlement Act to dispose of all Banks Peninsula, except for reserves and land already Crown-granted. Godley claimed that the French 'deeds', which he said he now held, showed that Ngai Tahu had sold the whole peninsula to the French.[72]

Nohomutu's widow and the chief Poharama wrote to Grey from Purau, complaining about European stock mixing with their own, saying: 'Let them graze upon the lands which properly belong to the Europeans and leave our lands for our own use, and our landing-place for the boats belonging to the Maoris.' They objected to their land being disturbed, because Poharama's children, his wife and younger brothers, 'twelve in number', were buried there. Kaikoura Whakatau wrote to Grey from Kaikoura, demanding to be paid for the Wairau purchase territory south of Te Paruparu (near Kaparatehau).[73]

Thus Ngai Tahu were taking their grievances to the Governor, as Mantell had advised.[74] But they did not know that Grey himself, in deference to the New Zealand Company's requirements, had been the author of them. Nor could they get their complaints into courts of law, since they lacked lawyers and interpreters. Kiriona Pohau, who had signed Kemp's deed, believed Kaitorete was outside Kemp's purchase, as we have seen. In 1868 he recalled what happened when European pastoralists moved on to Kaitorete:

I told them that this land was ours – not in Kemp's purchase. I went to turn the white man off. I went to the Christchurch Land Office, but there was no interpreter. The white men looked at me, and I looked at them. I wrote to the Government, to Mantell at Port Nicholson. Fox was Minister. I wrote perhaps twelve letters in a year. I got no answer then, but I got one lately.[75]

The thousand or so Canterbury Maoris were soon outnumbered by European immigrants,[76] who variously regarded them with amusement, indifference, or contempt.[77] In February 1851, the *Lyttelton Times* published a resolution from a public meeting in Wellington:

The Native race is fast becoming extinct, and there is no prospect of their becoming as a body sufficiently enlightened for the exercise of political privileges before the period of their extinction shall arrive. Nevertheless some participation may be allowed provided sufficient guarantees be given against the possibility of the superior intelligence of the Europeans being over-balanced by the ignorance of the uncivilized race.[78]

Despite being thus scorned in their own homeland, however, Maoris of southern New Zealand clung to their Maoritanga. Charles Creed, struggling at his Waikouaiti mission, sensed a defiant resurgence of Maoritanga, with the chief Kahuti organising clandestine haka parties at dead of night – 'obscene and horrifying', said Creed.[79] Kaikoareare, now living with his followers at Aramoana, was 'a curse to the whole district', according to Creed – 'a great scoffer at religion, and a daring Sabbath breaker'.[80]

John Tikao had moved to Pigeon Bay to be near his son's grave. But thanks to the refusal of a reserve by Governor Grey and Walter Mantell, Ngai Tahu were now the squatters there. Tikao, nearing the end of his life, his wife and children all dead, wrote in despair to Grey:

Greetings, Governor. Now then, listen to me. I will now begin speaking to you. You in turn will think upon what I have to say to you concerning my home at Akaroa which we gave to you as far as Pigeon Bay. You must give us a part of Pigeon Bay. Let it be 300 or 500 acres of that portion of land of mine which was given to you at Akaroa. Governor, if you accept this address, send Mr Kemp. We hear that Akaroa is to be surveyed first, and afterwards Pigeon Bay. Look upon us few humble people with pity. Enough. John Tikao.[81]

Tikao's letter went unheeded. By 1857, only thirteen Maoris remained at Pigeon Bay. In 1859, just one remained – a northerner renting one acre from a European.[82]

∾

Te Rauparaha's invasions had been warded off by Ngai Tahu, only to be resurrected in the form of Governor Grey's Wairau purchase. The occupation of Ngai Tahu land in violation of Kemp's deed now constituted a new invasion, even more disastrous. Grey, amid a mine-field of difficulties, maintained his ascendancy by keeping the New Zealand Company's colonists supplied with plenty of land, and by keeping Maoris divided.[83] The portion of land revenue intended for Maori welfare was at his disposal.[84] With it he gave presents to loyal chiefs, and favours to their tribes. For Te Wai Pounamu, he deemed it sufficient to confine these favours to Ngati Toa.

By the end of 1853, runholders had occupied as much of the plains, hills and mountains of Te Wai Pounamu as they could under-take to stock with sheep or cattle. The cheap terms on which they obtained this 'waste land' had followed from the theory that it was worthless without European capital and labour, and the great wealth that accrued to successful runholders ensured the popularity of the theory. The 100,000-hectare Waimakariri block, which Ngai Tuahuriri had wanted to retain, was allocated among just a dozen runholders. Among them was Charles Torlesse, whose surveying had enabled him to find out the best land. In 1851 he acquired Fernside, an 8,000-hectare estate adjoining Mantell's Tuahiwi reserve, and including much of the remaining podocarp forest.[85] Thus some five hundred Ngai Tuahuriri had to subsist on the 1,000 hectares that Mantell had allowed them, while their neighbour Torlesse had eight times as much for himself, and soon acquired more across the Ashley River.

Mantell had told Ngai Tahu that schools were the key to suc-cess in the European world. But runholding required no schooling. The only prerequisite for becoming 'squire' of dozens of square kilometres was £1,000 or £1,200 in ready money: 'For the young man with moderate capital, the Canterbury Settlement in its first few years presented opportunities unsurpassed in the whole history of British colonization.'[86] Runholders came from many walks of life – 'baronets, younger sons of good families, soldiers, sailors, par-sons, lawyers, tradesmen, shepherds, and farmers'.[87] The success-

230

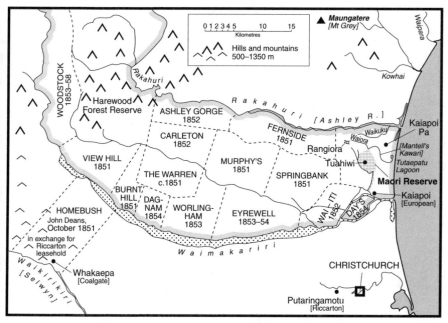

*The Waimakariri block and its allocation as pastoral runs
(after Acland 1975: 31).*

ful among these grew rich, and became the admired aristocrats of
colonial society. But Ngai Tahu, having no capital, and no means of
getting any, became poor, living as outcasts on their meagre, isolated reserves. The Maori prosperity observed by Shortland and
others during the 1840s, based on common land rights, was swept
away by the privatisation of the land into European hands. As had
happened in Britain, communal well-being was replaced by communal poverty and private wealth. With this transformation, a new
ethic crept into New Zealand affairs: deliberate lying by prominent
rangatira like Kemp and Mantell, and even by the ariki, Grey himself. To the Maori, this was beyond understanding.

Notes

1. Hocken Ms NZ Notes: 34ff.
2. Hight & Straubel 1957: 119; Grey–
   Fox, 11.12.1848, Canterbury
   Association Ms Papers 6/9: 1657.
3. Thomas–Fox, 28.2.1849, NAW
   NZC 107/1.

4. Hocken, op cit. Fox recalled: 'No
   more rides after this – but cool-
   ness.'
5. Fox–Grey, 9.4.1849, in Mackay
   1873 I: 250–51. The 'paper' was
   Godfrey's 1843 report.

6. Stokes–Grey, 4.5.1849, Stokes Ms 'Papers'.

7. Grey–Earl Grey, 5.5.1849, in *BPPNZ* 1850: 147ff; 15.5.1849, in *IUPBPPNZ* 6: 152ff.

8. Dillon–Fox, 27.4.1849, in Mackay 1873 I: 252; Domett–Mantell, 13.6.1849, Mantell Ms 83/150.

9. Tremewan 1990: 291ff.

10. Mantell–Domett, 28.5.1849, in Mackay 1873 I: 223.

11. Domett–Mantell, 13.6.1849, Mantell Ms 83/150.

12. MLCI 1B: 31.

13. Mantell Ms 1537: 105–6. The Akaroa Police consisted of two constables (Hill 1986 I: 265, 313).

14. Eyre–Grey (private), 29.5.1849, in *IUPBPPNZ* 6: 172.

15. Hay 1915: 8ff. Half the Maoris died at Pigeon Bay in this epidemic, says Hay, leaving the survivors 'quiet and peacefully disposed' instead of 'boastful and threatening'.

16. SNC 7/96: 732–33.

17. Mantell Ms 1537: 7–13.

18. Ibid. i.e., the knot of Gordius.

19. Hight & Straubel 1957: 117. Ogilvie (1970: 41) says the Rhodeses got 500 acres.

20. *AJHR* 1888 I-8: 36 q77.

21. DOSLIW Canterbury No. 5.

22. Mantell–Domett, 11.8.1849 (2), in Mackay 1873 I: 253–58.

23. Tikao–Mantell, 18.8.1849, Mantell Ms 1530.

24. Mantell Ms 1537: 31–32.

25. G. Mantell–W. Mantell, 31.1.1850, Mantell Ms 83/104.

26. Mantell Ms 1537: 31–32.

27. Mantell Ms 1536 'Tamakeke 25.8.1849'.

28. *NZS*, 22.8.1849.

29. Mantell Ms 1537: 42–43.

30. Mantell claimed that these chiefs, by departing, abandoned their claims (Mackay 1873 II: 199).

31. See Taylor 1950: 125.

32. Mantell Ms 83/150 and 1537: 45–53.

33. Domett–Mantell, 19.9.1849, Mantell Ms 83/159.

34. Domett–Mantell, 5.9.1849, NAW New Munster 49/771; Mantell Ms Letters and Memoranda 1848–56: 126ff.

35. DOSLIW Canterbury No. 2. Of the non-signatories, Mantell (Ms 1537) says the following attended at Port Levy: Tamakeke, Pohata Motunau, Te Aotewiria, Koti, John Pere, Waruwarutu, Maopo, Pohau, John Tikao, Paora Taki, Te Uki, Hupukuku, Huri, Te Ikawera, Metehau, Pokene, Te Muru, Te Oro, Okokorau and Petara.

36. Mackay 1873 II: 197.

37. Mantell–Domett, 28.11.1849, in Mackay 1873 I: 255.

38. Stokes–Fox, 23.6.1849, Stokes Ms Papers.

39. See SNC 3/8: 756ff.

40. Tiramorehu–Eyre, 22.10.1849 (transl), in Mackay 1873 I: 227–28. See Taiaroa Ms Papers/4a for copy of the Maori original, and Wai-27 T2.10–11 for transcript.

41. Torlesse–Thomas, 27.10.1849, in Thomas–Mantell, 29.10.1849, Mantell Ms 83/837; Torlesse 1958: 110–12.

42. Mantell–Domett, 28.11.1849, in Mackay 1873 I: 255.

43. WPS Minutes, 3.9.1881; Buller 1967: 164–66.

44. *Proceedings of the Zoological Society*, vol. 214, 1850; G. Mantell–W. Mantell, 29.10. 1850 & 25.11.1850, Mantell Ms 83/104. The living takahe was later classified as *Notornis hochstetteri*, to distinguish it from the fossil *N. mantelli* (Andersen Ms typed note).

45. DOSLIW Canterbury No. 1: two parchments each approximately A2 size.

46. Ibid, translation Te Aue Davis.

47. See e.g. Mackay 1873 I: 211–12. This mistakenly says that all signatures were taken at Otago.
48. See Evison 1993: 512ff.
49. Domett–Mantell, 24.12.1849, in Mackay 1873 I: 227.
50. Mantell–Domett, 24.1.1850, in Mackay 1873 I: 228.
51. Eyre–Kemp, 13.6.1850, in Mackay 1873 I: 229.
52. Kemp's deed plan, for example, indicates 185 people at Moeraki.
53. Haast 1938: 391; McHugh 1991: 108ff, 327ff.
54. See e.g. Tikao–Grey, 16.1.1850 (translation), in Mackay 1873 II: 7; and Tikao–Grey, 15.10.1850, Grey Ms Maori Letters: 618.
55. Mackay 1873 II: 6–7; draft in Mantell Ms 83/151.
56. Kettle–Cargill, 6.8.1850, Kettle Ms Letters.
57. Kettle–Mantell, 1.7.1852, Mantell Ms 83/152.
58. Grey–Earl Grey, 10.2.1849, in Mackay 1873 I: 212; Grey–Earl Grey, 15.5.1849, in *IUPBPPNZ* 6: 152ff.
59. Evison Ms 1952: 67ff; Wai-27 T1: 333–34; Creed Ms Journal, 8.7.1851; Woodhouse 1937: 57. In *AJHR* 1891 G-7: 57, Waruwarutu states: 'I used to run the cargo-boat to Timaru; got 8 shillings a bale for shipping wool, and made as much as £300 or £400 during a season. This work was afterwards taken up by the pakehas, and I lost the employment.'
60. *NTFSR*: 115ff.
61. Godley 1951: 137; Ward 1951: 104–9.
62. FitzGerald–Rintoul, 6.7.1851, quoted in Gardner 1971 II: 32.
63. *NZS*, 21.6.1851: 5. The Canterbury rental was 'impossibly high' (Macdonald 1956: 1).
64. Rutherford 1961: 190; Rice 1992: 63.

65. For lease terms in Nelson, Canterbury and Otago, see Acland 1975: 21ff; Beattie 1947a; Burdon 1938: chapter 3; Gardner 1971 II: chapter 2; Hall-Jones 1945: chapter 7; Hight & Straubel 1957: 186ff; McLintock 1949: 338ff; Pinney 1981; Sherrard 1966: 91ff.
66. Acland 1975: 29; Butler 1964: 39ff; Anon. 1976: 37 and passim.
67. Crawford 1981: 1–2 and passim.
68. Deans 1964: 75.
69. See Acland 1975: 329 and passim, Woodhouse 1937: map 'Pasturage Runs of Banks Peninsula'.
70. Domett–Watson, 15.4.1851, DOSLIW Ms Papers G4/290.
71. Watson–Godley, 19.5.1851 & 12.6.1851, DOSLIW Ms Papers G4/290(i); G4/741.
72. Godley–Watson, July 1851, Canterbury Assn Ms Letterbook B 18.7.1851–3.12.1851. Godley surrendered these1845 French 'deeds' to the government in 1852 (Godley–Domett, 17.9.1852, NAW NM8 52/1276). Their whereabouts is unknown.
73. Poharama and Wikitoria–Grey, 17.7.1852 and Whakatau–Grey, 25.7.1851, in Grey Ms Maori Letters: 523 (translation Te Aue Davis), 610.
74. *AJHR* 1888 I-8: 39q148.
75. MLCI 1B: 44.
76. There were 3,000 Europeans in Canterbury by 1852; more than 6,000 by 1856; more than 12,000 by 1859; and 20,000 by 1862 (Gardner 1971: 323).
77. See e.g. Sewell 1980 I: 129, 291–92, 435–36, 441; II: 130; Brooking 1984: 97, 98, 100 (cartoons); Stevenson 1900:130–31; Fitz-Gerald–Gladstone, 19.12.1851, Gladstone Papers 44371. Fitz-Gerald (an Irishman) wrote, 'The natives here [at Canterbury] are

quite as civilized as the English and much greater cheats.'

78. *LT*, 15.2.1851.

79. Creed Ms Journal, 8.7.1851 and 1–2.8.1851.

80 Creed–Mission Secretaries, 13.9.1851, Creed Ms Letters. Kaikoareare ran a popular ferry service on Otago harbour (Eccles 1944: 39–40).

81. Tikao–Grey, 30.12.1851 (translation), Grey Ms Maori Letters G622. The transcript in Wai-27 Z10: 12–13 mistakes Tikao's '1851' for '1857'.

82. Andersen 1927: 162; Mackay 1873 II: 127. Tikao died in 1852 (Tainui 1946: 228).

83. For Grey's North Island policy, see Dalton 1967: 47 and passim.

84. See *NTR*: 927ff.

85. Acland 1975: 31 (map), chapter 3 and passim.

86. Hight & Straubel 1957: 196ff.

87. Acland 1975: 24.

14

~

Honourable Proceedings

IN MURIHIKU by the 1850s the whaling industry had declined and the Maori population had diminished. But fifty years of sealing and whaling had given Murihiku a special character. More Europeans had married Maoris than elsewhere in Te Wai Pounamu. Horses, and European clothing, were in general use. Wheat, oats and tobacco were grown, besides potatoes. English was taught at the Reverend Johann Wohlers' Ruapuke school. Trade with Otago had enabled Maoris to get horses and cattle, and some hoped to get sheep. But old traditions survived. Potatoes were still grown in mounds, as in traditional kumara cultivation. The test of manhood was still to venture in open boats to the dangerous Fiordland and Poutini coasts in search of seals. The annual titi harvest sustained the ancient mahinga kai traditions, and contact with other Ngai Tahu.[1]

The establishment of the Otago settlement in 1848 soon threatened Murihiku with an influx of squatters seeking to avoid the New Zealand Company's high land prices. To avert this, Topi Patuki, while in Wellington in February 1849, had invited Governor Grey to Murihiku to discuss its purchase by the Crown. 'There we can talk and deliberate carefully about the area we will give up to you.' wrote Patuki. 'The larger area however must remain with us, the Maori people.' He added, 'Cease making mistakes as you did when you paid Rawiri Puaha in error for Kaiapoi.'[2]

When HMS *Acheron* arrived at Murihiku in March 1850 on its coastal survey mission, the Murihiku chiefs plied Captain Stokes with proposals, thinking he had come from Grey to buy land. Stokes was unaware that Patuki had told Grey that the Maoris wished to retain most of Murihiku, and reported to Eyre that they would sell it all, probably for £2,000. Stokes declared the district very suitable for colonisation, with 500,000 hectares of 'rich soil clothed with fine grass', and plentiful timber. Tuturau potatoes were perhaps the largest in the Southern Hemisphere, and Murihiku was 'fully a fortnight nearer England than any portion of New Zealand now under colonisation', urged Stokes.[3]

∾

Governor Grey moved from Auckland to Wellington early in 1851, and took over the Government House there from Eyre – whom he could no longer tolerate.[4] Walter Mantell was now in high favour with Grey, sharing his interest in science and his opposition to 'class settlements' like Otago and Canterbury. When Grey summoned Mantell on 10 March 1851 to discuss the purchase of Murihiku, Mantell proposed that the methods he had followed with Kemp's purchase should be repeated, describing them thus:

> In carrying out the spirit of my instructions on the block purchased by Mr Kemp, I allotted on an average ten acres to each individual, in the belief that the ownership of such an amount of land, though ample for their support, would not enable the Natives, in the capacity of large landed proprietors, to continue to live in their old barbarism on the rents of a uselessly extensive domain.[5]

Grey's presence in Wellington encouraged the formation of New Zealand's first scientific society – the New Zealand Society, founded on 2 July 1851 with Grey as president and Mantell as secretary.[6] Grey addressed the society as follows:

> We who stand in this country occupy an historical position of extraordinary interest. Before us lies a future already brilliant with the light of a glorious morn. Behind us lies a night of fearful gloom, unillumined by the light of written records, of picture memorials, of aught which can give a certain idea of the past. A few stray streaks of light in the form of tradition, of oral poetry, of carved records, are the only guides we have.[7]

In October 1851 Grey appointed Mantell Commissioner of Crown Lands for the New Munster Southern Districts, based at Dunedin, under the Crown Lands Amendment and Extension Ordinance of 28 July 1851. Mantell was also to purchase Murihiku for the Crown, first assessing the rights of each Maori claimant, and then awarding such reserves as he thought 'consistent with the public interest'. The price was not to exceed £2,000, paid in instalments over at least two years. Mantell was to report on the natural history of the region for Grey, and take a census.[8] Beyond these requirements, he had a free hand. Grey farewelled Mantell personally when he left for Dunedin. But on his arrival there, Mantell found his appointment being denounced. A leading newspaper declared that Otago had been insulted: 'A man whose disregard of morals and the ordinary decencies of life has made him conspicuous is hardly the person who should have been chosen to fill a high Government appointment.'[9]

Mantell left Dunedin for Murihiku on 3 December 1851 with two Europeans, and with Topi Patuki and his assistants. At Taieri, Mantell reported the rugged 2,310-acre reserve provided under the Otago purchase 'too large' for the twenty-three people living there. Arriving in Murihiku, he resumed his old methods. If he thought the Maoris asked too much, he gave them less. If they wanted reserves at places suitable for Europeans, he refused them. When the Tuturau chief Te Reko asked Mantell for 32,000 acres, the size of a large sheep run, Mantell awarded him 287 acres – and reported, 'Reko quite satisfied'.[10] At the Foveaux Strait settlements, Mantell held meetings and heard requests for reserves. In the Murihiku block of seven million acres he allocated seven Maori reserves totalling 4,875 acres, not all of it arable, for the 292 people he decided had valid claims.[11] This averaged 16.7 acres per head, when Europeans there were finding fifty acres insufficient for subsistence.[12]

Returning to Dunedin, Mantell sent to Grey asking for Charles Kettle (now in government employment) to survey the Murihiku reserves by May 1853, and for £1,000 with which to pay the first instalment on Murihiku by June.[13] Kettle surveyed the reserves in April, when most Maoris were away getting titi. The Murihiku purchase was now at a curious stage. The reserves were completed, yet there was no agreement to sell.

Meanwhile, six weeks after seeing Mantell off to Dunedin, Governor Grey received a complaint from Rawiri Puaha, Te Whiwhi and other Ngati Toa chiefs, about their old allies Ngati Rarua, Te Ati Awa and Ngati Raukawa claiming parts of Te Wai Pounamu.[14] Grey asked Major Mathew Richmond, now Superintendent at Nelson, to find out what these tribes were claiming. Richmond replied that

Ngati Tama and Ngati Rarua claimed the whole West Coast, and even Foveaux Strait and Ruapuke. Others claimed an interest in the Coast, some asking for £40,000 for the coal and gold there.[15]

Grey asked Te Whiwhi what land Ngati Toa still owned in Te Wai Pounamu. Te Whiwhi replied, 'Plenty.' They claimed it as far south as Banks Peninsula and Arahura, he said. They had been paid for Kaiapoi under the Wairau purchase, but not for the West Coast. Grey took Te Whiwhi to Nelson to inspect the survey maps. As they entered the Land Office, chiefs of Ngati Tama and Ngati Rarua were coming out with plans of land they had been offering to Richmond. Grey ordered the plans torn up. He arranged with Ngati Toa to meet him in Nelson in April 1852 to complete a purchase.[16]

Grey visited Canterbury in March 1852, and Ngai Tuahuriri publicly requested payment for the land north of Kaiapoi. Grey gave a conciliatory answer, but did not reveal his intention of paying Ngati Toa for the West Coast.[17] Three months later, Grey received an angry letter in Maori from Rawiri Puaha at Nelson, which translated as follows (in part):

> *E koro*, Governor in Chief, greetings. Sir, it is I again, I and my people living here. We are sick of staying in this place to arrange about the land. Sir, we think that the transference of the land to the European should be completed right away. We think that all this Island should be given up to you.

Puaha added:

> Sir, don't let us be here in vain, it was your word that was agreed to. If you were here, all the settlements would be agreed to at once. But you have vanished to Wellington and Richmond says you have the money. At Wellington you told us Richmond had it.[18]

But Grey had no funds to pay for the West Coast, or for Murihiku.

In the ensuing months Grey received a stream of Maori letters complaining about his land purchases in Te Wai Pounamu, past and impending. Whero Honira of Pipitea, Wellington, disputed Ngati Toa's claim. Taiaroa and Patuki wanted £1,200 for their share of Murihiku. Old Te Whaikai Pokene, angry that Ngati Toa were to receive yet more money for Te Wai Pounamu, demanded £4,400 for Ngati Raukawa's land at Waitohu,[19] where his son had been killed with Te Maiharanui in 1830. Ngati Toa had been paid for Kaiapoi because their people had been killed there, said Pokene, therefore he should be paid for Waitohu because of his son. Rawiri Puaha wrote scornfully of Taiaroa's claim to the West Coast:

Kei whakarongo koe ki te reo o te tangata e pohehe ana tana korero e rite ana ki te kawau, e noho ana i roto i te kohanga tana tangi Tororire tororire, Whaipo whaipo, mei kore te tikanga o te Atua raua ko te Kuini kua pohutu ia ki te moana. (Do not listen to the man's talk, he speaks in error. His talk is like a shag sitting in its nest, crying out, 'Tororire, tororire, Whaipo, whaipo,' as if it were not the plan of God and the Queen that he be splashed by the sea.) [20]

Hohaia Poheahea of Ngai Tahu asked £150 for Kaitorete and the same for Akaroa – since neither had been paid for, he said. Werita Tainui wrote that the land north of Kawatiri on the West Coast was not in Kemp's purchase, and urged Grey to pay for it 'this summer'. Te Aorahui wrote from Pigeon Bay in August 1852 denying Taiaroa's right to act for Ngai Tahu: 'Think not that Taiaroa is the only chief, there are other chiefs living here.' If Grey did not pay Ngai Tuahuriri for Kaiapoi, he said, the European settlers would be driven off. [21] This threat caused some alarm in Canterbury. [22]

~

Following the opening up of the Wairau block for European settlement, young Sir William Congreve had selected land at Waipapa, north of Kaikoura, in Ngati Kuri territory. In August 1852 Congreve wrote to Alfred Domett, the New Munster Colonial Secretary, protesting about 'natives, at present squatting on my Run at Waipapa, of whose aggressions I have already had cause to complain'. Domett urged Grey to 'check the aggression of the natives herein complained of, in the bud'. Other settlers were also being 'annoyed by the natives', said Domett. Grey replied: 'I have already ordered the Native Secretary [Kemp] to require these natives to return to their own reserve. Inform Sir W Congreve accordingly.' [23] But Ngati Kuri had no reserves, having sold no land, and they continued their protests.

In September 1852 Ngai Tuahuriri again asked Grey for payment for Kaiapoi and the land northward. [24] Charles Torlesse and another runholder reported that Maoris were threatening violence, and had 'the requisite ammunition'. [25] Grey declared that he would crush 'such acts of insubordination'. [26] Puaha and Ngati Toa now wrote to Grey, perhaps at his own prompting, claiming all Te Wai Pounamu by right of conquest – including Tuturau because Te Puoho had been killed there. No one could oppose them, they said. [27]

When Kaikoura Whakatau heard that Grey had agreed to sell to the whaler Alexander Fyffe the land he was squatting on at Kaikoura, he went to Wellington and asserted Ngati Kuri's rights to the land. Grey made Whakatau a native assessor and paid him £60.[28] This sum was recorded by Native Secretary Kemp as payment for 'all his [Whakatau's] claims in the vicinity of Kaikoura'. But Whakatau considered that he had been paid only for Fyffe's whaling station, and when an official was sent to survey the Crown's supposed Kaikoura purchase, Whakatau evicted him. Ngati Kuri continued harassing runholders on their lands.[29] Maori unrest over 'the land question' was also reported at Waikouaiti by the Reverend Charles Creed.[30]

When Resident Magistrate Charles Simeon at Lyttelton passed on to the government another Ngai Tahu request for payment for Kaiapoi, Kemp responded with the official view that 'according to their own usages' Ngai Tahu had no claim, as they had been 'driven off the land by the Ngatitoas'.[31] Grey now applied for leave to visit England, which he had not seen for twelve years. He appointed Donald McLean to head a new Native Land Purchase Department to deal with Maori land questions. Eyre had already left for England, to his own great relief.

Disregarding the claims of rival tribes, Grey now moved to open up the disputed 'waste lands' for European settlement. On 4 March 1853 he issued Waste Land Regulations authorising the sale of Crown land outside the original Nelson, Canterbury and Otago blocks, for ten shillings an acre, or, if the land was certified as not worth that, five shillings. Since these prices were a fraction of those applying within the original blocks, Grey's regulations were bitterly opposed by provincial leaders, but without success.[32]

In June 1853 Walter Mantell got Governor Grey's approval for a small Maori foreshore reserve on Princes Street near the heart of Dunedin, and another at Port Chalmers. These were designated as landing places and hostel sites for Maoris visiting town, and were both close to Free Church property.[33] But it was some time before the grants became generally known – to the great indignation of the Otago provincial authorities.[34] At about the same time, the British Government approved Grey's leave, provided he first implemented the 1852 New Zealand Constitution Act.[35]

∼

Chief Land Purchase Commissioner Donald McLean maintained Grey's policy of dealing only with Ngati Toa for the purchase of the remaining Maori land rights in Te Wai Pounamu (apart from Murihiku).[36] These rights he purchased on 10 August 1853, for £5,000, by means of the 'Waipounamu purchase'. Ngati Toa received £2,000 at once, and were to share the balance with tribes named in the deed as selling 'conjointly' with them: Te Ati Awa, Ngati Koata, Ngati Rarua, Rangitane and Ngai Tahu.[37] According to McLean, Taiaroa attended the Waipounamu purchase as 'chief of the aboriginal tribes' of Te Wai Pounamu. But neither Taiaroa nor anyone else held such a rank; nor did Taiaroa sign the Waipounamu deed.

Mantell now found that the Murihiku chiefs, tired of waiting for him to pay for their land, were negotiating with European squatters.[38] He therefore prepared a deed for the purchase of the Murihiku block for £2,000, to be paid later in two instalments. A further £600 was promised because of the delay. Mantell got the Otago chiefs to sign the Murihiku deed, without payment, on 18 August 1853 in Dunedin – eighty kilometres north of the Murihiku boundary. By getting the Otago chiefs to sign first, he could present the Murihiku chiefs with a fait accompli. Thus he again set one section of Ngai Tahu against another. Yet of the fifty Maori names written on the deed at Dunedin, only seventeen were signatures.[39]

It now suited Mantell's purpose to further humour Otago Ngai Tahu – and himself. He encouraged them to seek enrolment on the voting register for the forthcoming Otago provincial elections. In Dunedin this was seen as an affront to Captain William Cargill, the leading candidate for Superintendent, and Mantell was portrayed as toadying to the Maoris.[40] Under the Constitution Act, however, as Mantell must have known, Ngai Tahu could not vote, for they held their land in common.[41] The following month, Mantell paid the Otago chiefs their promised £1,000 instalment for Murihiku, which he had partly to borrow.

Grey, who the following year was to accept the governorship of South Africa's Cape Colony, now wrote to Mantell before departing for England:

> I am just upon the point of starting for Auckland, and therefore cannot write at much length to you – but I cannot refrain from expressing my warm approval of your having under the circumstances detailed in your letter of the 18th of August last, concluded the purchase of the Southern end of the Middle Island. Your proceedings upon that occasion have given me

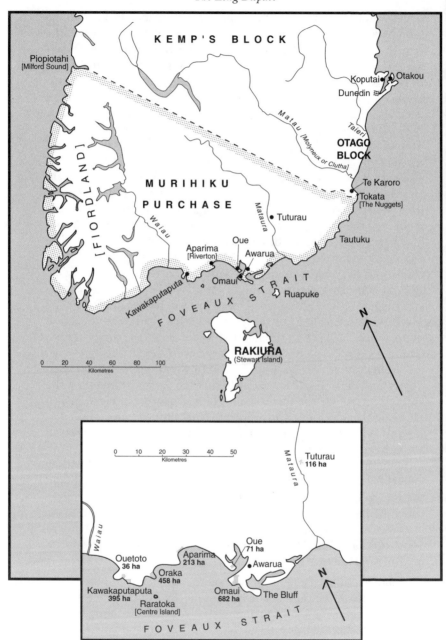

Mantell's Murihuku purchase, 1853, and Maori reserves.

very great pleasure, they are highly honourable to yourself, as also to me, as entirely justifying my appointment of you to so responsible an office as you hold. If I can do anything for you in England a letter addressed to me at the Athenaeum will reach me.

Grey concluded: 'I hope you will continue as good a course as you have begun, and be successful to your heart's content. Faithfully yours, G. Grey.'[42]

Four months after he had paid the Otago chiefs, Mantell paid the Murihiku chiefs £1,000 at Awarua, Foveaux Strait. He obtained their signatures not on the Murihiku deed, but on a receipt that did not say what the money was for. Thus there is no certainty that the Murihiku deed was ever seen in Murihiku, or that those who signed the receipt knew that under the deed they gave up everything except Mantell's reserves.[43] The promised additional £600, to be recouped from the sale of the former Maori land, was shared equally between Otago and Murihiku chiefs in November 1854. Mantell's Murihiku reserves proved inadequate for their Maori occupants, who were soon reduced to the same straits as those in Kemp's block.[44]

∼

After Grey left New Zealand, Donald McLean paid Te Ati Awa, as 'a conjoint tribe' under the Waipounamu purchase of 1853, a total of £1,000 for their claims. Tiramorehu heard of this from Kaikoura Whakatau, and wrote an angry letter to McLean and the Administrator, Colonel Robert Wynyard, saying that Ngai Tuahuriri had yet to be paid for the land north of Kaiapoi. 'I keep asking Mantell for payment,' said Tiramorehu. 'You do something about paying for the land.'[45] Two years later, despite Superintendent Richmond's urging, McLean had still done nothing about the claims of the so-called 'conjoint tribes', other than Te Ati Awa.[46] But he paid Taiaroa, in Wellington attending to his own interests, £85 to buy a horse. Taiaroa accepted this as an advance on the West Coast, claiming to be its 'sole owner'.[47]

McLean paid Ngati Toa another £2,000 for the Waipounamu purchase on 13 December 1854. From this they promised to 'satisfy and prevent the demands of all Natives whatsoever who may hereafter claim the land'. They settled for £2,000, instead of the £3,000 owing, because of their elderly chiefs dying in a measles epidemic – a disaster attributed to Grey's departure.[48] In return,

Ngati Toa gave up their claims to Te Wai Pounamu, including all lands they had 'not sold in former times'. Thus they surrendered the 117,250 acres of reserves they had retained under the Wairau purchase.[49] But their chiefs retained 'homesteads',[50] for which 2,940 acres were reserved in the Wairau district, and two chiefs received fifty-acre grants as well.[51]

There was great resentment among the tribes of Te Wai Pounamu at the news that McLean had paid Ngati Toa another £2,000 for their rights in Te Wai Pounamu before they themselves had received anything. Ngati Kuia stopped the government survey of their land, and protested:

> We consider that we are yet a people, a living people, and have a right to speak when our land is being sold without our consent, and no payment is received by us. Our conquerors did as they pleased before we became British subjects, but now we think we ought to have half the talking about it, and half of the payment for it.

Ngati Koata and Rangitane, like Ngati Kuia, refused to give up their land unless they were paid for it. The Ngati Rahiri hapu on Arapawa complained:

> Those Ngati Toas appear to do as they please with the Government. They ask for the loaf and it is given them without a word, but we have to beg for the crumbs, and wait a long time before they are thrown to us. However, we will let the Ngati Toas see that this land is our own and not theirs, and that the money they received the other day shall not be considered by us as any part of the payment for Arapawa.[52]

In 1856 McLean at last distributed £1,220 among northern tribes of Te Wai Pounamu – Ngati Tama, Rangitane, Ngati Kuia, Ngati Koata and Ngati Rarua – and another £500 among Te Ati Awa.[53] But Ngai Tahu, equally a 'conjoint tribe' under the Waipounamu deed, got nothing.

∾

Shrewd speculators had been quick to move on Grey's 1853 Waste Land Regulations, purchasing at ten shillings an acre the choicest lands adjoining the Nelson, Canterbury and Otago blocks. Crown leaseholders with ready cash made haste to buy the essential portions of their runs. Those without the cash found their best leasehold land bought from under their feet by rivals or speculators.[54] Among the first buyers were the Rhodes brothers on their 125,000-acre leasehold principality The Levels. They paid £4,260 for 8,520 acres of freehold, carefully selecting the most likely future town sites in South Canterbury, where a further 16,000 acres were selected by other buyers.[55]

Such bargain sales by Grey's Commissioners of Crown Lands offended the Otago Provincial Council. In November 1854 the council asked Superintendent Cargill to suspend Mantell's authority to sell land, until the General Assembly reviewed the rules. But Mantell publicly defied Cargill, referring to his 'age and temporary position'.[56] However, Mantell had already arranged with the government for leave of absence on half-pay,[57] having learned in 1853 of his father's death in London.[58] In March 1855 he left Dunedin for Wellington, taking with him a testimonial from seventy-one Otago citizens expressing their appreciation of 'his usefulness as a man of science, and also of his efficiency and impartiality as a Public Officer'.[59] Mantell also took the letterbook and official correspondence from the Otago Crown Lands office, leaving it in a 'denuded and helpless state'.[60]Cargill's angry protests found their way to the Colonial Office in London.

Schools and Christian instruction, according to Lord John Russell and the New Zealand Company, were to have been the major benefits of British colonisation for the Maori people,[61] funded either by the sale of Maori land, or (together with health care) by Maori endowment reserves under the abortive Native Trusts Act of 1844. Grey's abolition of the Protector's Department, according to him, was to have made these benefits more readily available.[62] The 1852 Constitution Act[63] provided for £7,000 to be spent annually for 'native purposes' under the Governor's supervision. Provincial governments therefore considered the central government alone responsible for Maori welfare such as schools and hospitals. But the Constitution Act did not make either the central or the provincial governments responsible for education or health. In colonial New Zealand there was little enthusiasm for free schools or hospitals.[64] When Grey authorised a government hospital at Dunedin in 1853, available to Maoris as well as to others, he was criticised in Otago for intruding on provincial authority.[65]

When the Reverend Johann Wohlers, in far-off Ruapuke, wanted a few pounds' worth of religious books for his school, Mantell advised him to apply to Colonel Wynyard, the Administrator. But state assistance for mission schools was controversial, and no funds had been voted for it. Wynyard declined Wohlers' request.⁶⁶ Nine months later, in May 1855, Mantell saw Wynyard and the Native Secretary John Jermyn Symonds in Auckland, and urged, for the first time, that the government should provide schools and hospitals for Ngai Tahu. Wynyard, keeping within his constitutional powers, advised Mantell to take up the question with the newly convened General Assembly, which had charge of finance.⁶⁷ Instead, Mantell returned to Wellington and arranged small consignments of religious schoolbooks for Wohlers and Tiramorehu at his own expense, aided by Chief Justice Martin and an Anglican missionary.⁶⁸

Before leaving for England in August 1855, Mantell informed Symonds officially that he had made his Akaroa award in 1849 in the belief that the Imperial Government would provide Ngai Tahu with 'schools, medical aid, &c', which he had been authorised to promise. Mantell now 'withdrew' this award and his report on it, he told Symonds, because the promises were still unfulfilled, and because Wynyard had referred him to the General Assembly where neither the Imperial Government nor Ngai Tahu were represented.

Mantell wrote again to Symonds privately, a day before leaving New Zealand, saying that Ngai Tahu had 'every right to demand the fulfilment of the promises' from the Imperial Government. He confided to Symonds about the 'sham of paternalism' and 'the yet unpurchased block of land at Akaroa and Wairewa' where Ngai Tahu were being turned off by the settlers. The government had no right to be selling this land to settlers, said Mantell, since Ngai Tahu had never agreed to his award.⁶⁹ Mantell then embarked for England, taking with him the Crown Land Office papers he had removed from Dunedin.

Yet Mantell, as we have seen, had told Ngai Tahu in 1849 that Banks Peninsula belonged to the Governor whether they agreed to his awards or not. In 1854 he had told William Guise Brittan, the Canterbury Crown Land Commissioner, that 'most emphatically the Natives have no right to any land in the Akaroa and Wairewa Block, beyond the reserves awarded by me'.⁷⁰

∽

Arriving in England, Mantell wrote on 5 February 1856 to the Colonial Office asking for an interview with the Secretary of State for the Colonies, Henry Labouchere, a great admirer of Sir George

Grey. But Labouchere had learned of Mantell's removal of official documents from the Otago Crown Lands Office,[71] and refused to see him until he had returned the documents and given an explanation. A four-month exchange of letters followed, with Mantell pressing for an interview and hinting at shortcomings in the New Zealand Government, while the Colonial Office demanded the missing documents and suspended Mantell's half-salary.[72] Mantell, hoist with his own petard, at length handed in what he said were the documents in question.

Mantell now wrote Labouchere an elaborate 'exposé', allegedly at the request of 'the Chief and subordinate Chiefs of the united tribes' in New Zealand.[73] His tone was highly moral. He had acquired 'about thirty million acres' from Ngai Tahu, he said, in return for 'small cash payments' and promises of 'schools, hospitals, and constant solicitude for their welfare and general protection on behalf of the Imperial Government'. The New Zealand Government had shifted responsibility for these promises to the General Assembly where the 'natives' and the Imperial Government were not represented, said Mantell.

Labouchere enquired who had authorised Mantell to promise schools, hospitals and general care, and whether he had officially complained in New Zealand. Mantell replied that Eyre had told him to make the promises, and that he had complained to Wynyard. Mantell haggled further, in characteristic style:

> In requesting your attention to the equitable claims of Natives, it was, I submit, not unnecessary to advert to the conduct of the Government toward them and to show how small was the prospect that a sufficient remedy could be obtained from that quarter without express instructions from a higher authority. If I have failed to make this clear to you I must, however reluctantly, reserve the irksome task of recording the peculiarities of the administration of the late Government of the Colony. But if, on the contrary, I have already said more than was necessary to your conviction, I beg to withdraw whatever may seem unrequired by the object I have now in view, on the understanding that such withdrawal is not in the least degree to be regarded as an admission of incorrectness in the statements I have made.[74]

Mantell then wrote to Tiramorehu reminding him about the promises of schools, hospitals and care, saying, 'These are the things which constitute the main payment for your lands.' Mantell informed

Tiramorehu that Wynyard had rebuffed him, and that he had gone to England, where he had told the 'Queen's Secretary',

> When you act justly towards my friends of Ngai Tahu in respect of my promises by reason of which the Queen became possessed of their lands, then only will I not be ashamed of the title 'a subject of the Queen'.[75]

Mantell told Tiramorehu to publish the letter.

Tiramorehu, years later at a royal commission hearing, recalled Mantell's promises of schools during his Kemp's purchase dealings:

> I said to Mantell, 'What are your schools for?' He said, 'To teach you to acquire knowledge, and also for the education of your children, so that they may be able to write in English, and speedily acquire all the knowledge which the Europeans possess.' I said to him, 'When are we to see the fulfilment of these words?' He said, 'After the last instalment of Mr Kemp's money has been paid.'[76]

What kind of school Mantell thought would impart such benefits to Ngai Tahu, he never explained. Nor did he explain how education, however sublime, could compensate Maoris for the loss of their land, or get them equality with Europeans in a colony founded on the principle that 'natives' were inferior and needed constant tutelage. The 'knowledge' that Ngai Tahu particularly needed, with their lands at stake, was that concerning their land rights under British law. John Tikao, Metehau and Tamakeke had challenged Mantell on these very matters. But Mantell, as we have seen, far from welcoming their claim to 'knowledge which the Europeans possessed', angrily denounced them as 'insolent'.

~

The Colonial Office told Mantell they could not interfere in New Zealand affairs without inviting the New Zealand Government's opinion. Mantell's request for confirmation in his appointment as a Crown Commissioner was also improper, they said, for he had been appointed in New Zealand. But since he had returned the documents, he could resume his half-salary 'if he thought it proper'. They referred his complaints to the new Governor, Colonel Thomas Gore Browne, who had reached New Zealand soon after Mantell's departure.[77]

Mantell at once answered the Colonial Office with a homily on Imperial duties, saying:

> Any civilized nation occupying the territory of a less civilized race, is in honour bound to provide for that race. No reference to the Local New Zealand Government can therefore be needed to convince Mr Labouchere that the common obligation of all colonising nations of higher civilisation and religion presses in this instance with double weight upon Her Majesty's Government.[78]

Without waiting for a reply, Mantell resigned his commissioner's appointment on the grounds that Labouchere had 'refused to entertain the claims of the Ngai Tahu natives', and because he could not approve of 'the principles upon which the acquisition of Native Lands is still conducted, nor of the policy of the Local Government toward the Natives in either Island'.

But Mantell's claim to the high moral ground was short-lived. An observant clerk in Dunedin noticed that Mantell's returned 'letterbook' bore a recent London watermark: thus it was a copy made in London, and not the original that Mantell had passed it off as. Soon Mantell found arrayed against him the strictures not only of his Otago enemies but those of the New Zealand Premier, Edward Stafford, and his Cabinet, and of Governor Browne himself.[79]

Mantell's correspondence with the Colonial Office dragged on acrimoniously until August 1857, when he grudgingly handed in the real letter book and retired from the fray. 'It is fortunate,' wrote Browne to Labouchere, 'that Mr Mantell has resigned his appointments, as the Provincial authorities at Otago are vehement in their complaints against him.' Regarding the promises of schools and hospitals, Browne remarked:

> I am satisfied that from the date of the Treaty of Waitangi promises of schools, hospitals, roads, constant solicitude for their welfare, and general protection on the part of the Imperial Government, have been held out to the Natives to induce them to part with their land. Nor does it appear to me that the obligation would be less imperative if no promise had ever been made. The difficulty is how to fulfil either the promise or the obligation.[80]

Mantell remained in London for two more years, occupied with science, family and private affairs. He worked on the moa with Professor Richard Owen at the British Museum.[81] In 1857 his younger brother's death in India left him responsible for the family estate.[82] His tilt at the Colonial Office won him admirers, as a champion of defenceless Maoris against bureaucratic indifference.[83] This reputation he cultivated for the rest of his life. His 'crusade' for schools and hospitals for Ngai Tahu was in the true spirit of the age. But it diverted attention from Ngai Tahu's desperate need for land, just as the last of the profitable pastoral lands within their former territory were being taken up by Europeans.

Great was the excitement in Otago and Murihiku late in 1856, when Tiramorehu received Mantell's letter saying he had gone to England to get his promises fulfilled. When Governor Browne visited Otago soon afterwards, the southern chiefs urged him to bring Mantell back. 'Te Tipa is the man for this Island,' they told him. Tiramorehu wrote to the Queen asking for Mantell's return. Letters went to Mantell from Haereroa, Merekihereka Hape, Topi Patuki and Tiramorehu, all expressing their affection, and urging him to be strong with the 'Queen's Secretary'. They wrote of their troubles with the Dunedin Scots. 'If there be no successful result to thy striving with the Queen's writer then shall we be ruined,' wrote Tiramorehu. But if Mantell was successful, he said, 'then shall we be saved'.[84]

Mantell at last replied to Topi and Tiramorehu from London on 16 February 1858. He had been constantly striving on their behalf, he said, but was not wearied. 'I will strive still until the conduct of the Government toward you be just,' he wrote, 'or until your loving friend Mantell dies.' [85] But despite these fine words, Mantell, as we have seen, had already abandoned his 'crusade'.

Notes

1. Mantell–Colonial Secretary, 18.3.1854, Mantell Ms Letter-books.
2. Patuki–Grey, 12.2.1849, Grey Ms Maori Letters.
3. Stokes–Eyre, 1.9.1850, in Mackay 1873 I: 269–70.
4. Rutherford 1961: 160–61.
5. Mantell–Grey, 13.3.1851, in Mackay 1873 I: 271–72.
6. Domett–Mantell, 14.4.1851, in Mackay 1873 I: 272; Fleming 1987: 7.
7. ATL illustration 920/112637½.
8. Domett–Mantell, 17.10.1851, Mantell Ms 83/151.
9. *Otago Witness*, 29.11.1851, quoted in McLintock 1949: 260.
10. Te Reko could map his former journey from Kaiapoi to Tuturau (Thomson 1867: 99).
11. Beattie 1947b: 112ff; Mackay 1873 I: 275–77.
12. Wai-27 O15: 12.
13. Mantell–Colonial Secretary, 19.2.1852, in Mackay 1873 I: 273.

14. Biggs 1959: 264ff.
15. See Richmond–Colonial Secretary, 5.1.1852, 21 & 31.5.1852, in Mackay 1873 I: 289ff.
16. SNC 4/27: 569ff.
17. *LT*, 27.3.1852; Hart 1887: 24.
18. Puaha–Grey, 29.5.1852, Grey Ms G425/271: 148.
19. For Waitohu, see Adkin 1948: 128 (map).
20. Puaha–Grey, 14.7.1852, Grey Ms 272/646: 439.
21. Grey Ms Maori Letters: nos 513, 646, 424, 538, 532, 507, 533, 510.
22. Sub-Inspector of Police–Resident Magistrate, 16.9.1852, NAW NM8 1852/1267.
23. Congreve–Colonial Secretary, 23.8.1852, in NAW NM8 52/1105.
24. Tau–McLean, 18.9.1852, McLean Ms 32/676.
25. Brown and Torlesse–FitzGerald, 15.9.1852, NAW NM8 52/1267.
26. Simeon–Colonial Secretary, 17.9.1852, NAW NM8 52/1267.
27. Biggs 1959: 264ff.
28. Sherrard 1966: 79; Domett–Commissioner of Crown Lands Wellington, 5.10.1852, NAW NM10/12: 171; Kemp–Domett, 24.10.1852, NAW NM81852/1376. Native assessors were paid a small stipend to assist magistrates in cases involving Maoris.
29. Hamilton–McLean, 8.1.1857, in Mackay 1873 II: 16; Sherrard 1966: 108.
30. Creed–Mission Secretaries, 13.9.1852, Creed Ms Letters.
31. Simeon–Kemp, 16.5.1853, NAW CS52/611.
32. Sewell 1980 I: 213ff.
33. Brooking 1984: 123.
34. *NTR* chapter 7. See Wai-27 F1, F2 for a detailed account of the Princes Street reserve.
35. Newcastle–Grey, 7.2.1853, Grey Ms Letters: 54.
36. McLean–Commissioner of Crown Lands, 15.12.1854, in Mackay 1873 I: 304.
37. 'Ngatitoa Waipounamu deed', in Mackay 1873 I: 307–8 (transcript). The original deed is missing.
38. Mantell–Domett, 18.8.1853, in Mackay 1873 I: 281–82.
39. DOSLIW CLO Otago 1.
40. See McLintock 1949: 350ff; Brooking 1984: 97ff.
41. See McLintock 1958: 417ff.
42. Grey–Mantell, 9.10.1853, Mantell Ms 83/288.
43. See Wai-27 Z41 for an analysis of the Murihiku deed and receipts.
44. See *NTR*: 616–18, 636ff.
45. Tiramorehu–McLean, 2.8.1854, McLean Ms 32/678B.
46. Richmond–Colonial Secretary, 14.9.1854, McLean Ms 32/4: 27; Richmond–McLean, 5.9.1855, McLean Ms 32/535. See also Gisborne 1897: 136ff.
47. Taiaroa–McLean, 29.11.1854 & 30.11.1854, Mantell Ms 83/169.
48. Thomson 1859 II: 213–14.
49. Ngati Toa receipt, 13.12.1854, in Mackay 1873 I: 311–12. Puaha evidently told the Marlborough Sounds tribes that Ngati Toa had retained their Wairau purchase reserves (Mackay 1873 I: 298).
50. DOSLIW Nelson No. 16.
51. Jellicoe 1930: 60–61.
52. Jenkins–Commissioner, nd, in Mackay 1873 I: 297ff; Richmond–McLean, 27.1.1855, McLean Ms 32/535.
53. Mackay 1873 I: 308–19 (transcripts of deeds); *AJHR* 1874 G-6 (boundaries).
54. According to Sewell (1980 I: 412), the surveyor Cridland picked out 2,000 acres in Canterbury for the stockowner Sidey for £1,000, and thus 'spoiled 200,000 acres of land'.
55. Woodhouse 1937: 120.
56. McLintock 1949: 391ff.

57. Wai-27 O20: 19.
58. R. Mantell–W. Mantell, 27.1.1853, Mantell Ms 83/438a. Gideon Mantell, worn out by spinal disease, died in November 1852 of an overdose of opiate (Mantell 1940: passim). Walter's younger brother Reginald was to attend to the estate.
59. John Hyde Harris and others–Mantell, Mantell Ms 83/142.
60. McLintock 1949, loc cit.
61. See Normanby–Hobson, 14.8.1839, in Mackay 1873 I: 15.
62. Grey–Earl Grey, 4.2.1847, in *BPPNZ* 1847: 92.
63. Clause 65 and Schedule, McLintock 1958: 429, 433. See also Dalton 1967: 12ff.
64. See Sewell 1980 II: 482–84; McLintock 1849: 373ff. The Canterbury Association briefly operated a Maori 'industrial school' at Kaiapoi (Gardner 1971: 369ff).
65. *Otago Witness*, 23.4.1853.
66. Colonial Secretary–Mantell, 17.8.1854, Mantell Ms 83/159.
67. Mantell–Labouchere, 31.7.1856, in Mackay 1873 II: 84–85; Mantell–Symonds, 21.8.1855 (draft), McLean Ms 32/446. Wynyard's response is inferred from the sources.
68. Mantell Ms 83/159.
69. Mantell–Symonds, loc cit.
70. Brittan, 4.1.1856, NAW IA I 56/367.
71. Ball–Mantell, 23.2.1856, Mantell Ms 83/143A.
72. See PRO/CO 209/140, 141, 146; 361/3; 406/14, 16; and Mantell Ms 83/143A.
73. Mantell–Labouchere, 5.7.1855, in Mackay 1873 II: 82–83. There seems to be no record of such a request from Ngai Tahu, nor of who the 'united tribes' and their chiefs were supposed to be.
74. Mantell–Merivale, 31.7.1855, in Mackay 1873 II: 83–84.
75. Mantell–Tiramorehu, 8.8.1856, in SNC 3/6: 261ff.
76. SNC 3/6: 249–51, 3/4: 205.
77. Merivale–Mantell, 11.8.1856, Mantell Ms 83/143A.
78. Mantell–Merivale, 12.8.1856, in Mackay 1873 II: 86.
79. See e.g. OP 5/1 Stafford–Otago Province, 1.12.56 & 11.12.57.
80. Mantell–Labouchere, 18.8.1856, PRO/CO 209/140: 626 (see also Mackay 1873 II: 87); Browne–Labouchere, 9.2.1857, PRO/CO 290/141: 35–38.
81. Oliver 1990: 268b.
82. Mantell Ms 83/439. Reginald Mantell died of cholera at the outbreak of the Indian Mutiny.
83. See Wilkes 1988.
84. Haereroa and Tiramorehu–Mantell, 22.7.1857 & 14.8.1857 (translation), Mantell Ms 83/166. See also Tiramorehu–Browne, 18.1.1856 (translation), loc cit.
85. Ngai Tahu–Queen, 23.9.1857 and Mantell–Patuki, 16.2.1858 (draft), Mantell Ms 83/166.

15

~

The Final Ngai Tahu Awards

COLONEL THOMAS GORE BROWNE arrived in New
Zealand as Governor in September 1855, at the age of forty-
eight. He was a conscientious professional soldier, but as a stranger
he was dependent on his advisers. In Maori affairs, the most influential of these was Chief Land Purchase Commissioner Donald
McLean, who had been maintaining Grey's strategy of playing off
rival tribes and hapu against one another so as to get Maori land
as cheaply as possible.[1] Brown appointed McLean also Native
Secretary.

The 1852 New Zealand Constitution Act had established six
provinces, each with its local government. Ngai Tahu tribal territory fell among the three South Island provinces – Nelson, Canterbury and Otago. But the constitution's property franchise, as we
have seen, disqualified Ngai Tahu from the elections. All six provinces had their elected superintendents and councils in office by
the time of Grey's departure at the end of 1853. But Grey did not
convene the New Zealand General Assembly. It was convened in
Auckland by the Administrator, Wynyard, on 24 May 1854. In
Canterbury and Otago respectively, Europeans now numbered about
6,000 and 4,000,[2] and the Maori population was only about a fifth
of the European. In Nelson, the Maori proportion of the population was smaller still – the Ngai Tahu portion comprising only the
small communities at Kaikoura and Kawatiri.

Governor Browne visited Lyttelton in January 1856, and heard
Ngai Tuahuriri again claim payment for Kaiapoi and the land north
of it. Browne told them, through his interpreter, that McLean (who
was present) would look into it.[3] At Akaroa, Browne received a
deputation of the local chiefs led by Hoani Papita Hakaroa. Banks
Peninsula land had now been allocated to European settlers by the

Canterbury authorities; but the Akaroa Maoris, to the settlers' annoyance, complained from the outset that they had never sold their territory. They now complained to Browne.[4] Browne, perhaps surprised at the vehemence of the small group confronting him, apparently remarked with military humour that his soldiers could polish them all off before breakfast. The chief Puaka, hearing the interpreter say the word parakuihi (breakfast), evidently thought he was being cursed in traditional fashion. He threatened the Governor. Hakaroa hustled him away, and the interview ended.[5]

After Governor Browne's party returned to Auckland, having also visited Dunedin, McLean sent J. G. Johnson to Akaroa as commissioner to enforce Mantell's 1849 award – 'which the natives should understand is final', said McLean.[6] But Johnson found that the Akaroa Maoris had never agreed to Mantell's award, nor to the French 'purchases' of 1845. He concluded, too, that Ngai Tuahuriri had a fair claim to the land from Kaiapoi northwards, now allocated to runholders. When Johnson told the Canterbury Superintendent, James Edward FitzGerald, of his findings, FitzGerald wrote to Governor Browne:

> I beg to represent strongly, that, if these matters are not now settled, the visit of Mr Johnson will be attended with great evils, by raising the expectations of the Natives, and inducing them to expect more hereafter: and that a great evil will have been created, which would not have existed had no Commissioner gone down.[7]

Johnson, true to official policy, advised McLean to pay Ngai Tuahuriri for their North Canterbury claim only on condition that they first induced the Akaroa chiefs to surrender their claims at Akaroa.[8] McLean entrusted this stratagem to William John Warburton Hamilton,[9] formerly of the *Acheron* and now resident magistrate at Lyttelton. Hamilton was highly respected in Canterbury. Aged thirty-one years, he was prominent in the Anglican community, an old boy of Harrow School, and a member of Christ's College Board and the Canterbury Provincial Council.[10] The form of deed that Hamilton received from McLean did not require a description of boundaries, or a map or plan. The Maoris, under the terms of McLean's deed, were to surrender nga wahi (the places, or pieces) 'in dispute at Akaroa', in return for Mantell's £150 and some reserves.[11] Negotiations were unnecessary, said McLean. Hamilton thought the Maoris hardly deserved the money, for he had witnessed Mantell pay them £500 at Akaroa in February 1849. But the payment he had witnessed, of course, was the second instalment for Kemp's purchase, not a payment for Akaroa.[12]

~

William Hamilton early in December 1856 engaged John Aldred, a Wesleyan clergyman, as his interpreter, and summoned a party of Ngai Tuahuriri from Tuahiwi for the job of 'softening' the Akaroa chiefs.[13] He did not know that the Akaroa chiefs had told Mantell that they wanted half the Akaroa block for themselves. Most of this half, apart from the heavily forested Wairewa basin, was now leased in three runs: Kinloch, of 15,000 acres, founded by Charles Barrington Robinson and a partner; Peraki, of 10,000 acres, founded by Robinson's successor John Watson; and Wakamoa, or Land's End, of 5,000 acres.[14]

When Hamilton and Aldred reached Akaroa with their Ngai Tuahuriri aides, they found the Akaroa chiefs unwilling to sell. Hakaroa and Mautai were adamant: £150 was too small a payment, they said. Besides, they still wanted to keep both sides of the Akaroa Heads and the southern bays of Banks Peninsula leased by the three runs. These areas would be necessary, the chiefs argued, to support their people, including the many absentees.[15] But Hamilton understood none of this, even from his interpreter.[16]

Each of the three Akaroa hapu had forty or fifty people in residence. The reserves Hamilton allowed them barely equalled McCleverty's old maximum of ten acres per person. Each hapu got a reserve of 400 acres, and £50 in coin. From this scanty allowance of acres and coins, under McLean's deed they had to meet the claims of their absentees and to surrender land for government roading on demand. Seeing no alternative, the Akaroa chiefs and their respective followers signed the deed on 10 December 1856. Hakaroa signed for Ngati Irakehu, Mautai for Ngati Mako of Wairewa, and Karaweko for Ngai Tarewa of Onuku. Paora Tau and Paora Taki of Ngai Tuahuriri signed with Mautai, and the Ngai Tuahuriri representatives shared in the meagre payment.[17] Without their influence, Hamilton reported, the deed would not have been signed, and 'this land question would probably have remained open for many years to come'. At his suggestion, McLean sent Ngai Tuahuriri £10 for their services.[18]

Hamilton maintained years later that he would have granted

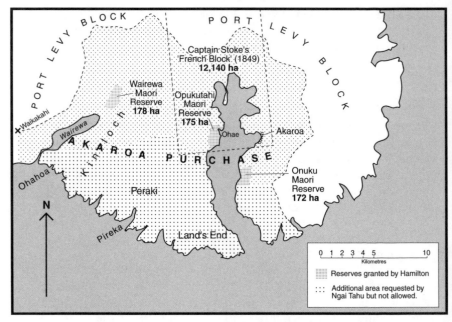

*Official boundary (shaded areas) of William Hamilton's Akaroa
purchase, 1856.*

Ngai Tahu any land that they had asked for in the Akaroa block. A
request by Mautai for 400 additional acres at Wairewa, however, to
graze 'ninety head of stock' had been expressed only after Mautai
had signed the deed – which was too late, said Hamilton, as it was
then a matter for the Canterbury Waste Lands Board. Mautai
applied to the board, but did not get his grazing land.[19]

When Kaikoura Whakatau heard that the government had
bought Akaroa, he went to Lyttelton with his supporters. There he
told Hamilton that the inclusion of Kaikoura and Kaiapoi in the
Wairau purchase had been wrong, because Ngati Toa had not remained in occupation of the disputed territory, and they had never
avenged the deaths of 'one canoe full' of their tribe at Oraumoa.
His hapu (Ngati Kuri) had been cultivating on the Kaikoura coast
ever since, he said. The government should pay Ngati Kuri for the
territory between Parinuiowhiti and Waiau-ua, and pay Poutini Ngai
Tahu for the West Coast, said Whakatau. Hamilton duly reported
this to Donald McLean.[20]

~

The Ngai Tuahuriri claims that William Hamilton was instructed to extinguish extended from Kemp's boundary at Kaiapoi, northward to the Hurunui River (the provincial boundary between Canterbury and Nelson). The territory between the Rakahuri and the Hurunui was now called 'North Canterbury'. Some Ngai Tuahuriri, including Tiramorehu, also had rights between the Hurunui and the Waiau-ua, along with Ngati Kuri of Kaikoura. North Canterbury comprised a million acres of plains, downlands, hills and mountains between the Main Divide and the east coast. It straddled the Waipara River, the original Canterbury Association boundary. North of this, it will be recalled, was Crown land that had been subject to Governor Grey's cheap land prices of 1853. South of the Waipara, the dearer Canterbury Association price had applied. In 1856 the price throughout the Canterbury province had been set at £2 per acre.[21] But from 1853 to 1856 the districts north of the Waipara and south of the Ashburton had been happy hunting grounds for wealthy land speculators.

All of the more attractive North Canterbury land had been sold or leased by 1857, despite Ngai Tahu's not having been paid for their interests in it. South of the Waipara, the easier land had been leased in nine runs, while north of it all the desirable territory as far as the Hurunui, about 370,000 acres, had been leased among seven or eight runholders, led by Clifford and Weld of Stonyhurst (about 62,000 acres) and Moore of Glenmark (eventually 150,000 acres). For tribal communities to use such extensive territories for food-gathering was deprecated as 'barbarism' by colonialists: but a single European runholder using the same area for grazing sheep was greatly admired, for none in civilised society were more respected than the landed gentry.

George Henry Moore had come from Tasmania in 1854 to buy sheep country on behalf of a partner. He spent £17,000 buying 40,000 acres in the Motunau and Hurunui districts at the Crown price of five to ten shillings an acre, thus securing the key portions of several leasehold runs. By the further acquisition of Crown leaseholds, Moore increased his holding to one of the largest and richest in the country. Thus was established Glenmark station, from which Moore was to gain 'probably the largest fortune' in New Zealand.[22]

Between the Ashburton River and the Waitaki, the 120 kilometres of coastal plains and downlands were now divided into twenty runs.[23] The Rhodes brothers, as we have seen, secured a huge station, The Levels.[24] The hundred Maori inhabitants of Arowhenua, crowded into Mantell's 600-acre reserve, were hemmed in on one side by The Levels, and on the other side by the Arowhenua station of 30,000 acres. At the Waitaki, Huruhuru and his whanau had been allowed only 376 acres by Mantell. Now their former territory was in the hands of three runholders – including the Studholmes, who held more than 75,000 acres by 1861.[25] South Canterbury runholders reported no animosity from the dispossessed Maoris.[26] Samuel Butler, runholding in the high country, and later to become a famous writer, wrote home to England:

> There are few Maoris here; they inhabit the North Island, and are only in small numbers, and degenerate in this, so may be passed over unnoticed. The only effectual policy in dealing with them is to show a bold front, and at the same time, do them a good turn whenever you can be quite certain that your kindness will not be misunderstood as a symptom of fear. [27]

Runholders with modest capital had to take land in the high country and endure some seasons of hardship before they could be comfortable.[28] But those who could afford land on the plains and downlands needed only a shrewd head, an eye for 'country', and the ability to command their men, in order to enjoy the life of a prosperous 'squire' as predicted by James FitzGerald. As their wealth increased, they built country mansions and town residences, sent their sons to Cambridge, endowed their daughters handsomely, bred and raced bloodstock, frequented the Christchurch Club,[29] perhaps took a turn at politics, and returned to England from time to time. Stock diseases and fluctuations in wool prices laid some runholders low, but wealthy runholders could usually ride out a slump by withholding their wool from sale until prices improved.

William Hamilton and his Wesleyan interpreter John Aldred went to Tuahiwi in February 1857 to purchase the North Canterbury block, from which the Crown had already received more than £15,000 in land sales revenue.[30] Ngai Tuahuriri had now waited ten years for their rights in the block to be acknowledged. Having lost to Mantell the Waimakariri block which they had originally wanted, they now expected from Hamilton at least some of the remaining North Canterbury Crown lease land so that they could at last take up pastoral farming on an equal footing with Europeans. They asked for land in the Motunau and Hurunui districts, whose fertile, rolling

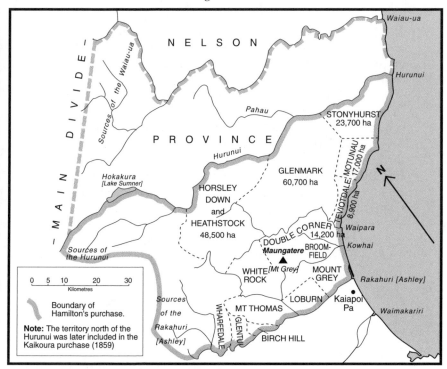

Hamilton's North Canterbury purchase, 1857, with pastoral runs (after Acland 1975: 31).

downlands and limestone ranges were ideal for pastoral farming, and were occupied by four mainly leasehold runs – Horsley Down, Glenmark, Stonyhurst and Motunau.

To share in this last opportunity to secure pastoral land in Canterbury, Ngai Tuahuriri invited chiefs from other hapu to the sale, including Hakaroa and Karaweko from Akaroa, Hoani Timaru from Taumutu, Mautai and Tamati Tikao from Wairewa, Pohio from Arowhenua, and Kaikoura Whakatau. But if Ngai Tuahuriri expected any favours from the Crown for bringing about the surrender of Akaroa, they were mistaken. Hamilton had been again instructed that the settlement of their claims was an award rather than a purchase, with the government laying down the terms. When Ngai Tuahuriri asked £2,000 for North Canterbury, Hamilton refused. He also refused them reserves of pastoral land at Motunau and Hurunui, telling them he had 'no instructions to entertain any question of reserves in this case'. The reserves Mantell had provided at Purau, Port Levy, Rapaki and Tuahiwi were 'all very ample', said Hamilton, and the Tuahiwi reserve alone was twice the size of all those he had just provided at Akaroa, where the Maori population was 'not much less' than at Tuahiwi, he said.[31]

The chiefs of Ngai Tuahuriri, in order to be rid at last of the incubus of the Wairau purchase, evidently saw no alternative to accepting Hamilton's harsh terms. On 5 February 1857 they signed a deed surrendering to the Queen their rights to North Canterbury for £200. Later, the government paid them another £200, and then a final £100 'as an act of grace'. Ngai Tuahuriri shared the meagre payments with their visitors. Like the Akaroa deed, the North Canterbury deed required the vendors to satisfy the claims of any absentees.[32] Only the site of the old Kaiapoi pa (which Mantell had not reserved, despite his promise to do so) was guaranteed to them. The deed also acknowledged the rights of Poutini Ngai Tahu to the West Coast.

William Hamilton had deliberately concealed from the Ngai Tahu chiefs assembled at Tuahiwi his real reason for refusing them reserves in North Canterbury.[33] 'By reserving any new tract for the Maoris,' Hamilton reported to McLean, 'serious complications might be created, and the necessity for reference to the Land Office would delay the purchase greatly.' He gave McLean further reasons, with which his official witnesses, the Reverend John Aldred and Sir William Congreve (now the provincial sheep-inspector), agreed:

> Having neither the means nor the knowledge to turn the land to account, it may be considered almost useless and valueless to themselves. It is greatly to their advantage that it should be in profitable occupation by ourselves, and that all questions about it should be closed at once. Our arrival among them has given such a value to their reserves that they may be considered to have been handsomely compensated for the surrender of what they could not use.[34]

But this Maori 'inability' to use the land was belied by Hamilton's subsequent report of November 1857, in which he said that Ngai Tahu were grazing stock at Akaroa, Kaikoura and Tuahiwi, and possessed 'considerable property and stock' which they were working at

'industriously'.[35] Tiramorehu had asked Eyre in 1849 for more grazing land for his cattle and sheep, as we have seen. Ngai Tahu already
had experience of stock-farming, whereas many European newcomers had none.[36] Maoris certainly had more knowledge of the country
and its climate than European newcomers had.

Thus the three Canterbury gentlemen – the magistrate, the
clergyman, and the baronet – deliberately deceived Ngai Tahu. But
Hamilton wore the breastplate of righteousness. He urged upon
Donald McLean that the Canterbury Maoris had no missionary,
school, interpreter or legal adviser. 'I do sincerely trust that you
will be able to move the General Government to take their case
into consideration,' he wrote, 'and have some competent person
sent among them to enquire and report upon their position with a
view to its amelioration.'[37]

Indeed, had Ngai Tahu been able to afford lawyers to get their
claims into the Supreme Court, Hamilton could not have denied
them their reserves so easily. As we have seen, the Court's 1847
judgment in *R. v. Symonds* had laid down that the Crown was not
entitled to brush aside requests by Maori customary owners for a
share of their own lands.[38] Yet Hamilton's deception was perfectly
acceptable to McLean and to the government. His North Canterbury purchase embodied the essence of colonialism. Ngai Tahu were
recommended for Christian instruction, schooling, and government
care, but were denied the economic self-sufficiency they had sought.

Since Donald McLean held both the key posts of Native Secretary
and Chief Land Purchase Officer, he was in no hurry to act on
Hamilton's advice that Ngai Tahu had valid claims to Kaikoura and
the West Coast. For McLean, the essence of policy was caution,
and judicious delay. Meanwhile, a son of his friend James Mackay,
a Nelson settler, had become interested in the Maoris of northern
Te Wai Pounamu. James Mackay junior was a tall, athletic, self-
confident young man who had come to New Zealand from Scotland with his father and family and his younger cousin Alexander in
1845.[39] In mixing with Maoris he had learned their language. He
had tried his hand at runholding in north-west Nelson, and had
prospected for grazing land in the rugged mountains there, becoming an expert bushman – 'the peer of them all', according to the
Canterbury surveyor Arthur Dobson.[40]

In 1857 James Mackay junior set out with Maori guides south-wards as far as Mawhera, on the hazardous route taken by Te Puoho in 1836. Thomas Brunner and Charles Heaphy had made this jour-ney in 1846, and had found thriving Maori communities. But by 1857 Poutini Ngai Tahu had been reduced, presumably by measles and influenza, to a mere hundred or two.[41] Mackay was courteously received at Mawhera by Wereta Tainui's older brother Tarapuhi – 'over six feet in height, and a very well-made, muscular man, of handsome countenance, and with a great reputation as an athlete and warrior'.[42]

When Mackay told Tarapuhi that his land had already been sold to the government by Ngati Toa under the 1853 Waipounamu pur-chase, Mackay was given a letter for Donald McLean, saying: 'Ngati Toa are thieves, as their feet have never trodden this ground. They are equal to rats, which when men are sleeping climb up to the storehouses and steal the food.' The payment that Puaha and Te Whiwhi had received for the Poutini Coast should be applied to other places instead, the Poutini chiefs told McLean.[43] They did not want Europeans coming to live on their land without paying for it, but they were prepared to sell the government the whole district, from Piopiotahi in the south, by way of the Main Divide to Lake Rotoroa, and thence to the coast at Kahurangi, south of Wanganui Inlet. In return they wanted £2,500, and a suitable share of the land for themselves, they said. Mackay returned to Nelson with the chiefs' letter, and samples of coal, and reported that on the West Coast there was land suitable for grazing.[44]

In 1858 Mackay's father wrote to McLean suggesting a govern-ment appointment for his restless son. Someone was needed to keep order on the burgeoning Aorere goldfields inland from Colling-wood, where payable gold had been found in 1856. James Mackay junior, at the age of twenty-seven, was thus appointed Assistant Native Secretary and Miners Warden at Collingwood. About 1,300 Europeans and 600 Maoris were now on the Aorere gold-diggings. Maori miners generally took their women and children and worked together in whanau, or even larger groups. They soon dominated some areas, and for a time 'a state of near war' existed between Maori and European miners.[45] But Mackay was a powerful man, and handy with his fists. He soon won a reputation for settling disputes quickly.[46] European miners came to respect their Maori rivals, who joined later in the pioneering of new goldfields on the Poutini Coast.[47]

Donald McLean, after a delay of nearly two years, decided to act on Hamilton's information regarding Ngai Tahu claims to Kaikoura and the West Coast. He needed a suitable land-purchaser for those rugged and little-known districts. His choice fell on James Mackay junior. In November 1858 McLean appointed Mackay Acting Land Purchase Commissioner to settle the Kaikoura and West Coast claims for £150 or £200 apiece, as Hamilton had suggested. These were to be awards, not purchases, extinguishing the claims of 'a few natives' in return for a token payment and reserves of from ten to a hundred acres per person, according to rank and according to the quality of the land. McLean thought five hundred acres would provide enough Maori reserves for the whole West Coast.[48] The vast 'wastelands' in the Kaikoura and West Coast districts, in the government's view, were already Crown demesne by virtue of British sovereignty. The Maori occupants would have to give up food-gathering, and subsist by cultivating small allotments.

Mackay set out from Nelson for Kaikoura with his cousin Alexander early in 1859, and rode down the coast from Kaparatehau telling the Maoris of his mission. Ngati Kuri now numbered little more than a hundred persons, but Mackay found that under the seasoned and capable Kaikoura Whakatau they were far from passive towards European encroachment on their lands. Maintaining their rights in their rugged country, with its towering mountains, fertile coastlands and rich sea fisheries and shellfish beds, was a matter of mana – a combination of duty and pride.[49] They were well aware that the government had made many thousands of pounds from selling or leasing the land to Europeans. The whole Kaikoura block of two and a half million acres that Mackay had been sent to acquire had already been leased or sold by the Land Office, except for the Kaikoura Peninsula and the nearby plains, and the remote headwaters of the Waiau-ua.[50]

Ngati Kuri asked £10,000 for their rights in the Kaikoura block, and requested the 125,000-acre block between the Tutaeputaputa and Kahutara Rivers, leased by three runholders, for themselves. But Mackay, in obedience to McLean's instruction, refused both requests. 'I have never yet in my life given in to a native,' he told McLean.[51] After a month of sporadic haggling,[52] Mackay reduced Ngati Kuri to accepting £300 for their claims, allowing them only some small coastal reserves totalling 5,560 acres, from which the

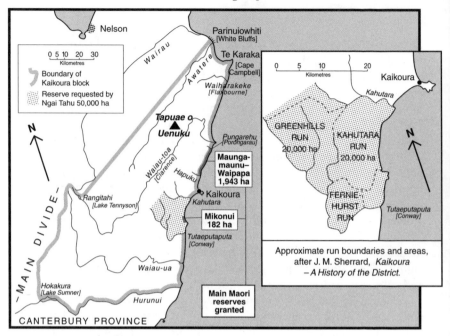

James Mackay's Kaikoura purchase, 1859.

deed required them to provide land for government roading on request, without compensation. The Kaikoura deed was signed on 29 March 1859.[53] The largest reserve, at Waipapa and Maungamaunu, was a long, precipitous coastal strip of about 4,795 acres that Ngati Kuri wanted for access to seafood and fishing grounds, and because of the karaka groves there. In excusing himself for providing such a 'large' reserve, Mackay reported to McLean that it was of 'the most useless and worthless description'.[54] To get enough pasture for their existing stock, said Mackay, the Maoris would have to buy land back from the government.

Thus Ngati Kuri, after their long wait, were debarred from run-holding. But Mackay, though 'as hard as stone', had acknowledged their tribal boundary to be at Te Parinuiowhiti, and thence inland to the headwaters of the Waiau-toa above Rangitahi, then along the mountain ranges to the Main Divide above Hokakura. Their protests against the Wairau purchase were thereby vindicated. The Europeans had the land, but the Maoris regained the mana.

∼

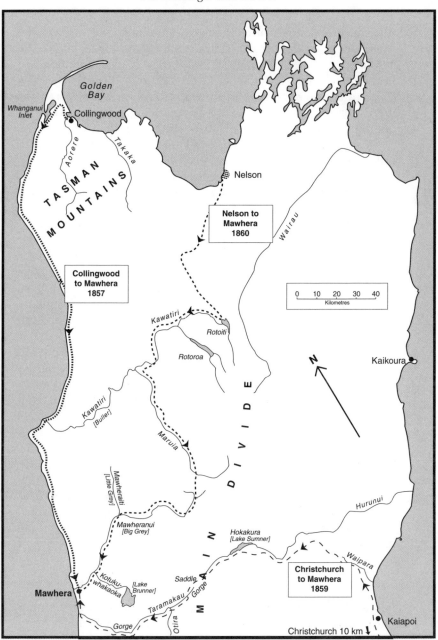

James Mackay's West Coast expeditions, 1857–1860.

To undertake the West Coast purchase, James Mackay and his cousin Alexander left Christchurch in the late autumn of 1859 to cross the Main Divide by the regular Maori route from the Hurunui to the Taramakau. A week later they arrived at the secluded mountain lake Hokakura (Sumner), nourisher of the Hurunui River. Early snow was on the ground, and John Rochfort's Nelson survey party was there working on the provincial boundaries. The two parties set out together for the Main Divide in wintry conditions.

A short distance upstream from Hokakura, the upper Hurunui valley joins the path of the great geological fault that runs for 160 kilometres west-south-west from near Kaikoura to the Main Divide, where a low notch marks its passage into the Taramakau. Here for the first time, above forested slopes, Mackay saw the broad alpine tops marking the south-western limits of his Kaikoura purchase, and the eastern boundary of the block he had come to buy. From the thousand-metre-high pass, the parties made the steep western descent to where the unforgiving Taramakau issues from its gloomy mountain gorge. The torrent was in full spate. Amid the splashing, slippery boulders overhung by dripping forest, Rochfort attempted a risky crossing and was swept away. Mackay, by dint of great strength and courage, saved him from 'the New Zealand death'.[55]

Parting from Rochfort and his party at the Otira, Mackay pressed on to Mawhera. There he found the West Coast purchase harder than he had expected. Tarapuhi had brought his brother Wereta Tainui from Kaikanui to join in the negotiations. Poutini Ngai Tahu were well aware that their Tuahiwi relatives had been left desperately short of land. As guardians of the pounamu, Poutini Ngai Tahu wished to keep the 375,000 acres of forested territory bounded by the Mawhera, Kotukuwhakaoka and Hokitika Rivers, with its mountains, plains and lakes – for here lay the famous Arahura pounamu. When James Mackay made his offer of £200, with just 800 acres in Maori reserves, it was scornfully rejected. After months of wrangling with the Maoris, he and his cousin left for home, reaching Nelson in September 1859 in Rochfort's schooner.[56]

⟲

James Mackay promptly went to Auckland and reported Poutini Ngai Tahu's refusal to Governor Browne, Donald McLean being away. Browne took it for granted that he was entitled to lay down the terms upon which Maoris were to surrender their land, and

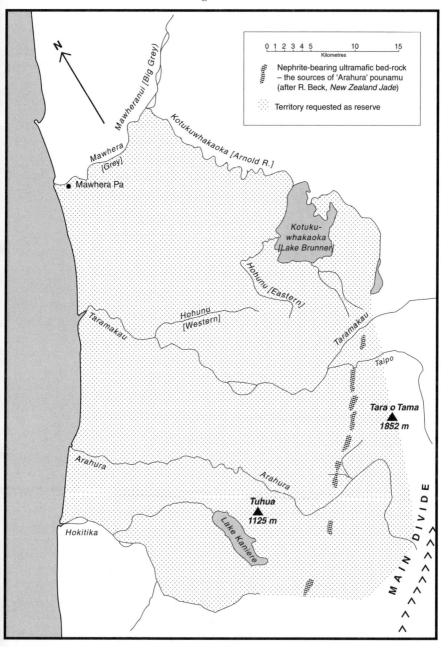

Territory requested as Maori reserve by Poutini Ngai Tahu, 1859–1860.

took no more notice of the guarantees in the Treaty of Waitangi than had Grey, Mantell and McLean. He authorised Mackay to pay Poutini Ngai Tahu £400, and to allow them 10,000 acres in reserves – 6,000 acres in individual allotments, and the rest as an endowment.

Returning to Mawhera overland from Nelson with this offer, Mackay again refused Poutini Ngai Tahu the 375,000 acres they wanted,[57] and offered them Governor Browne's 6,000 acres instead. Tarapuhi and his colleagues now knew that they were threatened from another quarter. Rochfort's survey party, with Maori assistance, had found gold in the Kawatiri, and news of the discovery had been published in Nelson.[58] Europeans were already on the West Coast seeking gold and pasture.[59] A rush by gold-diggers and squatters would overwhelm the tiny Poutini Maori communities unless they secured legal rights to at least some land. Reluctantly, the West Coast chiefs signed the Arahura deed on 21 May 1860 on Mackay's terms, on behalf of the Ngai Tahu tribe.[60] Maori rights to more than seven million acres thus passed to the Crown for £300. Tarapuhi got Mackay to reserve 250 acres at Mawhera pa, the best landing place on the river. Mackay agreed to Ngai Tahu's retaining the Arahura pounamu, together with land on both sides of the Arahura River. He wrote on his reserve plan:

> If on survey the land indicated in this sketch does not extend to Mount Tuhua, it had better be surveyed there, as the Natives are to be allowed to purchase any piece intervening. The whole of the river bed of the Arahura belongs to the Natives, to its source.[61]

But Mackay omitted this stipulation from the deed. The Arahura plan was not published, and Maori ownership of the pounamu was officially forgotten.[62]

Of the 10,225 acres reserved by Mackay for Maoris under the Arahura deed, 3,500 were for endowment and 6,725 for individual allotment – including some for a group of Ngati Apa at the Kawatiri. For the Poutini chiefs, however, the main achievement with the deed was that it officially recognised their rangatiratanga from Piopiotahi to Kahurangi, bounded inland by the Main Divide as far north as Lake Rotoroa. Mackay, a hard man, had upheld their claim against Ngati Toa's – which Grey and McLean had favoured.[63] Mackay returned to Nelson with the unused £100 from the £400 he had been authorised to pay. By his Kaikoura and Arahura purchases he had bought the Maori rights to a quarter of Te Wai Pounamu for £600.

Notes

1. See Oliver 1990: 255ff.
2. Gardner 1971: 323; Brooking 1984: 117.
3. *LT*, 12.1.1856: 6.
4. See also Hamilton–McLean, 18.1.1857, in Mackay 1873 II: 18, and Inhabitants of Akaroa–Governor Browne, 11.1.1856, PRO/CO/209/135: 58B.
5. SNC 6/74: 199ff; 6/75: 204ff. Tawha recalled: 'When Puaka got angry we all cleared out.'
6. McLean–Johnson, 25.4.1856, in Mackay 1873 II: 8.
7. Fitzgerald–Browne, 11.8.1856, in Mackay 1873 II: 11–12.
8. Johnson–McLean, 11.5.1856, in Mackay 1873 II: 8–11.
9. McLean Memo, 13.8.1856, in Steward–Hamilton, 16.8.1856 and McLean–Hamilton, 16.8.1856, in Mackay 1873 II: 12-13.
10. Scholefield 1940 I: 349ff.
11. DOSLIW Canterbury No. 3.
12. SNC 4/22: 52ff.
13. SNC 6/79
14. See Acland 1975: chapter 11.
15. SNC 4/21: 27ff; 6/65: 48–49; 6/73: 196–97; *LT*, 21.5.1879: 6b–c.
16. *LT*, 21.5.1879: 6c.
17. Tamanuiarangi, who carried the money for Hamilton, and was later elected as the first Member for Southern Maori, signed the deed thinking he was 'witnessing' it (SNC 6/79).
18. Hamilton–McLean, 11.12.1856 & 26.1.1857, in Mackay 1873 II: 15,19.
19. SNC 4/22: 57–59; 6/77: 278; Hamilton–McLean, 8.1.1858, in Mackay 1873 II: 17.
20. Hamilton–McLean, 8.1.1857, in Mackay 1873 II: 16ff.
21. See Gardner 1971: chapter 2; Wai-27 M5: 24 and passim.
22. Acland 1975: 275ff; Cresswell

1952: chapter 7; Gardner 1971: 37; Oliver 1990: 296–97.
23. Acland 1975: passim.
24. See Crawford 1981: passim.
25. Acland 1975: 23ff, 33 (map), 173, 195ff; Studholme 1954: chapter 2.
26. See e.g. Woodhouse 1937 and Studholme 1954.
27. Butler 1964: 115.
28. See e.g. Kennaway 1874 and Burdon 1938.
29. See Macdonald 1956; Acland 1975: 89, 392; Courage 1976: 246.
30. Hamilton–McLean, 5.2.1857, in Mackay 1873 II: 22.
31. Hamilton- McLean 5.2.1857, in Mackay 1873 II: 20ff. Since no Maori evidence is available on this purchase, we are dependent entirely on colonial sources.
32. DOSLIW Canterbury No. 4. The *Lyttelton Times* (28.2.1857: 6) reported, 'There is no doubt that the natives have been somewhat hardly used . . . The price we have had to pay is ridiculously small.' McLean's clause requiring the signatories of a deed to meet the claims of absentees was later called in question by William Rolleston: 'Can a number of joint owners sell a property without the knowledge and consent of the remainder?' What if the price paid was so far below the real value of the property that the sellers could not satisfy the claims of the absentees, asked Rolleston. 'It would seem that in equity the deed must be set aside,' he said (Memorandum, 14.12.1865, in Mackay 1873 II: 77–78). When he became Super-intendent of Canterbury in 1868, however, Rolleston evidently overcame his scruples about the North Canterbury and Akaroa deeds.

33. Hamilton–McLean, Minutes of Proceedings, 5.2.1857, in Mackay 1873 II: 21.
34. Ibid: 22.
35. Hamilton–McLean, 19.11.1857, in Mackay 1873 II: 28.
36. Acland 1975: 24.
37. Hamilton–McLean, 19.11.1857, in Mackay 1873 II: 28.
38. Haast 1938: 391ff.
39. See Oliver 1990: 252–53. James Mackay pronounced his surname 'Máckee', as indicated in his rendering of his name in Maori – 'Tiemi Make' (see e.g. Mackay 1873 II: 382, 385).
40. Lord 1939: 65; *NE*, 22.8.1857: 3.
41. *NE*, 26.8.1857: 3ff.
42. Dobson 1930:92.
43. Tarapuhi–McLean, 15.3.1857, McLean Ms Papers 681A.
44. See May 1962: 44ff; Lord 1939: chapter 6; McClymont 1959: 93ff. Other Europeans visited the Poutini Coast in 1857 after Mackay, including Leonard Harper (Harper 1946: 201ff).
45. Salmon 1963: 35ff: 'The speed with which the Maori learned the trade of goldminer was as disconcerting to the older settler as was the spirit of Maori independence to the new immigrant.'
46. Oliver 1990: 252–53. See also *NZ Railways Magazine*, 1.9.1933: 28.
47. Salmon loc cit. See also Philosophical Institute of Canterbury, 'Natural History of Canterbury' 1927: 39ff.
48. McLean–Mackay, 3.11.1858, in Mackay 1873 II: 33–34.
49. See Hamilton–McLean, 5.2.1857,
in Mackay 1873 II: 21; Mackay–McLean, 25.2.1859, 19.4.1859, in Mackay 1873 II: 34ff.
50. Wai-27 M6: 25 (map).
51. Mackay–McLean, 25.2.1859, McLean Ms Papers 32/421. Since no Maori evidence is available on the Kaikoura purchase, we are dependent entirely on Mackay's account.
52. See Wai-27 M10.
53. DOSLIW Marlborough No. 9.
54. Mackay–McLean, 19.4.1859, in Mackay 1873 II: 36.
55. Lord 1939: 73–74. The mortality among European surveyors on the West Coast by drowning was to become notorious. Their Maori assistants survived far better (see Dobson 1930: passim.).
56. Mackay–Native Secretary, 27.9.1859, Mackay Ms Collingwood Letterbook.
57. See Wai-27 N2.
58. *NE*, 24.12.1859. Rochfort's Kawatiri expedition foundered in a 'rise of flood 60 feet', with loss of canoe and instruments (BM Add Ms 31343 X/2 Rochfort).
59. Reid 1884: 14ff.
60. DOSLIW Westland No. 1.
61. Wai-27 D3: 15; D5: 41ff.
62. Mackay–McLean, 21.9.1861, in Mackay 1873 II: 40–42; Mackay, Memo, 8.6.1866, in Mackay 1873 II: 50; Arahura Deed Transcript and Reserve Schedules, in Mackay 1873 II: 385–89.
63. Mackay–Native Secretary, 27.9.1859, Mackay Ms Collingwood Letterbook: 52.

16

~

Civilising the Natives

IN INDIA in 1859 there drew to a close the greatest upheaval in the British Empire since the American Revolution of 1776. A local mutiny of Indian soldiers in May 1857 produced a widespread revolt against British rule. It led to the demise of the British East India Company which had controlled the sub-continent for nearly a century, and it hardened the Victorian attitude towards 'natives'. To the established idea of 'natives' as simple-minded inferiors were added, in the popular imagination, the sinister traits of treachery, ingratitude, and furtive, bestial cruelty. While military men criticised the policies thought to have provoked the revolt,[1] journalists stridently reviled it. But all agreed that 'natives' must be firmly governed, and (if possible) civilised.

In New Zealand, the evident failure of Maoris to embrace civilisation was attributed to their persistent communal land ownership. Leading colonists renewed Edward Gibbon Wakefield's call for the privatisation of Maori land. Henry Sewell of Canterbury believed that it would be 'the first real step to elevate and save the Native' from 'his present miserable state of tribal barbarism – a state of debasing socialistic communism'.[2] The Otago Native Reserves Commissioners, appointed under the 1856 Native Reserves Act, urged that the land retained by Ngai Tahu under the Otago purchase,[3] which was communally owned, should be privatised by dividing it into individual and separate Maori allotments. This would weaken tribal influence and encourage competitiveness, said the Commissioners, and thus promote the Maoris' moral and religious progress. 'The possession of an exclusive title to land,' they said, 'has a tendency to increase the desire for improving the worldly circumstances,' and encouraged 'self-respect and obedience, and respect for the ordinances of law and good government'.[4]

Christopher Richmond of Taranaki became New Zealand's first Minister for Native Affairs in August 1858, with Governor Browne still ultimately responsible for the portfolio. Richmond, on behalf of his government, prepared a lengthy memorandum for Browne, recommending the registration of tribal lands and the issuing of a private title for each individual Maori's share, as a necessary step towards civilisation. The Anglican leaders Bishop Selwyn, William Martin, and William Swainson also supported the privatisation of Maori land, so long as churches and schools got enough of it.[5] Browne, addressing the British Government, explained Richmond's memorandum thus:

> The subject has two aspects; the one relating to the civilization of the Natives, the other to the promotion of the settlement of the country by Europeans. Ministers hold that these two objects, truly viewed, are ultimately inseparable.[6]

James West Stack, the son of a Danish evangelist, had spent his childhood with the Church Missionary Society among Ngati Porou on the North Island east coast, and spoke Maori fluently. He went to England in 1848, aged thirteen. There, in 1851, he befriended Tamihana Te Rauparaha, who was in London with CMS missionaries who were trying to clear Henry Williams from Sir George Grey's accusations of corruption.[7] Stack trained with the CMS and returned to New Zealand with Tamihana.[8] In Canterbury in 1859, when Tamati Tikao and his wife started a free boarding school for Maori children at Wairewa,[9] the Anglican Church appointed Stack to establish a Maori mission at Tuahiwi. There Stack was concerned to find that 'indifference had taken the place of zeal for religion'.[10] Dunedin citizens, with the same concern, formed a 'Society for Elevating the Condition of the Maories in the Province of Otago', and sponsored a school at Otakou.[11]

The government now published a report by Francis Dart Fenton on the 'State of the Aboriginal Inhabitants of New Zealand', in which Fenton argued that privatising Maori land would rescue the Maori from decline by achieving 'the grand requisite of civilization: fixity of residence'.[12] The Otago Reserves Commissioners opposed the private Maori allotments being disposed of to non-Maoris, but Fenton argued that it would hasten the civilising of the Maori.

In December 1859, McLean appointed Walter Lawry Buller,

twenty-one-year-old son of James Buller, the prominent Wesleyan, as Canterbury Native Reserves Commissioner, with instructions to get Ngai Tuahuriri to privatise their reserves. From Tuahiwi, Buller reported that Ngai Tuahuriri's 'moral attainments' were inferior, but that Stack's mission would improve them.[13] He recited the official wisdom to McLean:

> Communism in land is admitted to be the great obstacle to the social and material advancement of the Maori people. It is very certain that under the present system of tenure the Natives will never be induced to give up their low Maori habits, and to adapt themselves to the requirements of a superior civilization.[14]

Buller found Maori disputes over timber rights at Tuahiwi, and urged the runanga to privatise the whole reserve.[15] Thinking this was an official directive,[16] the runanga in May 1860 grudgingly agreed to their arable land being divided for a year's trial into four-teen-acre sections, to be allocated regardless of rank. The forest too was subdivided. According to Buller, these subdivisions were opposed only by Metehau – 'a man of notoriously bad character'.[17]

Government troops had now started fighting Te Ati Awa in Taranaki to enforce a disputed purchase at Waitara. To rally sup-port for the government, and exhume the forgotten principles of the Treaty of Waitangi, Governor Browne and Donald McLean called a conference of Maori chiefs at Auckland in July 1860. McLean chaired the conference, and Walter Buller recorded its proceed-ings. About two hundred 'friendly' chiefs attended, including Pita Te Hori of Ngai Tuahuriri, and Taiaroa, now christened 'Matenga' (Marsden). When political equality for Maoris was proposed, McLean told the conference:

> Some of you have said that the laws for the Maori are not the same as the laws for the European. This is in some measure true. Children cannot have what belongs to persons of mature age; and a child does not grow to be a man in a day. [18]

∼

Walter Mantell returned to New Zealand from England in 1860, and Tiramorehu invited him to Moeraki to discuss the shortage of Maori land there.[19] But Mantell was too busy seeking election to the General Assembly. He took his seat in March 1861 for Wallace, a Murihiku electorate that appreciated his past activities and his pledge to support the efforts of 'Southland' to secede from his old adversary, Otago province.[20]

Buller returned to Tuahiwi in May 1861, and had 122 Maori allotments surveyed, mostly of fourteen acres. Seventy-five of the Tuahiwi allotments went to Tuahiwi people, and forty-seven to people from Rapaki, Port Levy and elsewhere. About fifty small bush allotments were also surveyed.[21] Mantell now became Native Minister in William Fox's government, and instructed Buller to allocate about a fifth of the Tuahiwi reserve to Moeraki people, including fifteen allotments already allocated to Tuahiwi men. The combined runanga of Tuahiwi, Rapaki and Port Levy objected. 'How are some to be provided with land when the others have got it?' was the question asked.[22] Tiramorehu wrote to Mantell accusing him of deceit. Recalling his request to Mantell in 1848 for a thousand more acres at Moeraki, he said, 'You stole it, Mantell.' He again asked for land at Waipara.[23] But Mantell had suddenly resigned as Minister because, he said, Cabinet had refused to provide schools and hospitals for Ngai Tahu. Mantell told his successor that the Tuahiwi Maoris knew 'perfectly well' that their reserve was 'made larger' to accommodate the Moeraki people.[24]

In 1861 the Taranaki War ended, and Sir George Grey succeeded Browne as Governor. Grey's professed mission in returning to New Zealand was to 'restore peace and good order amongst the Natives'.[25] But after a year in office, he envisaged a trial of strength between himself and the Waikato tribes. On 12 July 1863, spurred on by land-investment companies and land-hungry settlers, and by a rumoured Maori plan to sack Auckland, he ordered the British commander, General Cameron, to invade the Waikato. The news of war electrified the country. Many, like Donald McLean, saw the conflict as inevitable.[26] Throughout the colony it produced a surge of anti-Maori sentiment. Henry Sewell observed: 'The men of the Middle [i.e. South] Island are come up rabid about the Natives. Nothing but confiscation and if needs be extermination. War to the knife. These are the political ideas of the Middle Island.'[27]

Cameron's troops were soon joined by 'friendly' tribes wanting to fight their Waikato enemies. The 'rebel' tribes were overwhelmed in twelve months, although guerilla resistance continued throughout the 1860s. Large areas of Maori land were confiscated for European settlement. Ngai Tahu declared their loyalty to the Queen from the outset. But gunpowder smuggling rumoured at Stewart Island was readily attributed to their plotting to supply the 'rebels'.[28]

The South Island West Coast from Mawheranui (Grey River) south to Awarua (Haast River) was in Canterbury province, while the areas north of the Grey and south of the Haast were in Nelson and Otago respectively. All three provinces had offered rewards for the discovery of 'payable' and 'accessible' goldfields in their territories. Nelson and Otago had such goldfields operating by 1862, but not on the West Coast. There, European prospectors struggled with heavy rains, dense forests, forbidding gorges, dangerous rivers, turbulent seas, and general isolation, and often depended on local Maoris for their survival.[29] Poutini Ngai Tahu established their own gold-diggings. In December 1862, Tarapuhi's nephew Ihaia Tainui hurried over the Hurunui Saddle to Christchurch from the Maori diggings on the Hohonu in the lower Taramakau, with gold to claim the Canterbury province's £1,000 reward. A very strong man, he brought also a sealed packet from two Europeans – who (unknown to him) were also claiming the reward.

The Canterbury authorities inspected both samples brought by Ihaia, and deemed neither eligible for the reward.[30] But they took fresh interest in the West Coast. Herbert Howitt was sent to improve the Hurunui–Taramakau track. John Whitcombe was sent to prospect a pass from the Rakaia. Charles Townsend was sent to Mawhera to establish a government store there for prospectors and surveyors, and to repay Tarapuhi for past assistance.[31] The Canterbury provincial geologist Julius Haast reached the Coast from Wanaka over the pass now bearing his name. The Otago provincial geologist James Hector reached Kotuku (Martins Bay) in August 1863.[32]

The Canterbury Provincial Government now decided to have its West Coast territory surveyed. The northern section, from the Mawheranui south to Abut Head, was assigned to twenty-two-year-old Arthur Dobson, son of the Canterbury provincial engineer. Dobson sailed for the West Coast from Nelson in August 1863, but after a five-week voyage his schooner was wrecked on the Mawheranui River bar, the men and stores being saved by Tarapuhi, Townsend and their men. By now Whitcombe, Howitt and other Europeans had drowned. Townsend and others drowned on the Mawheranui bar soon afterwards. Fearful of their survival, the Canterbury southern West Coast survey party departed over the Haast Pass to Dunedin, losing another man on the way.[33] Dobson's European staff also left for home. Ihaia Tainui had remarked, 'This place is not fit for Europeans. There is too much water.'[34]

Adopting Rochfort's practice in Nelson province, Arthur Dobson now decided to employ only Maoris.[35] He was befriended by Tarapuhi, 'the most important chief on the Coast' and 'very active and strong' despite his seventy years. Dobson stayed for three weeks at Tarapuhi's Mawhera village of some forty huts, learning enough Maori to make himself understood. Maoris were then glad to join him for the pay, the cameraderie, and the tobacco. Dobson recalled:

> The Maoris were ideal bushmen, and they made very good chainmen, were quick to learn, and worked splendidly; in fact I could not have done this work under the same conditions with white men. They were always jolly and pleasant, could catch birds and eels, and knew where to find mussels on the rocks at dead low water. They could light fires and pitch tents under any conditions. They had canoes on every river.[36]

Tarapuhi, as a great chief, was above employment. But with his daughters Tireaki, Kaiwai and Waihuka, he canoed for Dobson on the Mawheranui.[37]

Dobson respected the Maoris, and the lonely magnificence of their mountains, lakes and forests. He admired Maori prowess in the bush, on the rivers, and at sea. He learned their navigational methods, and adopted their gear: the kawe for heavy back-packing, sandals for rough riverbeds and beaches, scanty clothing for working in water, poles for fording rivers, mokihi where there were no canoes, ladders of flax and lianes for negotiating cliffs and bluffs, and rat-proof whata for storing food. He admired the skill of an old Maori whom he engaged to build a canoe on the Hokitika River. With only axe and adze, and using no lines or templates, this craftsman fashioned his log perfectly symmetrically – and 'when put in the water it floated dead level, and was quite a clipper', recalled Dobson. Some of Dobson's Maori assistants could read and write, using 'broad flax leaves, scratching the letters on the shiny surface, and then folding the leaf up to about one foot in length'. In this way, Dobson recalled, 'The able-bodied young men that I had working for me sent word to the various pas down the coast that I was coming, and that I would pay for help for canoeing on the rivers.' Before the year's end (1863), Dobson had completed his contract.

Dobson once decided, against Tarapuhi's advice, to camp in worsening weather on a forested island, shunned by Maoris, on the secluded, meandering Kotukuwhakaoka River. Tarapuhi, despite his forebodings, insisted on staying with Dobson. The two took shelter in a derelict whare, to the dismal sound of heavy rain and the flooding river rushing by.

In the dead of night Tarapuhi said: 'Friend, I am afraid. Some evil thing approaches. May I come and lie by you?' Dobson replied: 'Certainly, come at once.' Tarapuhi crossed the hut and lay down, trembling. He whispered to Dobson: 'Tae-po, the evil spirit, now comes. He comes in the form of a little pig. He often comes like that. He is now putting his snout in between the bundles of raupo, and pushing his head right through, now his body, now he is all in. Cannot you see him? Now he is turning into a little man, now he is coming to the fire-log; alas, we shall perish. Now he stops, now he is sitting on the log warming his feet. It is well he is not looking this way.'

Despite Dobson's reassurances, Tarapuhi described the taepo's every movement, until at last it departed as it had come. 'He is gone, we are saved,' said Tarapuhi. Then, when he had recovered his composure: 'Tae-po does sometimes come like that, and not do any harm, but I told you this is a bad place.' Dobson recalled: 'I cannot account for this vision of Tarapuhi's; it was not a dream, as he was wide awake all the time. Of course I neither saw nor heard anything, but it was a solid reality to Tarapuhi, and he considered that we had had a miraculous escape.'[38]

Three months later, still active, Tarapuhi died at Mawhera. His devoted widow waited for Dobson's return to pass on some messages. Then, grieving for her husband, 'the best man in the world', she said her farewells and retired to a special hut, where she took no food and died a few days later.

The West Coast gold rush began in earnest early in 1865. Maori canoe-operators were superseded by Europeans operating whale-boats, and by roads, ferries, and eventually railways. The privatisation of land around mining, sawmilling and farming settlements hindered traditional Maori seasonal movements. But the Mawhera reserve remained the anchor stone of Tarapuhi's people. It soon accommodated much of Greymouth town, bringing its Maori owners £2,500 in annual rents by 1866 – a sore point with tenants.[39]

~

The Murihiku chiefs, apprehensive of European encroachment, now offered to sell Rakiura to the government. The Stewart Island purchase deed, signed on 29 June 1864, guaranteed Ngai Tahu the exclusive rights to certain titi islands.[40] Of the £6,000 purchase price, £2,000 was reserved for education. In 1868 the government substituted this £2,000 with 2,000 acres of land in the Hokonui hills, and leased it to a European farmer at £100 a year to fund a Maori school.[41] Thus 2,000 acres in the Hokonuis cost the Maoris nearly as much as Mantell had paid them for all of Murihiku fifteen years earlier.

William Fox became joint leader of the government, and Native Minister, late in 1863. Soon afterwards, he decided to nail Mantell down regarding his alleged promises to Ngai Tahu. His secretary (Edward Shortland) informed Mantell:

> [Mr Fox] cannot ascertain what those advantages were to be nor whether any specific plans for conferring them were ever devised or proposed by you to the Colonial Government, while you were a member of the Government or at any other time. Mr Fox will be much obliged if you will specify the precise nature of the pledges given or understood to be given by you to the Natives in question, in order that the Government may as far as possible, carry those pledges into effect.

Mantell, stung by these words, but without answering them, labelled Fox's inquiry as a 'repudiation' of his promises.[42] Late in 1864, with a change of government, Mantell became Native Minister under Frederick Weld as Premier. Mantell told his officials that Ngai Tuahuriri, whose complaints against him had never ceased, were really 'Peninsular Natives', with 'ample reserves' on Banks Peninsula.[43]

With the approval of Weld, Mantell appointed Francis Fenton as Chief Judge of the Native Land Court.[44] This new court was established under the Weld Government's Native Land Act of 1865 to privatise Maori communal land and thus hasten the familiar twin goals – the European settlement of Maori land, and the civilising of 'savages'.[45] Any ten Maori owners could apply for communal land to be subdivided into individual holdings, of which the ten would be trustees whether other owners supported them or not.

At Weld's request, Mantell now appointed an Under-Secretary for Native Affairs. This was William Rolleston, an austere, thirty-four-year-old Cambridge graduate and son of a prosperous English vicar. Rolleston had emigrated to Canterbury in search of a just

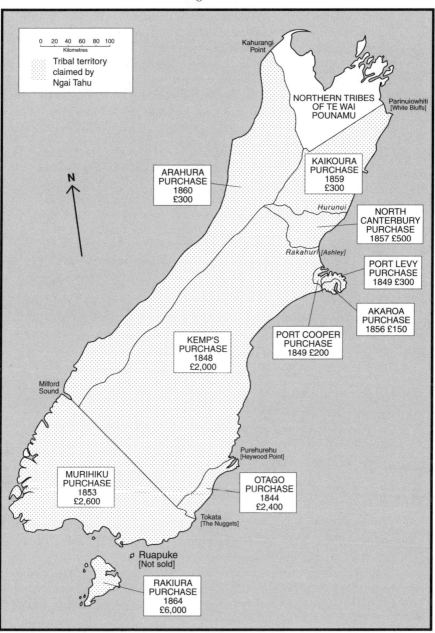

The ten official purchases of Ngai Tahu tribal territory, and payments, 1844–1864.

and virtuous society.[46] Anglican religion, classical education, scrupulous administration, moral righteousness, and the duty to civilise
'natives', were the articles of Rolleston's faith. Six years as a Canterbury settler had confirmed in him the colonialist attitude to Maoris.
Their isolation should be broken down, he said, by getting them to
sell their land and 'work for their subsistence'. Of the impoverished
Tuahiwi Maoris on their small allotments, surrounded by prosperous European settlers, Rolleston wrote:

> The circumstances of this small body of Natives, surrounded
> by a population of widely different pursuits and feelings, seems
> to foster their communistic habits even in a greater degree
> than is the case in the Northern Island. The principal object
> therefore in view, is to educate them to a change of ideas in
> respect of property in land, and at the same time to do away
> with the communism which pervades their other relations in
> life, and which forms the chief barrier between the two races.[47]

Soon after appointing Rolleston, Mantell resigned as Minister
for the third and final time, because (according to himself) a colleague had reneged on the question of Maori ownership of the
Princes Street reserve, which was being challenged by the Otago
province on the grounds that Governor Grey in 1853 had exceeded
his powers in granting the reserve. According to Weld, Mantell
confided to him that he (Mantell) 'could not *quite* justify this
resignation to *himself*'.[48] On 13 September 1865 the House of Representatives, despite Mantell's objections in the House, resolved that
the Princes Street reserve should be granted to the Otago province.
Mantell retired from the House with the dissolution of the 1861
Parliament, in January 1866.

∼

By 1866 gold rushes had brought the non-Maori population of
southern New Zealand to over a hundred thousand.[49] For most of
the Maori population, potatoes, flour and sugar had now replaced
fernroot and ti-kauru as staple foods; but because of their having
insufficient farmland they still depended on their traditional mahinga
kai for protein-rich foods, particularly eels, lampreys, inanga, weka,
and waterfowl such as putangitangi. European settlement was
steadily destroying these mahinga kai, especially by drainage and
pollution.[50]

Whether New Zealand wetlands produced more food in their natural state, than when drained for pasture, was of no concern to Europeans who preferred mutton, beef and dairy produce to 'Maori food'. Near Tuahiwi, the artesian-fed Waiora Stream, life-blood of the rich Tutae Patu lagoon, was permanently diverted by Europeans to drive a flourmill.[51] The European custom of discharging sewage and other refuse into streams, estuaries and foreshores, spoiled many mahinga kai for Maori use,[52] since Maoris would not knowingly eat what had been steeped in human excrement. The fencing of settlers' runs and farms, and the law of trespass, generally impeded Maori access to what mahinga kai remained. The weka, once plentiful on the plains, was dwindling, while the koreke was virtually extinct. Along with these misfortunes, lack of land prevented Maoris from raising capital for sea-fishing as a source of sustenance.[53]

European colonists, on their long and dangerous voyage to New Zealand, usually prayed thrice daily for survival. Once in New Zealand, their prayers answered, their biblical duty was to 'be fruitful, and multiply, and replenish the earth, and subdue it', and have dominion over every living thing.[54] Pastoralists enthusiastically burned the ancient vegetation of Te Wai Pounamu to provide pasturage for sheep and cattle.[55] 'I have seen no grander sight than the fire upon a country which has never before been burnt,' wrote Samuel Butler in 1860. 'The wild plants are few, and decidedly ugly,' he said.[56] Lady Barker, wife of another Canterbury runholder, wrote in 1865 of 'The Exceeding Joy of Burning'. She envied 'the good old times' when 'the tussocks were six feet high. What a blaze they must have made!'[57]

Runholders' fires inevitably reduced stability and moisture retention capacity in the subsoil, particularly on steep country where soils were generally skeletal. Runholders could ignore the manifest folly of such burning, for their political influence was pervasive. Their visible testimonials survive today in the desolate, scree-ravaged slopes of South Island mountains gripped by accelerated erosion, and the consequent choking of streams and rivers by silt, sand and shingle. These dreadful consequences emerged as early as 1868, in summer floods that brought Waimakariri waters into Christchurch:

> This was the flood that so greatly changed the face of Canterbury. Up till then most of the rivers were confined to fairly definite channels, and many were studded with permanent green islets; the Kowhai river, for instance, flowed among islets set with groves of yellow kowhai – whence the name of the river. But burning had been going on all over the country.

Not only the dense mass of decaying vegetation which held the water so that the rains filtered away slowly had gone up in widespread conflagrations, but thousands of acres of bush had been burned too, and that in summer, when the destruction of the bush and all it contained was most severe. Then, when the heavy rains fell, and the rains of 1868 were phenomenal, the water simply poured down the hills into the rivers, scouring the country, baring and loosening the shingle, and smothering up the riverbeds, creating the wide beds with braided water-channels later so characteristic of Canterbury. On the steeper hills were loosed the shingle-slides that now disfigure so much of the hill country, the damage being accentuated by heavy stocking and annual burning.[58]

British colonists had left behind them the 'poaching wars' of Britain, in which for generations the traditional taking of wildlife by common people, usually out of necessity, had been sternly suppressed.[59] In Europe, the right to go out with rod, gun and dog, and kill wild creatures for pleasure, was the privilege of gentlemen. But in the colonies, all classes of European could indulge this mania.[60] Because the native birds of Te Wai Pounamu were 'too tame for sport',[61] acclimatisation societies were formed to import British game birds and animals, and stock the rivers with Northern Hemisphere fish.[62]

Excessive lowering of the lake level at Waihora, as Maoris knew from centuries of experience, could adversely affect the natural stocks of shellfish, flatfish, eels and waterfowl. Nevertheless, the Canterbury provincial authorities proceeded to lower the lake and survey its shores in the interests of European settlement. The Ngai Tuahuriri runanga, meeting at Rapaki in 1865, deputed Natanahira Waruwarutu to protest to the central government, pointing out that under Kemp's deed Ngai Tahu had never sold Waihora, their greatest mahinga kai.[63]

In response, the Canterbury Provincial Government informed the central government that they had not changed the lake level, and only intended 'so far draining the lake that it shall not back up the river running into it, or overflow the land adjacent'. When Ngai Tuahuriri queried this self-contradictory explanation, the government referred the matter to Mantell, now a private citizen. Mantell effectively stymied the Maori protest by stating that he had told Taumutu chiefs in 1848 that 'the Government must be quite free to do as it pleased' with regard to the lake.[64]

To further discredit Kemp's deed, Mantell informed Native Under-Secretary Rolleston that Kemp's translation of the deed was incorrect, and that there was no proof 'either that those who signed were the owners of the land, or that the marks were made by those whose names are written beside them'. He did not say why he had waited eighteen years before revealing these startling facts, nor did he make them public. Instead, he gave the earnest Rolleston a conundrum, saying: 'The signatures of the vendors are, although added at the foot of the paper, not placed in such a position as to seem to be what they are.'[65]

∾

Edward John Eyre served in the West Indies after leaving New Zealand in 1853. In 1864 he became Governor of Jamaica and could again make a name for himself. But European colonists disliked him, and economic depression brought increasing unrest among the emancipated, impoverished Black majority. Amid rising tension, in October 1865 a local protest in eastern Jamaica, led by a Baptist landowner, was fired upon by police. In the ensuing riot, twenty-eight people were killed, black and white, including a magistrate. This was the 'Jamaica Rebellion'.

A frenzy of vengefulness seized the European population, mindful of past slave rebellions,[66] and fearful of a black republic such as Toussaint Louverture had established in Haiti seventy years before. Eyre proclaimed martial law in the eastern province. His troops burned homes, and hanged 354 persons after summary trial. Eighty-five were executed without trial, and six hundred were flogged, including women. An army captain reported: 'This is a picture of martial law: the soldiers enjoy it, the inhabitants here dread it. If they run on being approached, they are shot for running away.' Eyre had his chief opponent in the colonial assembly arrested and taken to the martial law area, where he too was hanged.[67]

When reports of this reached England, a 'Jamaica Committee' was formed to bring Eyre and his officers to trial, supported by prominent humanitarians and scientists, including John Stuart Mill, Herbert Spencer, Charles Darwin, Sir Charles Lyell and Thomas Huxley. Eyre was recalled amid a storm of criticism. But he arrived in England to a hero's welcome, at a public banquet held in his honour. Unwittingly he was now at the centre of one of the great controversies of the Victorian age. This reduced to a simple question: were Jamaican Blacks entitled to the rights of Englishmen? An 'Eyre Committee', which said 'No', was formed to defend Eyre, vigorously led by Thomas Carlyle and John Ruskin – the literary lions of Britain – and supported by Dickens, Tennyson, Kingsley and many of the aristocracy. *Punch* pilloried Eyre's critics as 'negromaniacs'.[68] A wave of anti-black hysteria swept England. Prosecutions of Eyre and his officers all failed. Successive governments paid his legal expenses and gave him a life pension, on which he went into dignified retirement. The 'Eyre controversy' added yet another current to the rising tide of race prejudice that now nourished British imperialism, in New Zealand as elsewhere.

The New Zealand Government in February 1867, at Rolleston's suggestion, paid Tiramorehu £200 for his Waipara claims, since he had not been party to the North Canterbury purchase.[69] Tiramorehu next went to Wellington to press for some pastoral land at the Waiau-ua, where he also had customary rights. He petitioned the General Assembly, reminding them of his previous requests for land, and describing a block on the Waiau-ua near the Main Divide. This, and the land south to the Kowhai River, said Tiramorehu, should be returned to Ngai Tahu for sheep runs ('he rana hipi moku' – 'sheep runs for myself', i.e. 'my tribe').[70] Mantell was now in the Legislative Council – a lifetime appointment – having been called there in June 1866 by Sir George Grey as Governor.

Tiramorehu asked Mantell to present his petition to the General Assembly. But Mantell presented an amended version which omitted the reminder of previous requests and the reference to sheep runs. A new passage appeared, translated thus:

> It was not I who gave my land over into the hand of the Pakeha; but it was all included in the boundaries of a block sold by another person altogether.[71]

There appears to be no evidence that Tiramorehu approved these curious changes in his petition. Horomona Pohio also petitioned Parliament for pastoral country north of Kemp's block, challenging the Wairau purchase and Hamilton's North Canterbury purchase. The petitions were rejected;[72] but for Ngai Tahu, petitioning Parliament had become another means of seeking redress.

Alexander Mackay in 1864 had became Commissioner of

Native Reserves and Civil Commissioner for the South Island, based in Nelson. Aged thirty-two years, he was more reserved than his cousin James Mackay junior, but he had an equal mastery of the Maori language, and was sensitive to Maori aspirations. The Tuahiwi runanga had now allocated nine of Buller's fourteen-acre sections to the Moeraki people, but refused to allow any more. Fitzgerald, who had replaced Mantell as Native Minister in August 1865, decided that in any case Maoris must pay the 'usual fees' before they could get Crown grants for the sections arranged by Buller.[73] That Maoris might have to sell land to meet these charges pleased Under-Secretary Rolleston, who told the Canterbury Maori Reserves Commissioner in October 1865:

> No impediment should be thrown in the way of their disposing of their lands, as any steps which tend to introduce a European population into the settlement and do away with the isolation which at present appears to prevent the social improvement of the Natives must be considered to be beneficial.[74]

In 1867 the General Assembly passed a Maori Representation Act adding four Maori seats to the House of Representatives, to be contested on manhood suffrage. Tamanuiarangi (John Patterson) of Tuahiwi won the Southern Maori seat, and Maoris of southern New Zealand were thus represented in the General Assembly for the first time. A Native Schools Act allowed £4,000 a year for Maori schools, provided that Maori parents gave land and financial support. The schools were to be open to all, for Under-Secretary Rolleston favoured a secular state education system.[75]

When Alexander Mackay went to Tuahiwi in November 1867 to investigate Buller's subdivisions, he encountered the bitter disputes that Mantell and Buller had sown among Ngai Tuahuriri. Those who had Buller's fourteen-acre sections were fearful of losing them to those who had none. Those who had no land resented those who had. Those who lived on the Tuahiwi reserve resented Mantell's efforts to give more of it to Moeraki people, and the Moeraki people resented not getting it. The Tuahiwi people, having allocated allotments to Rapaki and Port Levy people, expected the same in return. But the younger Rapaki people, themselves short of land, refused to give up any of their reserve.

Maori reserves could be enlarged only from adjoining land. But this was all now owned by Europeans, who would sell only at the market price, if at all. Alexander Mackay, knowing that the provincial and central governments would decline such expense, could only suggest as an alternative the reserving of some inferior Crown land away in the Canterbury foothills.[76] 'Civilising' Ngai Tahu by privatising their reserves had thus brought them more dissension, more poverty, and now the prospect of dispersal.

Notes

1. See Wood 1908: passim.
2. Sewell 1980 II: 258.
3. The 1867 Native Lands Act defined all such lands as 'reserves' if they had been named in a purchase deed. By 1870, even Ruapuke, which had never been sold, was a 'Native Reserve', since it was named as excluded in the Murihiku deed (Mackay 1873 I: 285–87).
4. Gillies, 21.6.1858, McGlashan Ms Papers.
5. Ward 1983: 32ff.
6. *AJHR* 1860 E-1: 7.
7. Scholefield 1940 and Oliver 1990 'J. W. Stack': passim.
8. Stack 1936: 103, 108ff.
9. Stack 1938: 58n.
10. Ibid. See Tau Ms 1992: passim.
11. Gillies, 21.6.1858, loc cit.
12. Fenton 1859: 41 and passim.
13. Buller–McLean, 6.3.1860, in Mackay 1873 II: 126ff.
14. *AJHR* 1862 E-5: 11.
15. Buller–McLean, 27.12.1859, in Mackay 1873 II: 128–29. For the origins and development of runanga among Ngai Tahu, see Tau Ms 1992.
16. Pita Te Hori, 24.4.1868, in Mackay 1873 II: 196.
17. *AJHR* 1862 E-5. Tau (op cit) says Buller's subdivisions were forced on Ngai Tuahuriri. For Europeans, 200 acres were now considered necessary (*NTR*: 940).
18. *AJHR* 1860 E-9: 7. For the Kohimarama Conference, see Sinclair 1957 and Orange 1987.
19. Tiramorehu–Mantell, 22.1.1861, Mantell Ms 83/194.
20. Wallace electors– Mantell, December 1860, Mantell Ms 83/142.
21. Mackay 1873 II: 196–97.
22. SNC 3/12: 411.
23. Tiramorehu–Mantell, 20.1.1862, in Mantell Ms 83/194 (translation Te Aue Davis).
24. Mantell Ms 83/150, Draft of Memo, nd.
25. Rogers–Hamilton, PRO/CO/381/58: 290.
26. Sinclair 1957: 271–72.
27. Ibid: 210.
28. Howard 1940: 142–49.
29. See Money 1871 for an account of early West Coast gold prospecting.
30. May 1962: chapter 3. West Coast Maoris generally used the Hurunui Saddle or Haast Pass to cross the Main Divide, although other passes were known to them (Andersen Ms 148: 34).
31. May 1962 loc cit.
32. Hall-Jones 1987: chapter 2.
33. May 1962, loc cit. See also e.g. Lauper 1960.
34. Quoted in May 1962: 96.
35. Dobson 1930: 84 and passim.
36. Ibid: 66, 90–91.
37. Ibid: 66.
38. Ibid: 93ff.
39. May 1962: 357.
40. DOSLIW Crown Land Deeds Otago No. 5; Wai-27 U3; Mackay 1873 II: 51ff.
41. Mackay 1873 II: 69ff.
42. Shortland–Mantell, 16.1.1864,

Mantell Ms 83/145.

43. Halse–Brown, 1.5.1865, in
    Mackay 1873 II: 106.
44. See Ward 1983: 180ff.
45. Ibid: 187.
46. See Stewart 1940, Rolleston 1971
    and Reeves 1973: 254. Reeves says
    Rolleston was 'a dignified figure in
    public life for at least 30 years',
    but 'a hard man to listen to'.
47. Rolleston–Tancred, 26.10.1865,
    in Mackay 1873 II: 109.
48. Weld–Grey, 19.7.1865, Grey Ms
    NZ Letters Vol 33: 114–16. See
    also *AJHR* 1888 I-8: 92/231.
49. The European population of the
    South Island was 138,540 in
    December 1867, with nearly
    50,000 in Otago (*AJHR* 1868 D-1).
    In 1868, the European population
    of Canterbury passed 40,000
    (Gardner 1971: 323), while the
    total Maori population of
    southern New Zealand was
    recorded as 1,626: Kaikoura 77,
    Buller 48, Westland 68, Tuahiwi
    176, Rapaki 76, Port Levy 52,
    Akaroa 29, Wairewa 87, Taumutu
    25, Arowhenua 86, Waimate 76,
    Moeraki 97, Waikouaiti 106,
    Purakaunui 19, Otakou 98, Taieri
    58, Molyneux 22, Tuturau 11,
    Aparima 64, Kawakaputaputa and
    Oraka 68, Oue 22, Omaui 23,
    Ruapuke 102, Stewart Island 88,
    Bluff 48. (Mackay 1873 II: 345).
50. See e.g. Dobson 1930: 27ff.
51. Evison 1993: 309. Tutae Patu has
    been bowdlerized as 'Tutai Paku'
    by official cartographers.
52. See e.g. Lamb 1963: chapter 4, and
    Wilson 1989: chapter 2. Wilson
    compares Deans's description of
    the Avon River in 1844 – 'a river of
    water clearer than crystal, indeed
    the finest water I ever saw' – with
    its seriously contaminated state in
    the 1860s.
53. *NTSFR*: 549.

54. Genesis 1: 28.
55. Jones (1933: 58) describes burning
    'quite 10,000 acres' of native
    'beech' forest at the Hope River
    for pasture – which trebled his
    sheep carrying capacity within a
    few years.
56. Butler 1964: 48, 56.
57. Barker 1883: 193–98.
58. Andersen 1949: 290–91.
59. See Hopkins 1985: passim.
60. Clark 1949: 266. See e.g. Earle
    (1966: 223), who witnessed the
    slaughter of nesting albatrosses by
    Englishmen on Tristan da Cunha
    in 1824: 'On the level ground they
    were completely at our mercy, but
    very little was shown them, and in
    a very short time the plain was
    strewn with their bodies, one blow
    on the head generally killing them
    instantly.'
61. Jones (1933: 129) describes
    shooting '100 to 200' putangitangi
    in one morning.
62. See Lamb 1964: passim.
63. Waruwarutu–FitzGerald, 9.9.1865,
    and ensuing correspondence, in
    Mackay 1873 I: 237ff.
64. Mantell–Rolleston, 12.4.1866, in
    Mackay 1873 I: 241–42.
65. Ibid.
66. See e.g. da Costa 1994: passim.
67. See Abrahams 1957 and Semmel
    1962.
68. *Punch*, Vol 49 and 10.2.1866,
    lampooned 'Quashi-Bungo the
    Black, who chops up white people
    and scoops out their brains'. Eyre
    was 'a brave man, daring to do his
    duty to his countrymen and
    countrywomen at a time when to
    have hesitated would have been to
    have invited butchery and some-
    thing worse'. *The Pall Mall Gazette*
    (see Desmond & Moore 1991: 541)
    said Eyre's critics 'bestowed on the
    negro that sympathetic recogni-
    tion which they are willing to

extend even to the ape as a man and a brother'.

69. Rolleston, 14.12.1865 et seq, in Mackay 1873 II: 75ff.
70. Tiramorehu–Parliament, 6.8.1867, Mantell Ms 83/198.
71. *AJLC* July–October 1867: 61.
72. NAW LE1 1867/13; *AJHR* 1866

F11: 7–8.
73. Brown–Mantell, 15.5.1865, in Mackay 1873 II: 106.
74. Rolleston–Tancred, 26.10.1865, in Mackay 1873 II: 109.
75. See Ward 1983: 210ff.
76. Richmond–Mackay, 22.11.1867 et seq, in Mackay 1873 II: 109ff.

17

~

A Whiff of Justice

CHIEF NATIVE Land Court Judge Francis Dart Fenton was
a hard-headed, testy, Yorkshire lawyer[1] who had found favour
with Sir George Grey and disfavour with Donald McLean – whom
Fenton regarded as a rival. From being a squatter in the Waikato,
Fenton had become a resident magistrate there in 1857, with the
mission of persuading Maori chiefs to accept the British judicial
system rather than the authority of the Maori King – in which task,
by his own account, he achieved some success.[2] In Fenton's view,
the British judicial system was just as necessary for the civilisation
of Maoris as was the privatisation of their land. He now aimed to
make the Native Land Court the means of sheeting home both of
these civilising principles to the Maori.

A number of Ngai Tahu applied to the Native Land Court early
in 1867 to have their succession rights in their reserve allotments
certified, and Tuahiwi Maoris applied also for a share in the Rapaki
reserve. The Court announced it would sit in Christchurch and
Dunedin in 1868. Here at last there appeared to be a chance for
Ngai Tahu to get their Kemp's deed grievances heard in a court of
law. Claims to the Native Land Court for mahinga kai and parts of
Kemp's block therefore followed. These produced a flurry of correspondence among central and provincial government officials.
Native Under-Secretary William Rolleston soon suspected that the
'whakarite' clause in Kemp's deed, promising further reserves, had
never been fulfilled. Yet Walter Mantell's 1848 report said the reserves had been 'finally arranged'. The government decided that
Mantell should explain himself in Fenton's court. Mantell showed
no enthusiasm for this, but under threat of subpoena he finally agreed
to attend the Court.[3]

On 20 April 1868 the first Native Land Court sitting in Te Wai

Pounamu opened in Christchurch before Chief Judge Fenton, with Henare Pukuatua of Te Arawa (a North Island tribe) as Native Assessor. Alexander Mackay attended as Native Reserves Commissioner, to assist Crown and claimants with technical information. The Crown was represented by Rolleston, with his nominee William Henry Wynn Williams, the Canterbury provincial solicitor and a member of the Canterbury Provincial Council, as legal counsel.[4] A Canterbury member of Cabinet, John Hall, attended with Rolleston, formerly his near-neighbour on the Rakaia sheep runs.

Maoris were unaccustomed to the British judicial system beloved by Fenton. It was based not on the principle of consensus customary on the Maori marae, but on the adversarial principle, which required each person to push his own interests against those of his fellow-man or risk being wiped out. Fenton ran his court punctiliously. When Wereta Tainui claimed that Mantell had promised the Kaikanui reserve to him, Fenton told him he should have subpoenaed Mantell as a witness. Succession claimants who came to court without their Crown Grant documents were told to get them. Those whose claims were contested by others were told to deposit money for court costs. Those who claimed their land had been sold to Kemp without their consent were told to complain to the government. Those who could not produce a survey plan of land they were claiming had their claims dismissed. Those who claimed land which had been sold by the Crown to Europeans were told the court had no jurisdiction. Those who were confused were told to get lawyers. By the end of the opening day many Maoris had left the court,[5] for the services of lawyers and surveyors were beyond their means.

When the Honourable Walter Mantell MLC[6] gave his testimony in the Native Land Court, he blamed the government for Ngai Tahu's lack of adequate reserves. He said the government had never intended fulfilling Kemp's deed. 'The Natives have been constantly writing to the Government and soliciting performance,' he told the Court. 'The claimants do not understand English, and the lawyers don't understand Maori, and, to frame my answer as respectfully as possible, it is not convenient for the Government to interfere.'

A Ngai Tahu claimant, Henare Pereita, claimed half the land between Christchurch and the foothills near John Hall's run. He 'wished to drive the Europeans off the land', he said, since he had not agreed to Kemp's purchase. Fenton dismissed his case, like others of the kind, because the Crown had already granted the land to Europeans. But Fenton, later, noted that Kemp's deed had never been fulfilled, and that 'It would be greatly to the honour and advantage of the Crown' if its guarantees were attended to without delay.[7]

~

In the second week of Fenton's hearings an area was claimed that had *not* been all Crown-granted to Europeans. This was Kaitorete, the 6,000-hectare strip of land, twenty-five kilometres long, between Waihora and the sea. Kaitorete was windswept and uninviting, but it was valuable to the Maori. Pingao grass provided fibre highly prized for traditional weaving and wall-panelling. On Kaitorete's lake shore, seasonal catches of high-quality eels were culled by digging blind channels in the shingle when eels were migrating to the sea to breed. Waterfowl, birds' eggs, and fish of various kinds were available in the lake.

Part of Kaitorete had been freeholded to Europeans. The rest was under Crown lease to the Rhodes brothers and other runholders. Heremaia Mautai, Pohau and Tawha claimed this part on behalf of their hapu, Ngati Mako. Mautai, a veteran of the Ngati Toa wars, and leader of the Wairewa community, had signed Hamilton's Akaroa deed in 1856, as we have seen. But he had not signed Kemp's deed or Mantell's receipts, nor had he accepted money from either commissioner, nor had he agreed to sell Kaitorete. Like Metehau at Tuahiwi twenty years earlier, he claimed his own right to the land despite others having sold theirs – a position described by Edward Shortland in 1844 as being perfectly in accordance with Maori custom.[8] Mautai recited to the court his six generations of whakapapa from Mako, all of whom had used Kaitorete. 'Kaitorete is mine,' said Mautai.

Mautai and his supporters, like Ngai Tuahuriri, maintained that the eastern boundary of Kemp's block followed the Otumatua–Taumutu line. They claimed that Mantell had ignored them at Kaitorete in 1848, and had not reserved their kainga nohoanga, and that hence Mantell had excluded Kaitorete from Kemp's block, for Kemp had promised that all kainga nohoanga in the block would be reserved. But Mantell then testified that he had told Mautai's people that Kemp's purchase included Kaitorete, and that they had not disputed it.

Williams now handed in Kemp's deed and Kettle's sketch map, the latter showing Kaitorete within the purchase. Mautai and his supporters had engaged a young Christchurch lawyer, William Cowlishaw, to represent them. When Cowlishaw was invited by the court to scrutinise the deed and sketch map, he missed their crucial defects. Unlike Mantell and Rolleston, he did not know that the signatures on the deed were dubious or defective. Nor did he recognise that the map's coast to coast 'Ngatitoa–Nelson block' boundary was incompatible with the fact that the Nelson block did not reach the West Coast. However, Pohau testified that when he signed Kemp's deed and Mantell's receipts he had seen no map, and Fenton then disallowed the map as evidence.[9] The court adjourned while Williams, Rolleston and Hall sought agreement with Cowlishaw.

By next day, 29 April, no agreement had been reached. Williams on behalf of the Crown then presented the court with an Order of Reference, under Section 83 of the 1867 Native Lands Act, by which Kemp's deed was referred to the court as an 'agreement' for adjudication and final settlement. The Crown, said Williams, would show what was needed for a settlement, and would agree to Ngai Tahu being awarded it provided that they promised to make no further claims under Kemp's deed.[10]

Cowlishaw, for Mautai, objected that the deed was not an 'agreement' under the act, since it did not properly define the boundaries. He declared: 'The contract is void for uncertainty. You cannot tell what is sold and what is not sold. The deed merely says, "The greater part of the land".'[11] Fenton overruled this objection. Cowlishaw then objected further, that whereas an Order of Reference required the authority of the Governor (Sir George Bowen), this order been signed only by 'John Hall'. Hall then came forward and added to his signature the words 'A member of the Executive Council of the Colony of New Zealand'. Fenton then admitted the order, saying that the court would presume that Hall had Bowen's authority, unless it was proved to the contrary.[12] When Cowlishaw sought to question Hall as to how he had got Bowen's authority when he (Bowen) was away in the north of the country, Hall suddenly left the court.[13]

On 5 May, Fenton delivered a lengthy judgment on Kaitorete.[14] Firstly, he said, 'the Ngai Tahu tribe, or the majority of them', had agreed to sell Kemp's block. Moreover, Mantell's phrase 'e mau nei te ahua' in the receipt on the back of the deed 'distinctly proved' that Kettle's map had been attached when that receipt was signed. Fenton ruled that the receipt translated as follows: 'Hakaroa, 22nd February 1849. On this day was paid to us the second payment for our land, the plan of which is here attached, £500 was paid to us.'[15]

Fenton admitted the map as evidence. Since it included Kaitorete in Kemp's block, judgment was given in favour of the Crown. Mautai's claim failed also, said Fenton, because his co-claimants Pohau and Tawha, and the 'majority' of chiefs, had signed Mantell's receipts. 'The Court cannot recognize individual ownership of Native land,' said Fenton. 'The land belonged to the tribe.' However, he said:

> There would be sufficient ground for a Court of Equity to compel a specific performance, and it will be the duty of the Court, under the Order of Reference, to ascertain all the terms of the contract, and to make such orders as will secure the due fulfilment of them, by the Crown on one side and the Ngai Tahu tribe on the other.

This ended the Kaitorete case, and Cowlishaw left the court with his clients.[16]

～

The remaining Ngai Tahu claimants conducted their own cases in Fenton's court. William Rolleston announced in advance that he would not oppose the granting of eeling rights if they did not inter-fere with roading or 'the settlement of the country'.[17] Horomona Pohio appeared for the people of Arowhenua, Waimate and Waitaki. They had been farming their existing reserves, said Pohio, and rais-ing horses, pigs, cattle and crops, and had leased none of their land to Europeans, but the land was quite exhausted. They wanted their reserves more than doubled in area and allocated to the people, not the chiefs – otherwise the chiefs would lease the land and keep the money. Pohio said:

> The Europeans' laws are not good. Some of them are made great gentlemen, and others very small. And there are some of them going about the streets whom the Maoris are feeding (Laughter).[18]

On 6 May 1868 Fenton questioned Mantell about his Arowhenua reserve. For the first time, Mantell had to relate under oath what he had done:

Fenton: Was it understood that these reserves were to extin-guish their claims?
Mantell: I think the Natives thought the reserves did not wind

the thing up. At that time I did, and reported so . . .

Fenton: Can you give an estimate of the extent of reserve that should now be made? Say Arowhenua – 86 people – 600 acres?

Mantell: I do not think it is sufficient.

Fenton: They use more land?

Mantell: Not only that, but their other means of living are diminished.

Fenton: Give us an idea of what should be the increase.

Mantell: I can only give an opinion. I should think the quantity should be doubled.

Fenton: What was understood about the eel weirs? Were they reserved as well?

Mantell: Certainly not. I said they would be removed when public convenience required it.

Fenton: (Objecting to this) – This was governed by the terms of the written contract or deed, which your subsequent proceedings could not vary. Did your reserves come under the kainga nohoanga clause or the whakarite clause?

Mantell: Both the clauses, but I acted under my instructions. [The instructions were read out, including the reference to 'sufficient' land being reserved for the Maoris.]

Fenton: What do you mean by 'sufficient' land?

Mantell: At that time my estimate was Colonel McCleverty's whom I consulted. The idea was, enough to furnish a bare subsistence by their own labour.

Fenton: When a man became old and could not work?

Mantell: I am not prepared to justify McCleverty's estimate or defend it.

Fenton: On what ground do you think the reserve made by you at Arowhenua was sufficient under the whakarite clause to satisfy the honour of the Crown?

Mantell: I have not said that I thought the reserve sufficient to satisfy the honour of the Crown, but according to McCleverty's opinion sufficient to live upon. Colonel McCleverty held a high official position.[19]

Alexander Mackay, as Native Reserves Commissioner, then testified that Mantell's reserves provided barely seven acres per person at Arowhenua, and only nine at Waimate and Waitaki. Until a little extra land had been provided by the government, he said, the people had been 'living in semi-starvation'.

Fenton, in accordance with the Order of Reference, now considered how much land the Arowhenua people deserved in satisfaction of Kemp's deed. He asked Mackay, not the Maoris, for guidance. Mackay thought of Buller's fourteen-acre sections and assumed that, as an average, Ngai Tahu could not hope for more. He said that an increase to fourteen acres per head would be 'amply sufficient'.[20]

Wiremu Naihira for the Tuahiwi people then claimed six eeling reserves along the coastal wetlands from Waipara to Christchurch, as well as fifty acres at Kuratawhiti for a weka preserve, twenty-five at Waihora for eeling, and 50,000 acres 'inland' for pastoral farming.[21] The Rapaki people claimed an extra 600 acres, because most of Mantell's 850-acre reserve was 'stone and precipice'. Irai Tihau, for Taumutu, claimed 250 acres to add to their eighty-acre reserve. Rapaki and Taumutu also claimed eeling reserves.

Fenton then gave judgment regarding the Arowhenua, Tuahiwi, Rapaki and Taumutu claims. Referring to the 'whakarite' clause in Kemp's deed, Fenton said: 'The discretion rests purely with the Crown, and accordingly we entirely follow them.' Mahinga kai did not include weka preserves or food-gathering rights, but only 'fixed works and operations'. The court would award such fishing easements and pieces of land as were agreed to by the Crown, to increase the Kemp's purchase reserves to fourteen acres per head average.[22]

Ngai Tahu boycotted the court the day after Fenton's judgments, except for Wiremu Naihira, who announced that the Tuahiwi people rejected the judgments, and the extra 650 acres Fenton had allowed them, because 'they were so numerous and the land was so small'.[23] Fenton said they could take it or leave it, since the court's order was in itself 'evidence of the satisfaction of their claims'. The location of the land to be awarded would be decided in Chambers, said Fenton. He thanked the Crown for their generosity, and the lawyers present, saying:

It is another proof of what I have constantly asserted – that Native matters are no mystery, and it only requires an educated English gentleman and not a Maori doctor to deal with such questions.[24]

Later he saw Naihira, Pohio and Tihau in Chambers with the Provincial Chief Surveyor. On behalf of their various runanga, they accepted Fenton's awards in the places that the Crown offered, amounting to 2,696 acres.[25] Natanahira Waruwarutu wrote to the Christchurch newspaper *The Press* saying:

We consider we have not been allowed by the Native Land

Court to speak for ourselves. In our view, the examination of witnesses has not been straight, being all one way.[26]

~

At Dunedin, from 14 May 1868, the Native Land Court heard more Maori claims regarding rights of succession, disputes over reserve rights, and the status of the Princes Street and Taiaroa Head lighthouse reserves. Mantell was questioned by James Livingstone Macassey, a brilliant young advocate, and counsel for Ngai Tahu claimants, on the Purakaunui reserve, where in 1848 Mantell had left forty-five people with 275 acres of poor land:

> *Mantell:* What I did was to get the Natives to agree to as small amounts as I could. The reserve at Purakaunui was sufficient for their immediate wants. I left their future wants to be provided for. The reserve was made, not so much as fulfilling either clause of the deed, but as the smallest quantity I could get the Natives to agree to.
>
> *Macassey:* What did you promise?
>
> *Mantell:* I was authorized to make a promise, and I told them that the Government would make schools, build hospitals, and appoint officers to communicate between them and the Government. I found those promises of great weight in inducing the Natives to come in – but these promises have not yet been fulfilled.
>
> *Macassey* (reading from Mantell's instructions): You were to 'inform them that the Crown will hereafter mark out for them such additional reserves as may be considered necessary for their future wants'?
>
> *Mantell:* I was not engaged to carry out the terms of Kemp's Deed, but was preparing for the execution of a new deed.
>
> *Macassey:* Did you make this promise?
>
> *Mantell:* I took refuge under this promise with the Natives . . .
>
> *Macassey:* Did the Natives believe your promise, and come to terms upon the strength of it?
>
> *Mantell:* Certainly.
>
> *Macassey:* How do you propose to keep that promise?
>
> *Mantell:* I have no power.
>
> *Fenton:* What would you do if you had the power?
>
> *Mantell:* I think a minimum of fourteen acres a head if I were a member of the Government, not as satisfying my own honour as a private individual.[27]

Fenton applied the Crown's Order of Reference in Otago as in Canterbury. Claimants under Kemp's deed had their reserves increased so as to average fourteen acres a head, and 2,100 acres were awarded in Otago. Since most Otago land fit for habitation was already allocated, Otago Ngai Tahu had to accept nearly half their award, for thirty-five claimants, at Tautuku on the remote south Otago coast. There the kai moana and timber at least were of some value to the Maori. But the Otago Superintendent, James Macandrew, bitterly opposed even the Tautuku award, on the grounds that the Otago province had not been heard in court.[28] For Rolleston, the month ended well. Having resigned as Under-Secretary for Native Affairs, he was elected Superintendent of Canterbury unopposed.[29]

∽

The Native Land Court proceedings left Ngai Tahu with a deep sense of injustice. Firstly, the Order of Reference had been introduced in response to the Kaitorete claim, yet it had been applied to the whole of Kemp's block.[30] Secondly, Fenton declared himself bound by the government's offer of a settlement, yet the settlement was never referred to Ngai Tahu as a tribe.[31] Even the Maoris attending the court had no warning of a final settlement, and were not expecting it. According to Alexander Mackay some years later, 'Many of them had only then heard for the first time of the conditions of Kemp's deed.'[32] The Maoris at Moeraki, Waikouaiti and Purakaunui were just as much affected by the Order of Reference as those who were at court, but they did not hear of it until after the judgment was delivered.[33] Finally, although Fenton had announced that under the Order of Reference 'it will be the duty of the Court to ascertain all the terms of the contract',[34] he did not ascertain all the terms. The most contentious of these, and crucial in the legal sense, were the boundaries of Kemp's block, regarding which Cowlishaw had claimed the deed was void for uncertainty. Yet Fenton did not attempt to ascertain the boundaries.

The Canterbury Ngai Tahu chiefs subsequently engaged lawyers to challenge the Order of Reference and Fenton's judgment in the Christchurch Supreme Court. The hearing of *Heremaia Mautai and Hoani Timaru v. The Queen* began on 6 October 1868 before Justice Gresson, whose country estate adjoined the Tuahiwi reserve. But the Crown lawyers avoided the Maori plaintiffs' arguments by denying the competency of the Supreme Court to hear an appeal from the Native Land Court. Justice Gresson ruled that since no appeal procedure was provided for in the Native Land Court's empowering act, the onus was on Mautai to prove that the Supreme Court had jurisdiction.[35]

The government of New Zealand was now led by Edward Stafford – since dubbed 'New Zealand's First Statesman'.[36] Learning of the Maoris' Supreme Court action, Stafford's government hurried a bill through Parliament to nullify it. This was the Ngaitahu Reference Validation Bill, designed to give the Order of Reference and Fenton's judgment the force of statute law and thus put both beyond the reach of litigation. On 6 October, the day of the Supreme Court hearing, the bill came before the Legislative Council for its final reading. Cowlishaw telegraphed Mantell begging him to oppose it. But Mantell merely recorded his dissent in the council, and 'did not ask honourable members to join with him'.[37] Instead, he had these words added to the bill:

> Provided that nothing in the said orders of the Native Land Court or in this Act contained shall be deemed to extinguish the claims of any Natives in respect of promises made to them by any officer of the Government of schools hospitals and other advantages to induce such Natives to consent to the sale of the said Ngaitahu Block.[38]

At first sight, this left alive the possibility of further claims under Kemp's deed. But the resulting Validation Act embodied a serious misrepresentation, which obstructed further claims. It stated that Fenton's court had 'investigated the title' to the lands 'delineated' on the deed map. To have done this, however, the court would have had to investigate the boundaries of Kemp's purchase. It had not done so, nor had it investigated the credentials of those who signed the deed. Thus not only the flaws in Kemp's purchase, but the flaws in Chief Judge Fenton's adjudication on them, received the sanction of Parliament and the force of law.

With the Validation Act passed, Mautai and Timaru could only seek costs against the Crown. This still required them to convince Justice Gresson that the Supreme Court had jurisdiction in the matter. Mautai engaged a senior counsel, Dr C. J. Foster, who advanced an interesting argument.[39] The Treaty of Waitangi was a contract between free and equal parties, said Foster, and guaranteed the Maoris all the rights of British citizens. It was a right of British citizens that their social customs and usages were in general incorporated in common law. Therefore, Maori social customs and usages were part of common law, he said. Then, since the Supreme Court was competent to hear cases involving common law, said Foster, it followed that the court was competent to hear Mautai's case involving Maori customs and usages. But Justice Gresson rejected this argument, and Ngai Tahu lost their claim for costs as well.[40]

A total of 4,795 acres was awarded to Ngai Tahu under Fenton's judgment in 'final extinguishment' of all claims under Kemp's deed in Canterbury and Otago.[41] But the Native Land Court had no power to compel the provincial governments to allocate this land promptly, if they could be made to allocate it at all. Ngai Tahu had no money to engage lawyers to get the land for them. Despite Rolleston's ready assurances of a 'settlement', and his influential position as Superintendent of Canterbury, many years were to pass before Ngai Tahu got the land that the Native Land Court had awarded.

Notes

1. See Gisborne 1897: 142; Oliver 1990: 121ff.
2. *AJHR* 1860 E-1C; Pocock 1965: 24ff.
3. Hall–Mantell, 16.5.1867, Haultain–Mantell, 28.4.1868, and associated communications, in Mackay 1873 II: 182–84.
4. Mackay 1873 II: 182–87; SNC 4/28: 585. See also Lamb 1963: 72–75 regarding Williams.
5. MLCI 1B: 1ff; Mackay 1873 II: 186ff. The official court record is in MLCI 1A and 1B, in Fenton's difficult handwriting. NTR: 509 refers to 'the printed record'. Only two 'printed records' exist, both incomplete and inconsistent with each other and with the court's minute books. One is Fenton's excerpts from his court notes in *AJHR* 1888 I-8: 34ff: the other is Mackay's court notes in Mackay 1873 II: 186ff. See also SNC 4/26: 567.
6. Member of the Legislative Council.
7. MLCI 1B: 39; Mackay 1873 II: 201–3.
8. Shortland 1851: 290–91.
9. MLCI 1B: 42–44; SNC 4/28: 584.
10. See *AJHR* 1921 G-5: 34ff.
11. MLCI 1B: 49.
12. MLCI 1B: 47; Mackay 1873 II: 206–7.
13. H. K. Taiaroa recalled: 'Cowlishaw got up in a state of excitement, in legal wardrobe, and pranced about the Court. But he failed to find the Honourable John Hall, because that gentleman had got on his horse, and went home to his own place, about fifty miles off.' (*NZPD* 38: 622, 21.7.1881).
14. For Mackay's transcript of Fenton's judgment, see Mackay 1873 II: 211ff.
15. i.e. that 'e mau nei te ahua' meant 'the plan of which is here attached'.
16. See MLCI 1B and Mackay 1873 II: 215ff, 6–7.5.1868.
17. MLCI 1B: 79.

18. Mackay 1873 II: 216.
19. MLCI 1B: 82–83.
20. Mackay 1873 II: 202, 210, 217; SNC 4/28: 592.
21. MLCI 1B: 84. The court minutes say 5,000 acres, but Naihira said he claimed 50,000 acres (*AJHR* 1891 G-7: 57).
22. MLCI 1B: 84–85.
23. Ibid: 88.
24. Mackay 1873 II: 218.
25. MLCI 1B: 90.
26. *The Press*, 9.5.1868.
27. MLCI 1A: 12ff.
28. Mackay 1873 II: 254ff. The Crown lawyer G. K. Turton gave Fenton the correct meaning of mahinga kai: 'Places for procuring or producing food – not only gardens, but pipi grounds, eel weirs, fisheries, &c' (Ibid: 232).
29. Oliver 1990: 373a.
30. Mackay 1873 I: 217.
31. Mackay 1873 II: 189–91. 'The Ngai Tahu tribe were represented by Mr Cowlishaw', according to Mackay (SNC 4/28: 579), but not according to Fenton's court minutes (MLCI 1B: passim.) See also SNC 4/28: 580–86.
32. MLCI 1B: 79ff; SNC 4/28: 580ff; 4/29: 601–5.
33. SNC 7/93: 722ff.
34. Mackay 1873 II: 215.
35. *The Press*, 8.10.1868.
36. E. Bohan, *Edward Stafford, New Zealand's First Statesman*, Christchurch 1994.
37. *NZPD* 4: 186 (1868).
38. Ngaitahu Reference Validation Act 1868. Fenton said later, 'I always thought that Act was a great mistake, and I told Mr Sewell so' (SNC 4/26: 567–68). Sewell was in England when the act was passed, but was afterwards Minister of Justice in New Zealand.
39. See Lamb 1963: 71–72 regarding Foster.
40. *The Press*, 21, 28.11.1868. Apparently no court record of this case has survived.
41. *AJHR* 1875 G-3.

18

⁓

In Naboth's Vineyard

NGAI TAHU'S tribal territory in 1840 had exceeded in area that of any other Maori tribe. But by 1870 there was hardly a New Zealand Maori tribe with less land than Ngai Tahu. In southern New Zealand, the former food-gathering preserves of the Maori were now the farmlands of the European. In sheltered places where kainga nohoanga might once have nestled, there now rose the mansions of the colonial gentry. Maoris of southern New Zealand were increasingly dependent on their dwindling reserves – everywhere inadequate and overcrowded. Fenton's 1868 awards had still not been allocated to Ngai Tahu by the colonial authorities. Many Maoris lost interest in farming and turned instead to seasonal wage labour for subsistence, leasing their reserve sections to Europeans. Alexander Mackay in 1872 blamed the Maoris for this:

> The civilization which now prevails around them, besides curtailing their liberties, has also compelled the adoption of a different mode of life, which, owing to their improvident habits, they find very difficult to maintain. All this is very perplexing and bewildering to the Maori, and it is not surprising that perceiving his incapacity to keep pace with his European neighbours, a want of earnestness should predominate in all he undertakes.[1]

While Maoris on the land grew poor, Europeans grew rich. North of the Waipara, most of the eighty kilometres of coastal territory – in which Ngai Tahu had been refused a share by Hamilton in 1857 – was now in the hands of two runholders: George Moore of Glenmark, and William ('Ready Money') Robinson of Cheviot – probably the wealthiest men in the South Island. Together they controlled more than 100,000 hectares. Robinson acquired the trappings of an English lord of the manor: a fashionable residence in Christ-church and another in Wellington, a two-storeyed seaside 'cottage' for his wife, expensive racehorses, and a forty-room country man-sion reckoned to be the finest in New Zealand.[2] As well as farmhands, he employed gamekeepers, gardeners, and a valet, and could afford to take his family to live in England.

The Canterbury and Otago provinces each supported over three million sheep by the 1870s, comprising more than half of New Zealand's flocks.[3] When wool prices fell, runholders on the fertile plains of Kemp's block turned to 'bonanza' wheat farming. This required equipment that Maoris could not afford. As arable farm-ing became more intensive, so did the destruction of mahinga kai, especially freshwater fisheries, provoking repeated Maori petitions to Parliament.[4]

In 1874 Alexander Mackay reported that Maori poverty was worsening in southern New Zealand, especially at Tuahiwi. But he no longer blamed only the Maoris:

> In former years, before the country was occupied by Euro-peans, they could roam all over it in search of edibles, but now they are hemmed in by civilization and have no chance of ob-taining the necessary supplies. Every year as the settlement of the country progresses, they are restricted to narrower and narrower limits. The settlers hunt down, for pastime or other purposes, the birds which constituted their food, or, for pur-poses of improvement drain the swamps and watercourses from which they obtained their supplies of fish. Their ordinary sub-sistence failing them, and lacking the energy or ability to sup-plement their means of livelihood by labour, they lead a life of misery and semi-starvation. All this might have been obviated in the case of the Southern Natives, had the precaution been taken to set apart land to provide for their wants, in anticipa-tion of the probable effect of colonization on their former hab-its. It would have been an easy matter for the Government to have imposed this tax on the landed estate, on the acquisition of Native territory. Such reserves would have afforded easy relief to the people who had ceded their lands for a trifle, and formed the only possible way of paying them with justice.

Mackay urged Parliament to compensate Ngai Tahu for their mahinga kai 'either in money or land or both', and charge the cost to the provinces that had 'benefited by the acquisition of the terri-tory'.[5] But his plea was disregarded.

~

Hori Kerei Taiaroa, originally named 'Huriwhenua' in honour of a Te Ati Awa chief who visited Otakou during his infancy,[6] was the only surviving son of Matenga Taiaroa. Matenga, before his death at Otakou in 1863, had dictated a 'testament' urging 'my tribe, my hapu and my son' to ensure that the promises made by Wakefield, Kemp and Mantell were fulfilled. He urged good treatment of Europeans, and respect for the Queen.[7] His son made these precepts his own. Matiaha Tiramorehu championed the Ngai Tahu claim from a Ngai Tuahuriri perspective. But H. K. Taiaroa adopted a southern emphasis, in keeping with his Ngai Te Ruahikihiki ancestry and his father's conciliatory attitude towards Ngati Toa. His ambitions for the claim did not extend north of the Waimakariri, or west of the Main Divide.

H. K. Taiaroa obtained the nomination for the Southern Maori seat in the House of Representatives in 1871, and was elected. He applied himself diligently, and within two years the Ngai Tahu claim was on the House agenda. He confided in Walter Mantell MLC; but Mantell, preoccupied with scientific interests, now had little political influence.[8] William Gisborne later wrote of Mantell:

> Politically he has been a disappointment. He seems to have had a natural distaste for politics. He was the Diogenes of Parliament, always alone in a cave, agreeing with no-one, scarcely with himself. He never heartily joined in the political tournament; he loved to be on the outskirts, and 'shoot folly as it flies'. Twice he has just joined Ministries and suddenly left them for some mysterious cause.[9]

Mantell once told the Legislative Council:

> I have had some experience of the acquisition of Native lands, and it was an experience the recollection of which I shall carry with me to the grave. I had no idea in those early days, when I was suddenly sent for and requested to go and compel the Natives who had been parties in the matter to come under a deed from which they derived no benefit – I had no idea at that time of the great amount of self-reproach I was laying in store for myself.[10]

~

European imperialism was in full cry in the 1870s. John Stuart Mill, the influential British liberal philosopher, had in 1862 expressed the view that small ethnic populations, for their own good, must abandon their identities and accept assimilation by larger nations.[11] This view was applied to the Maoris of southern New Zealand in 1872 by the Canterbury Anglican missioner James West Stack, a close friend of Francis Fenton.[12] Stack called for the abolition of Maori reserves and the dispersal of the occupants, so as to have 'every individual Maori's section surrounded by land in the occupation of white men'. Maoris would then 'become absorbed in the general population, and cease to regard themselves as a separate and foreign people',[13] said Stack.

On the world stage, the doctrine of European 'racial' supremacy had gained scientific respectability and fresh impetus in 1870, from the publication of Charles Darwin's *The Descent of Man, Selection in Relation to Sex*. This celebrated work expounded the great Victorian vision of human progress in terms of 'civilised races' replacing 'lower races'.[14] The idea that 'race' determined the course of history was congenial to European colonialists. A prominent Otago settler and provincial councillor wrote in 1874:

> The extinction of the Maori is a mere question of time. They feel they are a doomed race, and look forward to it with the resignation of the fatalist. The Maori feels he can no longer cope with the Anglo-Saxon. He sees that he is destitute of his energy and perseverance, that the European prospers where the Native would starve; that the white man is not a fighting man, but when he fights he is sure to win; that the prestige of the Maori is gone; that the land which his forefathers wrested from others has been wrested from himself by the gold of a race that will never die. He plainly sees that his countrymen are dwindling away, and that nothing can resuscitate the glory of the past. He has lost all hope, and become a confirmed fatalist, looking on the exterminating future as an invincible foe.[15]

But the Maoris of southern New Zealand, for their own part, were by no means apathetic. Tiramorehu, despite his poor health, took the lead in agitating for the fulfilment of the terms of Kemp's deed. Ngai Tahu held political meetings to prepare petitions for Parliament.[16] This annoyed the Reverend Stack, who had moved to Christchurch in 1870 when his house and school at Tuahiwi had burnt down. Stack had now accepted the duty of reporting to the government on the Canterbury Maoris. He denounced the Ngai

Tahu claim as 'a scheme for acquiring more land and money'[17] –
although he did not similarly denounce European schemes with
these objectives. In 1873, Stack wrote to Donald McLean, now
Native Minister:

> Sir, I think it is my duty to call your attention to the state-
> ments which are being made in every native village by Matiaha
> Tiramorehu as unless some steps are taken to correct the false
> impression he is producing upon the minds of all the Maoris
> who were not eyewitnesses to the signing of the Ngaitahu
> Kemp's deed a great hindrance will be thrown in the way of
> improving the natives here.
>
> On Thursday last I was invited to attend a meeting held at
> the Runanga house on the Kaiapoi reserve, in addition to the
> local population who were all present there were representa-
> tives from the different villages on the Banks Peninsula.
>
> Matiaha began by saying that the natives had never received
> payment for the land between the seaward range on the East-
> ern coast and the range on the Western – and that if they were
> strong enough the Maoris would occupy it, but not being pow-
> erful enough to do so they would take other steps to assert
> their ownership. He said that his claim was not a groundless
> one and in confirmation of his statement read an extract from
> a letter written to him by the Hon Mr Mantell some years ago.
>
> He said the Ngaitahu deed was fabricated by Mr Kemp on
> board ship; that when Mr Mantell came to survey the land he
> and others protested against the boundary going further west
> than the seaward range and that the justice of their protest was
> admitted; that the natives were repeatedly told that the money
> payment was only in part; that the Government are bound by
> the terms of the agreement to provide a site, building, and
> schoolmaster for each native village – and hospital buildings
> officers and attendance in every kainga – and further to give
> each man a 'share' in the land reserve.
>
> 'I am called,' he [Matiaha] said, 'an assessor and receive a
> salary. Why not give me a salary without calling me an asses-
> sor – it is only done to escape paying each Maori what is his
> due. I may die before these claims are admitted, but before I
> die I intend every Maori to know the rights of the case. I am
> one of the few left who were parties to the sale of our lands to
> the Government – but when I die there will be plenty to carry
> on the agitation for the restitution of our rights.'
>
> Matiaha has, I am informed, suggested that under various

pretences people should squat on the land they lay claims to, and quietly assert ownership. Matiaha's statements are just calculated to mislead those who have longed for some colorable pretext for preferring claims to further money payments for the land. They have an appearance of truthfulness about them and the golden visions they raise prevent the natives from settling down to honest toil. Day and night they talk of nothing else but '*whakaotinga o Niu Tireni*' – spending all their time in the runanga houses which have of late been erected in all their villages with a view to organising this agitation.

I think the best way to counter the evil effects of Matiaha's mission would be by a short official statement printed and circulated amongst the Maoris in the province and in Otago giving the real explanation of the Ngaitahu deed and the Hon Mr Mantell's promises, and the hopelessness of any illegal attempts to assert ownership to land now in the possession of the Crown.

I have the honour to be, Sir, Your obedient servant, James W. Stack.[18]

∾

Aroused by Tiramorehu's efforts, a hui of three hundred Maoris met at Tuahiwi in March 1874. The chiefs petitioned the General Assembly, declaring that Wakefield had promised 'tenths' at Otago, that the promises of Kemp and Mantell had been dishonoured, and that Fenton's court in 1868 had taken them unfairly by surprise. They admonished Parliament:

You may perhaps say to us, 'If all you say is true, how is it that you remained silent till now?' Why, you well know that we are not like you – quick in the race of mental attainments; we are lagging far behind in these things. When these land transactions took place our chiefs were scarcely able to read written language; they were often too ready to consent their names to be signed under writings the contents of which were either in part or totally absent from their minds. Judge for yourselves, honourable members of Parliament who listen to our complaints in this petition: Had the eyes of these our chiefs been open in those days, would they have consented to part with all the heritage that God has given them and their future offspring and descendants – all this vast territory – for the crumbs that fell from the white man's table – for this £2,000 odd? The daylight was slow in dawning upon us. It is only after one of our race entered Parliament that we became acquainted, little by little, with the ways by which the white man's land-purchases beguiled the whole Island from us. What these land-purchasers said to our elders who ceded the land is indelibly written in their and their children's minds, but this writing does not correspond to those of Mr Kemp in his deed. Nevertheless we are dispossessed of all the land. Is it because we are so few and powerless? No doubt, had Naboth been the stronger, Jezebel would not have gloried over his vineyard.[19]

The petition concluded:

The condition of the Maoris of Te Wai Pounamu is bad. As long as we have strength to work as servants to the Europeans, as long as the market is accepting that servitude, we are keeping ourselves and families above want. Should this strength and the market fail – and the time will come that it will – then we Maoris will be little better than a mass of paupers thrown upon the present lords of the land. The burden of our petition is that the white man has grasped at our fifty millions of acres in Te Wai Pounamu without any equitable return or provision for the Maori. We are debating before you, the honourable members of Parliament, the wrongs we suffer, relying firmly upon your honour and love of fair play for you to redress them, and take under your protection the semi-paupers and orphans of Te Wai Pounamu.[20]

At Moeraki, Waimate, Arowhenua and Banks Peninsula, parents refused to pay fees to the new Native schools, because Mantell had promised them free schools.[21]

∼

H. K. Taiaroa now sought to control the Ngai Tahu claim himself. A hui of 'the chiefs of the Ngai Tahu and Ngati Mamoe tribes' met at Otakou on 4 June 1875, and a handsome parchment had been prepared for their signature. Under this 'covenant' Taiaroa became sole organiser and permanent treasurer of the claim, with authority to raise funds, control expenditure, and appoint lawyers. Led by Topi Patuki, sixty-three persons signed the parchment, mostly from Otago and Murihiku, but including Wiremu Naihira from Tuahiwi, and Karaweko and Taare Tikao from Banks Peninsula. Many prominent chiefs did not sign, including Tiramorehu, Te Uki, Pohio, Waruwarutu and the Tainuis.[22] Taiaroa nevertheless claimed to have the support of 'the whole of Ngai Tahu'.[23] By 1877 he had banked some £3,000 that Ngai Tahu had struggled to raise for the claim.[24] In the process, many had leased out their land or gone into debt. Stock was sold, and crops sacrificed, for the cause.[25]

Meanwhile, Maoris of the Arowhenua-Moeraki district held another hui and petitioned the General Assembly for an inquiry into Kemp's purchase. A year passed without result. In May 1876 they warned the Governor, Lord Normanby, of further action:

> We humbly wish to bring before your Excellency's considera-
> tion that the denial of a trial of these our grievances, emanat-
> ing not from Her Majesty's representative but from the colo-
> nial Ministry of the day, as an interested party, has been the
> invariable rule in the dealings between the Government and
> us Maoris, first, because we are few, and bring no pressure to
> further our demands of justice; and secondly, the material wit-
> nesses being now well stricken in years, a short space of time
> will efface all evidence on the subject by their death. We ut-
> terly despair of any trial being instituted by the New Zealand
> Government in this matter, and as a last resort, we intend to
> take up our residence on the inland of this Island, the purchase
> of which land has never been accomplished either by Com-
> missioner Kemp or Mantell. We humbly lay this, our inten-
> tion, at your Excellency's feet.[26]

The Native Minister, Sir Donald McLean, after consulting Mantell,[27] asked Chief Judge Fenton to report on these petitions. Fenton did so and found little merit in them, least of all in their criticism of his own court. He told McLean:

> If the European race had never come into these seas the value
> of these Islands would still be only nominal. The immense value
> that now attaches to these territories is solely to be attributed
> to the capital and labour of the European.[28]

In Parliament, Taiaroa angrily denounced Fenton's report as 'deceit-ful and delusive'. McLean had put Fenton up to it, he said.[29]

～

In the winter of 1877, true to their promise, the Arowhenua people raised a heke and trekked two hundred kilometres inland to Te Ao Marama on the upper Waitaki, led by their prophet Te Maiharoa together with Horomona Pohio and Rawiri Te Maire. There they asserted their ownership of the Otago and Canterbury high country. They camped on a prominent leaseholder's run, in a windswept valley surrounded by snowy mountains.[30] The Reverend Stack disapproved, saying:

> The amount reserved for them is ridiculously small when compared with the average holdings of the colonists, but it is a question whether they ought to be allowed to take the law into their own hands to right themselves.[31]

Sir George Grey became Premier of New Zealand in October 1877. McLean's long influence on Native Affairs had ended with his resignation in December 1876, and he died soon afterwards. A young liberal, John Sheehan, was Grey's Native Minister and 'first-lieutenant' – the first New Zealand-born Cabinet minister. He promoted a 'Middle Island Half-Caste Crown Grants Act' allowing grants of ten acres per male and eight per female for landless Maoris of part-European descent. The government also agreed to pay £5,000 to Ngai Tahu in compensation for the back rents from the former Princes Street Maori reserve in Dunedin which a former government had paid to the Otago province.

But these concessions were accompanied by an ominous development. The judgment in *R. v. Symonds*, acknowledging a validity in customary ('aboriginal') Maori land title, had stood for thirty years. But in 1877 Chief Justice James Prendergast in the Wi Parata case delivered a contrary judgment. He ruled that the courts had no jurisdiction regarding customary Maori title, since (he said) such title did not exist. The Treaty of Waitangi was a 'simple nullity', as the chiefs who signed it had no sovereignty to cede, said Prendergast.[32] Prendergast remained Chief Justice until the end of the century.

Meanwhile Te Maiharoa's followers camping at Te Ao Marama aroused increasing hostility in the colonial press. In Maori eyes they were merely occupying what was theirs. But in the eyes of European runholders they were common lawbreakers, and there were accusations of sheep-stealing. John Sheehan had agreed, in principle, to set up a commission of inquiry on the Ngai Tahu claim. Taiaroa saw Te Maiharoa's heke as a threat to this prospect, and to his own ascendancy. Late in 1878 he went to Te Ao Marama with Sheehan to try to get the heke to leave, but without success.[33]

A royal commission was at last appointed on 15 February 1879 to investigate the Ngai Tahu claim. H. K. Taiaroa was appointed to the Legislative Council two days later, and the seat he vacated in the House was won in July by Ihaia Tainui. The royal commissioners, appointed after several nominees had declined the responsibility, were Judge Thomas Smith of the Native Land Court, and Francis Nairn, a Nelson settler. Their inquiry was restricted to the purchases that interested H. K. Taiaroa: Otago, Kemp's, Murihiku and Akaroa. Mantell's dealings at Port Cooper and Port Levy thus escaped scrutiny, as did the North Canterbury, Kaikoura and Arahura purchases arranged by McLean, and the Stewart Island purchase. Taiaroa engaged the prominent Wellington firm of Izard and Bell as his personal legal counsel, and had kaumatua record details of the hundreds of traditional mahinga kai and kainga nohoanga in the Otago and Kemp blocks. [34]

~

Commissioners Smith and Nairn entered upon their task assiduously. They set about hearing evidence from surviving Ngai Tahu witnesses to the four specified purchases, and from the Crown officials involved in them. The commission began its public hearings on 7 May 1879 at the public hall in the European town of Kaiapoi, to investigate Kemp's purchase. The first witness called was Henry Tacy Kemp. Kemp bore a longstanding grudge against Mantell for blocking his advancement (or so Kemp believed) when Mantell was Native Minister in 1865.[35] This missionary's son had now to swear upon the Bible as to what he had done at Akaroa in 1848. He seemed to find the experience unnerving, for his testimony was both confused and confusing,[36] and drew derisive laughter from the Maoris present.[37]

Mantell followed Kemp on the witness stand. He never gave a simple answer if he could help it. To the formal question, 'You are a member of the Legislative Council, residing in Wellington?' Mantell replied, 'I was recently residing in Wellington, and am a member of the Legislative Council. At present I am residing in Kaiapoi.' Mantell delivered more witticisms. He said that Eyre was at Akaroa only a day or two, but 'it appeared to me a very long time'. He was 'rather intimate' with Charles Kettle's sketch map, he said: 'I carried it about on my back for five months.'

When Mantell testified that Kemp's block had contained only 'nine hundred' Maoris, there was ironic laughter from the hall.[38] Recalling Metehau's attack on him he said, 'I nearly had to shoot one gentleman, but then my excuse was that he was nearly toma-hawking me.' While Mantell spoke, Metehau himself was in the hall – 'a highly respectable-looking, elderly gentleman speaking excellent English', according to the newspaper reporter sitting next to him. As the laughter at Mantell's joke subsided, Metehau said to the reporter: 'I'm damned sorry now I didn't do it!'[39]

The essence of Mantell's testimony[40] was what he had told Secretary of State Labouchere in 1856 – that on Eyre's instructions he had promised Ngai Tahu schools and hospitals and general care, but that the government had failed to honour these promises. As a member of the General Assembly, said Mantell, he did not wish to criticise Fenton's awards. He told Judge Smith:

> Although members of the Legislature are presumed to be quite competent to frame laws, the interpretation of them is com-mitted to the hands of other gentlemen, who, from their spe-cial training and keen intelligence, are supposed to be more fitted for the task.

On the second day of the commission's hearings at Kaiapoi, the elderly chiefs of Ngai Tuahuriri were called on for the first time to give their account of what had happened at Akaroa in June 1848. Natanahira Waruwarutu was first. He said that Kemp had prom-ised them the eel fisheries, the mahinga kai, the kainga nohoanga, the landing places, and a large portion of other land:

> The Maoris then thought the matter over, believing it was a promise made in all honour: they thought it was an honourable promise – the same as all promises made by great chiefs. The Maoris have since found that they did not get what had been promised, and it has given them food for reflection ever since.[41]

No map or plan had been shown them by Kemp, said Waru-warutu. Asked by Taiaroa's counsel, Izard, whether Mantell had promised schools or hospitals, Waruwarutu betrayed Ngai Tuahu-riri's resentment of Izard's presence, answering, 'Why should I repeat what Mr Mantell has already said?'

> *Izard:* Have any schools been established in accordance with the promises made?
> *Waruwarutu:* No! Where are they?
> *Izard:* Is there not a school at the Kaiapoi pa?
> *Waruwarutu:* Yes, but it was not established in fulfilment of the promises made.

Izard: Is there not one at Waikouaiti?
Waruwarutu: How can I tell?[42]

Matiaha Tiramorehu was called next. Kemp had left the hall during the Maori testimony. Tiramorehu related events on board HMS *Fly* at Akaroa in 1848. He told the commission:

> Tikao became obstinate because the payment of £2,000 was to extend over 4 years. Tikao said to Kemp, 'You will never get hold of Kaiapoi.' Tikao said, 'If you propose to pay us £500 now, £500 at a future time, £500 again, and £500 after that, you may keep your money.' Here Kemp in his turn got annoyed –'

Tiramorehu now became excited, exclaiming:

> Why don't you bring Kemp in to listen to what I am saying? Kemp said, 'Well, if you choose to keep hold of Kaiapoi, I shall take this money, and pay it over to Ngati Toa.' He said, 'If you are still obstinate, I will bring soldiers to occupy all your land.' This is what he meant, but he has turned it in another way of saying that a number of people from England were expected to arrive in New Zealand.[43]

Asked if hospitals had been provided, Tiramorehu shouted: 'Where are they?' Tiramorehu asked to see Kemp's deed, eyed it closely, and asked, 'What did you put the names in the deed for?' Receiving no reply, he said – 'I expect some of the names were signed on shore. There were not so many names as these signed on board the man-of-war.'[44] He said Kemp had produced no map or plan. Only the Maungaatua–Maungatere boundary had been agreed to. The 'Whaka-tipu Waitai' boundary must have been arranged secretly. Ngai Tahu had seen no map until Mantell showed it them. Mantell had failed to keep his promises. Tiramorehu threw on the table the letter Mantell had written him from England twenty years before: 'That letter was the final outcome of these promises,' he exclaimed. [45]

Te Uki next gave evidence. Kemp had shown them no map or plan, he said, but had threatened them with soldiers if they refused to sell. He and Tiramorehu had told Kemp that they wished to keep the land between the Waimakariri and Rakahuri, and their mahinga kai, eel weirs and sacred places. Kemp had promised them these. As Te Uki spoke, the vision of the lost lands and desecrated mahinga kai of his ancestors rose before his eyes – the eel fisheries drained, the life-giving waters diverted, the noble groves of cabbage trees destroyed by settlers' fires. He smote the table with his fist, startling his listeners, and exclaimed:

> Kemp promised us reserves, we were to have our fisheries, our burial places, mahinga kai, eel weirs anywhere, everywhere! These promises were made thirty years ago! Where is the fulfilment of them? Our mahinga kai were places where we used to get food, the natural products of the soil, such as cabbage trees, which grew right away from Kaiapoi to Purehurehu, and were used by the chiefs. If anyone of us, even a Maori, were to go and set fire to these trees, he would be killed at once! That was our law! The places from which we obtained food extended all the way from Kaiapoi to Purehurehu. It was all mahinga kai. Mr Kemp found us, when he came ashore, getting the roots of the cabbage tree. We used to get fern root. We used to catch ducks, and putangitangi. We had reserves where we used to catch some and leave others. We used to get food from all over our island! It was all mahinga kai! And we considered our island as in a far superior position to any other, because it is called Te Wai Pounamu, the Greenstone Island: the fame thereof reaches all lands!

Mantell had promised them a large final payment, said Te Uki, and hospitals and schools – but none had been built.

He now enlivened the subject with Maori humour:

> Mantell set aside fourteen acres on which I and my family and stock were to live. How am I to live on that? [Laughter.] He said larger reserves would be set apart. That was before Europeans settled over the country. Now, since that, the mahinga kai and eel weirs have gone and their place is taken by fields of wheat and houses. Subsequently at the Native Land Court there was a little bit of land about that size [placing his two hands about an inch apart], but the Government has got hold of it by the tail. [Laughter.] I am waiting to find out what this large consideration is to be. [Renewed Laughter.][46]

Next, Te Kahu told the commission that the shortage of land had set the people quarrelling – 'and they are still quarrelling'.[47] Kemp had shown them no map. Te Kahu knew of no hospital for Maoris.

> *Judge Smith:* If any of you fall sick, what do you do?
> *Te Kahu:* What can we do? Where are the hospitals?
> *Judge Smith:* Don't you go to the European hospitals?
> *Te Kahu:* If you go to the European hospitals you never come

out again. Some go, but all those who go never return. Hospitals are a bad institution, as people there never recover. In Otago, all our people sent to the hospital never recovered. [Laughter].[48]

In the course of eight days, the commission heard fourteen Maori witnesses on Kemp's purchase. Among them was a Maori clergyman who testified that more 'religious teaching' was needed. He was shouted down. When Judge Smith told him the subject was outside the scope of the commission, there were 'cries of satisfaction from the Maoris'.[49]

Te Maiharoa's heke was evicted from Te Ao Marama by armed police in the winter of 1879 – a measure long overdue according to J. W. Stack.[50] Yet, even then, they and other Ngai Tahu of Canterbury had not been put in possession of the land awarded them by Fenton in 1868.

In August 1879 Commissioners Smith and Nairn asked Henry Tacy Kemp to clarify in writing just what he had promised Ngai Tahu in 1848. Kemp wrote:

> I beg to state that the understanding between the Native sellers and myself as Crown Agent when the purchase of the Canterbury District was made, was to this effect, viz. – That in making a cession of the land, they were (in addition to the purchase money, the pas or places of residence, and the 'Mahinga kais' which were then and there reserved or guaranteed to them), to receive ample Reserves from which in course of time, they might derive considerable rents as a means towards their securing permanently the comforts and necessaries of civilized life. I think I am also bound to say, that without these promises, the cession of the land would have been delayed, if not withheld, for an indefinite period of time.[51]

Thus Kemp confirmed what Ngai Tahu had been claiming all along.

The commission sat in Auckland in September 1879 to hear Chief Judge Fenton testify.[52] Fenton had forgotten that in 1868 he had recorded in his court notes that Ngai Tahu were absent in protest at his award increasing their average holdings to fourteen acres a head.[53] He now said that everyone had agreed to fourteen acres. He was 'rather disappointed that they did not ask for more', and he blamed Alexander Mackay and Ngai Tahu themselves for it. Fenton had accepted Mackay's suggestion of fourteen acres because he thought Mackay was representing Ngai Tahu, he said. He was 'quite astonished' to hear otherwise. However, it was Ngai Tahu's fault: 'If the parties interested did not bring their affairs before the Court it is their own look-out, and they must suffer for their own lacks.'

The commissioners reminded Fenton that the Order of Reference had required him to investigate the boundaries of Kemp's purchase, but on his own admission he had not done so. Fenton at once blamed Ngai Tahu and their 'learned gentlemen'. If they did not raise the question, he said, the court was not required to consider it:

Having neglected the opportunity, they should not be allowed to complain, for it is their own doing. The Court was open to them. Why didn't they say, 'Define these boundaries'? That would have been a very serious thing. If they had said that 'the deed is void for uncertainty', it would have been a most important point to raise, – and I don't know what I would have said.

Judge Smith showed Fenton the northern boundary of Kemp's block on the deed plan:

Smith: We cannot trace how the line was drawn from Kaiapoi to Cape Foulwind.
Fenton: That question was not raised.
Smith: Had it been raised, you would have thought it necessary to have gone into it?
Fenton: I should have considered it a very important matter to go into.
Nairn: Equally important as any other question about the deed?
Fenton: More important.
Smith: I might mention that it has been urged that the Natives never understood they were doing more than selling the strip of land underneath the hills westward of the Canterbury Plains.
Nairn: I don't understand the boundaries given by Mr Kemp at all, and never have understood them. He mentions from Kaiapoi to Purehurehu, and then across to Wakatipu Waitai. Had the question of boundaries been raised, you would have considered it one to go into?
Fenton: Yes.
Nairn: You would have considered it an important one?
Fenton: Yes. I am struck with astonishment that the lawyers did not consider it.[54]

Mautai's lawyer Cowlishaw, as we have seen, had indeed submitted to Fenton in the Native Land Court at Christchurch that Kemp's deed was 'void for uncertainty' because it did not properly define the boundaries. Fenton had written it in his own court notes.[55] But Smith and Nairn did not know this, because they were relying on Mackay's account of the court proceedings,[56] which omitted the point. But Judge Smith, recalling that the Ngai Tahu Reference Validation Act indicated that Fenton had investigated the Kemp's purchase boundaries, whereas Fenton now agreed that he had not done so, remarked:

> The Ngai Tahu Reference Validation Act reads curiously in our present light.

Notes

1. Mackay 1873 I (ii): 53 ('Traditionary History').
2. Cresswell 1951: passim.
3. NZ Department of Agriculture 1947: 63 ff.
4. See e.g. SNC 4/29: 596.
5. *AJHR* 1874 G-2C: 2–3.
6. SNC 5/55: 144.
7. *AJHR* 1872 H-9: 8–9 (translation). Transcript of Maori original is in SNC 9.
8. Mantell was founding secretary of the New Zealand Institute in 1867, and a board member almost until his death. He was a member of the Wellington Botanic Garden Board until its demise in 1891, and lived near the garden on a large property in Sydney Street (Alington 1978: 68ff). He was sometime president of the Wellington Philosophical Society. Occasionally he deputised for the Director of the Colonial Museum, James Hector, when Hector was overseas (Shepherd & Cook 1988: passim). See also Buller 1967: 164–65.
9. Gisborne 1897: 152–53.
10. *NZPD* 19: 394 (12.10.1875).
11. Mill 1972: 363–64.
12. Oliver 1990: 123a.
13. *AJHR* 1872 E-3: 24.
14. Darwin 1870 I: 170, 239.
15. Adam 1874: 94–95.
16. There were hui at Otakou in January 1874 (*AJHR* 1874 G-2C: 2), Tuahiwi on 25.3.1874 (*AJHR* 1874 G-2: 23–24), and Arowhenua on 27.5.1875 (*AJHR* 1875 G-1A).
17. *AJHR* 1874 G-2: 23–24.
18. Stack–McLean, 15.9.1873, in Wai-27 T2: 132ff. Edward Gibbon (1993 II: 137) describes the Imperial informers of the fourth century thus: 'These official spies, who regularly corresponded with the palace, were encouraged, by favourable rewards, anxiously to watch the progress of every treasonable design, from the faint and latent symptoms of disaffection, to the actual preparation of an open revolt. Their careless or criminal violation of truth and justice was covered by the consecrated mask of zeal.'
19. *AJHR* 1876 G-7; *AJHR* 1888 I-8: 30–31. According to I Kings 21, Jezebel, wife of King Ahab,

had Naboth stoned to death for refusing to sell his vineyard to the King: 'And the word of the Lord came to Elijah the Tishbite, saying, Arise, go down to meet Ahab King of Israel, which is in Samaria: behold, he is in the vineyard of Naboth, whither he is gone down to possess it. And thou shalt speak unto him, saying, Thus saith the Lord, Hast thou killed, and also taken possession? And thou shalt speak unto him, saying, Thus saith the Lord, In the place where dogs licked the blood of Naboth shall dogs lick thy blood, even thine.'

20. *AJHR* 1876 G-7 (official translation).
21. *AJHR* 1874 G-8: 14.
22. Frank Lewis Mss: 'Taiaroa Covenant'. Te Uki's name is here marked by a cross: but earlier, known examples of his signature are all in autograph.
23. SNC 3/19: 51.
24. *NZPD* 27: 566.
25. *AJHR* 1891 G-7: 58. Stack in 1859 and 1861 noted the prosperous appearance of Ngai Tahu settlements (Stack 1972: 51; 1938: 50). In 1879 (after privatisation), he complained that many Ngai Tahu were leasing their land to Europeans for ready money (*AJHR* 1879 (I) G-1: 22 and passim).
26. *AJHR* 1888 I-8: 31.
27. See e.g. McLean–Mantell, 5.4.1876, Mantell Ms 83/164.

28. Fenton–McLean, 10.7.1876, in *AJHR* 1888 I-8: 31.
29. *AJHR* 1888 I-8: 40ff.
30. See Mikaere 1988: 69ff.
31. *AJHR* 1878 G-1: 17.
32. See McHugh 1991: 113ff.
33. Mikaere 1988: chapter 12 and passim.
34. See Wai-27 R30.
35. Kemp–Grey (private), 17.6.1893, Grey Ms NZ Letters, vol 20: 70; Kemp Ms 'For Private Circulation'. Kemp claimed that Mantell had resented his intervention in Mantell's alleged involvement with Maori women at Porirua in 1846.
36. See SNC 3/1.
37. *LT*, 8.5.1879: 6.
38. Ibid.
39. *LT* 10.5.1879: 6a.
40. See SNC 3/2.
41. *LT*, 9.5.1879: 6c.
42. Ibid.
43. *LT*, 9.5.1879: 6d.
44. Ibid.
45. *LT*, 13.5.1879: 5f.
46. SNC 3/7: 292ff; *LT*, 13.5.1879: 5g.
47. SNC 3/8: 396–97.
48. *LT*, 14.5.1879: 6c.
49. *LT*, 16.5.1879: 6f-g.
50. *AJHR* 1879 (I) G-1: 22.
51. SNC 4/25.
52. SNC 4/26.
53. MLCI 1B: 88.
54. SNC 4/26: 553–55.
55. MLCI 1B: 49.
56. Mackay 1873 II: 186ff.

19

~

Left Out of New Zealand

SIR GEORGE GREY'S government fell in October 1879. The new Premier was John Hall, known in southern Maori circles as 'Governor Hall' from his signing of the Ngai Tahu Order of Reference in 1868. William Rolleston was Minister of Lands. The Native Minister was John Bryce, a militant Wanganui settler who had fought against North Island Maoris in the wars of the 1860s. The new government believed in firmness for the Maori first, and justice afterwards.

Alexander Mackay, now Civil Commissioner for the South Island, testified before the Smith-Nairn Royal Commission in November 1879. He stoutly denied having been Ngai Tahu's 'agent' at the 1868 Native Land Court as Fenton had claimed. He said the local authorities that had since replaced the provincial governments in Canterbury and Otago had prevented Ngai Tahu from getting full possession of Fenton's awards. In Canterbury the authorities had drained eel fisheries, rendering them useless. 'A great injury had been done' to Ngai Tahu, said Mackay. In Otago they still had not got the thousand acres awarded them at Tautuku.[1]

Sir George Grey testified before the commission in December 1879, two months after losing office as Premier. His mood was expansive. He had intended much larger reserves for Ngai Tahu, he said:

> I imagined that Native gentlemen would arise in the country – men living in comfort – I did not imagine setting up a servile race with fourteen acres a head. Each chief would have as much property kept for him as would enable him to live comfortably as a European gentleman, and every native farmer should have a farm kept for him, with sufficient land to run their stock besides. That was decidedly my conception of what should be done, at the least.[2]

The royal commission reconvened in Wellington in January 1880 to question Walter Mantell further. Mantell now agreed that he had tried 'to keep the natives down below the McCleverty limit of ten acres per individual,' and that Ngai Tahu had complained then that the reserves were too small, and that his depriving them of kainga and cultivations was a breach of Kemp's deed. But he advanced a sophisticated explanation. He was indeed appointed 'to give effect to the deed', he agreed; but he was not responsible for 'fully carrying out the terms of the deed':

> There was a deed binding on the Government, and there were instructions binding on me which did not go to the extent of giving effect to the deed.[3]

His duty was to carry out his instructions, said Mantell. He had induced Ngai Tahu to surrender kainga and cultivations because 'It was an after-question as between the Government and the Natives' whether they would get them back. The fulfilment of the deed was 'left to the justice and liberality' of the Crown – which was not his responsibility.

But Judge Smith put an awkward question to Mantell. In writing to the Secretary of State in 1856, had not Mantell represented himself as having been a Commissioner of the Crown when acquiring these lands from Ngai Tahu? Did not that indicate that he was representing the Crown? To this, Mantell had only a lame answer. 'I presume that was my conception of the position at the time,' he said, 'and that of the natives.' Then he turned the blame elsewhere:

> I felt that I had been employed in what I understood to be an honourable transaction, but it turned out to be a disreputable fraud, and I think I have acted for the last twenty-five years under that belief pretty well. I retired from Ministries when they ceased to take that view of it.

But after the commission had adjourned for the day, Mantell found he disagreed with what he had just said, and deleted these last two sentences from his testimony.[4]

John Bryce, as Native Minister, now asked Smith and Nairn to hurry to their conclusion. They hurried, and examined another sixty-five witnesses in three months. But in April 1880 Bryce stopped their funds, and the commission went permanently into recess with their Murihiku hearings incomplete.[5]

In the Legislative Council in July 1880, H. K. Taiaroa criticised the Hall government's policy on Maori Assessors, who in return for a small fee sat with the judges of the Native Land Court. In reply, the Attorney-General, Frederick Whitaker, said that Taiaroa had not resigned his own assessorship on entering the Legislative Council the previous year. Therefore, said Whitaker, under the Disqualification Act of 1876, Taiaroa could be fined £50 for each day he had sat in the council. Although an assessor's fees were not clearly a 'salary' in terms of the Disqualification Act, Taiaroa thereupon left the council. But he denied receiving any assessor's fee since taking his seat, or knowingly breaching the Disqualification Act. After some days of uncertainty, the Speaker of the Council, Sir William FitzHerbert, announced that Taiaroa was indeed disqualified – 'in fact,' said FitzHerbert, 'he has never been a member of the Council, although he has sat in it'. On 25 August, the Council, by a majority, upheld FitzHerbert's ruling.[6]

Not all Legislative Councillors liked the Hall government's way of getting rid of Taiaroa. Several, including Mantell, defended his integrity. John Nathaniel Wilson of Hawke's Bay, a member of Sir George Grey's government the previous year, reminded the council that three members of the Lower House had been similarly disqualified then, but a special act had immediately been passed to enable them to resume their seats. 'They are of a different race from that to which Mr Taiaroa belongs,' said Wilson.[7] Ihaia Tainui, in a gesture of solidarity, resigned from the Lower House as Member for Southern Maori, enabling Taiaroa to be elected in that capacity once more. But to Taiaroa the shame of his expulsion from the Legislative Council was a blow to his mana that dogged him for the rest of his life.[8]

The Smith-Nairn Commission issued its report on 31 January 1881. It declared that Ngai Tahu had been entitled to the New Zealand Company's 'tenths' in the Otago, Kemp's and Akaroa blocks, as the Otago deed and Kemp's deed had been made out to the Company, and Grey had afterwards deemed Akaroa to be part of Kemp's purchase. Ngai Tahu, said the report, were therefore entitled to one-eleventh of the proceeds of the Crown's sale of land within the three blocks, with accumulated interest, less the value of the reserves and other benefits already received. Mantell's reserves, said the report, had been only a first instalment. The report was critical of Fenton's Native Land Court proceedings at Christchurch in 1868. Had Fenton properly informed Ngai Tahu on the Order of Reference, said the report, they would have challenged Kemp's boundaries. Instead,

Fenton had failed to hear the Ngai Tahu side of the case.[9]

Despite these startling conclusions, or because of them, the commission's report lay neglected throughout 1881. The colony's attention was directed to the crisis at Parihaka in Taranaki. There, John Hall's government had begun preparing confiscated Maori land for European settlement without first marking out Maori reserves that had been promised. The pacifist prophet Te Whiti-o-Rongomai encouraged passive resistance at Parihaka, and his followers pulled out survey pegs and fences, and ploughed up European pasture.

Maori passive resistance at Parihaka led to a widespread expectation of war. But John Bryce, who had wanted immediate reprisals against Te Whiti, had been replaced as Minister of Native Affairs by his colleague William Rolleston just before the Smith-Nairn report appeared. Rolleston failed to persuade Te Whiti to abandon his resistance, and came round to Bryce's view that the issue was one of 'law and order'. An armed force was prepared. Rolleston signed a proclamation requiring Te Whiti to comply or face the consequences. Rolleston then resigned, to allow Bryce to resume as Minister and subdue the pacifists.

On 5 November 1881 Bryce rode up to the undefended village of Parihaka at the head of 1,700 armed men – accompanied by Rolleston, the 'man of stern conscience'. Parihaka was laid waste, and its inhabitants were mostly arrested or dispersed.[10] Te Whiti and his lieutenant were imprisoned in the South Island and held without trial until 1883. Their plight aroused the sympathy of Ngai Tahu, and of some Europeans as well.[11]

Meanwhile Alexander Mackay continued to support the Ngai Tahu case in his official reports. He wrote:

> The small quantity of land held per individual – viz., fourteen acres, and in some cases the maximum quantity is less – altogether precludes the possibility of the Natives raising themselves above the position of peasants, when a European farmer finds even 100 acres too small to be payable. [12]

Early in 1882, H. K. Taiaroa asked what the government intended doing about the Smith-Nairn report. Bryce told the House:

> The Government regards the recommendations of the Commissioners – or perhaps I ought to say the opinions expressed by the Commissioners – as being utterly impracticable, and they therefore do not intend to take any action regarding them.

He added

> A great mass of evidence has been taken, and is lying in a box.
> It has never been read, and probably never will be, but there it
> is.[13]

The commission had been ' altogether unnecessary', said Bryce.

William Rolleston agreed with Bryce, and declared the report
'not worth the paper it was written on'. Rolleston told the House:
'The recommendations which it contains are, upon the face of them,
simply absurd, and not in accordance with any evidence that can be
produced in their favour.' Major Harry Atkinson, the Colonial Treasurer, distinguished in fighting Maoris in the Taranaki wars, added
his condemnation, with oblique reference to Taiaroa and Topi
Patuki: 'The question is simply this: that there are certain rich well-
to-do persons in the South Island, possessing ample means, who
have a claim, as they allege, of some three million pounds against
the Colony.'[14]

~

In 1883 Harry Atkinson became Premier, with William Rolleston
as his Minister of Lands and right-hand man, and John Bryce
as again Native Minister. This government took the message of
'stronger and weaker races' to Maori children by means of a school
textbook, *Health for the Maori*, by James Pope, the first Native
Schools inspector.[15] Pope's book, besides giving useful health hints,
urged Maori children to adopt European diet, give up the tangi in
favour of 'funerals', and abandon the haka and hui in favour of the
'picnic' and the 'tea-evening' enjoyed by 'sensible *pakehas*'. Pope
explained:

> When two different races of men have to live together, the
> race that, through any cause, is more ignorant, weaker in num-
> bers, and poorer than the other must learn the good customs
> of the stronger people or else it is sure to die out. We learn this
> from the history of other nations. If the weaker people take
> only to the bad habits of the stronger, and do not learn the
> good ones, these bad habits will soon kill them.

Pope wrote that 'drinking, and leading bad lives' would cause
the Maori to die out. He compared the Blacks in America with the
Tasmanians (already exterminated through government repression
and forced exile),[16] and with the North American 'Indians' (largely

exterminated through smallpox, measles and forced exile).[17] The Tasmanians and American 'Indians', declared Pope, had died because they chose 'the bad ways of the whites, but none of the good ones'. But the Blacks had not died out: 'Just because they were slaves, they were prevented from doing the things that have caused other races to decay,' said Pope. 'They could not be lazy; they were made to work.' He admonished Maori schoolchildren as follows:

> If the Maoris take to the best European customs, they will live and do very well, especially as they are far more clever than any of the people you have been reading about, perhaps quite as clever and as strong as the pakeha himself. But, if the Maori keeps to his own old ways, and adds to them the worst habits of the worst pakehas, he will be sure to die out, like the Tasmanians and so many of the Australians and Red Indians.[18]

The 1880s saw a deepening economic depression in New Zealand, which brought increasing hardship to the many Maoris who depended on seasonal or unskilled labour, as it did to unemployed Europeans. The Maori birth rate in southern New Zealand was healthy at forty-five to fifty live births annually per thousand people, but their infant mortality was more than four times that of Europeans. The average lifespan of Maoris of southern New Zealand during the period 1878–1896 was twenty-five to thirty years, while for Europeans it was nearly sixty years. In Canterbury and Otago, nine-tenths of European children lived to school age, but only half of Maori children did so.[19]

∽

Atkinson, Rolleston, Whitaker and Bryce, those stern chastisers of Maoris, were out of office by 1885, having lost the previous year's general election. John Hall (now a knight) had retired from politics through ill-health. Robert Stout was now Premier, with John Ballance as Native Minister. Taiaroa was again called to the Upper House, and Tame Parata, Haereroa's favourite nephew, became Member for Southern Maori. Parata pressed the new government for an answer on the Smith-Nairn report, while Taiaroa in the Upper House moved that its recommendations be adopted – but withdrew the motion on Mantell's advice, 'to enable fuller discussion next session'.[20]

Stout's government rejected financial compensation for Ngai

Tahu, but looked to settling their claim with further grants of land. To see how much land would be required for the purpose, the government appointed Alexander Mackay, now a Native Land Court judge, as a royal commission in May 1886. Mackay sent in his report a year later. It was sympathetic to Ngai Tahu, and described Mantell's methods of providing Maori reserves as follows: 'Instead of being consulted in respect of the land they desired to retain, they were coerced into accepting as little as they could be induced to receive.'

Mackay reported that the fishery easements awarded Ngai Tahu by Fenton in 1868 had been mostly spoiled by the acclimatisation societies' stocking of them with imported fish for sport. 'These fish are protected by special legislation,' said Mackay, 'consequently the Natives are debarred from using nets for catching the whitebait in season, nor can they catch eels or other native fish in these streams for fear of transgressing the law.' Mackay again recommended compensation for Ngai Tahu for the loss of their mahinga kai, and was the first to state officially that the Maori affinity for ancestral lands had a spiritual quality:

> The general sentiment of the Maoris in olden times with respect to their territorial possessions is not generally understood: it was not 'earth-hunger', but 'earth-love'. They felt keenly the parting with their rights over the land of their ancestors, when the soil, with all its memories and the dignity conferred by its possession, had passed over to the stranger, and in its place they had acquired only perishable goods, or money, which was speedily dissipated.[21]

Mackay recommended compensating Ngai Tahu with about 200,000 acres for their losses under the Otago, Kemp's, Murihiku and Akaroa purchases. Of this, he said, 130,700 acres should be awarded for Kemp's purchase, 100,000 acres of it as a permanent endowment. Added to the existing reserves, this would bring Maori land in Kemp's Block to about 150,000 acres – the area that should have been provided in the first place, said Mackay. With their population in 1848 at a thousand or more (underestimated, Mackay said, by Mantell), this would have provided about 150 acres a head. For Murihiku, Mackay recommended granting 55,412 acres, including 40,000 acres in endowment. For Otago he recommended a grant of 14,460 acres, the equivalent of one-tenth of the original 'New Edinburgh' block.

Alexander Mackay's report was very encouraging for Ngai Tahu. But again colonial politics intervened. Stout's government deliberated on the report, but lost the general election of October 1887. The new Premier was Sir Harry Atkinson, no friend of the Maori. One of his government's first measures was the Westland and Nelson Native Reserves Act, which gave lessees of certain Maori reserves, including the Mawhera reserve, the right of perpetual renewal, with rents fixed every twenty-one years. This deprived the Maori owners of the right to manage their own land, and of all prospect of ever reoccupying it.[22]

Mackay's report was referred in June 1888 to a joint parliamentary committee. William Rolleston, now out of Parliament, gave evidence. He bitterly attacked Mackay and his report. Rolleston knew all about the Ngai Tahu claim, he told the committee. Mackay had departed from his brief so as to give the Natives 'false expectations'. The proposed 150,000 acres compensation for Kemp's purchase was 'entirely untenable' and 'most mischievous', said Rolleston. The Ngai Tahu Reference Validation Act proved that Fenton's award was a 'final settlement' of the claim. 'I believe that the Europeans did the utmost they could, under very difficult circumstances,' said Rolleston, 'to help forward the civilization of the Natives.' It was astounding, he said, that whereas he as Native Under-Secretary had told Mackay in 1867 that the Maoris were to be assimilated, Mackay was now advocating that they should remain 'a separate race'. Schools and hospitals were available to Ngai Tahu, said Rolleston, but they had not used them:

> Continuously from the year 1865 every effort has been made by the Government to promote the civilization of the Natives, and any failure of the measures they have adopted has been not the fault of the Government, but the fault of the Natives.

Ten acres, said Rolleston, gave Ngai Tahu 'a far better position than they were in when the Europeans came, if they had habits of industry'. Leasing their lands had led to 'drinking and idleness', and more land would only encourage more of this, he said:

> It would tend, not to civilization, but to the creation of an idle and degraded race; and it is extremely desirable that no step should be taken to prevent a labouring-class from arising among the Natives. In the formation of that class among the Natives lies, to my mind, the future salvation of the race. [23]

Thus Rolleston made explicit the idea of a Maori under-class that had been implied in the New Zealand Company's final policy on 'tenths', in Governor Grey's enforcement of Kemp's purchase, and in the 'awards' of Mantell, Hamilton and James Mackay. The backwardness of 'natives' and the superiority of civilisation had now received fresh support from Lewis Morgan's new work on human evolution, which was enthusiastically endorsed by Friedrich Engels, the prominent Marxist. In this view, the 'evolution of man from the animal kingdom', and the 'development of the intellect', had been determined by methods of food production. The 'lowest stage' of human evolution was 'savagery' – the 'childhood' of the human race. The highest stage was 'civilization'. Australian Aborigines, Maoris, and most Polynesians, were only at the 'middle stage of savagery', characterised by the use of stone implements, ground ovens and cannibalism. The 'upper stage of savagery' was attained by using the bow and arrow, while advancement to 'barbarism', the next stage of advancement, required the use of pottery.[24]

A second Joint Parliamentary Committee on Middle Island Native Claims was set up in 1889, on the recommendation of the previous joint committee.[25] The new committee adopted Rolleston's approach. It recommended inquiring into the living conditions of South Island Maoris – 'and, if it be found that any have not sufficient land to enable them to support themselves by labour on it, to take power from time to time to make further provision by way of inalienable reserves to meet such cases'.[26] At length, in December 1890, Alexander Mackay was appointed again as a royal commission, this time to ascertain which South Island Maoris lacked sufficient land for their self-support. Eight days later, Atkinson's government was weakened in a general election. The parliamentary Opposition, soon to be known as the Liberal Party, came to power under John Ballance on their election pledge to 'put the small man on the land'. Ballance had promised a programme of land reform whereby the large landed estates, held largely responsible for the country's economic difficulties, would be acquired by the state and divided into small farms.

Alexander Mackay began his second royal commission investigation soon after Ballance took office, starting at Tuahiwi. There he got a cool reception. Ngai Tuahuriri told him they had raised a lot of money to help Taiaroa establish their claims, but no good had come of it. Previous commissions had produced no result, they said. The government knew what their grievance was, yet always avoided settling it. No doubt, said Ngai Tuahuriri, the reason for repeatedly counting their numbers and checking on their living conditions was to find out how soon they would become extinct.[27]

Mackay withdrew from Tuahiwi and started again at Murihiku. From there, in two months, he worked his way north through the main Maori settlements and returned to Tuahiwi, where he was then given a hearing. He submitted his report to the Governor in May 1891.[28] Of some fifteen hundred Maoris in Canterbury, Otago and Murihiku, he wrote, only Taiaroa and Topi Patuki had more than five hundred acres of land. Other Maoris with more than fourteen acres had got it through marriage or inheritance, said Mackay, but nearly half the people had no land.[29]

Most Maori reserve land, reported Mackay, had been initially inferior, and the rest had suffered from over-use. Unable to afford to fertilise their land or to leave it fallow, Maori owners increasingly leased their plots to Europeans who could afford to combine numerous small Maori holdings into economic farming units. Poverty had been a great leveller. Chiefly rank, while still recognised on social occasions and in determining rights of leadership, no longer had much economic significance. In most communities all had been dragged down together. H. K. Taiaroa and Topi Patuki were wealthy compared with the rest of Ngai Tahu, but their holdings ranked them only in the middle order of South Island landowners.

Alexander Mackay's report gave a harrowing account of the grinding poverty and despair that now gripped the Maoris of the original Murihiku, Otago, Kemp's and Akaroa blocks. Many had to be maintained by their relatives, which had the effect of keeping them all poor: 'There are no cases of entire destitution; but that is attributable in a great measure to the compassionate disposition of the Natives towards each other under circumstances of this kind.' Some of the younger men with insufficient land to support their families said it would be better for them to die, as there appeared no future for them. Every year it was harder for them to find employment. If employment became impossible, they would not be able to exist on their small portions of land. The eel fisheries that used to provide some food for their families were mostly destroyed by drainage or other causes, while streams and rivers were unavailable because of being stocked with imported fish.

At Waikouaiti, the exhausted soil was impossible to subsist on.

Able-bodied men who got seasonal work shearing and harvesting for the Europeans tried to improve their land, but they had also to support others, especially old people. People could not afford medical attention, and were heavily in debt to the storekeepers. When they died, their relatives had to pay their debts.

At Moeraki no one had enough land to live on, and all the mahinga kai had been destroyed by European settlement. If people tried gathering food, they were turned off by the landowners. Those employed by Europeans could eke out a livelihood, but others lived in semi-starvation. They could not afford medical care, and some, like Rawiri Te Mamaru, had died from the lack of it. They had waited patiently for the fulfilment of Mantell's promises, and then in despair had indebted themselves to pursue their claims. It had cost £400 to fence the Moeraki reserve into individual sections, and most of the reserve had been leased to Europeans to pay for the fencing. Anaru Pori had one acre to support himself and his two children. Thirty of Teone Mamaru's relatives had been omitted from Mantell's Moeraki reserve.

At Waitaki all mahinga kai were now cut off. Because trout had been put into all the rivers, the people could not catch flounders, whitebait or eels without risking fines or imprisonment. 'Some of us were nearly put in gaol for catching weka on some of the runs,' said Tamati Toko. The runholders had forbidden Maoris to catch weka, because they wanted them for game, or to kill the rabbits; but afterwards the weka were killed by dogs or poison, and had been lying dead on the runs in large numbers. Yet the runholders had threatened to shoot any Maori who went hunting weka. Wages for shearing and harvesting went to pay off debts. 'Many of us are in debt, even those who have land,' said Tamati. The winter was the time to catch weka, said Rawiri Te Maire, and the Maoris used to have *rahui* to protect them. But the Europeans killed them all the time, he said:

> The tuis and all other birds are gone, and the roots of the kauru and fern have been destroyed by fire, whereas our custom was to take only what was required. The Waitaki and all the other rivers have imported fish in them, so we are prevented from eeling or whitebaiting in season. We can get meat now only by paying for it, and we have no money for the purpose.

Maoris used to get fish and birds in season and preserve them for future use, Te Maire said. The land Mantell had reserved for them was of a poor, drought-prone type known as onekaha. Even Europeans could not grow crops on it.

At Arowhenua, where Tarawhata had treated Mantell hospitably in 1848, Mackay reported now seeing Tarawhata's widow, forty-three years later:

> An old woman, lives by herself, earns a few shillings by making kits. Owns 16 acres of land. Part of it is let for five shillings and eight pence an acre per year. Has to maintain all the visitors who visit Arowhenua. Tioi Anaha, blind and affected with gout, cannot work. His wife takes care of him, but she has a family of five girls all under age, and herself, to provide for.

Many Arowhenua people had lost their land when it was sold to Kemp by others, said Hoani Kahu, and Mantell had omitted a large number from his census, who also lost their rights. Now many could not support themselves, being landless. 'Something should be done for helpless women,' said Kahu. 'Kiti Kahu has only eight acres to support herself and four young children on.' The Waitarakao hapua was formerly a mahinga kai rich in eels, Kahu said:

> Now the Europeans go there and destroy large numbers of eels for 'sport', but do not use them. In former times our whata used to be full of food, but now we do not need whata because we have nothing to put in them, through everything being taken from us by the Europeans.

At Wairewa the Maoris tried to supply eels to other communities who had lost their fisheries. But all the eeling places at Wairewa now belonged to European settlers, and the Maoris were refused an eeling reserve of their own. Able-bodied men went shearing, harvesting or gathering cocksfoot grass-seed for a living, and others, including old people and widows with children, had to depend on them. Few had enough land.

Tuahiwi people could not live on Buller's fourteen-acre sections, either by cropping or grazing. Therefore those who could not go away to work for wages were plunged into debt. Hohepa Huria had to keep nine persons with his fourteen acres. Natanahira Waruwarutu, now elderly and living alone, found it difficult to manage even on ninety-eight acres. Wiremu Naihira, with 107 acres, had to keep nine persons. The extra land awarded by Fenton's court was near the foothills, thirty kilometres away, and too poor to live on. When Irai Tihau got ill, he had to mortgage his land to pay his debts. Many people got into debt raising money for the Ngai Tahu claim by letting their land in advance. Many of their eeling places had been lost through drainage and settlement. Waihora had formerly been their great eeling place, but now it was damaged through being lowered by the Europeans. Hoani Maaka said that the only way to make a living was by labouring hard for Europeans, but since Maoris had no skilled trades they could not earn much. He found cropping his land too expensive. It cost so much to work the land that there was not money enough to live on. Hoani Uru struggled hard to maintain his family, like all those with fourteen acres. He used to crop his land, then he let it, and now he could not get it back because the rent was drawn so far in advance. 'It would be better to be dead and out of the way,' he said, 'as there does not appear to be any place for us in the future.' [30]

Alexander Mackay's royal commission report of 1891 was the most eloquent testimony ever made to the Maoris' desperate need for land in southern New Zealand. But Ballance's government had other fish to fry. They had received a report of far more importance to the Liberal Party – that of the Royal Commission of Inquiry into Native Land Laws, chaired by Ballance's election organiser, the radical Auckland lawyer William Lee Rees, a great admirer of Sir George Grey. [31] Rees's commission, appointed when the Liberals took office, had been given an urgent task. North Island Maori tribes were regarded as among the great landowners whose land was needed for the 'small man' whom the government had promised to put on the land. Land reformers, including James Mackay junior, blamed the Native Land Court for a legal log-jam that prevented willing tribes from selling their lands. The Rees commission had to find out quickly how this log-jam could be freed, so that the government could honour its election pledge.

Rees, as chairman, dominated the Royal Commission on Native Land Laws, and was the only member who agreed with its report, which he wrote himself. The report praised communal Maori ownership of land, and proposed that it be reinstated. Privatisation of Maori land was a mistake, said the report. [32] Rees was strongly drawn to James Mackay's proposal for converting individual Maori land titles to hapu titles and then requiring the hapu to divide their lands into two parts, 'reserved land' and 'disposable land'. Government commissioners would then supervise the sale of the 'disposable land' to Europeans, and the whole process of getting Maori land for European settlement would be accelerated, according to this proposal.[33] The Rees Commission's terms of reference were confined to the North Island, and it found out nothing about the Maoris of southern New Zealand. Instead, its report was full of praise for the land purchase methods of Rees's idol, Grey, which had been followed so assiduously by Kemp, Mantell, Hamilton and James Mackay.[34]

At the same time as landless Maoris plumbed the depths of poverty and despair, a romantic movement idealising the 'old-time Maori' enthused New Zealand colonial society. Colonial writers and artists turned from the depressed, impoverished Maoris they saw around them, to the 'real' Maori of olden times. 'Those were the days,' said Fenton, giving evidence before Rees's commission, 'when the Maori chief was a gentleman.'[35] In Europe also, ancient ways of life were being idealised, or invented. Tennyson's revival of the Arthurian legends, and Wagner's operatic revivals of Germanic legends, were immensely popular.

Thomas Bracken, author of 'God Defend New Zealand', later to become the New Zealand anthem, found time from his duties as Member for Dunedin Central to publish *Lays of the Land of the Maori and Moa*, with stirring lines on 'The March of Te Rauparaha', and on Orakau – where 'Rewi bold and fearless' fought the British during the Waikato wars.[36] Edward Tregear published *The Aryan Maori*,[37] which proposed a respectable, or commendable, origin for the Maori. Josiah Clifton Firth, who had made and lost a fortune from 50,000 acres of confiscated Maori land at Matamata, published in London a handsome volume on *Nation Making, or Savagism versus Civilization*, which declared:

> The good qualities the Maoris possessed have been almost obliterated, while their bad ones are intensified . . . And yet Christian teachers, the English nation, and the Colonists, have laboured hard to cast out the unclean spirit from this poor savage.[38]

～

The Rees Commission's report was rather too strident for the Liberal government's liking, but it set in train a revision of the law on the purchase of Maori land. Meanwhile, other ways of putting the 'small man' on the land were pursued by the Minister of Lands, John McKenzie. In 1892 he guided through Parliament a Land Act offering applicants for Crown land a 999-year lease ('Lease in Perpetuity') at the extremely favourable fixed rental of four per cent of the valuation at time of lease,[39] and a Land for Settlements Act which authorised the government to resume (i.e. buy) large estates and subdivide them into small farms. The first to be resumed was the Cheviot estate of 85,000 acres, which adjoined land that Hamilton and James Mackay had refused Ngai Tahu in 1857 and 1859. Cheviot was purchased in 1893 under the Land and Income Assessment Act, for £260,220, and subdivided into about three hundred holdings, which were duly allocated to landless Europeans.

The Liberal's Native Minister, Alfred Cadman, toured the main Maori settlements of southern New Zealand during the 1892–1893 parliamentary recess, with maps and plans showing how the government proposed meeting the recommendations of Alexander Mackay's report. What Cadman revealed must have surprised even the most hardened Maori pessimists. A hundred thousand acres of vacant Crown land, including some of the most isolated bush country of western Southland and Stewart Island, was the government's offer in satisfaction of the Ngai Tahu claims. None of it was in Kemp's block or the Otago block. When Parliament resumed, Taiaroa declared that Ngai Tahu thought the land practically useless. Cadman had himself disagreed with the Ngai Tahu claims, said Taiaroa, and the land he offered confirmed this. Ngai Tahu would accept it as charity, but not in satisfaction of their claims.[40]

The government indicated, nevertheless, that it would proceed with Cadman's proposals. In December 1893 Judge Alexander Mackay and the Surveyor-General, Stephenson Percy Smith (a founder of the Polynesian Society), were appointed to work on Cadman's scheme. They were to match Mackay's estimate of the needs of thousands of South Island Maoris, with allocations in the blocks that the government was offering. Every Maori in the South Island had to be tabulated by name, ancestry and circumstances, and his or her entitlement assessed in terms of acres, to a maximum of fifty for adults and twenty for minors. This task Mackay and Smith agreed to undertake in their spare time – with what misgivings it is not known. It was to take them nearly twelve years. In April 1894 they were joined in the task by Tame Parata. They decided, with the approval of the Minister of Lands, that entitlement to the allocations of land would be restricted to persons born on or before 31 August 1896.[41]

~

During the upsurge of interest in the 'old–time Maori', the Reverend James Stack in 1893 published a book entitled *Kaiapohia – the Story of a Siege*, thus reviving in print the old Te Ati Awa curse against Kaiapoi. Generations of writers were to follow Stack in presenting 'Kaiapohia' to the public as a genuine Ngai Tahu name. As a parting gesture before finally leaving New Zealand for England, Stack organised the erection of a large concrete and stone 'Kaiapohia Monument' on the southern ramparts of the old pa site. It was unveiled by the Premier, Richard Seddon, on Easter Monday 1899.[42]

The closing decades of the nineteenth century marked the end of an era for the Maoris of southern New Zealand. Death silenced those who had championed the Ngai Tahu cause, and those who had opposed it. Heremaia Mautai had died on 5 December 1874, the last survivor of those who eluded Te Rauparaha at Onawe. His Christian grave overlooks shimmering Wairewa towards Kaitorete, which he so boldly claimed for his hapu in 1868. He did not live to see the allocation of Fenton's awards. Tiramorehu died in 1881, and William Hamilton in 1883. Wiremu Teone Te Uki and Teoti Wiremu Metehau (Pakipaki) died about the same time.[43] James Watkin died near Sydney in 1886, having been president of the Australian Methodist Conference in 1862. Edward Shortland died in England in 1893.

Walter Mantell died at Wellington in September 1895. Naihira died about the same time, and Waruwarutu in 1899 – the last survivor of those named on Kemp's deed, apart from Kemp himself.[44] Mantell's many secrets died with him, except for those scattered among his numerous private papers. He was regarded by colonial society as the benefactor of Ngai Tahu, to the end.[45] Sir George Grey died in London in 1898, and was buried in St Paul's Cathedral to honour his services to the Empire. Fenton died in the same year. Henry Tacy Kemp died in Auckland in 1901, a month before Edward Eyre who died in England. Rolleston died in 1903, much honoured for his services to his province.

The 1890s saw the climax of the Victorian Age. The great Queen's fiftieth jubilee in London in 1887 had been the occasion of patriotic outpourings in which colonial representatives from New Zealand joined others from Britain's far-flung empire. The role that Anglican missionaries had performed in preparing the Maori for British colonisation was freely acclaimed by Englishmen:

New Zealanders, whether Maori or European, owe a lasting debt of gratitude to that great Missionary Society which has given the Gospel to the Maoris, and by its influence so changed the character of that once savage race, that colonization became possible, and British energy has been able to metamorphose into the New Zealand of today. [46]

~

In 1893, after Richard John Seddon became Premier on the death of Ballance, William Rees quarrelled bitterly with Alfred Cadman, was challenged by him to a by-election, was defeated, and left politics. The Liberals were re-elected, and pressed on with their land reforms. The Native Land Court Act of 1894 eased the registration of Maori land titles and restored the Crown's 'right of pre-emption'. Armed with this statutory monopoly, the government purchased three million acres of North Island Maori land within twelve years, on average for under five shillings an acre, well below its market value.[47]

John McKenzie's second Land for Settlements Act was passed in 1894, enabling the more rapid purchase of large estates. An Advances for Settlers Act provided new settlers with cheap credit. While Ngai Tahu waited despondently for the remote bush sections they were to receive, a succession of profitable estates were resumed by the Crown for the benefit of landless Europeans. In twelve years the government spent £5 million on acquiring one million acres of farmland. £2 million of this was spent in Kemp's block, where sixty-six estates were resumed totalling over 370,000 acres. Several thousand working farmers were settled on this land, on farms ranging in size from about seventy-five acres to 430 acres, according to the quality of the land – mostly with leases in perpetuity.[48] The resumed estates cost the government on average £5 per acre.

The Liberal government's land-reform programme was widely acclaimed as a brilliant object lesson in social progress. But for the Maoris of southern New Zealand the lesson was a bitter one. While the government spent £5 an acre on land for landless Europeans, only the dregs of existing Crown land had been spared for landless Maoris – land that had attracted no European settlers. Most of it was worth less than £1 an acre, and some as little as five shillings.[49]

Ngai Tahu at Akaroa had been refused the 15,300 acres of the Kinloch and Morice estates by Mantell in 1849, and by Hamilton in 1856. Hamilton had allowed only 400 acres for each Akaroa block Maori community of forty or fifty people. The Kinloch and Morice estates were now resumed for £157,015 and divided into fifty-nine individual holdings averaging 260 acres, for landless Europeans.[50] The Arowhenua and Waimate Maoris, desperate for land, witnessed in their neighbourhood the greatest concentration of resumed estates, starting at Studholme and Pareora in 1893. But none of the land was offered them. Instead, they faced exile to the distant forests of Cadman's allocations, or a continued precarious existence labouring for Europeans.

William Rolleston's vision of 'natives' as a permanent labouring class was thus being realised – and not only in New Zealand. Cecil Rhodes, most acclaimed of English colonialists, had legislated to restrict black South Africans to McCleverty's old maximum of ten acres a head so as to force them into wage labour.[51] Well might Ngai Tahu, like their fellow 'natives' in South Africa, feel deliberately excluded from the prosperous future being arranged for colonial Europeans. At Arowhenua in 1905, the Ngati Huirapa hapu emblazoned a new meeting house with the name 'Te Hapa o Niu Tireni' – 'Left Out of New Zealand'.[52]

Notes

1. SNC 4/28; 4/29: 596; 4/30; Mackay 1873 II: 250. By 1889, the Tautuku land, in two 200-hectare blocks, had been allocated to 100 claimants (Public Trust Office – Macassey Kettle and Partners, 9.2.1889, 'Taiaroa Papers' in Frank Lewis Papers).
2. SNC 4/32.
3. SNC 4/33: 686–87 and passim.
4. Ibid: 698.
5. See *AJHR* 1888 I-8: 48ff.
6. *NZPD* 36: 358a–59b, 505–7.
7. *NZPD* 36: 547–54, 592; 37: 248b, 620–24.
8. *NZPD* 38: 622. Taiaroa said, 'I shall never forget it. It will always remain in my mind.'
9. *AJHR* 1888 I-8: 54–56.
10. See Rusden 1888: 86ff; Irvine & Alpers 1902: 300ff; Scott 1975;

Stewart 1940: chapter 16. Stewart cites J. C. Richmond on Rolleston: 'No man in the country is fitter to be trusted than Mr Rolleston in such a matter as this. Highly educated, exactly informed as to every detail of the history of Maori affairs – a man of stern conscience if New Zealand contains one.'
11. See *NZPD* 38: 620ff. The Grey government had also sent Parihaka prisoners south without trial.
12. *AJHR* 1881 G-8: 16.
13. *NZPD* 41: 62.
14. *NZPD* 42: 422ff.
15. Pope 1884.
16. Kociumbas 1992: 147–48.
17. See Catlin 1989 and Debo 1970.
18. Pope 1884: 31ff.
19. Wai-27 O15. *AJHR* 1892 G-1

gives Ngai Tahu population as 2,508 (with 'quarter-castes'). The Maori population of southern New Zealand increased by sixteen per cent between 1868 and 1896.

20. *NZPD* 52: 479, 596–99 and 53: 492–93.
21. *AJHR* 1888 G-1.
22. Wai-27 T1: 318ff.
23. AJHR 1888 I-8: 77ff.
24. Morgan 1877; Engels 1942: 13 and passim.
25. *AJHR* 1888 I-8.
26. *AJHR* 1889 I-10: 2.
27. *AJHR* 1891 G-7: 2ff.
28. Ibid.
29. Mackay found that forty-four per cent had no land, forty-six per cent had some but less than twenty hectares, with a further several hundred children unprovided for. Of the remaining ten per cent, ninety-five had twenty to forty hectares, twenty-eight had from forty to eighty, and nine had from eighty to 200. Two had more than 200 hectares: Topi Patuki with 460, and H. K. Taiaroa with 856.
30. *AJHR* 1891 G-7: passim.
31. *AJHR* 1891 G-1.
32. Ibid: xviii and passim. See Evison 1990a: chapter 6, and Williams 1969: 88.
33. See Mackay 1887.
34. *AJHR* 1891 G-1: vi.
35. Ibid.
36. Bracken 1884.
37. Published in Wellington, 1885.
38. Firth 1890: 80.
39. See Irvine & Alpers 1902: 357.
40. *NZPD* 79: 532, 81: 84.
41. Judge Rawson's report &c (Official Ms).
42. Pitama 1931. In Te Kahu 1901, S. P. Smith has 'Kaiapohia' throughout, saying 'Kaiapoi' was a corruption of 'Kaiapohia'. But Waruwarutu told Judge Smith in 1879: 'It is the ignorance of the northern Maoris which has induced them to call it Kaiapohia' (SNC 3/4: 196ff), and T. T.Tikao told Beattie, 'The name was never Kaiapohia. That name is purely a North Island invention. No self-respecting South Islander would use it' (Tikao 1939: 123). Stack's claim that 'Kaiapohia' was an original Ngai Tahu name is examined and rejected in Evison 1990b, the text of which unfortunately has many publishers' proof errors. Corrections were submitted, but the journal ceased publication.
43. Metehau died on 31.10.1883, aged sixty-five. His headstone at Tuahiwi reads 'Teoti Wiremu Pakipaki'.
44. See *AJHR* 1911 G-5: 9, 50.
45. See Gisborne 1897: 153–54, and Haast 1948: 271n.
46. Schaw 1893: 21. Schaw was a coastal defence expert, and active in the Bible in Schools movement (Scholefield 1940).
47. McCaskill 1962: 186ff; Oliver & Williams 1981: 238; *AJHR* 1907 G-1B: 4.
48. *AJHR* 1909 C-1. Estates resumed in Ngai Tahu purchase blocks totalled: Kemp's sixty-six, Kaikoura thirteen, North Canterbury three, Arahura three, Akaroa two, Otago four, Murihiku six, totalling about 500,000 hectares. See also Evison 1987: 64–65, and Scotter 1965: 124 (map).
49. *AJHR* 1914 G-2.
50. *AJHR* 1906/II C-1: 56; 1907 C-1: 62.
51. Omer-Cooper 1987: 135. This legislation was known as the Glen Grey Act (1894).
52. 'Hapa' – to be passed over; to be in need (Williams Dictionary).

20

The Twentieth Century

J UST AFTER Sir George Grey's death in 1898, William Pember
Reeves, a Lyttelton-born Liberal politician and writer, published
in London a popular history of New Zealand entitled *The Long White
Cloud*. 'The Long White Cloud' was a fanciful translation of the
Maori expression 'Aotearoa', recorded as a northern Maori name for
New Zealand, or some part of it.[1] 'Aotearoa' was promoted by Reeves,
James Cowan, and other colonial romantics, as the authentic Maori
name for New Zealand.

Reeves eulogised his native land, describing New Zealand's
climate and landscape as unrivalled. The Maoris were 'the finest
race of savages the world has seen', their chiefs 'like Homer's
heroes'. Edward Gibbon Wakefield, the 'founder' of the colony, was
the genius who had made New Zealand British, said Reeves. After
the Treaty of Waitangi, according to Reeves, it would have been
'just and statesmanlike' for Governor Hobson to have vigorously
acquired Maori land for settlement – but he neglected to do so.
Governor FitzRoy was next to blame, for leading New Zealand
'through weakness into war'. Then, in the nick of time, came 'good
Governor Grey'.

Grey, said Reeves, had the knightly virtues, in spite of his faults
('He never was frank; he never even seemed frank'). Grey was 'the
saviour and organizer of New Zealand, South Australia, and South
Africa'. He and his officials were 'clean-handed and competent',
asserted Reeves. His generosity and firmness won the Maoris' affec-
tions; but his good work was undone by others. During the North
Island wars, said Reeves, the Maoris struggled gallantly against 'our
overwhelming strength'. They were still uncivilised, he said, but
'could be rich farmers if they cared to master the art of farming'.
Reeves declared:

The average colonist regards a Mongolian with repulsion, a Negro with contempt, and looks on an Australian black as very near to a wild beast; but he likes the Maori, and treats them in many respects as his equals.[2]

Reeves's bold assertions and naked prejudices, in their simplicity, appealed to the colonial disposition. His confident portrayals of the heroic but savage Maori, the altruism of the Wakefield scheme, the 'noble and philanthropic' motives behind British annexation, the high quality of the New Zealand Company colonists ('one of the finest bodies of settlers that ever left England'), the honest but unimaginative Hobson, bad Governor FitzRoy and good Governor Grey, the obstinacy of the Maori tribes and their generous treatment after the wars, the Maoris' good fortune to be under British rule – all these stereotypes vindicated colonial New Zealand as it was. They became enshrined in school textbooks, and in New Zealanders' view of their past.

Another Canterbury-born writer, James Hight, a young university lecturer at Canterbury College, Christchurch, published a textbook in 1902 entitled *The English as a Colonising Nation*, for candidates for government services and teaching professions in Australasia. Hight wrote:

> Britain is at the head of the most progressive and most just of modern nations. It is therefore fitting that she should guide and control the destiny of new and infant countries; to her and no other should be committed the fate of the lower races of mankind, who are, many of them, engaged in an unequal struggle for very life with powers whose rule is not so merciful.[3]

The Englishman, declared Hight, was the 'ideal colonist and empire-builder' – sturdy, persevering, athletic, and unflinching:

> The Englishman, too, more than anyone else, loves order and justice; he has been accustomed to orderly government at Home, and he knows how to establish it in new lands. His kinder and more considerate treatment of conquered peoples gives him their support and trust.[4]

Hight's textbook too appealed to colonial sensibilities – particularly in his home province, that most 'English' of colonies. It remained in use for more than twenty years.

∼

The allocations of land proposed by Ballance's Liberal government for South Island landless Maoris were at last completed in 1905 by Alexander Mackay and S. P. Smith. They reported: 'In the end, lands have actually been found to meet all requirements as to area, but much of the land is of such a nature that it is doubtful if the people can profitably occupy it as homes.'[5]

Mackay and Smith prepared a draft bill that, with amendments, became the South Island Landless Natives Act of 1906, authorising the suggested allocations. For 4,064 Ngai Tahu in the South Island needing land, 142,465 acres were allocated, mainly in remote bush country. The maximum allowed per person was fifty acres.[6] The Liberal Native Minister, James Carroll, a Maori member of the House, told Parliament that the Act would 'clear our consciences and rid the records of any stigma attachable to the reputation of the colony and the Government'.[7] Kaiapoi-born Alfred Fraser, a former Native Land Court advocate and now Government member for Napier, was less sanguine:

> Tardy justice, we are told. Why, Sir, these Natives were robbed of their birthright forty or fifty years ago; it has been filched from them . . . We now propose to give them these small sections of fifty acres, some of them on hilltops, others in inaccessible parts of the South Island and Stewart Island – bush-covered, unapproachable by road or in any other way than by balloon, or in some cases by steamer.[8]

Tame Parata, Member for Southern Maori at H. K. Taiaroa's death in 1905, contrasted the desolate Landless Natives land with the 131,000 acres of good farmland the government had provided under the Land for Settlements Acts for landless Europeans in former Ngai Tahu territory in the previous twelve months. Yet, said Parata: 'I daresay that in many instances the Maoris who are entirely landless will be prepared to accept even this small portion that is offered to them in satisfaction of their cry to be provided with land.'[9]

Ngai Tahu gathered at 'Te Hapa o Niu Tireni' on 16 July 1907 to discuss what could be done about the Landless Natives fiasco. *Te Kereeme o Ngai-Tahu raua ko Ngati-Mamoe* ('The Claim of Ngai Tahu and Ngati Mamoe') was relaunched, with T. E. Green of Tuahiwi as chairman, J. H. W. Uru of Tuahiwi as secretary, and T. T. Tikao of Rapaki as treasurer. A committee was elected to collate documents, appoint legal advice, call meetings, and levy the runangas for a fighting fund. Their manifesto declared: 'The kaumatua have worked for a long time on this, and it will be a long time before it is finished. The people must have determination for the Claim to succeed.'[10]

∾

By 1909 most of the Maori titles to land allocated under the South Island Landless Natives Act had been issued, or were waiting to be uplifted. The act was then repealed under the Native Land Act 1909. In the same year, Alexander Mackay died. His cousin James, once among the most prominent of New Zealand's colonial frontiersmen, died at Paeroa in 1912, impoverished and forgotten.

Ngai Tahu now pressed for an investigation into the Landless Natives lands. In 1914, the resulting commission of inquiry reported that while some of the land allocated had been occupied, most of it was so unsuitable for settlement that its future use was doubtful. In the remoter bush country, the commission said, clearing the land would cost more than it would be worth when cleared – and even then, the sections would have to be at least five hundred acres to be economic, instead of the fifty acres allowed under the act.[11] None of the land allocated on Stewart Island to 730 persons from the South Island had been occupied. Those who had been awarded this land, it was observed later, 'preferred the comparative comfort of a destitute existence on the mainland'.[12]

The Great War of 1914–1918, fought to protect the weak from the strong, interrupted further official consideration of the Ngai Tahu claim. But by 1916 a number of Ngai Tahu had formally complained that they or their children had been wrongly omitted from the allocations of land under the 1906 act. The government legislated to allow their claims to be investigated,[13] and a hundred or more Maoris duly proved their eligibility and applied for land. But with the war over, the government found that 'every available and suitable block of Crown land is required at the present time for soldier settlement'.[14]

The government decided that these unsatisfied claims for South Island Landless Natives land would be legally met by paying the claimants in cash equivalent to the 1920 government valuation of the land that others had already been awarded. This valuation varied from between ten shillings and £3 per acre on the West Coast, to about two shillings per acre on Stewart Island. Claimants were

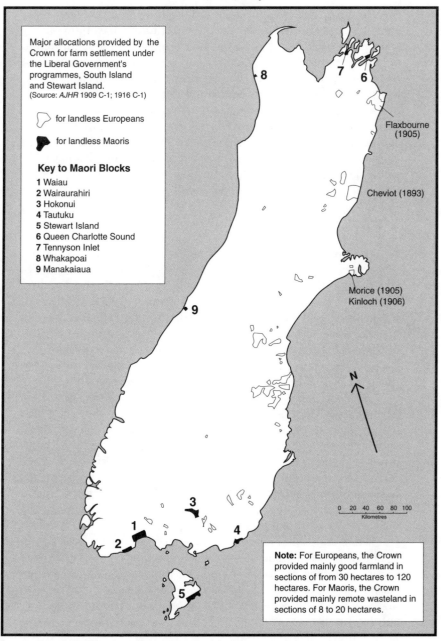

Major allocations provided by the Crown for farm settlement under the Liberal Government's programmes, South Island and Stewart Island.
(Source: *AJHR* 1909 C-1; 1916 C-1)

⬠ for landless Europeans

◆ for landless Maoris

Key to Maori Blocks

1 Waiau
2 Wairaurahiri
3 Hokonui
4 Tautuku
5 Stewart Island
6 Queen Charlotte Sound
7 Tennyson Inlet
8 Whakapoai
9 Manakaiaua

Flaxbourne (1905)

Cheviot (1893)

Morice (1905)
Kinloch (1906)

N

0 20 40 60 80 100
Kilometres

Note: For Europeans, the Crown provided mainly good farmland in sections of from 30 hectares to 120 hectares. For Maoris, the Crown provided mainly remote wasteland in sections of 8 to 20 hectares.

Official 'Lands for Settlement', European and Maori, 1892–1909.

therefore paid an 'average' of thirteen shillings and threepence per acre.[15] Those entitled under the 1906 Act to the maximum of fifty acres therefore got £33 2s 6d for their claims, and those entitled to twenty acres got £13 5s. The payments were duly gazetted, and the money was paid. Thus the real worth of the 1906 South Island Landless Natives Act grants was confirmed. After more than thirty years of parliamentary campaigning, and a royal commission recommendation that a substantial grant of land was justified, all that the average landless Maori adult in southern New Zealand had got in compensation from the Crown was £33 2s 6d, or rough land to that value. This amount, at best, could buy five or six acres of average farmland – hardly better than Mantell's awards of 1848.

Kemp's purchase was again investigated by royal commission in 1921. The report criticised Mantell's reserves and the 1868 proceedings of Chief Judge Fenton, and declared that the South Island Landless Natives Act was no solution to Ngai Tahu's claim. A substantial award was justified, said the commission. No land being available, the payment of £354,000 was recommended as compensation for the unfulfilled promises in Kemp's deed, based on the price per acre paid for the Otago purchase in 1844, plus seventy-two years' interest at five per cent.[16] The recommendation was disregarded.

Few New Zealanders of James Hight's generation, other than Maoris, took Maori grievances seriously. Victory in the Great War had inspired an even stronger belief in the virtues of being British, and of British colonial policy. Maoris and other 'natives' were commonly ridiculed. By 1930, collections of anti-Maori 'jokes', illustrated by fashionable New Zealand cartoonists, were national bestsellers. They portrayed Maoris as low-browed, heavy-featured, slovenly, and dimly but unsuccessfully groping to understand the civilised world around them.[17]

While 'coon humour' amused the semi-literate at the bookstands, sociologists in the academic world promoted a version of Darwin's theory of higher and lower 'races'. This was the theory of 'culture clash', according to which the weaker, 'unsuccessful cultures' were doomed to give way to the more 'successful'. The unsatisfactory cultures, in this view, were those of non-European 'races' – particularly 'natives'.

'Culture clash' and its consequences were expounded in 1927

by the Australian sociologist G. H. L. Pitt-Rivers.[18] 'The native problem,' he said, had arisen 'in every part of the world where European Christendom has taken over the control of the destinies of backward and dark-skinned races.' According to Pitt-Rivers, 'The native problem is the problem of the native.'[19] He described the Maoris as living examples of the 'failure of the Native' to cope with the superior European culture. This had induced 'psychological malaise' – a form of maladaptation, he said. He cited Darwin's examples of maladaptation leading to the extinction of organisms, as proof of the imminent extinction of the Maori:

> The psychological causes of depopulation are reflected in a general insouciance and depression of the native mind, accompanied by a growing disinclination to bear children. Thus, by destruction of their interest in life, natives become maladapted, a circumstance which throughout organic life leads to eventual extinction.[20]

Pitt-Rivers did not know that the New Zealand Maori population was going to double within thirty years.

The theory of Maori 'psychological failure' found support in the University of New Zealand. 'Maori problems,' wrote Professor Ivan Sutherland of Canterbury University College, 'are primarily psychological.'[21] Roger Duff, a prominent graduate of the college, in his Masters thesis *Tribal Maori and the Great Society*, identified the 'psychological failure' of Ngai Tahu as the reason why they now had so little land:

> The two sudden successive shocks of defeat and decimation at the hands of Te Rauparaha, followed by the mass settlement of Europeans, had a paralysing effect on the Maoris. To the primitive tribesman, able to envisage only two phases of relationship with foreigners – either that he dominated their mana, or that they dominated his – it would seem clear that his race was run. Land was docilely sold, practically given away, and in the middle fifties the Maori was already virtually landless, and an object of curiosity in his own homeland.[22]

Duff attributed this 'psychological collapse' of Ngai Tahu to their being faced with what he called 'the Great Society'.

Roger Duff echoed Johann Wohlers's conclusion that only intermarriage with Europeans had saved the Maori from extinction. The superior mana of European fathers in mixed marriages, said Duff, 'effectively barred off their wives and offspring from the fatal panic and despair which allowed the Maoris proper to die en masse'. Like Wohlers, Duff thought the 'European race' had a superior psychological strength. He wrote: 'They [the 'mixed bloods'] had inherited a spirit of enterprise from their fathers, which was wanting in the Maori proper, and were therefore better able to throw off despondency.'[23] Between the world wars, then, academics and journalists looked at Maori landlessness and poverty, and concluded that these were due to the inherent psychological weakness of the Maori.

∼

New Zealand historians in the 1930s still referred to Maoris as 'them', and to Europeans as 'us', as Pember Reeves had done in the 1898. In 1938, R. M. Burdon, for example, wrote that the Maori chiefs who had signed the Treaty of Waitangi 'recognized British sovereignty, though it was doubtful if they fully realized what they were doing', while 'We in return recognized the right of seventy or eighty thousand savages to the ownership of a country as large as England and Scotland'.[24] A widely used school history text, written by two liberal historians, began: 'No claims to the discovery of New Zealand prior to Tasman's visit in 1642 have been substantiated by reliable testimony or authentic record.' Having discussed the 'discovery' of New Zealand by Europeans, this book gave a chapter on 'The Aborigines'. The Maoris, it said, were in 'the unique position of an uncivilized race living in perfect amity and equality with the civilized race, and enjoying all the advantages of civilization'.[25]

New Zealand school books still referred to the colonial and imperial forces that had fought Maori 'rebels' in the 1860s, as 'our troops', and to the Maoris as 'the enemy'. Students were taught that 'on the whole, the Government of New Zealand has adhered to the Treaty of Waitangi with strict and scrupulous care', and that 'It would be hard to find elsewhere in the world another example of two peoples of different colour living together in such harmony and on such terms of equality'.[26] A school textbook written by two liberal university historians taught that, since the wars of the 1860s,

> There has never been any serious threat of conflict, though
> sections of the Maoris still consider that they have grievances,
> and take curious steps to have them righted. Such a step was
> taken in 1924 by the faith-healing Maori leader, Ratana, who

visited Britain and Geneva in order to charge the New Zealand Government with breaking the Treaty of Waitangi, and to appeal for redress to the British Government and to the League of Nations.[27]

Thus the textbooks of the 1930s reinforced the influence of Reeves and Hight on twentieth-century New Zealand opinion.[28]

In the early years of the World War of 1939–1945, New Zealand was both isolated and vulnerable. The Nazi and Japanese doctrines of 'racial' superiority appeared threatening to most New Zealanders. 'Race' as an explanation of human progress became less fashionable, and overt anti-Maori 'humour' became less evident. The readiness of Maoris to volunteer and fight overseas against the common enemy, and the courage and heavy sacrifices of Maori soldiers in battle, were viewed thankfully, and admired.

A year before the end of the war, New Zealand's first Labour government made a concession to Ngai Tahu. By the Ngai Tahu Claim Settlement Act of 1944, an annual payment to Ngai Tahu of £10,000 for thirty years was authorised, in 'final settlement' of all Kemp's purchase claims. This was based on the £354,000 recommended by the 1921 Royal Commission, adjusted down (not up) to 'round figures'. E. T. Tirikatene, the Government member for Southern Maori, canvassed the various Ngai Tahu runanga regarding this settlement, which was generally accepted on the principle that 'half a loaf is better than no bread'.[29] The act, however, did not purport to satisfy the terms of the Treaty of Waitangi with regard to Kemp's purchase or the other nine official Ngai Tahu purchases.

Under an act of 1946, a Ngai Tahu Maori Trust Board, elected regionally, was established to administer funds from the 1944 act for welfare purposes. In 1967 the trust board published lists of Kemp's deed beneficiaries alive at the time of the signing of the deed in 1848, verified before the Maori Land Court.[30] Proof of descent from one of these kaumatua was now necessary, and sufficient, for persons wishing to be registered as beneficiaries of the Board. In 1974 the annual payment to the trust board, already heavily depreciated by inflation, was confirmed in perpetuity.

∽

In 1972 the New Zealand Labour Party again came to power, after twelve years in opposition. The four members of Parliament for the Maori electorates, which had voted Labour since 1935, now regained some influence. For the first time in forty years, a Maori became Minister of Maori Affairs – Matiu Rata, Member for Northern Maori.[31] On Rata's initiative, a Treaty of Waitangi Act was passed in 1975. This set up a tribunal, chaired by the Chief Judge of the Maori Land Court, to hear Maori allegations of Crown breaches of the Treaty occurring after the passing of the act. Claimants had to establish that the Crown had breached the Treaty, and that as Maoris they had suffered as a result. If satisfied on these two counts, the tribunal was required to report to the government its findings as to the facts, and make recommendations as to settlement of the claim.

The fourth Labour government, in 1985, sponsored an amending act extending the Waitangi Tribunal's jurisdiction to Maori claims regarding alleged Crown Treaty breaches after 6 February 1840, when the Treaty was first signed. The amending act opened a door that had long been closed, making possible the hearing of historical claims for which Maoris previously had no statutory means of getting a hearing.[32] All claims were to be assessed by the 'principles', rather than the terms, of the Treaty. The Treaty was deemed to comprise the Maori and the English versions, regardless of which had been signed by the claimants' forebears.[33]

Late in 1986 Henare Rakiihia Tau of Ngai Tuahuriri lodged a Waitangi Tribunal claim jointly with the Ngai Tahu Maori Trust Board, alleging Crown breaches of the Treaty in respect of all ten official purchases of Ngai Tahu land, from the Otago purchase of 1844 to the Stewart Island purchase of 1864, and in respect of Ngai Tahu's fishing rights and a large number of other grievances.[34] In June 1987 the claimants lodged an amended claim regarding sea fisheries.[35]

Under the Fisheries Act of 1983, and an amendment of 1986, the government had established a 'quota management system' for New Zealand's commercial fisheries, ostensibly to prevent their indiscriminate or uncontrolled exploitation. The legislation sought to achieve this by the leasing of 'individual transferable quotas' (ITQ) for each commercial species so that the sum total of ITQ would not exceed the 'total allowable catch' per season, for the species concerned. ITQ could be sold, subleased or sold back to the government. The Ngai Tahu claimants objected to this privatisation of New Zealand fisheries as being contrary to Article Two of the Treaty of Waitangi.[36] They also claimed that they had not sold the interior of Te Wai Pounamu (sometimes referred to as 'the hole in the middle') under Kemp's purchase, nor Fiordland under the Murihiku purchase, nor more than half of the Akaroa block under Hamilton's purchase of 1856.

∽

Ngai Tahu's Waitangi Tribunal claim opened on the Ngai Tuahuriri marae at Tuahiwi in August 1987, and was immediately interrupted by members of Rangitane and the Kurahaupo Waka Society, who announced a cross-claim disputing Ngai Tahu's northern boundaries. The cross-claimants maintained that they, and not Ngai Tahu, were the customary owners of the Arahura and Kaikoura lands, or at least were entitled to an interest in them. They were soon joined by Ngati Toa, who claimed that Te Rauparaha had by rau patu established ownership, or else a 'sphere of influence', as far south as the Waimakariri and Hokitika Rivers.[37]

The Waitangi Tribunal had these cross-claims referred to the Maori Appellate Court. Subject to the court's findings, the tribunal proceeded to hear submissions on the Ngai Tahu claim from the claimants, from the Crown, from other interested parties, and from the tribunal's own consultants.[38] The Crown engaged historians, lawyers, and others, to pit their findings against those of the claimants and their advisers. The tribunal avoided the adversarial procedures of courts of law, preferring the more co-operative styles of the Maori marae. In place of formal cross-examination of witnesses by the contending parties, the contenders were invited to submit formal written commentaries in criticism or refutation of each other's submissions. In the case of the Banks Peninsula purchases, the Crown's initial submission[39] drew 169 items of criticism from the claimants,[40] and was subsequently replaced by another.[41] The tribunal's hearings, conducted mainly at Ngai Tahu marae, concluded late in 1989.

In June 1990 the cross-claimants brought their full case before the South Island Maori Appellate Court.[42] In support of their case, they cited letters from Ngati Toa chiefs to Governor Grey in 1851 and 1852 claiming Ngati Toa hegemony over Te Waipounamu as far south as Kaiapoi and Arahura, or even Tuturau.[43] Te Kanae's manuscript of 1888,[44] asserting that Kaiapoi belonged to Ngati Toa because Te Pehi and other Ngati Toa chiefs had been killed there, was again canvassed.[45]

The Maori Appellate Court delivered its judgment in November 1990, rejecting the cross-claims. It confirmed Ngai Tahu's northern tribal boundary as the Kahurangi–Rotoroa–Parinuiowhiti line recognised by James Mackay in his Kaikoura and Arahura purchases.[46] The Ngati Toa claim to own places where their chiefs had been killed was described by the court as a 'new také', and was firmly rejected. Thus Ngai Tahu, after 141 years, heard a judicial vindication of Tiramorehu's protests of 1849. The fateful incubus of Governor Grey's Wairau purchase was at last exorcised. The cross-claimants, disappointed with the judgment, appealed to the Privy Council in London, but without success.

With the cross-claims disposed of, the Waitangi Tribunal in February 1991 issued its findings on the Ngai Tahu land claims.[47] They found in favour of Ngai Tahu on the main grounds of their claim – that the Crown had breached the Treaty to their detriment – and stated:

> It cannot be disputed that, as a result of the Crown's numerous Treaty breaches, Ngai Tahu has suffered grievous economic loss. Moreover much of this loss has persisted for a century or more. Ngai Tahu is plainly entitled to very substantial compensation over and above any or all of the foregoing forms of redress i.e. the return of various categories of Crown land to the tribe. Such compensation would necessarily have to be financial. It would need to be sufficiently substantial to enable Ngai Tahu, now a numerous tribe, to be able significantly to enhance the social, educational and economic well-being of its people.[48]

The tribunal rejected about a third of several dozen grievances submitted by Ngai Tahu, including the claims that they had sold neither 'the hole in the middle' nor Fiordland, and that they had been entitled to the 'tenths' under the Otago purchase. On the other hand, the tribunal concluded that the Crown had yet to pay Ngai Tahu for 'at least 28,300 acres' of Captain Stokes's 'French block' of 1849.[49] In the light of the tribunal's report, the Crown and Ngai Tahu agreed to try to negotiate a settlement. The government meanwhile granted funds towards Ngai Tahu's legal costs.

∽

The Waitangi Tribunal's *Ngai Tahu Report* stated that in the 'new world' of European technology and market economy, the Crown had caused Ngai Tahu's 'relegation to the margins of that new world' by depriving them of adequate economic resources, and that this had also crippled Ngai Tahu politically.[50] Thus the doctrine advanced by Captain George Grey in 1839 and by William Rolleston in 1888, that 'natives' would benefit from being a labouring class on subsistence reserves, was again contradicted – as it had been by Alexander Mackay's 1891 royal commission report.

Yet in rejecting one old doctrine, the Waitangi Tribunal leaned towards another. They reported that after 1840 Ngai Tahu, as a small tribe, had 'to rely more on the Crown, than on their own resources' in order to cope with the effects of wholesale European settlement.[51] This echoed the view expressed by Lord John Russell in 1840, that 'natives' had an inherent difficulty in coping with European impact.[52] The Waitangi Tribunal's report also suggested that Ngai Tahu did not realise that they were going to be short of resources, until European settlers overran their lands in the 1850s.[53]

But as we have seen, Ngai Tuahuriri in 1848 had sufficient foresight to demand from Kemp some 100,000 hectares north of the Waimakariri, and either £5 million or the retention of all their mahinga kai and kainga nohoanga, for their future security. In Tiramorehu's words, they 'urged strenuously' that their share of the land 'ought to be large'. What took Ngai Tahu by surprise, by their own account, and which led to their ruin, was not 'wholesale European settlement' but the dishonouring of the solemn promises made by the Crown's commissioners, Kemp and Mantell. It was only after the Crown deprived Ngai Tahu of the economic resources promised them, that their prosperity, their industry, and eventually their morale, faltered. Yet the tribunal's senior historical consultant associated this failure with Ngai Tahu's 'not coping with the transition to a social and political world dominated by European values'.[54]

What are, or were, 'European values'? Official lying by Kemp, Mantell and Grey; the high-handedness or dishonesty of McLean, Hamilton and James Mackay; the arrogance or deviousness of Fenton and Rolleston – these had by 1870 effected the impoverishment of Ngai Tahu, as we have seen. Whether or not these 'values' were specifically 'European', the suggestion that Ngai Tahu could not cope with 'European values' echoes Pitt-Rivers's conclusion on 'culture clash' – that 'the native problem is the problem of the native'. Thus the doctrines of 'native' inadequacy, or 'inability to cope', intrinsic to the European colonisation of southern New Zealand, were still in vogue among 'cultural' historians in the late twentieth century.

∽

The Australian High Court on 3 June 1992 gave judgment in a case concerning Aboriginal land rights on the Murray Islands in Torres Strait, initiated by the Aboriginal land rights campaigner Eddie Mabo. The court decided that the application of the doctrine of *terra nullius* to Australia at the time of British annexation in 1788 was an injustice, the first of a number of against Aboriginals. The court ruled, in the light of the Australian Commonwealth Racial Discrimination Act of 1975, that where Aboriginals had maintained their customs with regard to land use, customary title must be upheld as legally valid. Thus ended two centuries of scepticism, or uncertainty, regarding Australian Aboriginal customary title. Two of the majority judges stated: 'The nation as a whole must remain diminished unless and until there is an acknowledgement of, and retreat from, those past injustices.'[55]

The Mabo decision reminded New Zealanders that they were not alone in experiencing claims and agitation for redress for colonialist suppression of customary aboriginal rights. Indeed, for decades, or generations, campaigns for such redress had already been waged in the Northern Hemisphere, with varying success – for example, by the Sami peoples of Fenno-Scandian Lapland and Russia, by the Inuit of Greenland, Canada, Alaska and Russia, and by the First Nations (the 'Indians') of North and Central America. The formation of a World Council of Indigenous Peoples in 1975 indicated a worldwide reaction against colonialism.[56] International conventions against colonialism, such as that on the Elimination of All Forms of Racial Discrimination, the International Labour Organization Convention of Indigenous and Tribal Peoples in Independent Countries (No. 169, 1989), and the United Nations Draft Declaration on the Rights of Indigenous Peoples, were representative of the mounting pressure on former colonial countries, to conform to international anti-colonialist opinion.[57] Colonialism, once triumphant, was on the defensive.

In the aftermath of the Mabo judgment, the Waitangi Tribunal in August 1992 issued its *Ngai Tahu Sea Fisheries Report*. This said that in 1840 Ngai Tahu had exercised effective rangatiratanga over their sea fisheries 'out to a distance of not less than twelve miles or so from the shore', and had successfully engaged in commercial fishing up to twenty or thirty miles offshore during the early decades of European settlement. But Ngai Tahu's impoverishment following the loss of their lands, said the tribunal, had prevented them from maintaining commercial fishing after the 1860s, except for individuals of mixed descent who had inherited sufficient resources from European forbears.[58]

The Waitangi Tribunal found that the quota management system favoured large against small operators in the fishing industry, and doubted whether the declared objective of protecting New Zealand's fishing grounds from overfishing was being achieved.[59] The tribunal said that the government's action in issuing 'quota' which guaranteed the 'full exclusive and undisturbed possession of the property right in fishing', was 'diametrically opposed' to the Treaty of Waitangi under which the Crown had already guaranteed this right to Maoris. Under the Treaty, said the tribunal, Ngai Tahu still had 'an exclusive Treaty right to the sea fisheries surrounding the whole of their *rohe* to a distance of twelve miles', and a Treaty development right to a reasonable and exclusive share of the sea fisheries beyond twelve miles and out to two hundred miles offshore.

The tribunal recommended that the Crown and Ngai Tahu should negotiate a settlement in the light of these conclusions, and that 'appropriate allowance should be made for the serious depletion of the inshore fishery off the Ngai Tahu rohe'. The Crown should return Waihora (Lake Ellesmere) to Ngai Tahu as an eel fishery when existing licences expired, said the tribunal, and compensate the current licence-holders (all of them non-Maori) for any resulting loss.[60]

The Waitangi Tribunal's examination of the Ngai Tahu Claim involved the painstaking consideration of complex historical evidence. In this respect the tribunal broke new ground. But in another respect the tribunal stayed with the past. Where nineteenth-century evidence was conflicting, the tribunal favoured official sources over Maori sources. As we have seen, both Ngati Toa and Ngai Tahu believed that Grey's Wairau purchase included Kaiapoi pa. But the Waitangi Tribunal did not believe it, preferring the evidence of Charles Kettle's sketch map showing 'Kaiapoi' at or near the mouth of the Hurunui River, north of the 43rd parallel. This, said the tribunal, was the true boundary of the Wairau purchase and of Kemp's purchase; and therefore the pa (being on latitude 43° 18') was not part of the Wairau purchase.[61]

The Waitangi Tribunal rejected the recorded testimony of Ngai

Tahu chiefs at the Smith-Nairn Commission, that Kemp had dealt with them dishonestly. Their evidence was, in the tribunal's view, unreliable – whether from lapse of memory, misunderstanding of language, 'conflation' of events, or other reasons left for conjecture.[62] But Kemp, Kettle and the other European witnesses to Kemp's deed were in the tribunal's view quite reliable when they 'witnessed' unsigned names on the deed as if they were signatures. Indeed, the fact that they did so, according to the tribunal, indicated that the Maoris represented by these unsigned names must have agreed with the deed. Otherwise, said the tribunal, the six European witnesses would not have certified the names – for the six were all 'reputable men'. The tribunal did not say the same of Tiramorehu, Waruwarutu or Te Uki. The tribunal's 'reputable men' were all British.[63]

The National government which took office in 1990 acknowledged that the Crown had an obligation to Ngai Tahu.[64] In 1996, the outgoing government signed with Ngai Tahu representatives a 'Heads of Agreement' specifying $170 million as the total value of the compensation due to Ngai Tahu under its Waitangi Tribunal claims. By this time the tribe's leadership was runanga-based, and operated a successful capitalist business structure. By 1997, the number of registered beneficiaries of Ngai Tahu descent exceeded twelve thousand, largely of part-European ancestry.

Notes

1. Grey 1956, passim. See also *ENZ* I: 53b. 'Aotearoa', whatever its provenance, was never a common Maori name for New Zealand; none was recorded by nineteenth-century ethnologists. In the Maori Treaty of Waitangi (1840), 'New Zealand' is rendered phonetically as 'Nu Tirani'. Likewise, Metehau's letter of 2.4.1849 has 'Nui Tireni', and the 1905 Arowhenua meeting house has 'Niu Tireni'.
2. Reeves 1973: passim.
3. Hight 1902: 10ff.
4. Ibid.
5. *AJHR* 1905 G-2; 1897 G-1, 1898 G-1, 1899 G-1.
6. *AJHR* 1904 G5; 1914 G-2: 3. See also Evison 1987: 66ff.
7. *NZPD* 137: 318a.
8. Ibid: 321b.
9. Ibid: 323b.
10. Ngai Tahu Claim Committee 1907.
11. *AJHR* 1914 G-2.
12. Howard 1940: 177.
13. Judge Rawson's Ms Report, 12.2.1918.

14. Under-Secretary–Minister of Lands, 13.4.1920, DOSLIW 22/1099/3.
15. Minister of Lands–Native Minister, 1.9.1920, DOSLIW 22/1099/3.
16. *AJHR* 1921 I G-5: 40 and passim. The commission comprised Jones, Strauchon and Ormsby.
17. See e.g. Lawlor 1926, 1927, 1930.
18. Pitt-Rivers 1927. Pitt-Rivers dedicated his book to Bronislav Malinowski, but it is not known what Malinowski thought of it.
19. Ibid: 25.
20. Ibid: 142.
21. Sutherland 1935: 104ff.
22. Duff in Sutherland 1940: 377 and passim; Duff ('Akin') Ms 1943: 23 and passim: here Duff says: 'The Maori when he worked, worked for his tribe; in the Great Society, when we work, we work for ourselves' (ibid: 29).
23. Duff in Sutherland 1940: 382. Duff later modified his views.
24. Burdon 1938: 13.
25. Shrimpton & Mulgan 1931: 7, 264–65.
26. Ibid: passim; Whitcombe & Tombs 1950: 83 and passim; Condliffe & Airey 1935: 73 and passim; McDonald 1972: 151.
27. Condliffe & Airey 1935: 138.
28. The present writer, while preparing a Masters thesis in 1948, was refused access to the Maori Affairs Department archives on the grounds that 'Maoris should be encouraged to look to the future, not the past' – a precept more congenial to officialdom than to historians.
29. W. D. Barrett, Tuahiwi, pers. comm., 1948. See *NTR*: 1020ff for an interpretation of this episode.
30. O'Regan 1994: passim.
31. Previous Maori Ministers had been James Carroll (1899–1912), and Apirana Ngata (1928–1931).
32. McHugh 1991: 309, 327–288. See also *NZ Statutes* 1993, Te Turewhenua Act, §406b.
33. See McHugh 1991: chapter 11, for an account of the legal aspects.
34. The Ngai Tahu Claim is number Wai-27 in the tribunal claims register.
35. See *NTSFR*: appendix 1.
36. See *NTSFR*: passim.
37. See e.g. M. J. Mitchell for the Runanganui o Te Tau Ihu o Te Waka a Maui, Maori Appellate Court, June 1990 (Re Waitangi Tribunal Reference, Ngai Tahu Claim: 4 South Island Appellate Court Minute Book: 697ff).
38. The tribunal members were Deputy Chief Judge Ashley McHugh (chairman), Monita (later Sir Monita) Delamere, Bishop Manuhuia Bennett, Georgina Te Heuheu, Professor Sir Hugh Kawharu, Sir Desmond Sullivan and Professor Gordon Orr.
39. Wai-27 L2.
40. Wai-27 M26.
41. Wai-27 R8.
42. Judge H. K. Hingston presiding, with Judges H. B. Marumaru and A. D. Spencer.
43. See Biggs 1959.
44. See Te Kanae Ms.
45. See R. Boast's evidence in Maori Appellate Court, Christchurch, June 1990.
46. Maori Land Court: 4 South Island Appellate Court Minute Book: 672ff.
47. *The Ngai Tahu Report 1991* 1991 (*NTR*), 3 vols.
48. *NTR*: 1056.
49. Ibid: 95 (map), 96. The tribunal here overlooked that much of Stokes's 'French Block' lay within the Port Levy block – which,

according to the tribunal's findings, had been effectively purchased by Mantell in 1849 (see Map 25, p. 219).

50. Ibid: 932–36, 944.
51. Ibid: 208.
52. See chapter 7 above; also Mikaere 1988: 19, 88, 125. According to Mikaere (a northern Maori), Ngai Tahu fell victim to the Crown's land purchase commissioners through 'inexperience', and 'signed away their heritage through ignorance'.
53. *NTR*: 835.
54. Wai-27 T1: 334.
55. *Eddie Mabo and Others v. The State of Queensland*, FC 92/014, 3 June 1992. See Bartlett 1993, Stephenson 1995, and *The Australian*, 4.6.1992.
56. See Valkeapaa 1983, and P. Jull in Goot & Rowse 1994.
57. See G. Nettheim in Stephenson 1995: 36–48.
58. *NTSFR*: 292ff.
59. Ibid: 375ff.
60. Ibid: 306ff.
61. *NTR*: 397, 427. According to Maori evidence (*LT*, 13.5.1879: 5e; MLCI 1B: 44; SNC 3/4: 192–94; 3/6: 241–42, 270–73; 3/7: 286; 3/10: 386), 'a great many spokes-men' told Mantell they objected to Kemp's boundary extending to the West Coast. But the Waitangi Tribunal concluded that this evidence was false because Mantell reported no such objections (NTR: 441). Again, the tribunal's report, citing 'contemporary'

European evidence, says that the land requested by Ngai Tuahuriri was 'between the Waimakariri and the Kawari, right across the island' (*NTR*: 74, 444, 477). But Maori evidence contradicts this (SNC 3/7: 278; 3/4: 199; *LT*, 9.5.1879: 6c). The tribunal says the 'Kawari' Stream mentioned by Mantell flowed into the Waimakariri (NTR: 73,480). But modern aerial photographs show that Mantell's 'Kawari' (CMA Map 140/8) was in fact the Waiora, which flowed into the Tutae Patu lagoon (see Evison 1993: 309).

62. Ibid: 443, 449.
63. Ibid: 416–18. The tribunal's report states: 'Given that the deed was witnessed by reputable men and that the signatures and marks are interspersed on the sheet, the tribunal can only conclude that those who were named but did not sign still gave their consent to the agreement.' However, Metehau, for example, whose unsigned name appears twice on the deed (as 'Te Hau'), was one of Kemp's strongest opponents, and did not board the *Fly*. Tiramorehu, a literate chief, testified that fewer names were originally on the deed, and thought the rest must have been added afterwards (SNC 3/5: 230–31; *LT*, 9.5.1879: 6d).
64. See e.g. *New Zealand Herald*, 8.6.1992, reporting D. A. Graham, Minister in Charge of Waitangi Tribunal Claim negotiations.

APPENDICES

~

1: The Treaty of Waitangi

1. The Maori Language Treaty signed at Waitangi in 1840

This version (with slight variations) was used for eight of the nine Treaty parchments, and was signed by the great majority of the Treaty signatories including Ngai Tahu and other South Island signatories.

TE TIRITI O WAITANGI

Ko Wikitoria te Kuini o Ingarani i tana mahara atawai ki nga Rangatira me nga Hapu o Nu Tirani i tana hiahia hoki kia tohungia ki a ratou o ratou rangatiratanga me to ratou wenua, a kia mau tonu hoki te Rongo ki a ratou me te Atanoho hoki kua wakaaro ia he mea tika kia tukua mai tetahi Rangatira hei kai wakarite ki nga Tangata maori o Nu Tirani. Kia wakaaetia e nga Rangatira maori te Kawanatanga o te Kuini ki nga wahikatoa o te wenua nei me nga motu. Na te mea hoki he tokomaha ke nga tangata o tona Iwi Kua noho ki tenei wenua, a e haere mai nei.

Na ko te Kuini e hiahia ana kia wakaritea te Kawanatanga kia kaua ai nga kino e puta mai ki te tangata maori ki te pakeha e noho ture kore ana.

Na kua pai te Kuini kia tukua a hau a Wiremu Hopihana he Kapitana i te Roiara Nawi hei Kawana mo nga wahi katoa o Nu Tirani e tukua aianei amua atu ki te Kuini, e mea atu ana ia ki nga Rangatira o te Wakaminenga o nga Hapu o Nu Tirani me era Rangatira atu enei ture ka korerotia nei.

Ko te tuatahi
Ko nga Rangatira o te Wakaminenga me nga Rangatira katoa hoki ki hai i uru ki taua Wakaminenga ka tuku rawa atu ki te Kuini o Ingarani ake tonu atu te Kawanatanga katoa o o ratou wenua.

Ko te tuarua

Ko te Kuini o Ingarani ka wakarite ka wakaae ki nga Rangatira ki nga Hapu ki nga tangata katoa o Nu Tirani te tino rangatiratanga o o ratou wenua o ratou kainga me o ratou taonga katoa. Otiia ko nga Rangatira o te Wakaminenga me nga Rangatira katoa atu ka tuku ki te Kuini te hokonga o era wahi wenua e pai ai te tangata nona te wenua ki te ritenga o te utu e wakaritea ai e ratou ko te kai hoko e meatia nei e te Kuini hei kai hoko mona.

Ko te tuatoru

Hei wakaritenga mai hoki tenei mo te wakaaetanga ki te Kawanatanga o te Kuini. Ka tiakina e te Kuini o Ingarani nga tangata maori katoa o Nu Tirani ka tukua ki a ratou nga tikanga katoa rite tahi ki ana mea ki nga tangata o Ingarani.

(signed WILLIAM HOBSON, Consul & Lieutenant-Governor)

Na ko matou ko nga Rangatira o te Wakaminenga o nga Hapu o Nu Tirani ka huihui nei ki Waitangi ko matou hoki ko nga Rangatira o Nu Tirani ka kite nei i te ritenga o enei kupu. Ka tangohia ka wakaaetia katoatia e matou, koia ka tohungia ai o matou ingoa o matou tohu.

Ka meatia tenei ki Waitangi i te ono o nga ra o Pepueri i te tau kotahi mano, e waru rau e wa te kau o to tatou Ariki.

2. A Modern English Translation of Maori Language Treaty*

Note: There is no precise English equivalent for certain Maori terms and expressions, such as 'tino rangatiratanga' and 'taonga'.

THE TREATY OF WAITANGI

Victoria, the Queen of England, in her concern to protect the chiefs and subtribes of New Zealand and in her desire to preserve their chieftainship and their lands to them and to maintain peace and good order, considers it just to appoint an administrator one who will negotiate with the people of New Zealand to the end that their chiefs will agree to the Queen's Government being established over all parts of this land and (adjoining) islands and also because there are many of her subjects already living on this land and others yet to come.

---

* Kawharu 1989: 319–21.

So the Queen desires to establish a government so that no evil will come to Maori and European living in a state of lawlessness.

So the Queen has appointed me, William Hobson a captain in the Royal Navy to be Governor for all parts of New Zealand (both those) shortly to be received by the Queen and (those) to be received hereafter and presents to the chiefs of the Confederation chiefs of the subtribes of New Zealand and other chiefs these laws set out here.

The first
The Chiefs of the Confederation and all the chiefs who have not joined that Confederation give absolutely to the Queen of England for ever the complete government over their land.

The second
The Queen of England agrees to protect the chiefs, the subtribes and all the people of New Zealand in the unqualified exercise of their chieftainship over their lands, villages and all their treasures. But on the other hand the Chiefs of the Confederation and all the Chiefs will sell land to the Queen at a price agreed to by the person owning it and by the person buying it (the latter being) appointed by the Queen as her purchase agent.

The third
For this agreed arrangement therefore concerning the Government of the Queen, the Queen of England will protect all the ordinary people of New Zealand and will give them the same rights and duties of citizenship as the people of England.

(Signed WILLIAM HOBSON, Consul and Lieutenant-Governor)

So we, the Chiefs of the Confederation and of the subtribes of New Zealand meeting here at Waitangi having seen the shape of these words which we accept and agree to record our names and marks thus.

Was done at Waitangi on the sixth of February in the year of our Lord 1840.

3. The English Language Treaty of 1840

This version was used for only one of the nine Treaty parchments, signed by thirty-nine signatories in the Waikato-Manukau district.

Note: There is no precise Maori equivalent for terms such as 'sovereignty' and 'pre-emption'. The term 'Confederation' in the

Treaty text refers to the 'United Tribes of New Zealand'organised
by the British Resident James Busby at the Bay of Islands in 1835.

THE TREATY OF WAITANGI

Her Majesty Victoria Queen of the United Kingdom of Great Britain and Ireland regarding with Her Royal Favour the Native Chiefs
and Tribes of New Zealand and anxious to protect their just Rights
and Property and to secure to them the enjoyment of Peace and
Good Order has deemed it necessary in consequence of the great
number of Her Majesty's Subjects who have already settled in New
Zealand and the rapid extension of Emigration both from Europe
and Australia which is still in progress to constitute and appoint a
functionary properly authorized to treat with the Aborigines of New
Zealand for the recognition of Her Majesty's sovereign authority
over the whole or any part of those islands – Her Majesty therefore
being desirous to establish a settled form of Civil Government with
a view to avert the evil consequences which must result from the
absence of the necessary Laws and Institutions alike to the native
population and to Her subjects has been graciously pleased to em-
power and to authorize me William Hobson a Captain in Her Majesty's Royal Navy Consul and Lieutenant Governor of such parts
of New Zealand as may be or hereafter shall be ceded to Her Majesty to invite the confederated and independent Chiefs of New
Zealand to concur in the following Articles and Conditions.

Article the First
The Chiefs of the Confederation of the United Tribes of New
Zealand and the separate and independent Chiefs who have not
become members of the Confederation cede to Her Majesty the
Queen of England absolutely and without reservation all the rights
and powers of Sovereignty which the said Confederation or Individual Chiefs respectively exercise or possess, or may be supposed
to exercise or to possess over their respective Territories as the sole
sovereigns thereof.

Article the Second
Her Majesty the Queen of England confirms and guarantees to the
Chiefs and Tribes of New Zealand and to the respective families
and individuals thereof the full exclusive and undisturbed possession of their Lands and Estates Forests Fisheries and other properties which they may collectively or individually possess so long as it

is their wish and desire to retain the same in their possession: but the Chiefs of the United Tribes and the individual Chiefs yield to Her Majesty the exclusive right of Pre-emption over such lands as the proprietors thereof may be disposed to alienate at such prices as may be agreed upon between the respective Proprietors and persons appointed by Her Majesty to treat with them in that behalf.

Article the Third
In consideration thereof Her Majesty the Queen of England extends to the Natives of New Zealand Her Royal protection and imparts to them all the Rights and Privileges of British Subjects.

(Signed WILLIAM HOBSON Lieutenant-Governor)

Now therefore We the Chiefs of the Confederation of the United Tribes of New Zealand being assembled in Congress at Victoria in Waitangi and We the Separate and Independent Chiefs of New Zealand claiming authority over the Tribes and Territories which are specified after our respective names, having been made fully to understand the Provisions of the foregoing Treaty, accept and enter into the same in the full spirit and meaning thereof in witness of which we have attached our signatures or marks at the places and the dates respectively specified.

Done at Waitangi this Sixth day of February in the year of Our Lord one thousand eight hundred and forty.

2: Signatures to Kemp's Deed, 1848

The next two pages (361–62) show facsimiles of Maori names written on Kemp's deed, reproduced by courtesy of the Department of Survey and Land Information, Wellington, who hold the original deed. The nineteenth-century official 'true copy' of the deed (DOSLIW L79/1153) followed Kemp in representing these names as forty signatures, including three by proxy.

At the time of Kemp's purchase many people were illiterate and their names had to be written down for them. They would then sign by drawing marks by their names. Illiterate Maoris generally marked their names with fairly elaborate and distinctive 'tohu', while literate Maoris signed by autograph.

As indicated on page 188 above, the present author regards only sixteen of the Maori signatures on Kemp's deed as genuine. Nineteen are entirely in Kemp's hand, without a Maori tohu. Two others are in Solomon Pohio's hand. In addition, Kemp wrote at the bottom of the deed (obscured on page 362) three names he claimed were signed by proxy by 'Tairoa & Solomon' – bringing Kemp's total to forty names.

The following summary gives the author's assessment of the names on the deed. Kemp's bold handwriting is easily recognisable from the first five names on page 362 which he wrote for Maoris signing by tohu – as well as from the deed itself and other documents he wrote. Kemp's 'signatures' for Karetai, te Hau [Metehau], Ihaia [Taihewa], Waruwarutu, and Wiremu [Naihira] can be discounted also because it is known from other sources that these could sign their own names (see Evison 1993: 509–11). The asterisks and ticks are not considered genuine Maori tohu, and were presumably added later. The grammatical prefix 'Ko' can be disregarded.

Page 361
Autographs: *John Tikao, John Pere, Matiaha [Tiramorehu], Korehe, Pukenui, te Uki.* (6)
Written by Kemp and unsigned: *Tiaki, te Hau, Ihaia, Waruwarutu, Taki, Rirawa, te Poriohua, Wiremu, Hape, Tuauau, Tuahuru, Te hau, Pukunui, Manahe.* (14)
Page 362
Signed by Tohu: *Taiaroa, Maopo, Paora Tau, Tainui, Koti, Potiki.* (6)
Autographs: *Pohau, Wiremu te Raki, Solomon Pohio, Tiare Weteri.* (4)
Written by Kemp, unsigned: *Karetai, Tare te Haruru, Haereroa, Tiraki, te Matahara.* (5)
Written by Solomon Pohio and unsigned: *Rangi Whakana.* (1)
Written by Solomon Pohio and Kemp and unsigned: *Te Whaikai Pokene.* (1)
'Proxies' by Kemp (who attributes them to 'Tairoa & Solomon'): *Topi, Kihau and Korako* (obscured). (3)

John Tekao

John Pere

Tiaki ✳

Ko t h au ✳

Matiaba

Ihaia

Warawarutu

Taki

Ka Rirawa

Lores

Ka te Korirhua

Wiremu

Ko Hape

Pukeros — Pukunui

Tuarau

Tuahuru

Manihe

Te Kau

Robuki

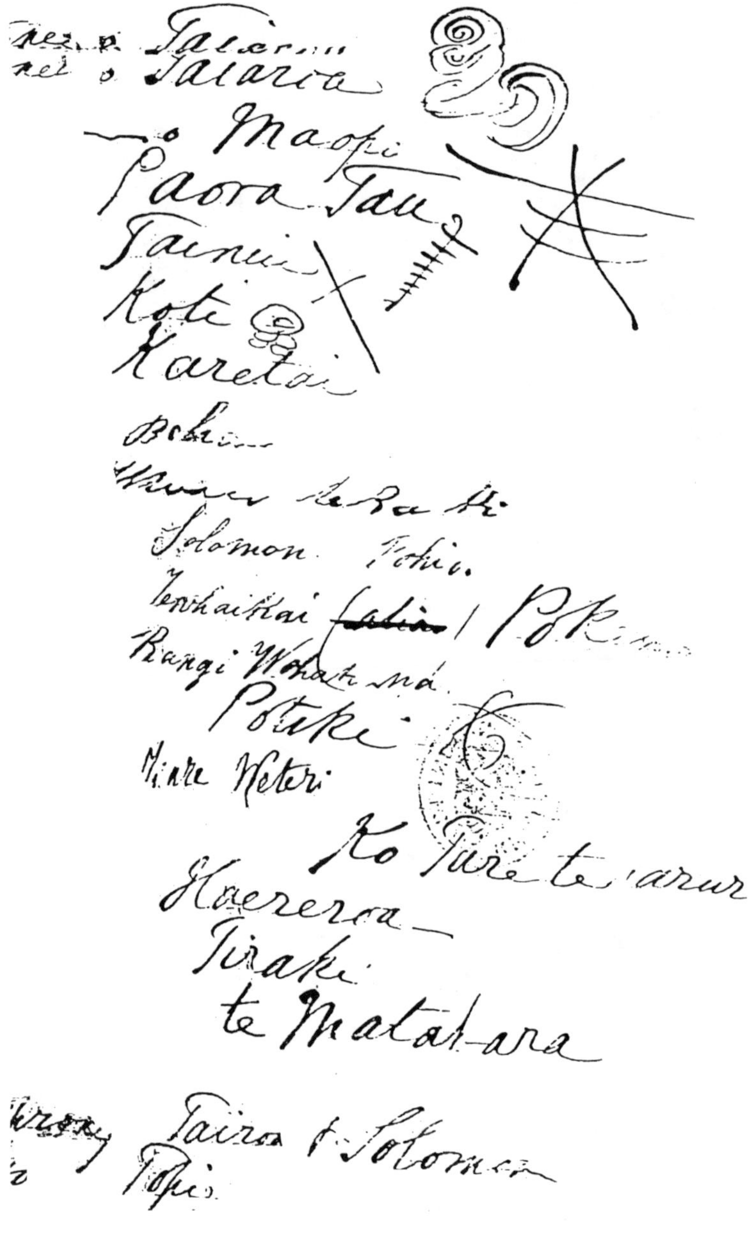
Paora Tau
Kote
Karetai
Solomon Pohio.
Potiki
Haereroa
Tiraki
te Matakara

GLOSSARY

The following Maori words and place names may be unfamiliar to some readers. (Some of these words have additional dictionary meanings.) Note that Maori nouns may be singular or plural, as indicated by the preceding definite article: *te* = singular, *nga* = plural. As used in the present text, Maori nouns must be judged singular or plural according to the context.

ahi kaa occupation rights
ahu mound, sacred mound
ariki high chief
aruhe edible bracken-fern root
atawhai care, liberality
atua god
awa river
haka rhythmic dance with chant (sometimes warlike)
Hakatere Ashburton River (p. 57 map)
hangi earth oven, and contents
hapu clan, subtribe
hapua coastal lagoon
hapuka groper (*Polyprion oxygeneios*)
harakeke New Zealand flax (*Phormium tenax*)
hau wind
heke migration
Hokakura Lake Sumner (p. 265 map)
Horomaka Banks Peninsula (p. 17 map)
huanga relatives
hui assembly
huri overturn
inanga whitebait (*Galaxias* juveniles); pale pounamu
iti small
iwi tribe
Kahutara River (p. 264 map)
kai food
Kai Huanga a Ngai Tahu feud of the 1820s

kai moana seafood
kainga unfortified settlement
kainga nohoanga customary camp site, permanent or seasonal
kaka bush parrot (*Nestor occidentalis*)
kakahu fine Maori cloak
kakapo night parrot (*Strigops habroptilus*)
kanakana lamprey (*Geotria australis*)
Kaparatehau Lake Grassmere (p. 62 map, inset)
karaka a nut-bearing tree (*Corynocarpus laevigatus*)
karakia prayer, religious chant
karakiabora European prayers or religious service
kaumatua elder
kauru sweet cake made from the pith or roots of the cabbage tree
kawanatanga right to govern
Kawatea Okains Bay (p. 219 map)
Kawatiri Buller River (p. 265 map)
kereru wood pigeon (*Hemiphaga novaeseelandiae*)
kina sea urchin (*Evechinus chloroticus*)
kiore New Zealand rat (*Rattus exulans*)
kiwi nocturnal flightless bird (*Apteryx* spp.)
ko digging-stick

koha gift
kokopu native trout (*Galaxias* spp.)
Koputai Port Chalmers (p. 116 map)
koreke New Zealand quail (*Coturnix novaezealandiae*)
korero discussion
koro old man ('*E koro*' = an affectionate form of address)
Kororareka Russell (p. 101 map, inset)
kotuku white heron (*Egretta alba modesta*)
Koukourarata Port Levy (p. 106 map)
koura crayfish, marine or freshwater (*Jasus* or *Paranephrops* spp.)
Kotukuwhakaoka Arnold River; Lake Brunner (p. 267 map)
kumara sweet potato (*Ipomoea batatas*)
Kuratawhiti part of eastern slopes of Torlesse Range
mahinga kai places for getting or producing food
Makarore Makarora (p. 73 map)
mana prestige
Maori ordinary (*Tangata Maori* = ordinary people, i.e. 'Maori' people)
Maoritanga Maori customs and culture
marae open meeting-place
Matau Clutha River (p. 17 map)
maunga mountain
Maungaatua Maungatua Range (p. 147 map)
Mangatawai Tophouse (p. 73 map)
Matau Clutha River (p. 17 map)
Maungatere Mount Grey (p. 57 map)
Mawhera (Pa) present site of Greymouth commercial centre (p. 265 map)
Mawheraiti Little Grey River (p. 265 map)
Mawhera(nui) (Big) Grey River (p. 265 map)
me resembling
mere war club

mere pounamu jade war club
moa large New Zealand ratite (Dinornithiformes)
mokihi canoe-shaped craft of bundled dry reeds or stalks
moko facial tattoo
Murihiku far south, or (sometimes) southern half, of South Island (p. 17 map)
muru retributive plundering
nga the definite article, plural
nohoanga a seat, or place to sojourn
nui big
onekaha hard soil, loess
Onekakara site of modern Moeraki boat harbour (p. 116 map)
Oraumoa Fighting Bay (p. 62 map, inset)
Otautahi a site in Christchurch city
Otumatua a prominence on the Port Hills (p. 181 map inset)
pa fortress, fortified village
Pahi's village near Pahia Point (p. 36 map)
Pakaariki site of modern Akaroa township (p. 42 map)
Pakeha Europeans
parakuihi breakfast
parekareka spotted shag (*Stictocarbo punctatus*)
patiki flatfish, flounder or sole (*Rhombosolea* or *Peltorhampus* spp.)
paua New Zealand abalone (*Haliotis* spp.)
pingao a wiry coastal grass (*Desmoschoenus spiralis*)
Piopiotahi Anita Bay, Milford Sound (p. 17 map, inset)
Pireka Peraki (p. 73 map)
po night, darkness
poha receptacle for storing preserved food
pohata wild turnip (*Brassica campestris*)
Pohatupa Flea Bay (p. 106 map)
Pohue Camp Bay (p. 42 map, inset)
poi to swing
pokeka rain-cape of undressed flax

Glossary

pora, bora large ocean-going vessel

Port Nicholson Wellington Harbour (p. 161 map)

pou a post (*pou whenua* = boundary post)

pounamu New Zealand jade or 'greenstone'

pu gun

Puari Ngai Tuahuriri pa at Port Levy (p. 106 map)

pukapuka written statement

pukapuka ruri survey plan or map (*ruri* = rule)

putangitangi New Zealand shelduck ('paradise duck' –*Tadorna variegata*)

Putaringamotu Lower Riccarton (Christchurch suburb) (p. 154 map)

rahui closed season

Rakahuri Ashley River (p. 42 map)

Rakaihautu a celebrated ancestral hero

Rakiura Stewart Island (p. 17 map)

rangatira chief

rangatiratanga chieftainship

Rangitahi Lake Tennyson (p. 264 map)

Rarotonga, Rarotoka Centre Island (p. 36 map)

Raukawa Moana Cook Strait (p. 17 map)

rau patu conquest

raupo bulrush (*Typha muelleri*)

Ripapa Ripa Island (p. 42 map)

rohe boundary

runanga council, assembly

taepo nocturnal goblin

taiwhatiwhati a bivalve mollusc (*Amphidesma* sp.)

takahe flightless New Zealand rail (*Notornis* spp.)

takahi taua punitive raiders

Takapuneke Red House Bay (p. 136 map)

take pretext, reason

take tuku purchased rights

take tupuna inherited rights

Tamatea An ancient voyager; Dusky Sound (p. 17 map)

Tangaroa taniwha of the sea

tangata people, man

tangata hara person(s) of no importance

tangata o te po people of the night; goblins

tangata pora Europeans ('pora people')

tangata whenua local inhabitants

tangi lament; a wake

tangiwai an exquisite, translucent bowenite

taniwha deities living in water

tapu sacred, sacredness

Tapuae o Uenuku highest peak of Inland Kaikoura Range (p. 17 map)

taramea speargrass (*Aciphylla* spp.)

taua war-party

tauaiti small war-party

tauanui great war-party

te the definite article, singular

Te Ahu Patiki Mount Herbert (p. 181 map, inset)

Te Ao Marama near modern Omarama

Te Awa Wakatipu Dart River (p. 17 map, inset)

Te Karaka Cape Campbell (p. 62 map, inset)

tenakoe a greeting (lit. 'there you are')

Te Ngarara outcrop of red rocks above Koukourarata (p. 219 map) (lit. 'the reptile')

Te Parinuiowhiti White Bluffs, Cook Strait (lit. 'the great cliff of Whiti') (p. 167 map)

Te Pohue Mount Evans (p. 42 map, inset)

Te Rautahi French Farm, Akaroa (p. 136 map)

Te Tai Poutini West Coast of the South Island (p. 17 map)

Te Tai Tapu coast of Golden Bay region (p. 47 map)

Te Wai Pounamu South Island of
New Zealand (p. 31 map)
tera yonder
ti cabbage tree (*Cordyline* spp.)
tikanga customary rights
ti-kauka cabbage tree (*Cordyline
australis*)
tino rangatiratanga absolute
unqualified chieftainship
tipa advance guard
titi young of the sooty shearwater
('mutton birds' – *Puffinus griseus*)
tohu a signed mark
tohunga priest, learned man
torua durable sandals of cabbage
tree leaf
totara Podocarpus totara, a durable
timber tree
Totaranui Queen Charlotte Sound
(p. 47 map)
tuangi cockle (*Austrovenus
stutchburyi*)
Tuhiraki Mount Bossu (p. 106 map)
tuku give up
tumatakuru matagouri (*Discaria
toumatou*)
tupuna, tipuna ancestors
Tutaeputaputa Conway River
(p. 264 map)
tutu a semi-prostrate shrub
(*Coriaria* spp.)
tutua commoner
upoko head
urupa burial ground
utu compensation, vengeance
wahi place, piece
wai water
Waiateruati ancient pa near
Arowhenua (p. 57 map)

Waiharakeke Flaxbourne
(p. 62 map, inset)
Waihora Lake Ellesmere (p. 42 map)
Waikakahi ancient pa site (p. 42 map)
waimaori fresh ('ordinary') water
Wairewa Lake Forsyth; also pa near
modern Little River (p. 42 map)
wairua spirit
waitai brackish or salt water
Waitarakao Washdyke (p. 133 map)
waka canoe; eponymous descendants
Wakatipu waimaori Lake Wakatipu
(p. 17 map)
Wakatipu waitai Lake McKerrow
(p. 17 map)
wakawaka division, section
wata see *whata*
weka woodhen (*Gallirallus australis*)
Whakaepa Coalgate (p. 42 map)
whakaotinga to finish
whakaotinga o Niu Tireni
to complete what is necessary for
New Zealand
whakapapa genealogy
Whakaraupo Lyttelton Harbour,
especially its upper reaches
(p. 42 map)
whakarite obligatory fulfilment
Whakatu Nelson district
(p. 122 map)
whakawaa adjudication
whanau extended family
whare hut, house
whata, wata elevated food store
whenua, wenua land
Whenua Hou Codfish Island
(p. 36 map)

LIST OF MAPS

Page

17   Southern New Zealand (unshaded) in pre-European times.
30   Voyage of the first British convict fleet to Australia.
31   The southern sealing grounds, 1790–1830.
36   Murihiku in the 1820s.
42   Scene of the Kai Huanga feud, 1824–1830.
47   Te Rauparaha's heke, with some tribal locations.
48   Northern Te Wai Pounamu.
57   Te Rauparaha's southern campaigns.
62   The Tauaiti and Tauanui field of operations, 1833–1834.
73   Te Puoho's raid, and shore whaling stations, 1836–37.
101   The Treaty of Waitangi in Southern New Zealand
      (Inset: Waitangi region).
106   The French at Banks Peninsula.
116   James Watkin's Wesleyan circuit, 1840–1844.
122   The Wairau Massacre and the Cook Strait region, 1843.
133   Edward Shortland's journey, January 1844.
136   Akaroa, 1843.
141   Early European colonisation and administration of New Zealand.
147   The Otago Purchase, July 1844.
154   Maori grazing leases, 1846.
161   Wellington district, 1846.
167   The Port Nicholson block, and Grey's Ngati Toa purchases.
181   Kemp's Purchase and the Port Cooper district, 1848.
187   Part of official copy of Kettle's sketch map for Kemp's purchase.
200   Mantell's Maori reserves for Kemp's purchase, 1848.
219   Mantell's Banks Peninsula purchases and reserves, 1849.
231   The Waimakariri block and its allocation as pastoral runs (after
      Acland 1975: 31).
242   Mantell's Murihiku purchase, 1853, and Maori reserves.
256   Official boundary of Hamilton's Akaroa purchase 1856 (shaded areas
      of land).
259   Hamilton's North Canterbury purchase 1857, with pastoral runs
      (after Acland 1975: 31).
264   James Mackay's Kaikoura Purchase 1859.
265   James Mackay's West Coast expeditions, 1857–1860.

267 Territory requested as Maori reserve by Poutini Ngai Tahu,
     1859–1860.
279 The ten official purchases of Ngai Tahu territory, and payments,
     1844–1864.
341 Official 'Lands for Settlement', European and Maori, 1892–1909.

LIST OF ABBREVIATIONS

AJHR	*Appendices to the Journals of the New Zealand House of Representatives*
AJLC	*Appendices to the Journals of the New Zealand Legislative Council*
AMIL	Auckland Museum and Institute Library, Auckland
APL	Auckland Public Library, Auckland
AONSW	Archives Office of New South Wales, Sydney
ARSCNZ	*Appendix to Report of 1844 Select Committee on New Zealand*
ATL	Alexander Turnbull Library, National Library, Wellington
BFAPS	British and Foreign Aborigines Protection Society
BM	The British Library, British Museum, London.
BPPNZ	*British Parliamentary Papers Relative to New Zealand*
CMA	Canterbury Museum Archives, Christchurch
CMS	Church Missionary Society.
CMSA	Canterbury Maori Studies Association, Christchurch
CO	Colonial Office, London.
CPL	Canterbury Public Library, Christchurch
DOSLID	Department of Survey & Land Information, Dunedin
DOSLIW	Department of Survey & Land Information, Wellington
ENZ	*An Encyclopaedia of New Zealand*, 3 vols, Wellington, 1966.
HCBB	*House of Commons Blue Book*
HL	Hocken Library, Dunedin
HRA	Historical Records of Australia
IUPBPPNZ	British Parliamentary Papers relating to NZ, Irish University Press, 1969
JPS	*Journal of the Polynesian Society*
LT	*Lyttelton Times*, Lyttelton/Christchurch
LTOS	Land Titles Office, Sydney
MAC	Methodist Archives, Morley House, Latimer Square, Christchurch
Mackay	A Compendium of Official Documents Relative to Native Affairs in the South Island by Alexander Mackay, 2 vols, Nelson, 1873.
Mantell Ms	Mantell, W. B. D., Ms Papers, Alexander Turnbull Library, Wellington.
MLCI	Maori Land Court Christchurch, Ikaroa District Minute Books
NAC	National Archives, Christchurch

NAW	National Archives, Wellington
NE	*Nelson Examiner*, Nelson
NSWSL	New South Wales State Library/Mitchell Library, Sydney
NTBB	Ngai Tahu Blue Book: Ngaitahu Kaumatua Alive in 1848, Ngai Tahu Maori Trust Board, Christchurch 1967
NTR	*Waitangi Tribunal Ngai Tahu Report*, Wellington, 1991
NTSFR	*Waitangi Tribunal Ngai Tahu Sea Fisheries Report*, Wellington, 1992
NZI	New Zealand Institute Proceedings, New Zealand Royal Society, Wellington.
NZPD	*New Zealand Parliamentary Debates (Hansard)*
NZS	*New Zealand Spectator and Cook Strait Guardian*, Wellington
OESM	Otago Early Settlers Museum, Dunedin
OP	Otago Provincial papers, National Archives, Wellington
PRO	Public Record Office, London
SIMAC	South Island Maori Appellate Court sitting in Christchurch 1989–1990, in Cross Claim by Rangitane, Ngati Toa and others v. Ngai Tahu Maori Trust Board, (4 SIAppCtMB 673).
SNC	Evidence of the Royal Commission of Smith and Nairn 1879–1880, National Archives, Wellington, Ms series MA 67.
Wai-27	Submissions to Waitangi Tribunal on the Ngai Tahu Claim 1987–1990.
Williams Dict.	*A Dictionary of the Maori Language* by H.W. Williams, Wellington, 1975.
WJ	James Watkin Ms Journal, Mitchell Library, Sydney.
WPS	Wellington Philosophical Society papers, Turnbull Library MSY3446, Wellington.

KEY TO SMITH-NAIRN COMMISSION REFERENCES

In the chapter notes, the abbreviation 'SNC' indicates an item of evidence taken by the Royal Commission of Judge Thomas Smith and Francis Nairn (1879–80). The numerals following 'SNC' in each case is the serial number of that item in the commission's records at the National Archives, Wellington. This key shows whose evidence is represented by these serial numbers.

SNC 3/1	Henry Tacy Kemp
SNC 3/2	Walter Mantell
SNC 3/3	Wiremu te Uki
SNC 3/4	Natanahira Waruwarutu
SNC 3/5	Matiaha Tiramorehu
SNC 3/6	Matiaha Tiramorehu
SNC 3/7	Wiremu te Uki
SNC 3/8	Taare Wetere Te Kahu
SNC 3/9	John Topi Patuki
SNC 3/10	Wiremu Naihira
SNC 3/11	Wiremu te Uki
SNC 3/12	Wiremu Naihira
SNC 3/17	Rawiri te Mamaru
SNC 3/19	Hori Kerei Taiaroa
SNC 4/21	Paurini Hirawea
SNC 4/22	W. J. W. Hamilton
SNC 4/25	Henry Tacy Kemp
SNC 4/26	Francis Dart Fenton
SNC 4/27	Matene te Whiwhi
SNC 4/28	Alexander Mackay
SNC 4/29	Alexander Mackay
SNC 4/30	Alexander Mackay
SNC 4/31	Sir George Grey
SNC 4/32	Sir George Grey
SNC 4/33	Walter Mantell
SNC 4/34	Walter Mantell
SNC 4/37	J. J. Symonds
SNC 4/38	Horomona Pohio

SNC 4/39	Rawiri te Maire
SNC 5/43	Hone Kahu
SNC 5/55	Hori Kerei Taiaroa
SNC 6/65	Hone Taupoki
SNC 6/68	Ihakara Tipia
SNC 6/73	Henere Te Paro
SNC 6/74	Henere Tawha
SNC 6/75	Tame Karangahape
SNC 6/77	W. J. W. Hamilton
SNC 6/79	Tamanuiarangi (John Patterson)
SNC 7/83	H. K. Taiaroa
SNC 7/84	Kiriona Pohau
SNC 7/93	Matiaha Tiramorehu
SNC 7/94	Ihaia Tainui
SNC 7/95	Ripene Te Rehe
SNC 7/96	Wiremu te Uki

BIBLIOGRAPHY

OFFICIAL PUBLICATIONS

Appendices to the Journals of the New Zealand House of Representatives (AJHR), Wellington.
Appendices to the Journals of the New Zealand Legislative Council (AJLC), Wellington.
British Parliamentary Papers Relative to New Zealand (BPPNZ), London.
British Parliamentary Papers Relating to New Zealand (IUPBPPNZ), Irish University Press, Shannon, 1969.
Compendium of Official Documents Relative to Native Affairs in the South Island, 2 vols, Compiled by Alexander Mackay, NZ Goverment, Nelson, 1873.
Encyclopaedia of New Zealand (3 vols), Wellington, 1966.
Historical Records of Australia (HRA), Sydney & Canberra, 1924 &c.
House of Commons Blue Books, London.
New Munster Gazette, Wellington.
New Zealand Parliamentary Debates – Hansard (*NZPD*), Wellington.
New Zealand Statutes, Wellington.
New Zealand Dept of Agriculture. *Farming in New Zealand*, Wellington, 1947.

OFFICIAL UNPUBLISHED PAPERS AND DOCUMENTS

Canterbury Land Office Records, CMA, Christchurch.
Colonial Office Papers, NSWSL, Sydney.
Colonial Office Papers, PRO, London.
Kettle, Charles. Field Book No. 33, DOSLID, Dunedin.
Lands & Survey Maps & Records, CMA, Christchurch.
Land Registrar Records, AONSW, Sydney.
Land Titles Records, LTOS, Sydney.
Mackay, James Jnr. Collingwood Letterbook, NAW MA Collingwood 2/1, Wellington.
New Munster Government Papers, NAW, Wellington.
New South Wales Governors' Despatches, NSWSL Microfilm series CY & PRO, Sydney.
New Zealand Government Papers, NAW, Wellington.
Otago Provincial Papers, NAW, Wellington.
Rawson, Judge W. E. Report 12.2.1918 ('South Island Landless Natives'), Minute Book & 'Brief History', DOSLIW, Wellington.

Royal Commission on Middle Island Native Land Purchases 1879–1880
(Smith-Nairn Commission), Evidence & Minutes (SNC), NAW MA/67,
Wellington.
Maps and deeds, DOSLIW, Wellington.
Treaty of Waitangi original parchments, NAW, Wellington.

COURT AND TRIBUNAL RECORDS

Maori Land Court Ikaroa Minute Books, MLCI, Christchurch.
Case Stated 4 SIAppCtMB folio 672 & 673, SIMAC, Christchurch.
Waitangi Tribunal, *Evidence and Submissions on Ngai Tahu Claim 1987-1990*
(Wai-27).
Waitangi Tribunal, *The Ngai Tahu Report 1991* (*NTR*), 3 vols, Wellington,
1991.
Waitangi Tribunal, *Ngai Tahu Sea Fisheries Report 1992* (*NTSFR*),
Wellington, 1992.

UNOFFICIAL PUBLISHED BOOKS AND ARTICLES

Abrahams, Peter. *Jamaica*, London, 1957.
Acland, L. G. D. (ed. Scotter). *The Early Canterbury Runs*, Christchurch,
1975
Adam, James *25 Years of Emigrant Life in the South of New Zealand*,
Edinburgh, 1874.
Adams, C. W. *A Spring in the Canterbury Settlement*, London, 1853.
Adkin, G. L. *Horowhenua: Its Maori Place-Names*, Wellington, 1948.
Alington, M. H. *Unquiet Earth*, Wellington, 1978.
Allan, R. M. *Nelson, A History of Early Settlement*, Wellington, 1965.
Andersen, J. C. *Jubilee History of South Canterbury*, Christchurch, 1916.
Andersen, J. C. *Place-names of Banks Peninsula*, Wellington, 1927.
Andersen, J. C. *Old Christchurch*, Christchurch, 1949.
Anderson, Atholl. *When All the Moa Ovens Grew Cold*, Dunedin, 1983.
Anderson, Atholl. *Te Puoho's Last Raid*, Dunedin, 1986.
Anderson, Atholl. 'The Chronology of Colonization in New Zealand',
Antiquity 65, 1991.
Anderson, Atholl, & McGovern-Wilson, R. (eds). *Beech Forest Hunters*,
Auckland 1991.
Anon. *The Canterbury Colony, Its Site and Prospects* (1852), HL, Dunedin,
1976.
Ballara, Angela 'The Role of Warfare in Maori Society in the Early Contact
Period', *JPS* 85, 1976.
Barker, Lady. *Station Life in New Zealand*, Christchurch, 1950.
Barratt, Glynn. *Bellingshausen, A Visit to New Zealand 1820*, Palmerston
North, 1979.

Bartlett, R. H. *The Mabo Decision*, Sydney, 1993.

Bathgate, M. A. 'Maori River and Ocean Going Craft in Southern New Zealand', *JPS* 78, 1969.

Beaglehole, J. C. *The 'Endeavour' Journal of Joseph Banks*, 2 vols, Sydney, 1962.

Beattie, J. H. *Early Runholding in Otago*, Dunedin, 1947a.

Beattie, J. H. *The Pioneers Explore Otago*, Dunedin, 1947b.

Beattie, J. H (ed. Anderson). *Traditional Lifeways of the Southern Maori*, Dunedin, 1994.

Beck, Russell. *New Zealand Jade*, Wellington, 1984.

Begg, A. C. & N. C. *The World of John Boultbee*, Christchurch, 1979.

Best, Ensign (ed. Taylor). *The Journal of Ensign Best*, Wellington, 1966.

Biggs, Bruce. 'Two Letters from Ngaati-Toa to Sir George Grey', *JPS* 68, 1959.

Boultbee, J. (ed. Starke). *Journal of a Rambler*, Wellington, 1986.

Bracken, Thomas. *Lays of the Land of the Maori and Moa*, London, 1884.

Brailsford, Barry. *The Tattooed Land*, Wellington, 1981.

British & Foreign Aborigines Society. *On the British Colonization of New Zealand*, London, n.d.

British & Foreign Aborigines Society. *Appeal of the British and Foreign Aborigines Protection Society*, London, 1840.

Brooking, Tom. *And Captain of Their Souls*, Dunedin, 1984.

Buck, P. (Te Rangihiroa). *The Coming of the Maori*, Wellington, 1950.

Buick, T. Lindsay . *The French at Akaroa*, Wellington, 1928.

Buller, W. L. (ed. Turbott). *Birds of New Zealand*, Christchurch, 1967.

Bunbury, Thomas. *Reminiscences of a Veteran*, 3 vols, London, 1861.

Burdon, R. M. *High Country*, Auckland, 1938.

Burns, Patricia. *Te Rauparaha – A New Perspective*, Wellington, 1980

Butler, J. (ed. Barton). *Earliest New Zealand*, Masterton, 1927.

Butler, Samuel. *A First Year in the Canterbury Settlement*, Auckland, 1964.

Butlin, N. G. *Economics and the Dreamtime*, Cambridge, 1993.

Carkeek, W. *The Kapiti Coast*, Wellington, 1966.

Catlin, George (ed. Matthiessen). *North American Indians*, New York, 1989.

Chisholm, Jocelyn. *Captain Cattlin Towards New Zealand*, Wellington, 1994.

Clark, A. H. *The Invasion of New Zealand by People, Plants and Animals* , New Brunswick, 1949.

Clarke, George. *Notes on Early Life in New Zealand*, Hobart, 1903,

Condliffe, J. B., & Airey, W. T. G. *Short History of New Zealand*, Auckland, 1935.

Couch, A. T. R. *Rapaki Remembered*, Christchurch, 1987.

Couch, W. (ed.). *Centenary of the Rapaki Church*, Christchurch, 1969.

Courage, S. A. *Lights and Shadows of Colonial Life*, Christchurch, 1976.

Coutts, P. J. F. 'Merger or Takeover – A Survey of the Effects of Contact Between European and Maori in the Foveaux Strait Region', *JPS* 78, 1969.

Cramp, K. R. *William Charles Wentworth of Vaucluse House*, Sydney, 1922.

Crawford, N. *The Station Years*, Cave, 1981.

Cresswell, D. R. *Squatter & Settler in the Waipara County*, Christchurch, 1952.
Cresswell, D. R. *The Story of Cheviot*, Cheviot, 1951.
Cumpston, J. S. *Shipping Arrivals and Departures, Sydney 1788–1825*, 2 vols, Canberra, 1977.
da Costa, E. V. *Crowns of Glory, Tears of Blood; The Demarara Slave Rebellion of 1823*, New York & London, 1994.
Dalton, B. J. *War and Politics in New Zealand 1855–1870*, Sydney, 1967.
Darwin, Charles. *The Descent of Man, Selection in Relation to Sex*, 2 vols, London, 1870–71.
Deans, J., J., & W., (ed. J. Deans). *Pioneers of Canterbury: Deans Letters 1840–1854*, Wellington, 1937.
Deans, John. *Pioneers on Port Cooper Plains*, Christchurch, 1964.
Debo, Angie. *A History of the Indians of the United States*, University of Oklahoma, 1970.
Delaporte, F. *Disease & Civilization: The Cholera in Paris 1832*, Cambridge Mass., 1986.
Desmond, A., & Moore, J. *Darwin*, London, 1991.
Dieffenbach, Ernst. *Travels in New Zealand*, 2 vols, London, 1843.
Dippie, B. W. *The Vanishing American*, Lawrence, Kansas, 1982.
Dobson, A. D. *Reminiscences*, Auckland, 1930.
Downes, T. W. *Old Whanganui*, Wanganui, 1915.
Durham, Lord. *Report on the Affairs of British North America*, London, 1912.
Durward, E. W. 'The Maori Population of Otago', *JPS* 42, 1933.
Earle, A. (ed. McCormick). *Journal of a Residence in Tristan da Cunha; Narrative of a Residence in New Zealand*, Oxford, 1966.
Eccles, A., & Reed, A. H. *John Jones of Otago*, Wellington, 1949.
Elvy, W. J. *Kaikoura Coast*, Christchurch, 1949.
Engels, Friedrich. *The Origin of the Family, Private Property, and the State*, Sydney, 1942.
Evison, H. C. *Ngai Tahu Land Rights* (3rd edn), Christchurch, 1987.
Evison, H. C. *The Treaty of Waitangi & The Waitangi Tribunal – Fact & Fiction*, Christchurch, 1990a.
Evison, H. C. 'Kaiapohia – The Story of a Name', *Te Karanga* (CMSA) 6/2, Christchurch, 1990b.
Evison, H. C. *Te Wai Pounamu, the Greenstone Island*, Wellington, 1993.
Evison, H. C. 'The Wentworth-Jones Deeds', *Turnbull Library Record*, Wellington,1995.
Fenton, F. D. *Observations on the State of the Aboriginal Inhabitants of N.Z.*, Auckland, 1859.
Findlay, G. G., & Holdsworth W. W. *The History of the Wesleyan Methodist Missionary Society*, 3 vols, London, 1921.
Firth, J. C. *Nation Making*, London, 1890.
Firth, Raymond. *Economics of the New Zealand Maori*, Wellington, 1959.
FitzRoy, Robert. *Remarks on New Zealand in February 1846*, London, 1846.
Fleming, C. A. *Science, Settlers and Scholars* Wellington, 1987.
Forster, J. R. (ed. Hoare). *The Resolution Journal of Johann Reinhold Forster*, 4 vols, London, 1982.

Fowell, N. (ed. Irvine). *The Sirius Letters* Sydney, 1988.

Fulton, R. V. *Medical Practice in Otago and Southland in the Early Days*, Dunedin, 1922.

Gardner, W .J. (ed.). *A History of Canterbury* Vol 2, Christchurch, 1971.

Gibbon, Edward. *The Decline and Fall of the Roman Empire*, 6 vols, London 1993–94.

Gisborne, William. *New Zealand Rulers and Statesmen 1840–1897*, London, 1897.

Gluckman, L. K. *Tangiwai*, Auckland, 1976.

Godley, Charlotte (ed. Godley). *Letters from Early N.Z. 1850–1853*, Christchurch, 1951.

Goot, M., & Rowse, T. (eds) *Make a Better Offer: The Politics of Mabo*, Sydney 1994.

Goya, Francisco (ed. Hofer). *The Disasters of War*, Cambridge Mass., 1967.

Grady, Don. *Guards of the Sea*, Christchurch, 1978.

Grey, George. *Journal of Two Expeditions of Discovery*, 2 vols, London, 1841.

Grey, George (ed. Bird). *Polynesian Mythology*, Christchurch, 1956.

Haast, H. F. von. *New Zealand Privy Council Cases 1840-1932*, Wellington, 1938.

Haast, H. F. von. *The Life and Times of Sir Julius von Haast*, Wellington, 1948.

Hall, T. D. H. *Captain Joseph Nias & the Treaty of Waitangi – a Vindication*, Wellington, 1938.

Hall-Jones, F. G. *King of the Bluff*, Invercargill, 1943.

Hall-Jones, F. G. *Historical Southland*, Invercargill, 1945.

Hall-Jones, John. *Fiordland Explored*, Wellington, 1976.

Hall-Jones, John. *Martins Bay*, Invercargill, 1987.

Hall-Jones, John. *Stewart Island Explored*, Invercargill, 1994.

Hamer, D. A., & Nicholls, R. *The Making of Wellington*, Wellington, 1990.

Hamilton, Henry *History of the Homeland*, London, 1947.

Harlow, Ray. *A Word-List of South Island Maori*, Dunedin, 1987.

Harlow, Ray. *Otago's First Book: The Distinctive Dialect of Southern Maori*, Dunedin, 1994.

Harper, A. P. *Memories of Mountains and Men*, Christchurch, 1946.

Hart, G. II. *Stray Leaves from the Early History of Canterbury*, Christchurch, 1887.

Harvey, Judge. *Native Land Court Report 1934*, in *AJHR* 1936 G-6B.

Havard-Williams, P. (ed.). *Marsden and the New Zealand Mission*, Dunedin, 1961.

Hay, James. *Earliest Canterbury and Its Settlers*, Christchurch, 1915.

Hempleman, G. (ed. Anson). *The Piraki Log*, London, 1911.

Heuer, Beryl. *Maori Women*, Wellington, 1972.

Hight, James. *The English as a Colonising Nation*, Christchurch, 1902.

Hight, James, & Straubel, C. R. (eds). *A History of Canterbury* Vol I, Christchurch, 1957.

Hill, R. S. *Policing the Colonial Frontier*, 2 vols, Wellington, 1986.

Hirst, J. B. *Convict Society and Its Enemies*, London, 1983.

Hobsbawm, E. J. & Rudé, G. *Captain Swing*, London, 1985.
Hocken, T. M. *Contributions to the Early History of New Zealand (Otago)*, London, 1898.
Hooker, R. H. *The Archaeology of the South Westland Maori*, Hokitika, 1986.
Hopkins, Harry. *The Long Affray – The Poaching Wars in Britain*, London, 1985.
Houghton, Philip. *The First New Zealanders*, Auckland, 1980.
Houghton, Philip. *People of the Great Ocean*, Cambridge, 1996.
Howard, Basil. *Rakiura – A History of Stewart Island*, Wellington, 1940.
Hughes, Robert *The Fatal Shore*, London, 1987.
Hurwitz, S. J. *Jamaica – A Historical Portrait*, New York, 1971.
Ironside, S. 'A Biography of James Watkin', *Wesleyan Methodist Magazine*, London, October 1891.
Irvine R. F., & Alpers O. T. J. *The Progress of New Zealand in the Century*, London, 1902.
Irwin, Geoffrey. *The Prehistoric Exploration and Colonisation of the Pacific*, Cambridge, 1992.
Jacobson, H. C. (ed.). *Tales [Stories] of Banks Peninsula*, Akaroa, 1914.
Jellicoe, R. L. *The New Zealand Company's Native Reserves*, Wellington, 1930.
Jones, E. *Autobiography of an Early Settler in New Zealand*, Wellington, 1933.
Kawharu, I. H. *Maori Land Tenure*, Oxford, 1977.
Kawharu, I. H. (ed.). *Waitangi: Maori and Pakeha Perspectives of the Treaty of Waitangi*, Auckland, 1989.
Kemp, H. T. *Revised Narrative of Incidents and Events in the Early Colonizing History of New Zealand*, Auckland, 1901.
Kennaway, L. J. *Crusts*, London, 1874.
Knight, H., & Coutts, P. *Matanaka, Otago's First Farm*, Dunedin, 1975.
Kociumbas, Jan. *The Oxford History of Australia*, Vol 2, Melbourne 1992.
Lamb, R. C. *Early Christchurch*, Christchurch, 1963.
Lamb, R. C. *Birds, Beasts and Fishes*, Christchurch, 1964.
Lauper, Jakob (ed. Pascoe). *Over the Whitcombe Pass*, Christchurch, 1960.
Lavaud, Charles. *Akaroa*, Christchurch, 1986.
Lawlor, Pat. *Maori Tales*, Sydney, 1926.
Lawlor, Pat. *More Maori Tales*, Sydney, 1927.
Lawlor, Pat. *Still More Maori Tales*, Sydney, 1930.
Lord, E. I. *Old Westland*, Auckland, 1939.
Lubbock, Adelaide. *Owen Stanley, R.N.*, Melbourne, 1968.
McBryde, Isabel. *Guests of the Governor*, Sydney, 1989.
McCaskill, M. (ed.) *Land & Livelihood*, Christchurch, 1962.
McClymont, W. G. *The Exploration of New Zealand*, London, 1959.
Macdonald, G. R. *The Christchurch Club*, Christchurch, 1956.
McDonald, K. C. *History of North Otago*, Oamaru, 1940.
McDonald, K. C. *Our Country's Story* (2nd edn), Christchurch, 1972.
McHugh, Paul. *The Maori Magna Carta*, Auckland, 1991.
Mackay, James. *Our Dealings With Maori Lands*, Auckland, 1887.
McKillop, H. F. *Reminiscences of Twelve Months Service in New Zealand*, London, 1849.

Bibliography

McLean, Gavin. *Moeraki*, Dunedin, 1986.
McLintock, A. H. *The History of Otago*, Dunedin, 1949.
McLintock, A. H. *Crown Colony Government in New Zealand*, Wellington, 1958.
McNab, Robert. *Murihiku and the Southern Islands*, Christchurch, 1907.
McNab, Robert. *Historical Records of New Zealand*, 2 vols, Wellington, 1908 & 1914.
McNab, Robert. *The Old Whaling Days*, Christchurch, 1913.
Mahuika, Api. 'Leadership: Inherited and Achieved', *Te Ao Hurihuri* (ed. King), Auckland, 1981.
Maling, P. B. *Early Sketches and Charts of Banks Peninsula*, Christchurch, 1981.
Malthus, Thomas R. (ed. E. Wrigley & D. Souden). *An Essay on the Principle of Population*, 8 vols, London, 1986.
Mantell, Gideon (ed. Curwen). *The Journal of Gideon Mantell*, London, 1940.
Marsden, S. (ed. Elder). *The Letters & Journals of Samuel Marsden 1765– 1838* , Dunedin, 1932.
Martin, William. *The Taranaki Question*, Auckland, 1860.
Mathew, Felton (ed. Rutherford). *The Founding of New Zealand*, Wellington, 1940.
May, P. R. *The West Coast Gold Rushes*, Christchurch, 1962.
Meredith, G. L. *Adventuring in Maoriland in the Seventies*, Sydney, 1935.
Mikaere, Buddy. *Te Maiharoa and the Promised Land*, Auckland, 1988.
Mill, J. S. *Utilitarianism, Liberty, and Representative Government*, London, 1910 repr. 1972.
Mingay, G. E. (ed.). *The Agrarian History of England and Wales*, Vol 6, Cambridge, 1989.
Molesworth, W. *Report from the Select Committee on Transportation*, London, 1838.
Money, C .L. *Knocking About in New Zealand*, Melbourne, 1871.
Morgan, Lewis. *Ancient Society, or Researches in the Lines of Human Progress from Savagery, through Barbarism to Civilisation*, Chicago & London, 1877.
New Zealand Company. *Fifteenth Report of the Directors*, London, 1844.
Ngai Tahu Claim Committee. *Te Kereeme o Ngai-Tahu raua ko Ngatı-Mamoe*, Arowhenua, 1907.
Ngai Tahu Maori Trust Board. *Ngaitahu Kaumatua Alive in 1848* ('Ngai Tahu Blue Book'),' Christchurch, 1967.
Ogilvie, Elisabeth. *Purau*, Christchurch, 1970.
Ogilvie, Gordon. *Pioneers of the Plains: The Deans of Canterbury*, Christchurch, 1996.
Oldham, W. (ed.Oldham). *Britain's Convicts to the Colonies*, Sydney, 1990.
Oliver, W. H. (ed.). *The Dictionary of New Zealand Biography*, Vol I, Wellington, 1990.
Oliver, W. H. & Williams B. R. (eds) *The Oxford History of New Zealand*, Wellington, 1981.

Omer-Cooper, J. D. *History of Southern Africa*, London, 1987.

Orange, Claudia. *The Treaty of Waitangi*, Wellington, 1987.

Orange, Claudia. *An Illustrated History of the Treaty of Waitangi*, Wellington, 1990.

O'Regan, T. (ed.) *Whakapapa Ngai Tahu: The Establishment of the Ngai Tahu Beneficial Register*, Christchurch, 1994.

Orbell, Margaret. *The Natural World of the Maori* (Illustr. Moon), Auckland, 1985.

Owens, J. M. R. *Prophets in the Wilderness*, Auckland, 1974.

Patuki, John Topi. Petition, *AJHR* 1878 J-3.

Philosophical Institute of Canterbury. *Natural History of Canterbury*, Christchurch, 1927.

Pinney, Robert. *Early North Otago Runs*, Auckland, 1981.

Pitama, T. A. (ed.). *Kaiapohia Pa Centenary Souvenir*, Kaiapoi, 1931.

Pitt-Rivers, G. H. L. *The Clash of Cultures and The Contact of Races*, London, 1927.

Pocock, J. G. A. (ed.). *The Maori in New Zealand Politics*, Wellington, 1965.

Pool, D. I. *The Maori Population of New Zealand*, Auckland, 1977.

Pool, D. I. *Te Iwi Maori*, Auckland, 1991.

Pope, J. H. *Health for the Maori*, Wellington, 1884.

Power, W. T. *Sketches in New Zealand with Pen and Pencil*, London, 1849.

Prichard, M. F. L. (ed.). *The Collected Works of Edward Gibbon Wakefield*, Auckland, 1969.

Pybus, T. A. *The Maoris of the South Island*, Wellington, 1954a.

Pybus, T. A. *Maori and Missionary*, Wellington, 1954b.

Reeves, W. P. *The Long White Cloud*, London 1898, Auckland reprint 1973.

Reid, R. C. *Rambles on the Golden Coast*, Hokitika, 1884.

Rice, G. W. (ed.). *The Oxford History of New Zealand*, Auckland, 1992.

Richards, Rhys. *Murihiku Re-Viewed*, Wellington, 1995.

Rolleston, R. *William & Mary Rolleston*, Wellington, 1971.

Rose, F. G. G. *The Traditional Mode of Production of the Australian Aborigines*, Sydney,1987.

Ross, Angus. 'The Purchase of the South Island', *Otago Daily Times*, Dunedin, 24.2.1940.

Ross, J. O. C. *William Stewart – Sealing Captain Trader and Speculator*, Canberra, 1987.

Rusden, G. W. *Aureretanga – The Groans of the Maoris*, London, 1888.

Rutherford, J. *The Treaty of Waitangi and the Acquisition of British Sovereignty in New Zealand*, Auckland, 1949.

Rutherford, J. *Sir George Grey – A Study in Colonial Government*, London, 1961.

Salmon, J. H. M. *A History of Goldmining in New Zealand*, Wellington, 1963.

Savage, John. *Some Account of New Zealand*, London, 1807.

Schaw, H. *The Metamorphosis of Maoriland*, Wellington, 1893.

Scholefield, G. H. *Captain William Hobson*, Oxford, 1934.

Scholefield, G. H. *A Dictionary of New Zealand Biography*, 2 vols, Wellington, 1940.

Scott, Dick. *Ask That Mountain*, Auckland, 1975.

Scotter, W. H. *A History of Canterbury*, Vol III, Christchurch, 1965.

Selwyn, G. A. *Annals of the Diocese of New Zealand*, London, 1847.

Selwyn, G. A. *A Journal of the Bishop's Visitation Tour 1848*, London, 1849.

Semmel, Bernard. *The Governor Eyre Controversy*, London, 1962.

Sewell, Henry (ed. McIntyre). *The Journal of Henry Sewell 1853–7*, 2 vols, Christchurch 1980.

Sharp, Andrew. *Ancient Voyagers in the Pacific*, Harmondsworth, 1957.

Shepherd, W., & Cook, W. *The Botanic Garden*, Wellington, 1988.

Sherrard, J. M. *Kaikoura – A History of the District*, Kaikoura, 1966.

Sherrard, O. A. *Freedom from Fear*, London, 1959.

Shortland, Edward. *The Southern Districts of New Zealand*, London, 1851.

Shortland, Edward. *Traditions & Superstitions of the New Zealanders*, London, 1856.

Shortland, Edward. *Maori Religion and Mythology*, London, 1882.

Shrimpton, A. W. & Mulgan, A. E. *A History of New Zealand*, Auckland, 1931.

Simpson, Tony. *Te Riri Pakeha: The White Man's Anger*, Auckland, 1986.

Sinclair, Keith. *The Origins of the Maori Wars*, Wellington, 1957.

Skinner, W. H. 'History and Traditions of the Taranaki Coast', *JPS* 19, New Plymouth, 1910.

Smith, Adam. *An Inquiry into the Nature and Causes of the Wealth of Nations*, London 1890.

Smith, S. P. *History & Traditions of the Maoris of the West Coast*, New Plymouth, 1910.

Spokes, Sidney. *Gideon Algernon Mantell*, London, 1927.

Stack, J. W. *Kaiapohia – The Story of a Siege*, Christchurch, 1893.

Stack, J. W. (ed. Reed). *More Maoriland Adventures of J.W. Stack*, Dunedin, 1936.

Stack, J. W. (ed. Reed). *Further Maoriland Adventures of J.W. Stack*, Dunedin, 1938.

Stack, J. W. (ed. Reed). *Through Canterbury and Otago with Bishop Harper*, Christchurch, 1972.

Stephenson, M. A. (ed.). *Mabo: The Native Title Legislation*, St Lucia, Queensland, 1995.

Stevenson, E., & others. *Canterbury Old and New*, Christchurch, 1900.

Stewart, W. D. *William Rolleston*, Christchurch, 1940.

Studholme, E. C. *Te Waimate*, Wellington, 1954.

Sutherland, I. L. G. *The Maori Situation*, Wellington, 1935.

Sutherland, I. L. G. (ed.). *The Maori People Today*, Wellington, 1940.

Sutton, D. G. *The Origins of the First New Zealanders*, Auckland, 1994.

Sweetman, Edward. *The Unsigned New Zealand Treaty*, Melbourne, 1939.

Tainui, Rahera (ed. J. M. McEwen). 'Notes Relating to Ngai-tahu', *JPS* 55, 1946.

Tau, T. M., Goodall, A., Palmer, D., & Tau, H. R. *Te Whakatau Kaupapa*, Wellington, 1990.

Taylor, W. A. *Lore and History of the South Island Maori*, Christchurch, 1950.

Te Kahu, T. W. (ed. S. P. Smith). 'The Wars of Kaitahu and Katimamoe', *JPS* 10, 1901.

Tench, Watkin. *Sydney's First Four Years*, Sydney, 1979.

Thompson, E. P. *Customs in Common*, London, 1993.

Thomson, A .S. *The Story of New Zealand*, 2 vols, London, 1859.

Thomson, J. T. ('Otagonian'). *Rambles with a Philosopher*, Dunedin, 1867.

Thomson, J. T. 'Extracts from a Journal Kept During the Performance of a Reconnaissance Survey of theSouthern Districts of the Province of Otago, N.Z., 1858,' *Journal of the Royal Geographical Society* 28, London, 1858.

Thomson, M. G. (ed. A. Eccles). *A Pakeha's Recollections*, Wellington, 1944.

Tikao, T. T. (ed. Beattie). *Tikao Talks*, Auckland, 1990.

Tiramorehu, M. 'Te Aro, February 7, 1849', *NZS* 17.2.1849.3.

Torlesse, Charles (ed. Maling). *The Torlesse Papers*, Christchurch, 1958.

Tortell, Philip. *New Zealand Atlas of Coastal Resources*, Wellington, 1981.

Travers, W. T. L. *The Stirring Times of Te Rauparaha*, Christchurch, 1906.

Tremewan, Peter. 'King Chigary: The Missing Links', *Te Karanga* (CMSA) 5/2., August 1989.

Tremewan, Peter. *French Akaroa*, Christchurch, 1990.

Tremewan, Peter. *Selling Otago*, Dunedin 1994.

Trevor-Roper, H. *The Rise of Christian Europe* (2nd edn), London, 1966.

Trotter, M., & McCulloch, B. *Unearthing New Zealand*, Wellington, 1989.

Turner, G. M. 'The Mutton-Birders', *Wanderlust*, Auckland, September 1930.

Urlich, D. 'The Introduction & Diffusion of Firearms in New Zealand', *JPS* 79, 1970.

Valkeapaa, Nils-Aslak (transl. Wahl). *Greetings from Lappland: The Sami, Europe's Forgotten People*, London 1983.

Vallance, T. G. 'Gideon Mantell 1791–1852', *Royal Society of N.Z.* 21, Wellington, 1984.

Vayda, A. P. *Maori Warfare*, Wellington, 1960.

Wade, William R. *A Journey in the Northern Island of New Zealand*, Hobart, 1842.

Waite, Fred. *Port Molyneux*, Balclutha, 1940.

Waite, Fred. *Maoris and Settlers in South Otago*, Dunedin, 1980.

Wakefield, E. G. *A Letter from Sydney and Other Writings*, London, 1929: (a) *A Letter from Sydney*, 1829; (b) *The Art of Colonization*, 1833.

Wakefield, E. G. & Ward, H. G. *The British Colonization of New Zealand*, London, 1837.

Wakefield, E. J. *Adventure in New Zealand*, 2 vols, London, 1845.

Ward, Alan. *A Show of Justice*, Auckland, 1983.

Ward, Edward. *The Journal of Edward Ward 1850–51*, Christchurch, 1951.

Ward, Louis E. *Early Wellington*, Auckland 1928.

Wards, Ian. *The Shadow of the Land*, Wellington, 1968.

Watkin, James (ed. Pratt). 'Journal of James Watkin', *The Press*, Christchurch, 1931 (various dates).

Whitcombe and Tombs (publ.). *Our Country*, Christchurch, 1935.

Wilkes, Joanne. 'Walter Mantell, Geraldine Jewsbury, and Race Relations in New Zealand', *NZ Journal of History* 22/2, Auckland, 1988.

Williams, Eric E. *Capitalism & Slavery*, Chapel Hill Nth Carolina, 1961.

Williams, Henry (ed. Rogers). *The Early Journals of Henry Williams*, Christchurch, 1968.

Williams, H. W. *A Dictionary of the Maori Language*, Wellington, 1975.

Williams, J. A. *Politics of the New Zealand Maori*, Auckland, 1969.

Williams, Trevor. 'James Stephen and British Intervention in New Zealand, *Journal of Modern History* 13/1, Chicago, 1941.

Williams, T. C. *A Letter to the Rt Hon W. E. Gladstone on behalf of the Ngati Raukawa Tribe*, Wellington, 1873.

Williment, T. M. I. *John Hobbs*, Wellington, 1985.

Wilson, Eva. *Titi Heritage*, Invercargill, 1979.

Wilson, John. *From Swamp to City*, Christchurch, 1989.

Wilson, John (ed.). *He Korero Purakau Mo Nga Taunahanahatanga a Nga Tupuna*, Wellington,1990.

Wilson, J. O. *New Zealand Parliamentary Record*, Wellington, 1985.

Winiata, Maharaia. *The Changing Role of the Leader in Maori Society*, Auckland, 1967.

Wohlers, J. (transl. J. Houghton). *Memories of the Life of J. F. H. Wohlers*, Dunedin,1895.

Wood, Evelyn. *The Revolt in Hindusta*n, London, 1908.

Woodhouse, A. E. *George Rhodes of the Levels*, Christchurch, 1937.

Woods, J. F. T. *History of the Discovery and Exploration of Australia*, 2 vols, London,1865.

Woolmington, J. (ed.). *Aborigines in Colonial Society 1788–1850*, Armidale NSW, 1988.

Wright, H. M. *New Zealand, 1769–1840*, Cambridge Mass., 1967.

Yate, William. *An Account of New Zealand*, London, 1835.

Ziegler, P. *The Black Death*, London, 1982.

Facsimiles of the Treaty of Waitangi, Wellington, 1976.
The Holy Bible, King James Version, Cambridge.

NEWSPAPERS AND PERIODICALS

Journal of the Polynesian Society, *(JPS)*, New Plymouth & Wellington.
New Zealand Institute Proceedings *(NZI)*, Wellington.
The Australian, Sydney.
The Lyttelton Times *(LT)*, Christchurch.
The Nelson Examiner, Nelson.
The New Zealand Railways Magazine, Wellington.
The New Zealand Spectator and Cook Strait Guardian *(NZS)*, Wellington.

The Otago Daily Times, Dunedin.
The Otago Witness, Dunedin.
The Press, Christchurch.
Proceedings of the Zoological Society, London.
Punch, London.
The Sydney Gazette and New South Wales Advertiser, Sydney.
Wesleyan Methodist Magazine, London.

UNOFFICIAL, UNPUBLISHED MANUSCRIPTS, THESES,
AND OTHER PAPERS

Andersen, Johannes. Ms 148, ATL, Wellington.
Andersen, Johannes. Typed Note in copy of *The Notornis*, Forest & Bird Feb
    1949, AMIL, Auckland.
Anderson, Atholl. 'Mahinga Kai and the Economic Organization of Ngai
    Tahu', a paper read at the NZ Historical Assn. Conference,Christchurch,
    11 May 1991.
Burns, Thomas. 'Diary, 1849', OESM, Dunedin.
Canterbury Association Papers. CMA, Christchurch.
Carrington, A. H. 'Ngaitahu: The Invasion & Occupation of the South
    Island' (1934), ATL,Wellington.
Comber, H.W. 'Journal', Macmillan Brown Library, Christchurch;
    typescript kindly supplied by Prof W. D. McIntyre, 1994.
Creed, Charles. 'Journal & Letters', MAC, Christchurch.
Duff, R. S. ('Akin'). 'Tribal Maori & The Great Society', University of New
    Zealand MA thesis, Christchurch 1943.
Elizabeth 1830 Ship's Articles. NSWSL Ms Ae17, Sydney.
Evison, H. C. 'A History of the Canterbury Maoris (Ngai Tahu) with
    Special Reference to the Land Question', University of New Zealand
    MA thesis, Dunedin,1952.
Fly, HMS, 'Letterbook 1847–1851', ATL qMs, Wellington.
'Gladstone Papers'. BM AddMs, London.
Green, T. E. 'Papers', Private Collection, Tuahiwi.
Greenwood, Joseph H. 'Diary 1841–1847', ATL, Wellington.
Grey, George. 'Diary of Sir George Grey', APL GNZ Mss3, Auckland.
Grey, George. 'Letters', APL GNZ Mss38 & 201, Auckland.
Grey, George. 'Letterbook 1846–1853', APL GNZ Mss227, Auckland.
Grey, George. 'Maori Letters', APL GNZMA (Mmss), Auckland.
Haast, Julius von. 'Papers', ATL Ms37, Wellington.
Hansard, George A. 'The Acheron Journal': see John L. Stokes, below.
Harwood, Octavius. 'Journal', HL M1 438/3, Dunedin.
Heberley, James. 'Reminiscences 1809–1843', ATL qMs, Wellington.
Hocken, Thomas M. 'New Zealand Notes', HL Ms 37, Dunedin.
Hocken, Thomas M. 'Hocken Papers', HL Ms90, Dunedin.
Karetai. Ms 108/90, Ms 808A-B, HL, Dunedin.
Kemp. H. T. 'For Private Circulation', GNZ Ms 201, APL, Auckland.

Kent, John Rodolphus. 'Journal of the Proceedings of HM Colonial Cutter Mermaid, 8 May to 15 August 1823, and Remarks', Ms A4037 (Micro CY1167), NSWSL, Sydney.

Kettle, Charles. 'Letters' (Transcript), HL, M 183, Dunedin.

Kettle, Charles. 'Fieldbook No. 3', DOSLID, Dunedin.

Lands & Survey Papers. CMA, Christchurch.

Lavaud, Charles. 'Voyage et Essai de Colonisation à L'Ile du Sud de la Nouvelle-Zélande', ATL, Wellington

Lewis, Frank. 'Papers', Private Collection, Port Levy.

McGlashan, John. 'Papers', HL Ms M1 463/7, Dunedin.

Mackay, James. 'Collingwood Letterbooks', NAW, Wellington.

McLean, Donald. 'Papers', ATL Ms 32, Wellington.

Mantell, G. A. 'Journal', Ms 1504–1507, ATL, Wellington.

Mantell, W. B. D. 'Papers, Ms83 & various', ATL, Wellington.

Methodist Register of Baptisms & Marriages. Waikouaiti 1840ff MAC, Christchurch.

'Peel Papers'. BM AddMs 4071, London.

Price, Joseph. 'Reminiscences' (transcr. Andersen), CMA Fr361, Christchurch.

Rhodes Family. 'Papers', CMA, Christchurch.

Robinson, Charles Barrington. 'Letters', NAW IA 1 42/1284, 43/255, 43/1425, Wellington.

Selwyn, G. A. 'Journal' (transcript) & 'Letters', CMA, Christchurch.

Selwyn, G. A. 'Map', ATL 830a 1841 (Acc. No. 22,123), Wellington.

Shepherd, T. 'Journal', NSWSL Ms A1966 (Micro CY479) pp 334–387, Sydney.

'Sherborn Autographs'. BM Add Mss 42583, London.

Shortland, Edward. 'The Annexation of New Zealand', HL Ms 489, Dunedin.

Shortland, Edward. 'Middle Island Census', HL Ms 90, Dunedin.

Shortland, Edward. 'Diaries & Journals 1842–1844', APL, Auckland.

Shortland, Edward. 'Letters', HL Ms 86A & B, Dunedin.

Shortland, Edward. 'Middle Island Journal', HL Ms 23, Dunedin.

Shortland, Edward (transl.). 'Narrative of the Origin and Progress of the Wars of Ngatitoa and others with Ngaitahu, by Tamihana son of Te Rauparaha', HL Ms 96, Dunedin.

Shortland, Edward. 'Waiata Book', HL Ms 489, Dunedin.

Stack, James W. 'Report on the Christchurch Diocesan Maori Mission for 1882–1883', HL Ms F & J 6/50, Dunedin.

Stanley, Owen. 'Letters', CPL, Christchurch.

Stokes, John L. 'Journal of the Voyage of the Acheron 1849 to 1851' (reputedly by G. A. Hansard), HL Ms Vol 157, Dunedin.

Stokes, John L. 'Papers', ATL Mss, Wellington.

'Taiaroa Papers'. CMA, Christchurch.

Taki, Paora. 'Events as Told by Paora Taki', transl. Te Aue Davis: Ngai Tahu Submission, S.I. Maori Appellate Court in re Cross Claim Kurahaupo Waka Society & M. N. Sadd, Christchurch, 1990.

Tamihana Te Rauparaha. 'History of Te Rauparaha Written by Tamihana Te Rauparaha at his Father's Dictation 1845', APL GNZ Mmss 27, Auckland.

Tamihana Te Rauparaha. Typed transcription of above, APL GNZ Mmss 27a, Auckland.

Tamihana Te Rauparaha. Translation of above by George Graham 1915–1918, APL GNZ Mmss 27b, Auckland. (Copies also at ATL MSy 2073, Wellington, and HL Ms 874A, Dunedin.)

Tau, Rawiri Te Maire. 'Kurakura Ngai Tahu', University of Canterbury MA thesis, 1992.

Te Kanae, Wiremu Naera. 'Life and Times of Te Rauparaha', (Porirua 1888), transl G. Graham, Grey MNZ Ms, APL, Auckland.

Tuhawaiki. 'Declaration of ownership of Robucka Island by John Touwaick' (Tuhawaiki's Proclamation 28.3.1840), HL Ms 808B, Dunedin.

Waruwarutu, Natanahira. 'Ms Narrative' translated by Te Aritaua Pitama, T.E. Green Mss in Pitama family papers, private collection, Tuahiwi.

Watkin, James. 'Pity Poor Fiji', NSWSL Ms A381, Sydney.

Watkin, James. 'Journal', NSWSL Ms A834–5 (Micro CY189), Sydney.

Watkin, James. 'Letters', MAC, Christchurch.

Watkin, James. 'Letters', HL Ms 1 440/7, Dunedin.

Watkin, James. 'Register of Baptisms', Transcript, HL Ms M1 543/U.

Weller Brothers. 'Letters', NSWSL Ms A1609 (Micro CY117), Sydney.

'Weller Papers'. HL Ms 440.5, Dunedin.

Wellington Philosophical Society. 'Papers' ATL (under 'Royal Society'), Wellington.

'Wentworth-Jones Deeds'. ATL MSO 4947, Wellington, & NSWSL Ms Aw51, Sydney.

'Williams Papers'. AMIL Ms 91/75, Auckland.

Williams, Edward Marsh. 'Journal of a voyage to the Northern and Southern Islands of N.Z. in HMS Herald 1840', ATL Ms 2407, Wellington.

Wills, Alfred. 'Letters' 1848, NZ Company Correspondence, NAC Ch290-7/7 box 2/4, Christchurch.

INDEX

Page numbers in italics refer to maps. The abbreviation 'n' is used after a page reference to refer to a note on that page.

Aboriginal Australians 35–36, 350
Acheron 205, 208, 235, 254
Advances for Settlers Act 334
ahi kaa 23
Akaroa 32, 103–8, 123–25, 128–29,
    131–32, 135, *136*, 152, 159, 172,
    179, 194–95, 202–3, 205, 221,
    253
Akaroa purchase 255–56, *256, 279*,
    310
Aldred, John 255, 258, 260
Anglem, Captain 68–69
Aorere goldfields 262
Aotearoa 337, 352
Arahura purchase 266, 268, *279*,
    310
Atkinson, Harry 321, 325
Aube 103–5
Australian Patriotic Association 79

Ballance, John 323, 326
Banks Peninsula 98, 103, 104–5,
    106, 107, 123–24, 128–29, 137,
    153, 159, 171, 174, 215–16, *219*,
    228, 253–54, *see also* Horomaka
Barker, Lady Mary Anne 281
Barrett, Dicky 60
Beagle 139
Bell, Francis Dillon 142, 189
Belligny, Pierre de 104, 107–8,
    128–29, 135, 152–53, 160, 216,
    219
Bérard, Auguste 123, 129, 137,
    152, 160, 219
Boulcott's farm, attack on 162–63

Boultbee, John 40, 41, 43
Bourke, Richard 54, 69, 75, 79
Bowen, Sir George 292
Bracken, Thomas 331
Britannia 31
British and Foreign Aborigines
    Protection Society 85
British and Foreign Bible Society
    120
Britomart 103–4
Brittan, William Guise 246
Brown, Colonel Thomas Gore 248,
    253–54, 266, 272–73
Browne, Gordon 53
Bruce, Captain James 79, 91, 179,
    188
Brunner, Thomas 262
Bryce, John 318–19, 321
Buffalo 97
Bull, Lieutenant 188
Buller, James 273–74
Buller, Walter Lawry 272–73
Bunbury, Major Thomas 97, 98,
    99, 102, 107
Bunn and Company 50
Burdon, R. M. 344
Busby, James 69, 102
Butler, Revd John 34
Butler, Samuel 258, 281

Caddell, James 33–39
Cadman, Alfred 332, 334
Cameron, General 274
cannibalism 21, 33, 34, 37, 43, 49,
    50, 51, 52, 53, 58, 88

Canterbury 202, 214
Canterbury Association Lands
    Settlement Act (1850) 225, 228
Canterbury Association 202, 225–
    27, 257
Canterbury settlement 202, 214,
    230, 236
Cargill, Captain William 241, 245
Carrington, Octavius 217, 218, 220
Carroll, James 339
Cass, Thomas 202
Catholic mission 118
Cattlin, Captain 89, 90
Cécille, Captain 77
Chapman, Henry 224
Chatham Islands 104
Cheviot station 301, 332
Christchurch 227, *see also*
    Putaringamotu
Church Missionary Society 34,
    74–75, 89, 92, 110, 120, 131, 160,
    161–62, 272
Clarke, George (Chief Protector)
    110, 159, 161–62, 175n
Clarke, George (junior) 142, 148,
    155
Clayton, Captain 77, 80, 124
Clementson, chief mate of *Elizabeth*
    52–54
Clifford, Charles 164, 226
Cloudy Bay 65, 75, 100
colonisation schemes 39, 83–86,
    103, 139, *141*, 202, 338
Comber, Henry 100
Comte de Paris 103, 105
Congreve, Sir William 239, 260
Constitution Act (1852) 245, 253
convicts 27, 29–31, 35, 49, 113
Cook, Captain James 24–25, 27, 29
Cook, William 40, 50
Cooper, Holt and Rhodes 80, 123
Cowan, James 337
Cowell, master of *Elizabeth* 52–54
Cowlishaw, William 292, 298, 316
Creed, Charles 120, 144–45, 229, 240
crime and punishment, in 18th
    century Britain 28–31

Crocombe, Joseph 151
Crown Lands Amendment and
    Extension Ordinance (1851) 227
Crown pastoral leases 227

Darling, Governor Ralph 53-54, 69
Darwin, Charles 139, 283, 303, 342
Deans family 127, 129, 153, 178,
    179, 195, 198, 225–26, 227–28
Deborah 144–46
Department for the Protection of
    Aborigines 110
Disqualification Act (1876) 320
Dobson, Arthur 275–77
Domett, Alfred 239
Driver 159, 160, 163
Dromedary 34
Druid 89
Duff, Roger 343–44
Durham, Earl of 84
Dusky Sound 32

East India Company 27, 31, 32
Edwardson, Captain William 34
Elizabeth 37, 39, 52–54, 69
Ellesmere, Lake *see* Waihora
Engels, Friedrich 326
Evans, Dr George 87
Eyre, Edward John 170–71, 173–
    74, 189, 193–94, 202–5, 207, 209,
    217, 221–22, 223–24, 236, 240,
    247, 283–84, 333

Favorite 107
Fenton, Francis Dart 272, 278,
    289–91, 295, 297, 301, 303, 308,
    314–15, 318, 320, 330, 349
Fighting Bay, *see* Oraumoa
firearms: and southern Maoris 37,
    38–39; consequences of introduc-
    tion 49; musket trade 40, 60;
    northern musket wars 46; use by
    Te Whakataupuka 41–42
Firth, Josiah Clifton 331
Fisheries Act (1983) 346
FitzGerald, James Edward 226, 254
FitzHerbert, Sir William 320

FitzRoy, Captain Robert 129, 139–
44, 147, 151–53, 158, 337–38
flax, *see* harakeke
Fly 173, 178–79, 183, 186, 194–95,
312
food, Maori: 1840s agriculture 177;
damage to mahinga kai 281, 328–
29; gathering 20; kumara 19;
potatoes 33; preparation of 21;
putangitangi 61; regional specialties
19; sources of 18; staple foods of
1860s 280–81; titi 18, 20, 37; tutu
135; usual diet 39, 130, 226, 235;
vegetable crops 33
Foster, C. J. 298–99
Fox, William 202–4, 207, 214–15,
216, 222, 273, 278
Fraser, Alfred 339
French Farm, *see* Te Rautahi
Fyffe, Alexander 240

General Gates 34, 37
Gilfillan murders 168
Gipps, Sir George 79, 86, 89, 90,
97, 102, 104, 110–11, 115–16,
125, 140, 151, 160
Gisborne, William 303
Glenmark station 257, 259, 301
Godfrey, Lt-Col Edward 115–16,
123, 124, 129, 159
Godley, John Robert 226, 228
gold mining 262, 275, 277, 280
Grassmere, Lake, *see* Kaparatehau
Green, T. E. 339
greenstone, *see* pounamu
Greenwood brothers 128, 135–37,
142, 153
Gresson, Justice 297-8
Grey, Captain George 152, 158–
76, 193, 198, 199, 214, 222, 224,
230, 253, 272, 349; in Australia
111–12; appointed Governor of
New Zealand 158; quells Heke's
uprising 153, 158–60; Hutt
Valley disputes 160–61, 162–63;
grants Otago block 161; and
CMS missionaries 161–62;

befriends Ngati Toa chiefs 163;
seizes Te Rauparaha 163;
appointed Governor-in-Chief
165; purchases Porirua and
Wairua blocks 166–68; and Eyre
170–71; releases Te Rauparaha
171; meets Ngai Tahu at Akaroa
(1848) 172-3; reports on waste
lands 178; sets price for Ngai
Tahu payment 178; open letter
from Tiramorehu 204–5;
response to Te Rauparaha's and
Metehau's letters to Queen 208–
10; extends Crown leases 227–28;
and Mantell 236–37; receives
Maori complaints 237–40; leaves
New Zealand 241, 243; second
term as Governor 274; becomes
Premier 309; at Smith-Nairn
commission 318; death of 333;
Reeves's assessment of 337–38
Grey, Earl (Lord Howick) 165,
166, 173
Grose, Major Francis 31
Guard, John 60, 64, 68–69, 76

Haast, Julius 275
Hadfield, Revd Octavius 89, 119–
20, 142, 164
Haereroa 61, 79, 91, 92, 201, 250
Hakaroa, Hoani Papita 59, 129,
153, 223, 253, 255, 259
Hall, John 290, 292, 321
Halswell, Edmund 113, 114
Hamilton, William John
Warburton 205, 254–55, 256,
257, 258, 259, 333, 349
Hape, Merekihereka 250
harakeke: British use of 18; Maori-
European trade in 35, 36, 37–38;
Maori use of 18
Harlequin 65
Harriet 68
Hawea 20, 74
Hawes, Benjamin 165
Hay, Ebenezer 127, 129, 171
health, Maori: 1880s statistics 323;

diseases as cause of death 70–71,
149; effect of contact with whalers
76, 149; epidemics 78, 149–50,
232n, 243; European-introduced
diseases 71, 74; pre-European
24; provision of hospitals 245–
46; swamps and disease 150
Heaphy, Charles 262
Hector, James 275
Heke, Hone 153, 158–60
Hempleman, George 77, 79, 88
Herald 96, 97, 98, 99, 100, 103
Herd, Captain James 39
*Heremaia Mautai and Hoani Timaru
v. The Queen* 297
Heroine 77
Hesketh, Henry 89, 91, 99
Hight, James 337
Hobson, Captain William 75, 86,
89, 95–96, 103–4, 106, 110, 114,
123, 337–38
Honekai 25, 32, 33, 38
Honira, Whero 238
Hope, G. W. 159
Horomaka 76–80, 81n, *106, see also*
Banks Peninsula
Howitt, Herbert 275
Howland, Seth 220
Huruhuru 132–34, 207
Hutt Valley dispute 153, 160, 162–63

Inflexible 168–73
Ironside, Samuel 118, 120, 123
Iwikau 98, 105, 107, 124, 129
Iwikau, Haukeke 56, 197
Izard and Bell 310

jade, *see* pounamu
Johnson, J. G. 254
Joint Parliamentary Committee
(1889) 326
Jones, John 71, 79, 89, 90, 92, 117,
120, 124–25, 126n, 145–46, 151,
201
Kahuti (Blueskin) 201, 207, 229
Kai Huanga feud 38, *42,* 43, 50, 56,
60

Kai Tahu 26n
Kaiapohia 56, 333, 336n
Kaiapoi 166, 172–73, 180, 196,
235, 239, 240, 260, 351; defences
of 50, fall prophesied 55–56,
origin of name 20, siege and fall
of 56–58, skirmish with Ngati
Toa 50–51
Kaihope 105, 124
Kaikoareare 59, 60, 93n, 201, 223,
229
Kaikoura 188, 240, 256, 263
Kaikoura purchase *264, 279,* 310
Kaikoura Whakatau 228, 240, 243,
256, 259, 263
Kaitorete 70, 166, 172, 198, 228–
29, 239
Kaituna 218–19
Kakapo Bay 60
Kakongutungutu 105, 124, 156n,
171
Kaparatehau 61, 63, 64
Kapiti Island 46, 49, 53
Karaki 78
Karaweko 255, 259, 307
Karetai 61, 68, 69, 79, 93n, 100,
148–49, 173, 179, 185, 190, 207
Katu, *see* Tamihana Te Rauparaha
Kawatiri 239
Kekerengu 50
Kelly, Captain James 68
Kemp, Henry Tacy 162, 169, 173–
74, 177–92, 193, 209–10, 240,
310, 312, 314, 333, 349
Kemp, James 162
Kemp's deed (1848) 183-8, 194,
206, 223, 225, 283, 289–92, 295,
297
Kemp's purchase 177–92, *181,* 205,
215, 222–23, 228–29, 255, *279,*
298, 310, 313, 315, 324, 345, 351
Kent, Captain John 36, 37, 39
Kettle, Charles 173, 179, *187,* 188,
225, 237
Kettle's sketch map 183, 186, 191n,
195–97, 206–7, 223, 291–92, 351
Kihau 202, 206, 207

Koeti 186, 223
Koputai (Port Chalmers) 148
Korako, Hoani Wetere 100, 120
Korehe 185
Koroko 71, 79-80, 116, 120, 131, 134
Kororareka 96
Koti 185
Kukurarangi 55

Labouchere, Henry 246–47, 249
Lambton 39
land, Maori reserves 155, 161, 166, 182, 183, 188–90, 193–94, 198, 199, *200*, 202, 207, 217, *219*, 220–22, 230–31, 236–37, *242*; abolition called for 304; Akaroa 255; Arowhenua 257–58, 293–95, 329; Grey's intention towards 318; Kaikoura 263–64; Kaitorete 291; Kemp's confirmation of 314; Mackay's recommendations 324, 327; Mantell's Banks Peninsula reserves *219*; Mantell's Maori reserves for Kemp's purchase 198–201, *200*; Mawhera 276–77, 325; Moeraki 199, 222–25, 273–74, 328; Murihiku 237, 243, 324; North Canterbury 259–61; perpetual leases 325; Pigeon Bay 229; Port Chalmers 240; Port Levy 220, 260, 285; Princes Street 240, 280, 296, 309; Purakaunui 296; Purau 218, 260; Rapaki 218, 260, *285*, 295; surrendered by Ngati Toa 244; Taiaroa Head lighthouse 296; Taieri 237; Taumutu 198–99, 295; territory requested by Poutini Ngai Tahu 267; Tuahiwi 260, 274, 285, 295, 329; Waikouaiti 201, 225, 327–28; Wairewa 329; Waitaki 294, 328; West Coast 263, 266, *267*, 268; whakarite clause 289, 295
Land Claims Commission 89, 91, 123

Land Claims Ordinance Act (1841) 115, 121, 217
Land for Settlements Acts (1892 & 1894) 332, 334, 339
Lands for Settlement 340, *341*
land purchases (listed individually), *see* Akaroa, Arahura, Kaikoura, Kemp's, North Canterbury, Rakiura, Waipounamu, Wairau, Wentworth-Jones
Langlois, Captain Jean 77, 103–5, 152
Lavaud, Captain Charles 103–4, 107–8, 114, 123
Leathart, Captain 77, 80, 98, 123
Love, John, *see* Tikao
Lyttelton 225; *see also* Port Cooper

Macandrew, James 297
Macassey, James Livingstone 296
McCleverty, Lt-Col William 162, 166, 169, 193
Mackay, Alexander 261, 263, 266, 284–85, 290, 295, 297, 301–2, 415, 318, 321, 324–25, 326–27, 330, 332, 339, 340
Mackay, James (junior) 261–64, *264*, *265*, 266, 268, 330, 340, 349
Mackay, James (senior) 261
McKenzie, John 332, 334
McKillop, Midshipman 163
McLean, Sir Donald 188, 240–41, 243–44, 253, 256, 261, 263, 272–73, 308–9, 349
Magnet 79, 91
Malthus, Thomas 83
Mantell, Dr Gideon 87–88, 143, 170, 222
Mantell, Walter Baldock Durrant 87–88, 143, 162, 169–70, 171, 193–213, 228, 230, 236–37, 240–41, *242*, 243, 245-9, 273–74, 278, 280, 282–83, 284, 289–90, 296–97, 298, 303, 310–11, 319, 333, 349
Maopo 185, 219–20
Maori: burial customs 24, 64;

conversion to Christianity 119–20; customary land rights 22–23; economy in 1840s 130; importance of travel to 23; language, southern dialect 25, 92–93, 117, 131; seafaring 40, 124, 132–34; settlement of New Zealand 15; religious beliefs 18–19, 24, 277; *see also* food, health, population, social structure, warfare,

Maori Appellate Court 347

Maori Representation Act (1867) 285

Marsden, Revd Samuel 34, 54, 68, 75, 110

Martin, William 165–66, 224, 246, 272

Matilda 37

Maungaatua 146, *147*, 148

Mautai, Heremaia 59, 107, 129, 153, 190, 223, 255-6, 259, 291, 293, 298, 333

Measly Beach 70

Mermaid 36

Metehau, Teoti Wiremu 169, 179–80, 182, 195, 197, 198, 203, 205, 208–10, 213n, 223, 248, 273, 310–11, 333, 354

Mill, John Stuart 303

Moki 20

Momo 56, 58, 70

Monro, Dr David 144–46, 150

Moore, George Henry 257, 301

Moore, W. H. 53–54

Morgan, Lewis 326

Motukikarehu 218

Muaupoko 46

Murihaka 38

Murihiku 15, 16, 33, 34, *36*, 37, 235–37, 241, *242*, 278, *279*, 310

Murphy, Michael 104, 105

muskets, *see* firearms

Naihira, Wiremu 190, 223, 295, 307, 329, 333

Nairn, Francis 310, 314

Nanto-Bordelaise Company 77, 103–4, 108, 124, 159, 216, 222

Native Land Act (1865) 278

Native Land Act (1909) 340

Native Land Court 278, 289-90, 296-8, 318, 330

Native Land Court Act (1894) 334

Native Land Purchase Department 240

Native Lands Act (1867) 292

Native Reserves Act (1856) 271

Native Reserves Commissioners 271, 272, 273

Native Schools Act (1867) 285

Native Trusts Act (1844) 245

'natives', European view of 27, 85, 86, 110–11, 113, 117–18, 140, 146, 150, 151–52, 229, 271, 273, 325–26, 331, 335, 337-8, 342-45

Nelson 113–14, 143–44

New Edinburgh settlement 139, 143, 146, 154–55, 161; *see also* Otago settlement

Nene, Waka 169

New Munster 165, 170, 202, 214, 227, 236, 239

New Ulster 165, 227

New Zealand Association 84, 97

New Zealand Company 39, 96, 102, 113, 115, 121, 151, 171, 178, 188, 202, 218; acres purchased 159; 'buys' land from Te Rauparaha 88–90; buys out Nanto-Bordelaise Company 216; ceases operation 225; 'compensation' for Maoris 159; driven from Wairau 121–23, 140–44; finances 155; Hutt Valley dispute 160; Kemp's purchase 193–94, 215; Nelson settlement 114-15, 226; New Edinburgh settlement 139, 143–44, 146, 154–55; New Munster 170; North Island settlements *141*; Otago purchase 161; Pennington's awards 159; Port Nicholson settlement 84–85, 86–87, 113; Royal Charter 113; squatters 127–28, 226;

'tenths' 85, 112–13, 114, 154, 306; undermines FitzRoy 158; Wanganui settlement 164
New Zealand Constitution Act (1846) 165
New Zealand Constitution Act (1852) 240
New Zealand Land Claims Act (1840) 102, 115
New Zealand Society (1851) 236
Nga Puhi 46
Nga Roimata 52-53
Ngai Tahu: 1832 population of 60; 1834 tauanui 64–65; 1839–1840 taua 88; and 'European values' 349; and *Elizabeth* affair 52–55; and French at Akaroa 106–7; Cadman's scheme 332; chiefs 'sell' land 79, 90, 105; Claim Settlement Act (1944) 345; claim taken to Native Land Court (1868) 289–97; counterattack on Ngati Toa 61–65, *62*; division over Banks Peninsula 105; division over Kemp's purchase 190; dominance of 25; Eyre dismisses grievances 204; fall of Kaiapoi 55–58; farming expertise 260–61; 'Heads of Agreement' 352; hospitality of 135; impoverishment of 230–31, 302; Kaikoura claim 263; land allocations (1906) 339–42, *341*; land claim 304–8; land leased to squatters 153; land ownership dispute with Ngati Toa 164, 168; land purchased 279; Mackay Royal Commission (1886) 324; Maori Appellate Court judgment 347–48; Maori Trust Board 345, 346; marriage alliance with Ngati Mamoe 25; measles epidemic 70; meeting with Grey at Akaroa 172; meeting with Kemp at Akaroa 179–80; meeting with Mantell at Akaroa 203; *Ngai Tahu Report* 348–49; *Ngai Tahu*

Sea Fisheries Report 350-1; no payment from McLean 244; Otago purchase 148–49; Parinuiowhiti boundary 65; plunder of Otakou whaling station 68; population 60, 253, 352; privatisation of land 271–72; protest against Kettle's map 195; 'psychological failure' 343–44; raid by Te Puoho 72–74, *73*; regain Poutini coast 74; royal commission (1921) 342; Smith-Nairn Royal Commission 309–19, 321, 323; Supreme Court appeal 297–99; territory of 20; Tiramorehu airs dispute 204–5; Treaty signatures 109n; tribal territory in 1870 301; Waitangi Tribunal claim 346–48
Ngai Tahu Claim Settlement Act (1944) 345
Ngai Tahu Reference Validation Act (1868) 298, 316, 325
Ngai Tarewa 52
Ngai Te Ruahikihiki 303
Ngai Tuahuriri 20, 39, 41, 51, 56, 58, 61, 64, 70, 78, 105, 110, 153, 166, 172, 179–80, 194–95, 196–97, 198, 230, 238, 253–54, 255–57, 258–59, 273, 282, 311, 346
Ngati Apa 46, 48, 50
Ngati Awa 65n
Ngati Haua-te-rangi 162
Ngati Huirapa 56, 61, 335
Ngati Irakehu 38, 52
Ngati Koata 241, 244
Ngati Kuia 48, 55, 244
Ngati Kuri 20, 24, 48, 50, 166, 168, 239, 240, 263
Ngati Mako 59, 291
Ngati Mamoe 20, 25
Ngati Mutunga 64
Ngati Rahiri 244
Ngati Rangatahi 160
Ngati Rarua 55–56, 64, 74, 75, 241, 244
Ngati Raukawa 48, 64, 238

Ngati Ruanui 65, 68–69
Ngati Tama 55, 72, 100, 244
Ngati Toa 46, 50, 51, 53, 55, 61,
  63, 64, 70, 78, 80n, 88, 100, 121,
  123, 142, 163, 164, 168, 172, 196,
  204, 230, 237, 239, 241, 243–44
Ngati Wairangi 20
Ngawhakawa 74
Nias, Captain Joseph 96–100
Niho 55–56, 72, 74
Nohomutu 107, 128, 217
Nohorua 100, 166
Normanby, Lord 86, 99, 194, 308
North Canterbury 257, 258, *259*,
  260
North Canterbury purchase *259*,
  279, 310
North Star 140
Notornis mantelli 170, 222, 232n

Oliver, Commander 173, 188
Omihi, capture of 50
Onawe, siege and fall of 58–59
Onekakara 76
Onuku 32
Oraumoa, battle at 64
Oriental 88, 143
Otago 146, 148; *see also* Otakou
Otago Provincial Council 245
Otago purchase 139–57, *147*, 156n,
  161, 173, *181*, *279*, 310, 346, 348
Otago settlement 171, 173, 179,
  235, 236
Otakou 37, 145–47, 272; *see also*
  Otago
Owen, Professor Richard 199, 249

Pahi 34, 37
Paitu 78, 207
Paka, Noa 207
Pakaariki Bay 32, 108, 124, 128,
  152
Pakipaki, *see* Metehau
Parapara 72
Parata, Tame 323, 332, 339
Parihaka 321
Parure 59, 129

Patuki, Topi 74, 79, 91, 94n, 202–3,
  204, 205, 207, 219, 235, 237, 238,
  250, 307, 327
Peel, Sir Robert 164
Pennington, J. A. 113-14, 121, 124,
  158–59
Pere, John 53–54, 185, 207
Pereita, Henare 290
Phillip, Captain Arthur 29, 30, 31,
  35
Pigeon Bay 127, 171, 172, 229–30,
  232n, 239
Piopiotahi 16
Pireka 88
Pitt-Rivers, G. H. L. 343
Poharama 228
Pohau, Kiriona 185, 198, 203, 205,
  206–7, 219–20, 228, 291, 292, 293
Poheahea, Hohaia 239
Pohio, Horomona (Solomon) 120,
  185, 199, 201, 204, 259, 284, 293,
  295, 307–9
Pohue 124
Pokene, Te Whaikai 61, 93n, 185,
  195, 220, 223, 238
Pope, James 321–22
population, Maori: at Port Levy
  198; decline in 149–50; in 1854
  253; Ngai Tahu in 1832 60; Ngai
  Tahu in 1997 352; Ngati Kuri
  263; Poutini Ngai Tahu 262; pre-
  European 16, 20; Shortland's
  census 1843 130–31; southern
  tribes in 1834 67n
Porirua purchase 164, 166, *167*, 168
Poroutawao 164
Port Bunn 50, 60, 76
Port Cooper 127, 144-5, 153, *181*,
  202, 214–16, 218, *279*
Port Greenwood, *see* Purau
Port Jackson 30, 31
Port Levy 128, 214–16, 218, 220,
  279
Port Nicholson 84–85, 87, 98–99,
  113, 163, *167*
Port Pegasus 39–40, 99
Potiki, Wiremu 185, 201

pounamu 16, 17, 20, 110, 130, 266, 268
Poutini Ngai Tahu 20, 55, 74, 110, 260, 262, 266, 267, 268, 275
Prendergast, James 309
Prince of Denmark 39
Protectorate Department 111, 160, 165, 245
Puaha, Rawiri 163, 164, 166, 168, 169, 235, 237–38, 239, 262
Puaka 254
Puari 110, 196–97
Pukenui, Apera 107, 185, 218–21
Puketeraki 196
Purau 128, 135, 142
Putaringamotu 127, 153, 195, 198

Queen Charlotte Sound, *see* Totaranui

R v. Symonds 309
Rakaihautu 180
Rakiihia 25
Rakiura purchase *279*
Rangitane 46, 48, 50, 121, 241, 244
Rangiwhakatia 61
Rapuwai 20
Rata, Matiu 346
Rattlesnake 75
rau patu 23, 175n
Raven, Captain William 31
Rees, William Lee 330–31, 334
Reeves, William Pember 337–38
Regia 92
Rennie, George 139 40
Rhin 135, 137
Rhodes family 80, 98, 103, 123, 153, 178, 226, 227–28, 245, 257–58, 291
Richmond, Christopher 272
Richmond, Major Mathew 115–16, 125, 142, 153, 160, 164, 237–38, 243
Riggs, Captain Abimelech 34
'right of discovery' 29, 86, 97, 99, 107
Ripapa pa 38, 43

Robinson, Charles Barrington 104, 105, 107–8, 128–29, 130, 137, 152–53, 156n, 216, 221, 255, 301–2
Rochfort, John 266, 268
Rolleston, William 269n, 278–80, 283, 285, 289–90, 292–93, 298, 318, 323–22, 325–26, 333, 349
Rosanna 39
Royal Charter (1846) 165
Royal Commission on Native Land Laws 330
Royal Commissions regarding Ngai Tahu claim: 1879, 309–22; 1886, 324; 1890, 326–30; 1914, 340; 1921, 342
Ruaparae 59, 153
Ruapuke Island 34, 69, 91, 99, 100, 146, 149
runholders, Canterbury 257–58, *259*, 281, 301–2
Russell, Lord John 96, 102, 110–14, 121, 139, 165, 245

Scotia 145
Scott, David 146, 155
sealers *31*, 32, 33, 34, 37, 39–40
seals, Maori use of 18
Seddon, Richard 333-4
Selwyn, Bishop George Augustus 114, 137, 144, 165-6, 189–90, 272
Servantes, Lieutenant 166, 168
Sewell, Henry 271, 274
Sheehan, John 309
Shortland, Edward 120–24, 128–38, *133*, 138n, 142, 148, 152, 162, 197-8, 278, 291, 333
Shortland, Lt Willoughby 123
Simeon, Charles 240
Sinclair family 127, 129, 152, 156n, 159, 171, 218
Sisters 152
slavery 27, 110
Smith, Adam 83
Smith, Stephenson Percy 332, 339
Smith, Thomas 310, 313, 314–15, 319

Smith-Nairn Royal Commission 309–19, 320, 323, 352

Snapper 34

social structure, Maori: class distinctions 22; effect of Christianity on 190; iwi 22; male and female roles in 22; marriage alliances 25; role of ariki in 22, 38; southern, in 1840s 130

Sophia 68

South Island Landless Natives Act (1906) 339, 340, 342

Spain, Commissioner William 114, 115, 121, 142, 148, 163–64, 168

Stack, James West 272, 303–6, 309, 314, 333

Stafford, Edward 249, 298

Stanley, Lord 121, 152, 154, 158–59, 160, 215, 216

Stanley, Owen 103–4, 105–6, 128

Stewart Island 99

Stewart Island purchase 310, 346

Stewart, Captain John 52-4

Stewart, William (adventurer) 39, 98, 99

Stewart, William (cartographer) 39

Stokes, Captain John Lort 205, 207, 215, 221, 235–36, 348

Stout, Robert 323–24

Success 89

Sutherland, Professor Ivan 343

Swainson, William 272

Sydney Cove 33

Sydney Packet 71

Symonds, John Jermyn 143, 145, 148, 154–55, 159, 162, 246

taepo 18, 277

Taetae 186, 223

Taiaroa, Hori Kerei 303, 307–8, 309–10, 320, 321, 323, 327, 332

Taiaroa, Matenga 37, 38, 39, 41, 43, 56, 60, 65, 68, 74, 79, 88, 90, 93n, 105, 123, 144, 146, 148, 182–83, 185, 197, 201, 203, 205, 206, 219, 238–39, 241, 273

Taieri Plain 146–47

Tainui, Ihaia 275–76, 310, 320

Tainui, Wereta 185, 198, 239, 266, 290

takahe (*Notornis hochstetteri*) 222, 232

Takapuneke 38, 52

take tupuna 23

take tuku 23

Takere 55

Taki, Paora 223, 255

Tamakeke 59, 107, 129, 219–20, 221, 223, 248

Tamanuiarangi (John Patterson) 285

Tamatea 24, 25, 76

Tangaroa 19

Tangatahara 51, 58–59, 61

Tapuae o Uenuku 15, 25n

Taranaki War (1861) 274

Tarapuhi 223, 262, 266, 268, 275–77

Tarawhata 61, 134–35, 199, 207

Tau, Henare Rakiihia 346

Tau, Paora 180, 183, 185, 195–97, 206, 255

Taumutu 32, 38, 44

Taununu 38, 41, 43

Tautuku 297

Tawera 196

Tawha 291, 293

Taylor, Revd Richard 169–70

Te Ahu Patiki 76

Te Aorahui 239

Te Ati Awa 48, 55, 65n, 78, 88, 100, 169, 241, 243, 244, 273

Te Awaiti 51

Te Hau Tapunuiotu 25, 32

Te Hiko 52, 56, 59, 75, 206

Te Hori, Pita 273

Te Kahu, Tiare Wetere 120, 185, 313

Te Kanae 347

Te Karoro 150

Te Maiharanui 38, 44, 45n, 51–53, 64, 177

Te Maiharoa 308–9, 314

Te Maire, Rawiri 223, 308–9, 328

Te Mamaku 162, 163, 164, 168
Te Mamaru, Rawiri 207
Te Matahara 223
Te Pai 34, 37
Te Parinuiowhiti 19
Te Pehi Kupe 50, 51–52, 55
Te Poka 228
Te Puoho o te Rangi 72, 73, 74
Te Raho, 63
Te Raki, Wiremu 177, 185
Te Rangihaeata 50, 121, 122, 140,
  160, 163, 168
Te Rauparaha 44, 160; character
  46; leads heke south 46, 47; takes
  Kapiti 46-8; captures Hotuiti 46;
  captures Kaikoura 48–49; trades
  from Kapiti 49; and brig *Eliza-
  beth* 52–53; takes Ngai Tahu
  captives to Kapiti 53; invades
  South Island (1831–1832) 55, 57;
  sacks Tuahiwi 56; besieges
  Kaiapoi 56; South Island
  victories 57; warned by Te Raho
  63; near capture by Ngai Tahu
  63–64; counterattack by Ngai
  Tahu (1834) 64–65; prepares for
  invasion of Murihiku 69; sends
  peace embassy to Ngai Tuahuriri
  70; falls out with Te Ati Awa 78;
  enmity towards southern Ngai
  Tahu 78–79; 'sells' land to New
  Zealand Company 88–90;
  releases prisoners 89; signs
  Treaty 99; consents to Nelson
  settlement 114; Wairau Massacre
  122–23, 142; abducted by Grey
  163; captivity 168; release 170–
  71; letter to Queen 208
Te Rauparaha, Tamihana (Katu) 89,
  119, 123, 163, 164, 166, 168, 272
Te Rautahi 124, 152
Te Rehe 59, 134, 223
Te Reko 237
Te Ruaparae 129, 223
Te Tai Poutini 16
Te Tai Tapu 121
Te Uki, Wiremu Teone 153, 172, 180,

182, 183, 185, 198-9, 203, 205, 207,
  217, 222, 307, 312–13, 333
Te Wai Pounamu 15, 16
Te Wera 34, 37, 39
Te Whakarukeruke 81n, 107, 183,
  185, 190, 195, 203, 217, 223
Te Whakataupuka 38, 40–41, 43,
  44, 50, 59, 60, 61, 64, 65, 68, 69–
  70, 71, 177
Te Whe 52
Te Wherowhero 169, 170
Te Whiti-o-Rongomai 321
Te Whiwhi (Henare Matene) 89,
  119, 123, 163, 166, 168, 237–38,
  262
terra nullius 29, 350
Thierry, Charles de 39
Thomas, Captain Joseph 202–3,
  214, 216, 220
Thompson, Henry 122, 142
Tiakikai 217
Tihau, Irai 293, 295
Tikao (John Love): signs Treaty of
  Waitangi 98; signs French deed
  (1840) 107; champions Maori
  land rights 128, 134–35; and
  Governor Grey 173; and Kemp's
  purchase 180–83; signs Kemp's
  deed 185; and Mantell 195, 203–5,
  248; and Eyre 204; signs Kemp's
  purchase receipt 206; opposes
  Mantell's Bank's Peninsula
  purchases 218–21; protests at
  Wairau purchase 224; writes to
  Governor Grey 229; dies 234n
Tikao, Teone Taare 307, 339
Tikao, Tamati 259, 272
Timaru, Hoani 259, 298
Tioriori 196
Tiramorehu, Matiaha: mana 78;
  settles at Moeraki 78; Wesleyan
  convert 120; and Shortland 131;
  and river-crossing 138n; and
  Kemp's deed 180–85, and
  Mantell, 1849 195, 199; and
  Kemp's purchase payments 199,
  207, 223; and Mantell's reserves

203, 273; launches Ngai Tahu
claim 204; protests to Grey 204–
5; protests to Eyre 221–24;
protests to McLean and Wynyard
243; books from Mantell 246; and
Mantell's promises 248; writes to
Queen 250; northern land rights
257, 284; petitions General
Assembly 284; pursues Ngai Tahu
claim 303, 305–7; at Smith-Nairn
Commission 312; dies 333
Tirikatene, E. T. 345
Toetoe 39
Tohowaiki 90, 94n
Tokitoki 34, 35
Tongan Wesleyan Mission 71-2
Torlesse, Charles 202–3, 208, 214,
222, 230, 239
Tory 85, 88
Totaranui (Queen Charlotte Sound)
25, 33
Townsend, Charles 275
trade, Maori–European: in flax 35,
36, 37–38, 39; in muskets 40,
46–48, 60; in preserved heads 49,
53, 64, 68, 75; in produce, wool
and meat 177; with settlers 226;
with whalers 76
Treaty of Waitangi (1840) 355;
adjudged a 'nullity' 309; allegations of Crown breaches 346; at
Onuku 98; British sovereignty
proclaimed 98, 99, 100; English
version 96; guarantee of tino
rangatiratanga 115; Hobson
claims 'universal adherence' 98–
99; obtaining signatures 96;
prevents French purchase of
Banks Peninsula 107; provisions
of 95–96; 'right of pre-emption'
96–97; select committee report
on 151–52; signing 95; South
Island signatures 99–100, *101*,
107; Treaty of Waitangi Act
(1975) 346; Waitangi Tribunal
346
Treaty of Waitangi Act (1975) 346

Tregear, Edward 331
Tu Te Hounuku 38, 64–65
Tua Marina 122
Tuahiwi 56, 280, 306
Tuahuriri 20, 196
Tuahuru 223
Tuauau 32, 59, 77, 79, 107, 124,
129, 223
Tuckett, Frederick 123, 143–50,
154, 155n
Tuhawaiki: leads Tauaiti 61;
ambushes Te Rauparaha 63;
Oramoa battle 64, Tauanui 65;
visits Sydney 68; defeats Te
Puoho 74; Peter Williams's
permit 76; Sydney land sales 79;
1839 taua 88; and Governor
Gipps 89–90; Wentworth-Jones
'purchase' 90–91, 93n; Ruapuke
proclamation 91; signs Treaty of
Waitangi 99–100, 108n, 109n;
commercial pursuits 110; and
Watkin's mission 117, 119; Land
Claims Commission 124–25;
meets FitzRoy 144; Monro's
description 144–45; Otago
purchase 146–49; dies 149
Tuhuru 74, 186, 223
Tukaha 217
Tukawa 93n
Turakautahi 20
Tutae Patu lagoon 281
Tuturau 74, 239

Undine 189
Uru, Hoani 330
Uru, J. H. W. 339

Waiateruati 56, 59, 134
Waiharakeke 63
Waihora 18, 145, 282, 351
Waikanae 142
Waikato War (1863) 274
Waikouaiti 91, 92, 125, 145, 240
Waimakariri 195–97, 230, *231*, 258
Waingongoro 170
Waipounamu purchase 241, 243, 262

Wairau 'Massacre' 121–23, *122*, 140, 142

Wairau purchase 121, 164, 166, *167*, 168, *181*, 188, 195, 215, 224, 228, 230, 239, 244, 256, 264, 348, 351

Waitaha 20

Waitangi Tribunal 346–52

Waitara 273

Wakefield scheme 139, 226

Wakefield, Captain Arthur 114, 122, 140

Wakefield, Colonel William 85, 88–89, 121, 143–44, 148-9, 154–55, 159–60, 163, 171, 173–74, 178, 202, 215

Wakefield, Daniel 146

Wakefield, Edward Gibbon 83–85, 111, 112, 114, 271, 337–38

Wanganui 164, 169, 188

warfare, Maori: effect on food-gathering 21; effect on non-combatants 21; fighting season 20, 110; honour of 20, 21; inter-tribal 20; justification for 20; musket 49; spoils of 21; traditional 49; treatment of captives 58

Waruwarutu, Natanahira 64, 190, 282, 295, 307, 311–12, 329, 333

Waste Land Regulations (1853) 240, 244

waste lands 83–84, 121–22, 135, 158, 165–66, 178, 240, 244–45

Watkin, James 71–72, 92, 100, *116*, 116–20, 131, 144–45, 333

Watson, John 153, 179, 188, 205, 218, 222, 228, 255

Weld, Frederick 278

Weller brothers 68–70, 76, 80, 90

Wellington 113, 114, 160, *161*; *see also* Port Nicholson

Wentworth, William Charles 54, 79, 90, 97, 102

Wentworth-Jones 'purchase' 90–92, 93n, 97, 102

Wesley, John 28

Wesleyan mission 75, 92, 116–18

Wesleyans 28–29

Westland and Nelson Native Reserves Act 325

Whakaepa 39

Whakana, Rangi 185, 223

Whakatau, Kaikoura 228, 239–40, 243, 256, 259, 263

Whakatu 121

whaling: at Murihiku 235; at Onekakara 76; at Preservation Inlet 50; at Te Awaiti and Port Bunn 60–61; Cloudy Bay stations attacked 65; depletion of whale populations 75; effect on Maori population 149; employment of Maoris 76; French whalers 77; Kakapo Bay station destroyed by Ngai Tahu 63–64; Maori patronage of stations 60–61, 68; shore-based 73, 75–76; Weller brothers' station plundered 68; whaleboats prized by Maoris 60

Whitaker, Frederick 320

Whitcombe, John 275

Williams, Edward Marsh 97, 98

Williams, Peter 41, 50, 60, 76, 125

Williams, Revd Henry 89, 97, 99, 100, 160, 161, 272

Williams, W. H. Wynn 290, 292

Wills, Arthur 193–97, 198–201

Wilson, John Nathaniel 320

Wohlers, Johann 144, 146, 150, 235, 245–46

Wynyard, Colonel Robert 243, 245–46, 253